LIABILITY FOR ENVIRONMENTAL HARM TO THE GLOBAL COMMONS

This book examines liability for environmental harm in Antarctic, deep seabed and high seas commons areas to highlight a unique set of legal questions: Who has standing to claim for environmental harm in global commons ecosystems? How should questions of causation and allocation of liability be addressed where harm arises from a wide range of activities engaging diverse state and non-state actors? What kinds of harm should be compensable in global commons ecosystems, which are remote and characterized by high levels of scientific uncertainty? How can practical concerns such as ensuring adequate funds for compensation and access to dispute settlement forums be resolved? *Liability for Environmental Harm to the Global Commons* provides the first in-depth examination and evaluation of current rules and possible avenues for future legal developments in this area of increasing importance for states, international organizations and commercial actors, as well as legal and governance scholars.

Neil Craik is Professor of Law at the Balsillie School of International Affairs, University of Waterloo, Canada. He has published widely in the fields of international and Canadian environmental law and the law of the sea, and is co-editor of *Global Environmental Change and Innovation in International Law* (Cambridge University Press, 2018).

Tara Davenport is an assistant professor at National University of Singapore (NUS), where she teaches principles of property law, law of the sea and international regulation of shipping. Her research interests are in law of the sea, the global commons and maritime disputes. She is also co-head of the oceans law and policy team at the Centre for International Law and Deputy Director of the Asia-Pacific Centre for Environmental Law at NUS.

Ruth Mackenzie is Reader in International Law at the University of Westminster, where she teaches and researches in the fields of international environmental law, law of the sea and international courts and tribunals. Ruth is a member of the IUCN World Commission on Environmental Law.

CAMBRIDGE STUDIES ON ENVIRONMENT, ENERGY AND NATURAL RESOURCES GOVERNANCE

Cambridge Studies on Environment, Energy and Natural Resources Governance publishes foundational monographs of general interest to scholars and practitioners within the broadly defined fields of sustainable development policy, including studies on law, economics, politics, history and policy. These fields currently attract unprecedented interest due both to the urgency of developing policies to address climate change, the energy transition, food security and water availability and, more generally, to the progressive realization of the impact of humans as a geological driver of the state of the Earth, now called the "Anthropocene."

The general editor of the series is Professor Jorge E. Viñuales, the Harold Samuel Chair of Law and Environmental Policy at the University of Cambridge and the Founder and First Director of the Cambridge Centre for Environment, Energy and Natural Resource Governance (C-EENRG).

Liability for Environmental Harm to the Global Commons

NEIL CRAIK
University of Waterloo

TARA DAVENPORT
National University of Singapore

RUTH MACKENZIE
University of Westminster

CAMBRIDGE
UNIVERSITY PRESS

CAMBRIDGE
UNIVERSITY PRESS

Shaftesbury Road, Cambridge CB2 8EA, United Kingdom

One Liberty Plaza, 20th Floor, New York, NY 10006, USA

477 Williamstown Road, Port Melbourne, VIC 3207, Australia

314–321, 3rd Floor, Plot 3, Splendor Forum, Jasola District Centre, New Delhi – 110025, India

103 Penang Road, #05–06/07, Visioncrest Commercial, Singapore 238467

Cambridge University Press is part of Cambridge University Press & Assessment, a department of the University of Cambridge.

We share the University's mission to contribute to society through the pursuit of education, learning and research at the highest international levels of excellence.

www.cambridge.org
Information on this title: www.cambridge.org/9781108496223

DOI: 10.1017/9781108866477

First published 2023

A catalogue record for this publication is available from the British Library.

A Cataloging-in-Publication data record for this book is available from the Library of Congress

ISBN 978-1-108-49622-3 Hardback

Contents

Acknowledgements

This book has its origins in a research project examining dimensions of liability arising from deep seabed mining activities in the Area, that is, the seabed and ocean floor and subsoil beyond the limits of national jurisdiction which was developed in 2017 by the Centre for International Governance Innovation (CIGI), the Commonwealth Secretariat and the Secretariat of the International Seabed Authority (ISA). To carry out this project legal experts were invited to form the Legal Working Group on Liability for Environmental Harm from Activities in the Area (LWG). We were fortunate enough to be part of the LWG and we benefitted tremendously from the discussions and insights of the other members of the LWG. The other members of the LWG (and their affiliations at the time the project was undertaken) were as follows:

- Alfonso Ascencio-Herrera, Deputy Secretary-General, ISA
- Christopher Brown, Legal Officer, ISA
- Eden Charles, Independent Consultant on International Law, and Former Ambassador, Trinidad and Tobago
- Elie Jarmarche, Special Advisor on the Law of the Sea, and Member of the Legal and Technical Commission, ISA
- Hannah Lily, Legal Advisor, Commonwealth Secretariat
- Stephen Roady, Professor of the Practice of Law, Duke University School of Law
- Andrés Sebastián Rojas, Ministry of Foreign Affairs and Worship, Argentina
- Dire Tladi, Professor of Law, University of Pretoria, and Member, International Law Commission
- Guifang (Julia) Xue, Professor, KoGuan Law, Shanghai Jiao Tong University.

In addition to our colleagues on the LWG, we are particularly grateful to the three partner organizations for their financial and logistical support of the activities of the

LWG. The work of the LWG was presented in a series of reports published by CIGI in 2018,[1] and has been further developed in a subsequent publication that draws on the work of the LWG.[2]

The research and ideas contained in this book were presented at workshops and seminars at the Lauterpacht Centre for International Law, University of Cambridge; and the University of New South Wales Law School. We are grateful to the participants for their insights and interest in this project. All views, errors and omissions in the book are attributable to the authors only.

Neil Craik's work on this book was generously supported by the Social Sciences and Humanities Research Council of Canada through an Insight Grant ('The International Law of the Global Commons: Towards a Global Constitutional Framework'), as well as through support provided by CIGI through a Senior Fellowship. Tara Davenport's work was supported by the Faculty of Law at the National University of Singapore (NUS) and in particular the research institutes, the Asia-Pacific Centre for Environmental Law and the Centre for International Law. Ruth Mackenzie's work was supported by Westminster Law School.

Our research for this book and our preparation of the manuscript benefitted greatly from the work of a number of student research assistants. We are grateful to Kristine Gu (University of Calgary Law School); and Sebastian Aguirre, Lee Wei Ting, Ashley Teo, Tiwana Manamol, Gracia Goh, Joy Chen and Jiang Zhifeng (National University of Singapore).

The preparation of this book was greatly impacted by the global pandemic, which affected our professional and personal lives in many ways. We owe a huge debt of gratitude to Matt Galloway of Cambridge University Press for his steadfast perseverance and patience in the face of numerous delays in completing the manuscript. Thank you, as well, to Jadyn Fauconnier-Herry and the production staff at Cambridge University Press.

We are all especially grateful to our family and friends who provided support, encouragement and much appreciated (at least in hindsight) distractions, as we worked to complete this book. Neil is particularly thankful to Janet, his wife, for trying (with marginal success) to get him to work less, and his parents, Fergus and Anne, who politely stopped asking when this book might be completed. Ruth expresses special thanks to Sylvia Mackenzie for her spirit, humour and constant support. Tara thanks Paul, Kaiden, Talia and Avana for their unwavering patience and constant support.

[1] The work of the LWG is summarized in Neil Craik and others, 'Liability for Environmental Harm: Synthesis and Overview' CIGI, Liability Issues for Deep Seabed Mining Series Paper No 1, 13 July 2018. The complete set of papers of the LWG can be found online: <www.cigionline.org/series/liability-issues-deep-seabed-mining-series>.

[2] Neil Craik, 'Liability for Environmental Harm from Deep Seabed Mining: Towards a Hybrid Approach' (2019) 33 Ocean Yearbook 315–338.

Table of Cases

Permanent Court of International Justice

Factory at Chorzów (Germany v Poland) (Merits) [1928] PCIJ Rep Series A No 17

SS Wimbledon (United Kingdom, France, Italy & Japan v Germany) [1923] PCIJ Rep Series A No 1

International Court of Justice

Ahmadou Sadio Diallo (Republic of Guinea v Democratic Republic of the Congo) (Compensation), Judgment [2012] ICJ Rep 324

Allegations of Genocide under the Convention on the Prevention and Punishment of the Crime of Genocide (Ukraine v Russia), Application Instituting Proceedings, 26 February 2022

Application of the Convention on the Prevention and Punishment of Genocide (The Gambia v Myanmar), General List No 178, Preliminary Objections, Judgment of 22 July 2022

Armed Activities on the Territory of the Congo (Democratic Republic of the Congo v Uganda), Judgment [2005] ICJ Rep 168

Armed Activities on the Territory of the Congo (Democratic Republic of the Congo v Rwanda), Jurisdiction and Admissibility [2006] ICJ Rep 6

Armed Activities on the Territory of the Congo (Democratic Republic of the Congo v Uganda), (Order of 8 September 2020) [2020] ICJ Rep 264; (Order of 12 October 2020) [2020] ICJ Rep 295

Armed Activities on the Territory of the Congo (Democratic Republic of the Congo v Uganda), General List No 116, Judgment, 9 February 2022

Barcelona Traction, Light and Power Company, Limited (Belgium v Spain), *Second Phase* [1970] ICJ Rep 3

Case Concerning Aerial Herbicide Spraying (Ecuador v Colombia) (Application Instituting Proceedings), General List No 138 [2008] ICJ Rep 4

Case Concerning the Application of the Convention on the Prevention and Punishment of the Crime of Genocide (Bosnia and Herzegovina v Serbia and Montenegro), Judgment [2007] ICJ Rep 43

Case Concerning East Timor (Portugal v Australia) [1995] ICJ Rep 90

Certain Activities Carried Out by Nicaragua in the Border Area (Costa Rica v Nicaragua) *and Construction of a Road in Costa Rica along the San Juan River* (Nicaragua v Costa Rica), Judgment [2015] ICJ Rep 665

Certain Activities Carried Out by Nicaragua in the Border Area (Costa Rica v Nicaragua), *Compensation Owed by the Republic of Nicaragua to the Republic of Costa Rica*, Judgment [2018] ICJ Rep 15

Certain Phosphate Lands in Nauru (Nauru v Australia), Preliminary Objections [1992] ICJ Rep 240

Construction of a Road in Costa Rica along the San Juan River (Nicaragua v Costa Rica), Judgment [2015] ICJ Rep 665

Corfu Channel Case (United Kingdom v Albania), Judgment [1949] ICJ Rep 4

Eletronica Sicula, S.p.A (ELSI) (United States of America v Italy), Judgment [1989] ICJ Rep 15

Gabčikovo-Nagymaros Project (Hungary v Slovakia), Judgment [1997] ICJ Rep 7

Interpretation of the Agreement of 25 March 1951 between the WHO and Egypt, Advisory Opinion [1980] ICJ Rep 73

Legal Consequences of the Construction of a Wall in the Occupied Palestinian Territory, Advisory Opinion [2004] ICJ Rep 136

Legal Consequences of the Separation of the Chagos Archipelago from Mauritius in 1965, Advisory Opinion [2019] ICJ Rep 95

Legality of the Threat or Use of Nuclear Weapons, Advisory Opinion [1996] ICJ 226

Military and Paramilitary Activities in and against Nicaragua (Nicaragua v the United States of America), Judgment [1986] ICJ Rep 14

Monetary Gold Removed from Rome in 1943 (Italy v France, United Kingdom and United States), Judgment [1954] ICJ Rep 19

Nuclear Tests Case (Australia v France), Judgment [1974] ICJ Rep 253

Nuclear Tests Case (New Zealand v France), Judgment [1974] ICJ Rep 457

Obligations Concerning Negotiations Relating to Cessation of the Nuclear Arms Race and to Nuclear Disarmament (Marshall Islands v United Kingdom), Preliminary Objections, Judgment [2016] ICJ Rep 833

Pulp Mills on the River Uruguay (Argentina v Uruguay), Judgment [2010] ICJ Rep 14

Questions Relating to the Obligation to Prosecute or Extradite (Belgium v Senegal), Judgment [2012] ICJ Rep 422

Reparation for Injuries Suffered in the Service of the United Nations, Advisory Opinion [1949] ICJ Rep 174
Southwest Africa Case (Ethiopia v South Africa; Liberia v South Africa) Second Phase, Judgment [1966] ICJ Rep 6
Whaling in the Antarctic (Australia v Japan: New Zealand Intervening), Judgment [2014] ICJ Rep 226

International Tribunal for the Law of the Sea (ITLOS) and UNCLOS-Related Arbitral Tribunals

Arctic Sunrise Arbitration (Netherlands v Russia), Provisional Measures, ITLOS Case No 22 [2013]
Dispute Concerning Delimitation of the Maritime Boundaries between Mauritius and Maldives (Mauritius v Maldives), Preliminary Objections, Judgment, ITLOS Case No 28 [2021]
The M/V 'NORSTAR' Case (Panama v Italy), Judgment, ITLOS Case No 25 [2019]
Request for an Advisory Opinion submitted by the Sub-Regional Fisheries Commission (SRFC), Advisory Opinion of 2 April 2015, ITLOS Case No 21 [2015]
Responsibilities and Obligations of States Sponsoring Persons and Entities with Respect to Activities in the Area, Advisory Opinion of 1 February 2011, ITLOS Case No 17 [2011]
South China Sea Arbitration (The Republic of Philippines v The People's Republic of China), Award, Oxford Reports on ICGJ 495 [PCA 2016]

Other Inter-state Arbitrations

Bering Fur Seals Arbitration, Award RIAA vol XXVIII, 263 [1893]
Iron Rhine Arbitration (Belgium v Netherlands) Award RIAA vol XXVII 23 [2005]
Lake Lanoux Case (France v Spain) RIAA vol XII 281 [1957]
Trail Smelter Arbitration (Canada v United States) RIAA vol III 1905 [1941]

United Nations Compensation Commission

UNCC 'Report and Recommendations on the First Instalment of "F4" Claims' (2001) UN Doc S/AC 26/2001/16
UNCC 'Report and Recommendations made by the Panel of Commissioners concerning the Second Instalment of "F4" Claims' (2002) UN Doc S/AC 26/2002/26

UNCC 'Report and Recommendations made by the Panel of Commissioners concerning the Third Instalment of "F4" Claims' (2003) UN Doc S/AC 26/2003/3

UNCC 'Report and Recommendations made by the Panel of Commissioners concerning the Fifth Instalment of "F4" Claims' (2005) UN Doc S/AC 26/2005/10

Inter-American Court of Human Rights

The Environment and Human Rights, Advisory Opinion OC-23/17, Inter-American Court of Human Rights Series A No 23 (15 November 2017)

Investment Disputes

Perenco Ecuador Limited and The Republic of Ecuador, ICSID Case ARB/08/6 Award of 27 September 2019

Domestic Case Law

AG v PYA Quarries Ltd [1957] 2 QB 169 (UK)

Alfred L Snapp & Son, Inc v Puerto Rico ex rel Barez, 458 US 592 (1982)

Anns v Merton London Borough Council [1977] UKHL 4, [1978] AC 728

AWA Ltd v Daniels t/as Deloitte, Haskins and Sells (1992) 7 ACSR 759

British Columbia v Canadian Forest Products Ltd 2004 SCC 38

British South Africa Co v Companhia de Moçambique [1893] AC 602 (HL)

Bonnington Castings v Wardlow [1956] AC 613

Cambridge Water Co Ltd v Eastern Countries Leather plc [1994] 1 All ER 53

Dow Chemical Co v Aifares 286 SW2d 674, 688–689 (Tex 1990)

Environmental Defense Fund v Massey (1992) 986 F 2d 528 (US)

Friends of the Earth Netherlands (Milieudefensie) v Royal Dutch Shell, District Court The Hague (Judgment of 26 May 2021) Case No C/09/571932

Hilton v Guyot (1895) 159 US 113

Juliana v United States 217 F.Supp.3d 1224 (D. Or. 2016)

Juliana v United States 447 F.3d 1159 (9th Cir. 2020)

Just v British Columbia [1989] 2 SCR 1228

La Generale des Carrieres et des Mines v FG Hemisphere Associates LLC, [2012] UK PC 27, para 29

McGhee v National Coal Board [1972] 3 All ER 1008

National Audubon Society v Superior Court of Alpine County 33 Cal (3d) 419 (1983) [Mono Lake]

Pakootas v Teck Cominco Metals, Ltd (2006) 452 F.3d 1066 (9th Cir) (US)

Pfizer, Inc v Government of India 434 US 308
Principality of Monaco v Mississippi (1934) 292 US 313 (US), 323
RJR Nabisco Inc v European Community (2016) 136 S Ct 2101 (US)
Rylands v Fletcher (1868) LR 3 HL 330
The Schooner Exchange v McFadden (1812) 7 Cranch 116
Selma Pressure Treating Co v Osmose Wood Preserving Inc, 271 Cal. Rptr 596, 606 (Cal. Ct. App. 1990)
Spiliada Maritime Corp v Cansulex Ltd [1986] UKHL 10, [1987] AC 460
State v Jersey Central Power & Light Co 336 1A.2d 750, 759 (N.J. App. Div. 1975)
The State of the Netherlands v Urgenda Foundation, The Supreme Court of the Netherlands (20 December 2019), case 19/00135
The State of the Netherlands v Urgenda Foundation, The Hague Court of Appeal (9 October 2018), case 200.178.245/01
'*Water Use Permit Applications, Re*, 9 P (3d), 409, 450 (2002)'

Table of Treaties and Instruments

Year	Full Reference	Abbreviation
1945	Charter of the United Nations (adopted 26 June 1945, entered into force 24 October 1945) 1 UNTS XVI	UN Charter
1946	General Convention on the Privileges and Immunities of the United Nations (adopted 13 February 1946, entered into force 17 September 1946) 1 UNTS 15, 90 UNTS 327	UN Privileges and Immunities Convention
1946	International Convention for the Regulation of Whaling (adopted 2 December 1946, entered into force 10 November 1948) 161 UNTS 72	ICRW
1947	Convention on Privileges and Immunities of Specialized Agencies (adopted 21 November 1947, entered into force 2 December 1948) 33 UNTS 261	Specialized Agencies Privileges and Immunities Convention
1959	Antarctic Treaty (adopted 1 December 1959, entered into force 23 June 1961) 402 UNTS 71	1959 Antarctic Treaty
1960	Convention on Third Party Liability in the Field of Nuclear Energy (adopted 29 July 1960, entered into force 1 April 1968) 956 UNTS 251	1960 Paris Convention
1963	Vienna Convention on the Civil Liability for Nuclear Damage (adopted 21 May 1963, entered into force 12 November 1977) 1063 UNTS 265	1963 Vienna Convention
1969	International Convention Relating to Intervention on the High Seas in Cases of Oil Pollution Casualties (adopted 29 November 1969, entered into force 6 May 1975) 970 UNTS 211	1969 Intervention Convention
1969	International Convention on Civil Liability for Oil Pollution Damage (adopted 29 November 1969, entered into force 19 June 1975) 973 UNTS 3	1969 Oil Pollution Liability Convention

(continued)

(*continued*)

Year	Full Reference	Abbreviation
1971	International Convention on the Establishment of an International Fund for Compensation for Oil Pollution Damage (adopted 18 December 1971, entered into force 16 October 1978) 110 UNTS 57	1971 Fund Convention
1972	Convention on International Liability for Damage Caused by Space Objects (adopted 29 March 1972, entered into force 1 September 1972) 961 UNTS 187	1972 Space Liability Convention
1972	Stockholm Declaration, Declaration of the United Nations Conference on the Human Environment (1972) UN Doc A/Conf.48/14/Rev.1	1972 Stockholm Declaration
1972	Convention for the Conservation of Antarctic Seals (adopted 1 June 1972, entered into force 7 April 1982) 11 ILM 251	1972 Seals Convention
1972	London Convention for the Prevention of Marine Pollution by Dumping of Wastes and Other Matter (adopted 29 December 1972, entered into force 30 August 1975) 1046 UNTS 120	1972 London Convention
1974	Nordic Convention on the Protection of the Environment (adopted 19 February 1974, entered into force 5 October 1976) 1092 UNTS 279	1974 Nordic Convention
1976	Convention for the Protection of the Marine Environment and the Coastal Region of the Mediterranean (adopted 16 February 1976, entered into force 1 February 1979) 15 ILM 290 as amended June 1995, UNEP(OCA)/MED IG.6/7 (entered into force 9 July 2004)	1976 Barcelona Convention
1976	Convention on Limitation of Liability for Maritime Claims (adopted 19 November 1976, entered into force 1 December 1986) 1456 UNTS 221	1976 LLMC
1980	Convention on the Conservation of Antarctic Marine Living Resources (adopted 20 May 1980, entered into force 7 April 1982) 1329 UNTS 47	CCAMLR
1981	Protocol between the Government of Canada and the Government of the USSR (2 April 1981) 20 ILM 689	–
1982	World Charter for Nature (adopted 28 October 1982) UN Doc A/RES/37/7	–
1982	United Nations Convention on the Law of the Sea (adopted 10 December 1982, entered into force 16 November 1994) 1833 UNTS 397	UNCLOS
1988	Convention on the Regulation of Antarctic Mineral Resource Activity (adopted 2 June 1988) 27 ILM 868	CRAMRA
1989	Basel Convention on the Control of Transboundary Movements of Hazardous Wastes and Their Disposal (adopted 22 March 1989) 1637 UNTS 9	1989 Basel Convention

Year	Full Reference	Abbreviation
1990	International Convention on Oil Pollution Preparedness, Response and Cooperation (adopted 30 November 1990, entered into force 13 May 1995) 1891 UNTS 77	OPPRC Convention
1991	Convention on Environmental Impact Assessment in a Transboundary Context (adopted 25 February 1991, entered into force 10 September 1997) 1989 UNTS 309	–
1991	Protocol on Environmental Protection to the Antarctic Treaty (adopted 4 October 1991, entered into force 14 January 1998) 30 ILM 1461	1991 Antarctic Protocol
1992	Convention on the Protection and Use of Transboundary Watercourses and International Lakes (adopted 17 March 1992, entered into force 6 October 1996) 1936 UNTS 269	1992 Watercourses and Lakes Convention
1992	Convention on the Transboundary Effects of Industrial Accidents (adopted 17 March 1992, entered into force 19 April 2000) 2105 UNTS 457	1992 Convention on Industrial Accidents
1992	Convention on the Protection of the Marine Environment of the Baltic Sea Area (adopted 9 April 1992, entered into force 17 January 2000) 2099 UNTS 195	1992 Baltic Sea Convention
1992	Convention on the Protection of the Marine Environment of the Black Sea Against Pollution (adopted 21 April 1992, entered into force 15 January 1994) 1764 UNTS 4	1992 Black Sea Convention
1992	Convention for the Protection of the Marine Environment of the North-East Atlantic (adopted 22 September 1992, entered into force 25 March 1998) 2354 UNTS 67	OSPAR Convention
1992	Protocol to Amend the 1969 International Convention on Civil Liability for Oil Pollution Damage (adopted 27 November 1992, entered into force 30 May 1996) 1956 UNTS 255	1992 Oil Pollution Liability Convention
1992	Protocol to Amend the International Convention on the Establishment of an International Fund for Compensation for Oil Pollution Damage (adopted 27 November 1992, entered into force 30 May 1996) 1953 UNTS 330	1992 Fund Convention
1992	Rio Declaration on Environment and Development, Report of the United Nations Conference on Environment and Development (1992) UN Doc A/Conf.151/26/Rev.1, Annex I	1992 Rio Declaration
1992	Convention on Biological Diversity (adopted 5 June 1992, entered into force 29 December 1993) 1760 UNTS 79	–

(continued)

(*continued*)

Year	Full Reference	Abbreviation
1992	United Nations Framework Convention on Climate Change (adopted 9 May 1992, entered into force 21 March 1994) 1771 UNTS 107	UNFCCC
1993	Lugano Convention on Civil Liability for Damage Resulting from Activities Dangerous to the Environment (adopted 21 June 1993, not yet entered into force) 32 ILM 1228	1993 Lugano Convention
1994	Agreement Relating to the Implementation of Part XI of the United Nations Convention on the Law of the Sea (adopted 28 July 1994, entered into force 28 July 1996) 1836 UNTS 3	1994 Implementation Agreement
1995	Agreement for the Implementation of the United Nations Convention on the Law of the Sea of 10 December 1982 Relating to the Conservation and Management of Straddling Fish Stocks and Highly Migratory Fish Stocks (adopted 4 August 1995, entered into force 11 December 2001) 34 ILM 1542	1995 Fish Stocks Agreement
1996	Protocol of 1996 to Amend the Convention on Limitation of Liability for Maritime Claims, 1976 (adopted 2 May 1996, entered into force 13 May 2004) Can TS 2008 No 18	1996 LLMC
1996	International Convention on Liability and Compensation for Damage in Connection with the Carriage of Hazardous and Noxious Substances by Sea (adopted 3 May 1996, not yet entered into force) 35 ILM 1415	1996 HNS Convention
1996	Protocol to the Convention on the Prevention of Marine Pollution by Dumping of Wastes and Other Matter, 1972 (adopted 7 November 1996, entered into force 24 March 2006) ATS 11	1996 Dumping Protocol
1997	Convention on the Law of the Non-Navigational Uses of International Watercourses (adopted 21 May 1997, entered into force 17 August 2014) 36 ILM 700	1997 Watercourses Convention
1997	Protocol to Amend the Vienna Convention on Civil Liability for Nuclear Damage (adopted 12 September 1997, entered into force 4 October 2003) 2241 UNTS 270	1997 Vienna Convention
1997	Convention on Supplementary Compensation for Nuclear Damage (adopted 12 September 1997, entered into force 15 April 2015) 36 ILM 1473	1997 Nuclear Supplementary Fund Convention
1998	Convention on Access to Information, Public Participation in Decision-Making and Access to Justice in Environmental Matters (adopted 25 June 1998, entered into force 30 October 2001) 2161 UNTS 447, 38 ILM 517	1998 Aarhus Convention

Year	Full Reference	Abbreviation
1999	Basel Protocol on Liability and Compensation for Damage Resulting from Transboundary Movement of Hazardous Wastes and Their Disposal (adopted 10 December 1999) UNEP/CHW.1/WG/1/9/2	1999 Basel Liability Protocol
2000	Cartagena Protocol on Biosafety (adopted 29 January 2000, entered into force 11 September 2003) 2226 UNTS 208	Cartagena Protocol
2000	International Seabed Authority, Regulations on Prospecting and Exploration for Polymetallic Nodules in the Area (13 July 2000) Doc No ISBA/6/A/18 (13 July 2000)	PMN
2001	International Convention on Civil Liability for Bunker Oil Pollution Damage (adopted 23 March 2001, entered into force 21 November 2008) UNTS No 47	2001 Bunker Oil Convention
2001	International Law Commission, 'Draft Articles on Responsibility of States for Internationally Wrongful Acts, with Commentaries' (2001) UN Doc A/56/10	ASR
2001	International Law Commission, 'Draft Articles on Prevention of Transboundary Harm from Hazardous Activities, with Commentaries' (2001) UN Doc A/56/10	Draft Articles on Prevention of Transboundary Harm
2003	Protocol of 2003 to the International Convention on the Establishment of an International Fund for Compensation for Oil, (adopted 16 May 2003, entered into force 3 March 2005) 92FUND/A.8/4 Annex 1	2003 Supplementary Fund Convention
2003	Protocol on Civil Liability and Compensation for Damage Caused by the Transboundary Effects of Industrial Accidents on Transboundary Waters (adopted 21 May 2003, not yet entered into force)	UNECE Protocol on Liability for Industrial Accidents
2003	Protocol on Strategic Environment Assessment to the Convention on Environmental Impact Assessment in a Transboundary Context (adopted 21 May 2003, entered into force 11 July 2010) 2865 UNTS 140	2003 Kiev SEA Protocol
2004	European Council, Environmental Liability Directive 2004/35/CE (entered into force 30 April 2004) OJ L 143	Liability Directive
2005	Annex VI to the Protocol on Environmental Protection to the Antarctic Treaty on Liability Arising from Environmental Emergencies (adopted 17 June 2005) (2006) 45 ILM 5	Liability Annex
2006	International Law Commission, 'Draft Principles on the Allocation of Loss in the Case of Transboundary Harm Arising Out of Hazardous Activities, with Commentaries' (2006) UN Doc A/61/10	Draft Principles

(continued)

(*continued*)

Year	Full Reference	Abbreviation
2007	Nairobi International Convention on the Removal of Wrecks (adopted 18 May 2007, entered into force 14 April 2015) 46 ILM (2007)	2007 Wrecks Convention
2008	Guidelines for the Determination of Liability and Compensation for Damage Resulting from Pollution of the Marine Environment in the Mediterranean Sea Area' (2008) UNEP(DEPI)/MEDI G.17/10	Barcelona Convention Guidelines
2010	Nagoya-Kuala Lumpur Supplementary Protocol on Liability and Redress to the Cartagena Protocol on Biosafety (adopted 15 October 2010, entered into force 5 March 2018) (2011) 50 ILM 105	2010 Nagoya-Kuala Lumpur Supplementary Protocol
2010	International Seabed Authority, Regulations on Prospecting and Exploration for Polymetallic Sulphides in the Area, Doc No. ISBA/16/A/12/Rev.1 (7 May 2010)	PMS
2010	Protocol to the International Convention on Liability and Compensation for Damage in Connection with the Carriage of Hazardous and Noxious Substances by Sea (adopted 30 April 2010, not yet in force)	2010 HNS Convention
2011	International Law Commission, 'Draft Articles on the Responsibility of International Organizations, with Commentaries' (2011) II (2) ILC Yearbook 1	DARIO
2012	Amendments to the Protocol of 1996 to Amend the Convention on Limitation of Liability for Maritime Claims, 1976 (adopted 19 April 2012, entered into force 8 June 2015) IMO Resolution LEG.5(99) (2012)	2012 LLMC
2013	International Seabed Authority, Regulations on Prospecting for Cobalt-rich Ferromanganese Crusts in the Area, Doc No. ISBA/19/C/17 (22 July 2013)	CFC
2013	Warsaw International Mechanism for Loss and Damage Associated with Climate Change Impacts (31 January 2014) UN Doc FCCC/CP/2013/10/Add.1	WIM
2014	Protocol to the Athens Convention relating to the Carriage of Passengers and Their Luggage by Sea (Consolidated text of the 1974 Athens Convention relating to the Carriage of Passengers and their Luggage by Sea and the 2002 Protocol to the Convention), (adopted 1 November 2002, entered into force 23 April 2014) Cmnd 8760	2014 Athens Convention
2015	Paris Agreement (adopted 12 December 2015, entered into force 4 November 2016) UN Doc FCCC/CP/2015/10/Add.1	Paris Agreement

Year	Full Reference	Abbreviation
2019	Draft Regulations on Exploitation of Mineral Resources in the Area, Prepared by the Legal and Technical Commission, ISBA/25/C/WP.1 dated 22 March 2019	DER
2022	Further revised draft text of an agreement under the United Nations Convention on the Law of the Sea on the conservation and sustainable use of marine biological diversity of areas beyond national jurisdiction, Note by the President UN Doc A/CONF.232/2022/5, 1 June 2022	2022 Draft ILBI Text
2023	Draft agreement under the United Nations Convention on the Law of the Sea on the conservation and sustainable use of marine biological diversity of areas beyond national jurisdiction, Advance, Unedited text, 4 March 2023	2023 BBNJ Agreement

Abbreviations

ABNJ	areas beyond national jurisdiction
AJIL	American Journal of International Law
ATCM	Antarctic Treaty Consultative Meeting
ATCP	Antarctic Treaty Consultative Party
BBNJ	biodiversity beyond national jurisdiction
CCAMLR Commission	Commission on the Conservation of Antarctic Marine Living Resources
CCLR	Carbon and Climate Law Review
CEP	Committee for Environmental Protection
CHH	common heritage of humankind
CLJ	Cambridge Law Journal
COP	Conference of the Parties
CRISTAL	Contract Regarding an Interim Supplement to Tanker Liability for Oil Pollution
DRC	Democratic Republic of the Congo
ECF	Environmental Compensation Fund
EEZ	exclusive economic zone
EIA	environmental impact assessment
EJIL	European Journal of International Law
EPL	Environmental Policy and Law
EPG	Environmental Policy and Governance
GAIRS	generally accepted international rules and standards
GRIR	Geneva Risk and Insurance Review
GYIL	German Yearbook of International Law
HEA	habitat equivalency analysis
IAEA	International Atomic Energy Agency

ICGJ	International Courts of General Jurisdiction
ICJ	International Court of Justice
ICLQ	International and Comparative Law Quarterly
IJLMA	International Journal of Law and Management
IJMCL	International Journal of Marine and Coastal Law
ILBI	internationally legally binding instrument
ILC	International Law Commission
ILM	International Legal Materials
IMO	International Maritime Organization
IOPC Funds	International Oil Pollution Compensation Funds
IPCC	Intergovernmental Panel on Climate Change
ISA	International Seabed Authority
ITLOS	International Tribunal for the Law of the Sea
IUCN	International Union for Conservation of Nature
JEL	Journal of Environmental Law
JIDS	Journal of International Dispute Settlement
JLS	Journal of Legal Studies
LJIL	Leiden Journal of International Law
LPICT	The Law and Practice of International Courts and Tribunals
LTC	Legal and Technical Commission
MJEAL	Michigan Journal of Environmental and Administrative Law
MJIL	Melbourne Journal of International Law
MJSDL	McGill Journal of Sustainable Development Law
NEA	Nuclear Energy Agency
NGO	non-governmental organization
NILR	Netherlands International Law Review
NYIL	Netherlands Yearbook of International Law
OECD	Organization for Economic Cooperation and Development
P&I	protection and indemnity
PCA	Permanent Court of Arbitration
PCIJ	Permanent Court of International Justice
RECIEL	Review of European, Comparative & International Environmental Law
RFMA	Regional fisheries management arrangements
RFMO	Regional fisheries management organization
SDC	Seabed Disputes Chamber

TOVALOP	Tanker Owners Voluntary Agreement Concerning Liability for Oil Pollution
UN	United Nations
UNCC	United Nations Compensation Commission
UNGA	United Nations General Assembly
UNTS	United Nations Treaty Series
UTLJ	University of Toronto Law Journal

1

Introduction

1.1 INTRODUCTION

On 10 November 1988, the oil tanker *Odyssey* broke apart in the North Atlantic, 700 miles off the Canadian coast. The *Odyssey* was carrying 132,000 tons of crude oil, which was released into the marine environment – making the *Odyssey* one of the largest oil spills to have ever occurred. Since the spill occurred on the high seas and the released oil did not reach the shores of any state, no response actions were taken.[1] This is not to suggest that environmental harm did not occur. It most certainly did.[2] However, the spill did not trigger the same legal response as one which damages the marine environment in areas within the national jurisdiction of states. The different legal treatment arises for several reasons. First, the harm itself was to the environment *per se*, as opposed to impacting the economic interests of a particular state or private actor. Even if the environmental harm that arose could be quantified and recognized as compensable, it is not clear what legal entities would have the right to recover for the loss suffered. The ambiguity surrounding the issue of legal standing to pursue claims for harms in areas beyond national jurisdiction (ABNJ) is a function of the nature of global commons, such as the high seas, whereby the harm is in one sense suffered by all states, perhaps by all humankind. However, in the absence of some legal actor that is authorized to act on behalf of these collective interests, legal responsibility is not easily recognized.

The legal rules governing liability for environmental harm in ABNJ have often been bracketed or placed outside the boundaries of the more familiar terrain of inter-state liability rules and practices.[3] Emblematic of this gap is the lack of progress on realizing

[1] CEDRE, 'Odyssey – Spill Report', online <wwz.cedre.fr/en/Resources/Spills/Spills/Odyssey> accessed 15 October 2022.

[2] Advisory Committee on Marine Pollution of the Seas of the International Council for the Exploration of the Sea, 1990 *Marine Pollution Yearbook* (Pergamon 1990) 9.

[3] For example, the civil liability rules and processes governing spills from oil transport explicitly exclude environmental harm to areas beyond national jurisdiction: see International Convention on Civil Liability for Oil Pollution Damage (adopted 29 November 1969, entered

the objective of Principle 13 of the Rio Declaration on Environment and Development, which states in part that '[s]tates shall also cooperate in an expeditious and more determined manner to develop further international law regarding liability and compensation for adverse effects of environmental damage caused by activities within their jurisdiction or control to areas beyond their jurisdiction'.[4] Article 235 of the 1982 United Nations Convention on the Law of the Sea (UNCLOS) similarly calls on states to cooperate 'in the … further development of international law relating to responsibility and liability for the assessment of and compensation for damage' caused by pollution to the marine environment.[5] Yet, development of liability rules addressing areas beyond national jurisdiction very much remains unfinished business.

This book, in examining the existing, emerging and prospective international legal rules addressing liability for environmental harm to areas beyond national jurisdiction, takes as its starting point the increased salience of addressing the impacts on the environment in areas beyond the national jurisdiction of any state – many miles out to sea, in the ocean depths, or in the Antarctic.[6] This salience is a function of the expanding pressures on the environment in areas beyond national jurisdiction flowing from the increased intensity of ongoing economic activities in these areas and the emergence of new environmental risks from novel activities, such as deep seabed mining and marine geoengineering. Reports of the impacts of marine debris, overfishing and pollution from shipping and from offshore resource exploitation, amongst others, challenge policymakers to act effectively to prevent environmental harm and to restore ecosystems and ecosystem services when harm occurs. These challenges are compounded by climate change and widespread biodiversity loss, as well as increasing recognition of the fundamental role that oceans and the Antarctic play in maintaining earth systems.[7] Liability – by which

into force 19 June 1975) 973 UNTS 3 (1969 Oil Pollution Liability Convention), amended by the 1992 Protocol to Amend the 1969 International Convention on Civil Liability for Oil Pollution Damage (adopted 27 November 1992, entered into force 30 May 1996) 1956 UNTS 255 (1992 Oil Pollution Liability Convention) art II. The 1969 International Convention Relating to Intervention on the High Seas in Cases of Oil Pollution Casualties only affirms the right of coastal states to take such measures on the high seas as may be necessary to prevent, mitigate or eliminate danger to its coastline or related interests from pollution by oil after a maritime casualty but does not address liability *per se*. See International Convention Relating to Intervention on the High Seas in Cases of Oil Pollution Casualties (adopted 29 November 1969, entered into force 6 May 1975) 970 UNTS 211 (Intervention Convention).

4 Report of the United Nations Conference on Environment and Development (1992) UN Doc A/Conf.151/26/Rev.1, Annex I (1992 Rio Declaration), principle 13.

5 United Nations Convention on the Law of the Sea (adopted 10 December 1982, entered into force 16 November 1994) 1833 UNTS 397 (UNCLOS) art 235.

6 ES Brondizio, J Settele, S Díaz and HT Ngo (eds), *Global Assessment Report on Biodiversity and Ecosystem Services of the Intergovernmental Science-Policy Platform on Biodiversity and Ecosystem Services* (IPBES Secretariat 2019); Intergovernmental Panel on Climate Change (IPCC), *Special Report on the Ocean and Cryosphere in a Changing Climate* (CUP 2019).

7 IPCC, *Special Report* 2019 (n 6). See also Will Steffen and others, 'Planetary Boundaries: Guiding Human Development on a Changing Planet' (2015) 347 (6223) Science 736.

we mean to refer to the rules and procedures governing compensation to the international community, states or other affected persons for damage caused to environment – offers a crucial element for governing the global commons by strengthening legal accountability for environmental risks and providing resources for ecological restoration.

Liability for environmental damage has been addressed in a piecemeal fashion in international environmental law. Specific rules on state liability for environmental damage remain relatively underdeveloped, beyond the general rules on state responsibility. While rules on state responsibility apply as a matter of principle to wrongful acts occasioning significant environmental harm in areas beyond national jurisdiction, the legal framework of state responsibility provides an incomplete and uncertain response.[8] Numerous agreements have been adopted establishing civil liability regimes in respect of various sectoral activities and the principles governing compensation for environmental harm to areas within national jurisdiction under such agreements, such as those governing oil pollution from tankers, are well understood.[9] However, many of the civil liability regimes have not entered into force, and coverage of environmental damage outside of areas under national jurisdiction remains inadequate. The potential transposition of these rules to areas that are not subject to national jurisdiction, or the development of alternative approaches, raises a unique set of legal questions that has not previously been the subject of any extended analysis.[10]

Some commentators have questioned whether liability and compensation approaches are appropriate for the global commons,[11] or as a tool for environmental

8 See Phoebe Okowa, 'Responsibility for Environmental Damage' in Malgosia Fitzmaurice, David M Ong, and Panos Merkouris (eds), *Research Handbook on International Environmental Law* (Edward Elgar 2010) 303; Alan E Boyle, 'Remedying Harm to International Common Spaces and Resources: Compensation and Other Approaches' in Peter Wetterstein (ed), *Harm to the Environment: The Right to Compensation and the Assessment of Damages* (OUP 1997) 83; and Katja Creutz, *State Responsibility in the International Legal Order: A Critical Appraisal* (CUP 2020) 19, 163–166.

9 See Jan Albers, *Responsibility and Liability in the Context of Transboundary Movements of Hazardous Wastes by Sea* (Springer-Verlag 2015); Julian Barboza, *The Environment, Risk and Liability in International Law* (Brill 2011); Michael Faure (ed), *Civil Liability and Financial Security for Offshore Oil and Gas Activities* (CUP 2016); Wu Chao, *Pollution from the Carriage of Oil by Sea: Liability and Compensation* (Kluwer Law International 1996).

10 See Kathy Leigh, 'Liability for Damage to the Global Commons' (1992) 14 Aust YBIL 129; Meher Nigar, 'Environmental Liability and Global Commons: A Critical Study' (2018) 60(2) IJLMA 435; Xue Hanqin, *Transboundary Damage in International Law* (CUP 2003) 191–266; Malgosia Fitzmaurice, 'Liability for Environmental Damage Caused to the Global Commons' (1996) 5 RECIEL 305; Nicholas Gaskell, 'Liability and Compensation Regimes: Pollution of the High Seas' in Robert C Beckman, Millicent McCreath, J Ashley Roach and Zhen Sun (eds), *High Seas Governance: Gaps and Challenges* (Brill 2018) 229–272.

11 Boyle (n 8) 99–100; Louise de La Fayette, 'The Concept of Environmental Damage in International Liability Regimes' in Michael Bowman and Alan Boyle (eds), *Environmental Damage in International and Comparative Law: Problems of Definition and Valuation* (OUP 2002) 149, 187–188.

protection.[12] As the legal response to the *Odyssey* oil spill suggests, applying liability rules to the global commons does raise complex questions concerning the kinds of harm that ought to be compensable and how any damages are to be calculated, the standards of behaviour that ought to attract legal responsibility and which entities have the standing to pursue legal remedies for harm to the commons environment. The emerging patterns of activities in the global commons such as deep seabed mining, bioprospecting and scientific research engage a diverse group of international, state and non-state actors, who could attract liability for their operational activities, but also for their failure to provide proper oversight of these activities. In addition to raising novel legal questions, liability rules implicate a range of practical concerns about how to ensure the availability of adequate funds for compensation (through insurance or compensation funds) and access to dispute settlement forums to resolve complex, multi-party incidents. It is these questions that this book sets out to address.

1.2 DEFINING THE GLOBAL COMMONS OR AREAS BEYOND NATIONAL JURISDICTION

The phrase 'commons' has its origins in medieval times when pastures were reserved for the joint use of villagers, and eventually were transferred to private ownership in various stages between the sixteenth and nineteenth centuries.[13] From a legal perspective, the 'commons' denotes an area or resources that are shared amongst a group and to which access cannot be denied to a member of the group. It has also been defined as 'a resource to which no single decision-making unit holds exclusive title' or as a 'resource domain in which common pool resources are found'.[14] Global commons are differentiated based on the identity of the relevant decision-making units, states and the scale of the system (involving all states). Thus, global commons have been defined as 'resource domains to which all nations have legal access'.[15] This definition focuses on the commons as a category of property. Our interest extends beyond the legal implications of ownership and includes questions of authority or jurisdiction. In other words, we are interested in the structure of liability rules in areas where no state has the exclusive right to exercise authority over the area or resources located in these areas which are also described as areas beyond national jurisdiction or ABNJ. We use the term 'global commons' in this book in the

[12] Jutta Brunnée, 'Of Sense and Sensibility: Reflections on International Liability Regimes as Tools for Environmental Protection' (2004) 53(2) ICLQ 351.

[13] Jerome Blum, *The End of the Old Order in Rural Europe* (Princeton University Press 1978) (describing transformation of common property through enclosures). But see Elinor Ostrom, *Governing the Commons: The Evolution of Institutions for Collective Action* (CUP 1990) ch 3 (describing enduring communal tenure systems).

[14] Susan Buck, *The Global Commons: An Introduction* (Island Press 2012) 5.

[15] ibid 5.

limited sense of the coverage of the book, and interchangeably with the term 'areas beyond national jurisdiction'.

The scholarly literature generally considers there to be four distinct global commons systems: Antarctica, the oceans, the atmosphere and outer space.[16] Our interest, and the focus of this book, is on two of these systems, the Antarctic and the oceans. We address the latter under the distinct legal regimes governing the high seas and deep seabed, owing to the unique status of each. The focus on these three interrelated global commons, that is, Antarctica, the deep seabed and the high seas, is deliberate. Each has a distinct legal regime governed by international law which addresses the legal nature of the various commons and their respective governance in unique ways. An underlying premise of this book is that examining these different contexts provides a more complete picture of how liability rules apply to areas beyond national jurisdiction, and allows for cross-regime comparison. This latter point allows the analysis to engage more deeply with questions of how the differing institutional and legal settings influence liability rules and procedures.

Because our interest is in examining how international law addresses liability for environmental harm to areas not under state jurisdiction, we exclude outer space and the atmosphere. The existing liability rules associated with space activity focus on impacts to state territory, and not to areas of the environment beyond state jurisdiction.[17] While a number of commentators have argued that the atmosphere is properly viewed as a form of commons, as a legal classification this view is contested.[18] In any event, for the purposes of addressing liability for environmental harm, it is the impact of climate change on the environment of commons areas that is of interest.[19] Thus, global atmospheric change is considered to the extent that certain impacts of climate change constitute a driver of environmental damage in the three global commons areas that are addressed.

To situate the examination of the key elements of the liability rules and processes examined in this book, we provide a preliminary overview of each of the three key

[16] ibid; John Vogler, *The Global Commons: A Regime Analysis* (Wiley & Sons 1995).

[17] Convention on International Liability for Damage Caused by Space Objects (adopted 29 November 1971, entered into force 1 September 1972) 961 UNTS 187.

[18] See discussion in ILC, 'Second Report on the Protection of the Atmosphere, by Shinya Murase, Special Rapporteur' (2015) UN DocA/CN.4/681, para 56, noting that '[a]lthough the concept of the atmosphere, which is not area-based, does not conform to that of "areas beyond the limits of national jurisdiction", it is nonetheless clear that the atmosphere existing above those areas is now covered by principle 21 of the Stockholm Declaration'; the International Law Association Committee on Legal Principles relating to Climate Change referred to the 'global climate system' as a 'common natural resource' ILA Resolution 2/2014 *Declaration of Legal Principles Relating to Climate Change* <www.ila-hq.org/en/committees/the-legal-principles-relating-to-climate-change> accessed 12 October 2022.

[19] Boyle (n 8) 86 'in so far as we can point to "harm" in the context of climate change or loss of biological diversity this will of necessity either be harm which affects states, or, in the case of oceans and Antarctica, it will be harm to common spaces and their ecology. It is not plausible to conceive of "harm" to the climate or biodiversity which has no such impacts'.

commons regimes, addressing their respective legal status as global commons, institutional structures, the principal activities being undertaken that pose environmental risks and the principal treaty rules addressing responsibility and liability for environmental harm.

1.2.1 *Antarctic*

1.2.1.1 Legal Status as Global Commons

Antarctica lies entirely within the South Pole and an ice sheet covers 98 per cent of the continent. It forms about 10 per cent of the earth's land surface. Since its initial discovery in the eighteenth century, seven states (Argentina, Australia, Chile, France, New Zealand, Norway and the United Kingdom) have asserted sovereignty over some portion of the Antarctic on various grounds including discovery, contiguity and occupation.[20]

Antarctica is governed by its own, relatively self-contained legal regime established under the Antarctic Treaty System, consisting of the 1959 Antarctic Treaty,[21] the 1972 Convention for the Conservation of Antarctic Seals,[22] the 1980 Convention on the Conservation of Antarctic Marine Living Resources (CCAMLR);[23] and the 1991 Protocol on Environmental Protection to the Antarctic Treaty (1991 Antarctic Protocol),[24] under which a series of Annexes has been adopted, including Annex VI addressing liability.[25] The preamble of the 1959 Antarctic Treaty recognizes that 'it is in the interest of all mankind that Antarctica shall continue forever to be used exclusively for peaceful purposes and shall not become the scene or object of international discord'.[26] The Antarctic Treaty aimed to address the major concerns in the management of Antarctica, namely, the demilitarization of Antarctica, the promotion of scientific research

20 Christopher C. Joyner, *Governing the Frozen Commons: The Antarctic Regime and Environmental Protection* (University of South Carolina Press 1998) 46.

21 Antarctic Treaty (adopted 1 December 1959, entered into force 23 June 1961) 402 UNTS 71.

22 1972 Convention for the Conservation of Antarctic Seals (adopted 1 June 1972, in force 7 April 1982) 11 ILM 251. The 1972 Convention for the Conservation of Antarctic Seals is no longer operational as there is no more commercial sealing in the Antarctic. Commercial whaling has also been phased out in the Southern Ocean because of a moratorium adopted in 1982 under the International Convention for the Regulation of Whaling, although Japan has continued to whale, ostensibly for purposes of scientific research which is allowed under the ICRW.

23 Convention on the Conservation of Antarctic Marine Living Resources (adopted 20 May 1980, entered into force 7 April 1982) 1329 UNTS 47 (CCAMLR).

24 Protocol on Environmental Protection to the Antarctic Treaty (adopted 4 October 1991, entered into force 14 January 1998) (1991) 30 ILM 1461 (1991 Antarctic Protocol).

25 Annex VI to the Protocol on Environmental Protection to the Antarctic Treaty on Liability Arising from Environmental Emergencies (adopted 17 June 2005) (2006) 45 ILM 5 (Liability Annex).

26 Antarctic Treaty 1959 (n 21) preamble.

and to hold all claims to territorial sovereignty in abeyance.[27] These sovereignty claims are strongly contested[28] and, while the terms of the 1959 Antarctic Treaty do not displace these claims, they do not allow them to be asserted through acts or activities taking place while the Treaty remains in force.[29] Moreover, Argentina, Australia, Chile, France, New Zealand, Norway and the United Kingdom have made maritime claims, although these claims have not been accepted by the international community and are *prima facie* held in abeyance under the 1959 Antarctic Treaty.[30]

While much of the Antarctic remains subject to unresolved and contested claims of sovereignty,[31] the current approach to the governance of the Antarctic is to treat it as a form of commons. The commons status of the Antarctic is supported in practice by, *inter alia*, the approach to freedom of scientific research, and the designation of the Antarctic 'as a natural reserve, devoted to peace and science' under the 1991 Antarctic Protocol.[32] The 1959 Antarctic Treaty applies to the area south of 60 degrees South Latitude including all ice shelves but article VI provides that nothing should affect states' rights under international law with regard to the high seas (which would include UNCLOS and other rules of customary international law).[33]

1.2.1.2 Institutional Arrangements

The Antarctic Treaty System is decentralized and there is no separate international organization with independent legal personality. Instead, the Antarctic Treaty provides for governance through periodic consultative meetings of the parties (Antarctic

27 ibid arts I, III–IV.

28 For example, Joyner argues that not all of Antarctica rests on *terra firma* and does not qualify as *terra nullius* in its entirety and invites the question as 'to whether frozen water can qualify as having the same legal status as land for purposes of acquiring valid claims to sovereign title over territory'. Further he contends that 'true and effective occupation, demonstrated through permanent settlement, remains to be convincingly demonstrated in Antarctica by any claimant government' and '[s]overeignty claims legally premised on Antarctica being *res nullius* are therefore questionable'. Joyner, *Governing the Frozen Commons* (n 20) 46.

29 Antarctic Treaty (n 21) art IV. Despite the freezing of the claims, claimant states have sought to exercise their rights under UNCLOS to claim maritime entitlements from their territory and this has been objected to by other states on the basis that their sovereignty claims have no basis in international law: Karen N Scott and David VanderZwaag, 'Polar Oceans and Law of the Sea' in Donald Rothwell and others (eds), *The Oxford Handbook of the Law of the Sea* (OUP 2015) 724, 738–739.

30 Both France and Australia have proclaimed an Exclusive Economic Zone off their Antarctic territories and all seven states have either submitted preliminary information, partial submissions or full submissions to extended continental shelf claims before the Commission on the Limits of the Continental Shelf: Scott and VanderZwaag (n 29).

31 See, for example, Joyner, *Governing the Frozen Commons* (n 20) 46–47; Philippe Sands and Jacqueline Peel, *Principles of International Environmental Law* (4th edn, CUP 2018) 12.

32 1991 Antarctic Protocol (n 24) art 2.

33 1959 Antarctic Treaty (n 21) art VI.

Treaty Consultative Meetings or ATCMs) and other informal arrangements. It established a two-tiered system of membership, the Antarctic Treaty Consultative Parties (ATCP) and non-consultative parties. The ATCP consist of the original twelve members plus additional states that demonstrate their interest in the region by conducting substantial scientific research activity there, such as the establishment of a scientific station or the dispatch of a scientific expedition.[34] There are presently twenty-nine ATCP members that are entitled to attend and participate in decision-making in annual ATCMs. Non-consultative parties, which now number twenty-five, are allowed to attend ATCMs but cannot vote at meetings. Decisions, Resolutions and Measures are adopted at the ATCM by consensus to implement both the Antarctic Treaty and the 1991 Antarctic Protocol but only Measures are legally binding on Consultative Parties once they have been approved by all Consultative Parties. The Committee on Environmental Protection was established under the 1991 Antarctic Protocol and meets concurrently with the ATCM to address matters relating to environmental protection and management and provide advice to the ATCM. The other relevant institutional body is the Commission for the Conservation of Antarctic Marine Living Resources (CCAMLR Commission) which is an international commission that establishes conservation measures for the use of marine living resources in the Antarctic.

1.2.1.3 Resources, Activities and Risks

From a resource perspective, the Antarctic continent itself does not contain many readily exploitable resources due to its inhospitable conditions. That said, it is estimated that about three-quarters of the world's total supply of fresh water is trapped in the polar ice caps and may present a future exploitable resource.[35] The most promising economic resources lie in the Antarctic Ocean, home to an abundance of marine living resources such as krill, seals, whales and squid.[36] While the 1959 Antarctic Treaty preserves freedoms of the high seas, including freedom of fishing (in other words, an open-access regime), marine living resources are governed by CCAMLR and the conservation measures issued by the CCAMLR Commission.

There have been reports of minerals and hydrocarbon resources in the Antarctic Ocean but their existence and extent has been subject to much debate.[37] Indeed, developing states mooted the idea that the common heritage of humankind principle (discussed in Section 1.2.2) should also be applied to resources in

[34] ibid art IX(2).

[35] John Vogler, *The Global Commons: Environmental and Technological Governance* (2nd edn, Wiley 2000) 76.

[36] Christopher C Joyner, 'The Antarctic Legal Regime: An Introduction' in Christopher C Joyner and Sudhir K Chopra (eds), *The Antarctic Legal Regime* (Martinus Nijhoff 1988) 2.

[37] ibid 2; Vogler, *The Global Commons: Environmental and Technological Governance* (n 35) 76.

Antarctica.[38] However, it was agreed that Antarctica would be excluded from negotiations in the Third UN Conference on the Law of the Sea (UNCLOS III) provided that it would be discussed by the ATCPs after UNCLOS III was concluded.[39] In 1988, the Convention on the Regulation of Antarctic Mineral Resource Activities (CRAMRA), which provided a regime for the exploration and exploitation of mineral resources, was adopted.[40] CRAMRA, however, never entered into force, due to opposition from environmental non-governmental organizations (NGOs) and states, such as France and Australia, bolstered by a renewed emphasis on the importance of conservation of the Antarctic. CRAMRA was ultimately displaced by the 1991 Antarctic Protocol which, amongst other things, prohibits any activity relating to mineral and oil resources other than scientific research within the fifty years initial timeframe of the Agreement.[41] Until 2048, the 1991 Antarctic Protocol can only be modified by unanimous agreement of all the Consultative Parties of the Antarctic Treaty and the prohibition of mineral resource activities can only be removed if a binding legal regime on Antarctic mineral resources is in force.[42]

Other activities that take place in Antarctica not directly related to resource exploration and exploitation include scientific research and small-scale, but growing, tourist activities. In relation to scientific research, there has been developing interest in bioprospecting for genetic resources in Antarctica.[43] It is important to note that the Antarctic Treaty Regime affirms the rights of both state and non-state operators to conduct activities in Antarctica. Notwithstanding, the moratorium on mining activities and limitation of activities, there remain risks to the Antarctic environment, chiefly from the operation of scientific research stations, associated flights and, increasingly, tourism-related shipping which raises risks relating to fuel oil spills, a risk which was manifested in 1989 when the *Bahia Paraiso*, an oil tanker ran aground three kilometres from Palmer Station with 810 tons of diesel oil aboard.[44] There may also be risks related to fisheries and associated ship traffic. There are, of course, much broader risks to the Antarctic environment arising from climate change.[45]

38 See, for example, statement of President of Malaysia, Mahathir Bin-Mohammad, in the United Nations General Assembly that there was a strong case for Antarctica to be the common heritage of mankind: United Nations General Assembly Official Records, 37th Session, U.N. Doc/A/37/P.V. 10 (1982) 17–20 (Statement of Mahathir Bin-Mohammad).

39 Buck (n 14) 62.

40 Convention on the Regulation of Antarctic Mineral Resource Activity, 2 June 1988 27 ILM 868 (not yet entered into force) (CRAMRA).

41 1991 Antarctic Protocol (n 24) arts 7, 25 (5).

42 ibid art 25(5).

43 Dagmar Lohan and Sam Johnston, *Bioprospecting in Antarctica* (UNU-IAS, 2005), online <www.cbd.int/financial/bensharing/g-absantarctic.pdf> accessed 14 October 2022.

44 CEDRE, 'Bahia Paraiso – Spill report', online <wwz.cedre.fr/en/Resources/Spills/Spills/Bahia-Paraiso> accessed 13 October 2022.

45 Intergovernmental Panel on Climate Change, *Special Report on the Ocean and Cryosphere in a Changing Climate* (CUP 2022) <www.ipcc.ch/srocc/> accessed 13 October 2022. ATCM XLIV – CEP XXIV Report Volume I, Resolution 4 (2022) Antarctic Climate Change and the

1.2.1.4 Existing Environmental Protection and Liability Framework

The 1959 Antarctic Treaty contains no provisions on the protection of the terrestrial or marine environment in Antarctica. However, the ATCM created a vast array of recommendations which included regulation of the environment, although these were non-binding and prompted concerns about compliance.[46] In the mid-1970s, in line with increasing global awareness of the environment and the use of Antarctic tourist activities and mineral resource surveys, the idea of Antarctica as a 'world park' was mooted by countries such as New Zealand and by NGOs.[47] The 'world park' agenda of conservation played an instrumental role in shifting focus from exploitation to environmental protection and also led to the rejection of CRAMRA. This provided the catalyst for negotiations of the 1991 Antarctic Protocol.

The 1991 Antarctic Protocol marked a 'qualitative change in the approach to environmental issues in the Antarctic and replaces the [previous] ad hoc and unwieldy network of measures'.[48] In addition to designating 'Antarctica as a natural reserve, devoted to peace and science', it obliges states to commit to 'comprehensive protection of the Antarctic Environment and dependent and associated ecosystems'.[49] Article 3 (1) states,

> The protection of the Antarctic environment and dependent and associated ecosystems and the intrinsic value of Antarctica, including its wilderness and aesthetic values and its values as an area for the conduct of scientific research, in particular research essential to the understanding of the global environment, shall be fundamental considerations in the planning and conduct of all activities in the Antarctic Treaty area.

The Protocol takes an ecosystem approach, and requires parties to cooperate in planning and conducting activities in the Antarctic Treaty Area, undertake environmental impact assessments (EIAs) for potentially harmful activities according to detailed requirements as well as contingency planning for emergencies.[50] It also establishes the Committee for Environmental Protection (CEP) as an expert advisory body to provide advice and formulate recommendations to the ATCM.[51] The Protocol has six annexes: Annex I (EIA), Annex II (Flora and Fauna), Annex III (Waste Disposal), Annex IV (Marine Pollution), Annex V (Protected Areas) and Annex VI (Liability Annex). Activities are subject to environmental scrutiny, largely

Environment: A Decadal Synopsis and Recommendations for Action Report <https://documents.ats.aq/ATCM44/fr/ATCM44_fr011_e.pdf>.

46 Vogler, *The Global Commons: Environmental and Technological Governance* (n 35) 85.

47 ibid 82.

48 L Elliot, *International Environmental Politics: Protecting the Antarctic* (Palgrave MacMillan 1994) 196.

49 1991 Antarctic Protocol (n 24) art 2.

50 ibid arts 8 and 15; Annex I (EIAs).

51 ibid arts 11, 12, 15.

through the EIA process, but the Antarctic institutions play no formal regulatory role, in the sense of being either an approval authority or an oversight body.

It should also be noted that UNCLOS provisions apply to Antarctica (including Part VII on the high seas and Part XII on the protection of the marine environment), but their exact relationship with the Antarctic Treaty System is 'equivocal'.[52] UNCLOS preserves the rights and obligations of parties under other agreements provided that those rights do not affect rights provided for under UNCLOS and/or any agreements modifying the operation of UNCLOS are compatible with the object and purpose of UNCLOS.[53] The 1959 Antarctic Treaty and the Antarctic Protocol provisions on the environment and marine scientific research are viewed as compatible with the object and purpose of UNCLOS.[54] While there is some debate on whether the seabed in Antarctica is considered part of the 'the Area' under UNCLOS, there is some evidence to suggest that it was agreed in UNCLOS negotiations that Part XI of UNCLOS that governs the deep seabed would not apply to Antarctica.[55]

The issue of liability first arose in the context of the CRAMRA, where the proposed mineral exploitation activities gave rise to clear environmental risks. The final text of the CRAMRA included a provision on liability imposing strict liability on operators arising from their mineral resource activity.[56] When the CRAMRA failed to achieve support for ratification and negotiations on the Antarctic Protocol began, the issue of liability remained on the table. Ultimately, liability was identified in article 16 of the 1991 Antarctic Protocol, but details of the requirements were put off for further negotiation of a liability annex.

Subsequently, there were debates during the negotiations of the liability annex on whether to take a comprehensive approach whereby all elements of a liability regime were included in one annex or a step-by-step approach, with the first step being response action to environmental emergencies.[57] Ultimately, pragmatism won out and the step-by-step approach was preferred.[58] The 2005 Liability Annex (Annex VI to the 1991 Protocol) only covers damage resulting from 'environmental emergencies' which have been defined as 'any accidental event that has occurred, having taken place after the entry into force of this Annex and that results in, or imminently threatens to result in any significant and harmful impact on the Antarctic environment'.[59] However, the parties affirmed their commitment to taking future steps

52 Scott and VanderZwaag (n 29) 740.
53 UNCLOS (n 5) arts 311 (1) and (2).
54 Scott and VanderZwaag (n 29) 740.
55 ibid 741.
56 CRAMRA (n 40) art 8.
57 ATCM, 'Liability – Report of the Group of Legal Experts' (1998) XXII ATCM/WP1.
58 Michael Johnson, 'Liability for Environmental Damage in Antarctica: The Adoption of Annex VI to the Antarctic Environmental Protocol' (2006) 19(1) Geo Int'l Envtl L Rev 33, 38.
59 Liability Annex (n 25) art 2(b).

towards a comprehensive liability regime in a Decision adopted together with Annex VI,[60] although no further action has been taken to date.[61] Moreover, in the Final Act of the Eleventh Antarctic Treaty Special Consultative Meeting at which the 1991 Antarctic Protocol was adopted, the ATCPs agreed that the Arbitral Tribunal established under the Protocol would not make a determination on damages relating to liability arising from activities taking place in the Antarctic Treaty Area until a binding legal regime had entered into force through an Annex pursuant to article 16.[62]

The focus of the liability requirements in the 2005 Liability Annex is on ensuring that response measures are taken in the event of an environmental emergency. Parties are required to ensure that operators under their jurisdiction take prompt and effective response actions.[63] Failure to do so results in the strict liability of the operator to pay the costs of any response measure that was or ought to have been undertaken.[64] The Liability Annex addresses a variety of implementation issues, such as exemptions to liability, limits on liability, the creation of a fund to address uncompensated response actions.[65] However, the Liability Annex is not yet in force and does not appear likely to enter into force in the near future.[66]

1.2.2 *Deep Seabed*

1.2.2.1 Legal Status as Global Commons

Since J. L. Mero estimated that there was over one trillion tons of manganese nodules on the Pacific deep seabed in 1965,[67] there has been great interest in mineral resources of the deep seabed. Part XI of UNCLOS, as modified by the 1994 Agreement Relating to the Implementation of Part XI of UNCLOS (1994

60 ATCM XXVIII, 6–17 June 2005, Final Report of the Twenty-Eighth Antarctic Consultative Meeting (17 June 2005), part II, Decision I.

61 See discussion in Alan D Hemmings, 'Liability Postponed: The Failure to Bring Annex VI of the Madrid Protocol into Force' (2018) 8(2) Polar J 315, 327–328.

62 Final Session of the Eleventh Antarctic Treaty Special Consultative Meeting, 32.

63 Liability Annex (n 25) art 5.

64 ibid art 6.

65 ibid arts 8, 9, 12.

66 At ATCM XLIV in 2022, it was agreed to revisit the matter of establishing a timeframe for the resumption of negotiations on liability in 2025, Final Report of the Forty-fourth Antarctic Treaty Consultative Meeting, vol 1 (Preliminary Version), paras 151–158, Decision 2 (2022) <www.ats.aq/devAS/Info/FinalReports?lang=e> accessed 13 October 2022. A summary of previous ATCM and CEP resolutions and measures relating to remediation and liability was provided to ATCM XLIV: document SP009, Annex 1 <www.ats.aq/devAS/Meetings/DocDatabase?lang=e> accessed 13 October 2022.

67 GP Glasby, 'Deep Seabed Mining: Past Failures and Future Prospects' (2002) 20(2) Marine Georesources & Geotechnology 161, 161. Mero's predictions proved to be based on a deeply flawed premise.

Agreement),[68] establishes a detailed regime for 'activities in the Area', that is, the exploration and exploitation of the mineral resources of the Area.[69] The Area is defined as the 'seabed and ocean floor and subsoil beyond the limits of national jurisdiction',[70] which are designated, along with the mineral resources found therein, as the common heritage of mankind (hereinafter referred to as the 'common heritage of humankind' or 'CHH').[71] No state or natural or juridical person (as the case may be) shall claim or exercise sovereignty or sovereign rights or appropriate any part of the Area or its resources.[72] Part XI, however, preserves the high seas status of the superjacent waters and the seabed for other uses – such as for submarine cables and pipelines and freedom of scientific research.[73]

Apart from the non-appropriation element, which the CHH shares with the freedom of the high seas, what does the CHH mean? From its inception, the CHH has been a 'controversial legal concept',[74] and there existed no agreement of a workable definition.[75] The troubled attempts to implement the CHH principle in various treaty regimes from law of the sea, to outer space, to Antarctica, the atmosphere and biological diversity either met with failure (atmosphere, Antarctica, biological diversity), inchoate implementation (outer space) or a significant modification from what it started out to be (as exemplified in the UNCLOS and the 1994 Implementation Agreement).[76] The most robust implementation of the CHH principle can be found in UNCLOS, despite the modification of Part XI by the 1994 Implementation Agreement. The CHH principle as implemented in UNCLOS has a definite legal meaning. As articulated by Ambassador Arvid Pardo,[77] it consists of

68 Agreement relating to the implementation of Part XI of the United Nations Convention on the Law of the Sea of 10 December 1982 (adopted 28 July 1994, entered into force 28 July 1996) UNTS vol 1836 (1994 Implementation Agreement) Annex, s 2(1–2).

69 Resources refers to 'all solid, liquid or gaseous mineral resources *in situ* in the Area at or beneath the seabed, including polymetallic nodules': see UNCLOS (n 5) art 133 (a).

70 ibid art 1(1).

71 ibid art 136.

72 UNCLOS (n 5) art 137(1).

73 ibid art 135.

74 Prue Taylor, 'The Concept of the Common Heritage of Mankind' in Douglas Fisher (ed), *Research Handbook on Fundamental Concepts of Environmental Law* (Edward Elgar 2016) 306, 306.

75 Jeffrey Loan, 'The Common Heritage of Mankind in Antarctica: An Analysis in Light of the Threats Posed by Climate Change' (2004) 1 NZ Yearbook Intl L 149, 157.

76 For a discussion on the way in which the common heritage of humankind (CHH) principle has been implemented in various regimes, please refer to Kemal Baslar, *The Concept of the Common Heritage of Mankind in International Law* (Martinus Nijhoff 1998). For a discussion on how the CHH implemented in UNCLOS was modified, see, for example, Alfredo C Robles Jr, 'The 1994 Agreement on Deep Seabed Mining: Universality vs. the Common Heritage of Humanity' (1996) 12 World Bulletin 20 at 61. The voluminous literature on the CHH has been compiled in a bibliography: Prue Taylor and Lucy Stroud, *Common Heritage of Mankind: A Bibliography of Legal Writing* (Fondation de Malte 2013).

77 Arvid Pardo, 'Law of the Sea Conference – What Went Wrong' in Robert L Friedheim (ed), *Managing Ocean Resources: A Primer* (Westview Press 1979) 137 at 141. See also, for example,

non-appropriation;[78] shared management of the resources on behalf of the international community;[79] sharing of benefits for the whole of humankind;[80] peaceful purposes;[81] and preservation and protection of the marine environment from the effects of activities in the Area.[82] The framing of the principle in terms of 'humankind' also imports an intergenerational element.[83] While the extent to which each of these has been implemented under UNCLOS is an ongoing process (and also subject to debate),[84] these five elements are generally accepted as giving legal flesh to the CHH principle. This has implications for institutional arrangements, access to resources and environmental protection which are addressed below.

1.2.2.2 Institutional Arrangements

The International Seabed Authority (ISA), one of the three institutions established under UNCLOS,[85] is the intergovernmental organization which organizes, carries out and controls 'activities in the Area' for and on behalf of humankind as a whole.[86] Related to the CHH principle is that the rights in the resources of the Area are 'vested in mankind as a whole, on whose behalf the Authority shall act',[87] which suggests that the ISA has trust-like duties that it owes to the international community. Currently, the main organs of the ISA are the (1) Assembly composed of all states parties to the UNCLOS, (2) Council with thirty-six member states and (3) a Secretariat. There are also subsidiary bodies made up of experts, the Legal and Technical Commission (LTC), responsible to the Council, and the Finance Committee, responsible to the Assembly. The ISA also has a mining arm, the Enterprise (which is currently non-operational), to organize, carry out and control activities in the Area on behalf of humankind.[88] The Seabed Disputes Chamber

Christopher C Joyner, 'Legal Implications of the Concept of the Common Heritage of Mankind' (1986) 35(1) ICLQ 190, 191, which states that five principal elements appear to characterize the notion of common heritage of mankind 'when applied to common space areas'. See also Taylor (n 74) 319–320.

78 UNCLOS (n 5), art 137(1).

79 ibid arts 137(2), 153(1), 157.

80 ibid arts 137(2), 140.

81 ibid art 141.

82 ibid arts 145, 150(b).

83 Marie Bourrel, Torsten Thiele and Duncan Currie, 'The Common Heritage of Mankind as a Means to Assess and Advance Equity in Deep Sea Mining' (2018) 95 Mar Pol'y 311.

84 See, for example, Michael Lodge, 'The Common Heritage of Mankind' (2012) 27 IJMCL 733, 734; Aline Jaeckel, Jeff A Ardron and Kristina M Gjerde, 'Sharing Benefits of the Common Heritage of Mankind – Is the Deep Seabed Mining Regime Ready?' (2016) 70 Mar Pol'y 198, 200.

85 UNCLOS (n 5) art 156.

86 ibid art 153(1).

87 ibid art 137(2).

88 Under the 1994 Implementation Agreement, the functions of the Enterprise have been conferred on the Secretariat until it begins to operate independently of the Secretariat, until

(SDC) of the International Tribunal for the Law of the Sea (ITLOS) was also established under Part XI to determine disputes arising from activities in the Area.[89]

In contrast to the decentralized system of governance in Antarctica, the ISA is a separate international organization with international legal personality,[90] and has been given 'competence and regulatory control to an extent so far unparalleled in international law'.[91] The ISA has been given a broad mandate to regulate a variety of matters relating to activities in the Area, including the regulation of (1) the system of exploration and exploitation;[92] (2) the protection of the marine environment from harmful effects arising from activities in the Area;[93] (3) the equitable sharing of financial and other economic benefits derived from activities in the Area through any appropriate mechanism;[94] (4) the distribution of revenues to states parties from the exploitation of the outer continental shelf, on the basis of equitable sharing criteria.[95] To fulfil its mandate, the ISA has been afforded a considerable degree of discretion in the adoption of rules, regulations and procedures to govern activities in the Area – UNCLOS only sets out the core elements of the deep seabed regime, 'leaving the ISA with a significant degree of operational competence to further develop governance arrangements'.[96]

1.2.2.3 Resources, Activities and Risks

As mentioned above, the Area and its resources (currently consisting of polymetallic nodules, polymetallic sulphides and cobalt-rich ferromanganese crusts) are the CHH. These resources are said to provide a variety of raw materials such as manganese, nickel, cobalt, copper, zinc, lithium and rare earth elements.[97] Activities in the Area may be carried out by the Enterprise (currently non-operational)[98] and, in association with the ISA, states parties or state enterprises or natural or juridical persons[99] ('contractors'). For natural or juridical persons to carry

such time as the Council issues a directive permitting the Enterprise to function independently: 1994 Implementation Agreement (n 68) section 2 (1).

89 UNCLOS (n 5) art 186.

90 ibid art 176.

91 Richard Collins and Duncan French, 'A Guardian of Universal Interest or Increasingly Out of Its Depth? The International Seabed Authority Turns 25' (2019) 17(3) Int Org Law Rev 1, 3.

92 UNCLOS (n 5), art 153 (1); art 160 (2) (f) (ii); art 162 (2) (o) (ii); Annex III, art 17 (1).

93 ibid art 145, art 209 (1); Annex III, art 17 (1) (b) (xii) and art 17 (2) (f).

94 ibid art 140 (2), art 160 (2) (f), art 162 (o) (i).

95 ibid art 82(4).

96 Collins and French (n 91) 24.

97 The turn to electric vehicles has created a surge in demand for key deep seabed minerals, such as cobalt and lithium, leading to a debate as to whether deep seabed mining is necessary for broader sustainability transitions, see Christopher Pala, 'Can Mining the Seabed Help Save the Planet?' Foreign Policy, 7 November 2021 <https://foreignpolicy.com/2021/11/07/seabed-mining-marine-life-climate-change-electric-cars-pacific-nauru/> accessed 13 October 2022.

98 1994 Implementation Agreement (n 68), Annex, section 2.

99 UNCLOS (n 5) art 153(2).

out activities in the Area, they must possess the nationality of states parties or be effectively controlled by them or by their nationals and must be sponsored by states parties ('sponsoring state[s]').[100] Contractors have to apply for a licence to explore and exploit resources which will be reviewed by the LTC, who will then make a recommendation to the Council on whether the licence should be approved.

The ISA's development of the legal regime governing activities in the Area has been executed in an evolutionary and incremental manner, determined by what needed to be regulated in each phase of development of activities in the Area and further shaped by technology and increasing knowledge of the deep sea environment. The first phase of the ISA's work focused on the regulation of exploration,[101] and the second phase is currently focused on the development of regulations on the *exploitation* of mineral resources of the Area.[102] At the time of writing, the LTC had issued Draft Regulations on Exploitation of Mineral Resources in the Area (DER)[103] which are under consideration by the Council. The rules on prospecting, exploration and exploitation will constitute the Mining Code that will govern activities in the Area.

The contract is the basis upon which title to minerals passes to the contractor upon recovery. The rights to exploit and acquire rights with respect to the minerals recovered are protected by security of tenure, as such the ISA cannot unilaterally revise, suspend or terminate a contract (except in cases of non-compliance).[104] The contract provides the basis of legal control by the ISA over the contractor and the mining activities, whereby the contractor agrees to be bound by the ISA's regulations and the plan of work approved by the ISA. It is envisaged that the contractors will have to pay a portion of their profits to the ISA, which is responsible for devising a system for the equitable sharing of financial and other economic benefits derived from activities in the Area.[105]

[100] ibid art 153(2)(b); Annex III, art 4.

[101] The ISA has issued three sets of regulations on exploration: ISA, Regulations on Prospecting and Exploration for Polymetallic Nodules in the Area (13 July 2000), Doc. No. ISBA/6/A/18 (13 July 2000) (PMN). In 2013, the Regulations for Polymetallic Nodules were amended to be consistent with the regulations adopted in 2010 and 2012 for the other resources. ISA, Regulations on Prospecting and Exploration for Polymetallic Sulphides in the Area, Doc No. ISBA/16/A/12/Rev. 1 (7 May 2010) (PMS); ISA, Regulations on Prospecting for Cobalt-Rich Ferromanganese Crusts in the Area, Doc No. ISBA/19/C/17 (22 July 2013) (CFC) [collectively the 'Exploration Regulations']. At the timing of writing, thirty-one contracts for exploration have been issued pursuant to the Exploration Regulations.

[102] See ISA Website available at <www.isa.org.jm/legal-instruments/ongoing-development-regulations-exploitation-mineral-resources-area>

[103] Draft Regulations on Exploitation of Mineral Resources in the Area, Prepared by the Legal and Technical Commission, ISBA/25/C/WP.1 dated 22 March 2019 (DER).

[104] UNCLOS (n 5) art 153(6); Annex III, arts 18 and 19.

[105] UNCLOS (n 5) art 140(2).

In relation to mineral resource exploitation in the deep seabed, much attention has focused on risks to vulnerable and unique marine organisms and ecosystems of the deep seabed. While the increased interest in deep seabed mining has led to its increased scientific study, there remains significant scientific uncertainty, which is a function of the limited amount of baseline data and knowledge of broad system interactions, as well as the novelty of the mining activity itself.[106] While impacts may vary in effect and intensity, according to the type of mining activity involved, they may include direct habitat destruction, elimination of local biodiversity and degradation of surrounding environments through indirect impacts such as sediment plumes, noise and vibration from pumps, platforms, vessels and light.[107] Mining activities in the Area might also give rise to loss or damage to mineral resources of the Area, themselves part of the common heritage of humankind, and part of the geophysical environment of the deep seabed ecosystem, as well as losses stemming from impacts to other marine users.

1.2.2.4 Environmental Protection and Environmental Liability

A central obligation that falls on the ISA and sponsoring states is to ensure the effective protection of the marine environment.[108] Since this is a shared responsibility, both the ISA and sponsoring states are required to put in place effective regulatory requirements, including 'administrative measures … reasonably appropriate for securing compliance'.[109] The ISA regulations and the plans of work will provide the core environmental protection requirements. The ISA also has administrative tools, such as the ability to issue emergency orders to contractors, to prevent serious harm to the marine environment.[110] The basic structure of responsibility for environmental protection is that the contractors are obliged to comply with the regulatory requirements and will be liable for 'any damage arising out of wrongful acts in the conduct of its operations'.[111] Article 139 of the UNCLOS and article 4(4) of Annex III expressly provide that sponsoring states will be liable for their failures to 'ensure' that contractors carry out their activities in accordance with its obligations. The duty to ensure was identified as part of the obligation of due diligence by the SDC in its 2011 Advisory Opinion on Activities in the Area.[112] The ISA has similar

[106] Lisa Levin, Diva Amon and Hannah Lily, 'Challenges to the Sustainability of Deep Seabed Mining' (2020) 3 Nature Sustainability 784.

[107] Lisa A Levin and others, 'Defining "Serious Harm" to the Marine Environment in the Context of Deep-Seabed Mining' (2016) 74 Mar Pol'y 245, 250–255.

[108] UNCLOS (n 5) art 145.

[109] ibid Annex III, art 4(4).

[110] ibid art 162(2)(x).

[111] ibid Annex III, art 22.

[112] *Responsibilities and Obligations of States Sponsoring Persons and Entities with Respect to Activities in the Area* (Advisory Opinion of 1 February 2011) ITLOS Reports 2011, 10 (*Activities in the Area* Advisory Opinion), para 110.

responsibilities to ensure and is identified as being liable for any damage arising out of its wrongful acts in the exercise of its powers.[113] No further elaboration of liability rules or mechanisms have been enacted by the ISA, although both the Exploration Regulations and DER reflect the responsibility and liability of the contractor and ISA as set out in UNCLOS and described above.

As the environmental liability provisions contained in Part XI UNCLOS, and any coverage of liability in the DER under development by the ISA, relate to environmental damage arising from 'activities in the Area', these provisions should apply also to any such environmental damage to the water column (i.e. the high seas). However, they do not cover damage to the deep seabed environment (either the seabed or water column) from other causes not related to activities in the Area.

1.2.3 *High Seas*

1.2.3.1 Legal Status as Global Commons

Article 86 of UNCLOS states that Part VII on the high seas applies to 'all parts of the sea that are not included in the exclusive economic zone, in the territorial sea or in the internal waters of a State, or in the archipelagic waters of an archipelagic State'. The high seas is open to all states and no state can validly purport to subject any part of the high seas to its sovereignty.[114] The prevailing principle, absent other rules of international law to the contrary, is freedom of the high seas; examples of which are non-exhaustively listed in UNCLOS and include the freedom of navigation, overflight, the laying of submarine cables and pipelines, fishing and scientific research.[115] The freedom of the high seas is subject to a general limitation that they be exercised with due regard for the interests of other states in their exercise of high seas freedoms, and also with due regard for the rights under UNCLOS with respect to activities in the Area.[116] Each enumerated freedom also has specific limitations set out in the Convention, and are subject to other internationally agreed upon obligations addressing specific activities.[117] The primary means in which UNCLOS establishes public order in the high seas is through the principle of exclusive flag state jurisdiction over vessels on the high seas.[118]

[113] UNCLOS (n 5) art 153; Annex III, art 22.
[114] UNCLOS (n 5) arts 87 and 89.
[115] ibid art 87(1).
[116] ibid art 87 (2).
[117] For example, the freedom of navigation is limited by flag state jurisdiction; freedom of fishing is subject to the conditions laid down in section 2 on Part VI and other limitations.
[118] UNCLOS (n 5) art 92. As observed in the MV Norstar, 'the principle of exclusive flag State jurisdiction prohibits not only the exercise of enforcement jurisdiction on the high seas by States other than the flag State but also the extension of their prescriptive jurisdiction to lawful activities conducted by foreign ships on the high seas'. *The M/V 'NORSTAR' Case (Panama v Italy)*, Judgment, 10 April 2019, para 225.

1.2.3.2 Institutional Arrangements

UNCLOS does not create a treaty body to act as the 'supreme body' of the Convention in the same manner as the United Nations Framework Convention on Climate Change or the Convention on Biological Diversity.[119] Article 319 does provide for meetings of the parties, but without identifying the role and nature of the meetings of the state parties.[120] UNCLOS does create the International Tribunal for the Law of the Sea, which along with other forums identified in Part XV of UNCLOS provides a venue for the settlement of disputes arising under UNCLOS. The ITLOS has addressed questions bearing on the legal responsibilities and liabilities of states under UNCLOS, most notably in the SDC's Advisory Opinion on Activities in the Area[121] and the Advisory Opinion requested by the Subregional Fisheries Commission.[122]

Beyond these general institutional arrangements, there has been no specific international organization, body or equivalent process that addresses the governance of the high seas. Instead, a number of sectoral activities in the high seas are governed by existing treaty regimes and institutions, including a series of species and regional fisheries treaties and arrangements as well as some regional seas conventions, with associated governance bodies, such as regional fisheries management organizations and commissions. However, the various regimes are fragmented, sometimes overlapping, lack any coordinating mechanism and leave significant gaps in governance of the high seas, reinforcing the belief that high seas governance represented an 'unfinished agenda' of UNCLOS.[123]

These concerns, and particularly concerns about the protection of marine biodiversity eventually led to the UN Informal Consultative Process on Oceans and the Law of the Sea to establish an Ad Hoc Open-ended Informal Working Group in 2004 to study issues relating to conservation and sustainable use of marine biological diversity beyond areas of national jurisdiction (BBNJ Working Group). In 2011, the BBNJ Working Group, after much debate in previous sessions, agreed to work towards the establishment of an intergovernmental negotiating process that would 'address the conservation and sustainable use of marine biodiversity in areas beyond national jurisdiction, in particular, together and as a whole'. Four issues were to be considered as a package deal, namely marine genetic resources including questions on the sharing of benefits;

[119] See Robin Churchill and Geir Ulfstein, 'Autonomous Institutional Arrangements in Multilateral Environmental Agreements: A Little-Noticed Phenomenon in International Law' (2000) 94(4) AJIL 623.

[120] UNCLOS (n 5) art 319; see James Harrison, 'The Law of the Sea Convention Institutions' in Donald R Rothwell, Alex G Oude Elferink, Karen N Scott and Tim Stephens (eds), *Oxford Handbook on the Law of the Sea* (OUP 2014) 373, 377.

[121] *Activities in the Area* Advisory Opinion (n 112).

[122] *Request for an Advisory Opinion submitted by the Sub-Regional Fisheries Commission (SRFC)* (Advisory Opinion of 2 April 2015) ITLOS Reports 2015 (SRFC Advisory Opinion).

[123] David Freestone, 'International Governance, Responsibility and Management of Areas beyond National Jurisdiction' (2012) 27 IJMCL 191, 195.

area-based management tools, including marine protected areas, environmental impact assessments; and capacity-building and transfer of marine technology. In 2015, the BBNJ Working Group recommended to the United Nations General Assembly (UNGA) that it 'develop an internationally legally-binding instrument under the Convention on the conservation and sustainable use of marine biological diversity of areas beyond national jurisdiction'.[124] The text of this Agreement was agreed in March 2023 (2023 BBNJ Agreement).[125] The Agreement establishes a Conference of the Parties, a Scientific and Technical Body, a clearing house mechanism and a secretariat.[126] The Conference of the Parties (COP) will meet for the first time no later than one year after the entry into force of the Agreement, and will develop these institutional arrangements, including the terms of reference and modalities of operation of the Scientific and Technical Body. Amongst its functions, the COP is to review the adequacy and effectiveness of the provisions of the Agreement within five years of entry into force and at intervals thereafter, and may propose means to strengthen implementation.[127] The Agreement will enter into force 120 days after the sixtieth instrument of ratification, approval, acceptance or accession is deposited.[128] It is to be interpreted and applied in a manner consistent with UNCLOS, and in a way 'that does not undermine relevant legal instruments and frameworks and relevant global, regional subregional and sectoral bodies and that promotes coherence and coordination with those instruments, frameworks and bodies'.[129] The relationship between the Agreement and other relevant legal instruments, frameworks and bodies is taken up in more detail in provisions addressing area-based management tools and environmental impact assessment.[130]

1.2.3.3 Resources, Activities and Risks

Part VI (high seas) of UNCLOS only expressly deals with fisheries resources and recognizes the freedom of fishing as a freedom of the high seas. Thus, in principle,

[124] For a history of the developments leading up to the negotiations of a new international legally binding instrument under UNCLOS on the conservation and sustainable use of marine biological diversity in areas beyond national jurisdiction, see Glen Wright, Juliette Rochette, Kristina Gjerde and Isabel Seeder, 'The Long and Winding Road: Negotiating a Treaty for the Conservation and Sustainable Use of Marine Biodiversity in Areas beyond National Jurisdiction', IDDRI Study No. 18, August 2018 <www.iddri.org/sites/default/files/PDF/Publications/Catalogue%20Iddri/Etude/201808-Study_HauteMer-long%20and%20winding%20road.pdf> accessed 13 October 2022.

[125] Draft agreement under the United Nations Convention on the Law of the Sea on the conservation and sustainable use of marine biological diversity of areas beyond national jurisdiction, Advance, Unedited text, 4 March 2023 ('BBNJ Agreement').

[126] ibid arts 48–51. A financial mechanism will also be established, art 52.

[127] ibid art 48(7).

[128] ibid art 61.

[129] ibid art 4.

[130] See, for example, arts 14(b), 18, 19, 20 ante, and 23.

living resources are open to access and appropriation by any state, subject to due regard for the interests of other states.[131] Part VII limits these high seas freedoms by imposing certain obligations on states with regard to the conservation of the living resources of the high seas, and a number of other international and regional instruments impose additional rules, including in relation to straddling and highly migratory species.[132] The status, collection and utilization of marine genetic resources of areas beyond national jurisdiction are addressed in the 2023 BBNJ Agreement.[133] No state may claim or exercise sovereignty or sovereign rights over such resources, and activities with respect to such resources may be carried out by all parties to the Agreement and natural or juridical persons under the jurisdiction of parties, in accordance with the provisions of the Agreement on notification and information sharing through the clearing house mechanism and fair and equitable sharing of benefits arising from activities with respect to such resources.

Non-resource related activities in the high seas are numerous, some are explicitly recognized in UNCLOS such as shipping, marine scientific research and the laying of submarine cables and pipelines, but others are emerging such as geoengineering, or the large-scale ocean clean-up which aims to clean up plastic debris in the oceans.

In the high seas, a multitude of activities pose risks of environmental harm. These include impacts on marine species and ecosystem services arising from pollution of the marine environment. Such pollution can derive from a range of sources: vessels; land-based sources; offshore mineral resource exploitation activities within national jurisdiction or, prospectively, in the Area; or from activities related to pipelines and cables. Environmental harm can include the impacts of noise pollution (e.g. sonar). Marine biodiversity of the high seas may also be impacted directly or indirectly by over-exploitation of marine living resources and by non-selective and/or destructive fishing practices, such as bottom-trawling, which can also damage the physical environment itself. Potential climate change impacts include ocean acidification and coral bleaching, as well as more fundamental change to marine ecosystems in light of ocean warming and sea level rise. Measures intended to mitigate climate change, such as marine geoengineering, may also give rise to adverse changes to marine biodiversity.[134]

131 UNCLOS (n 5) art 87 (1) (e) read with art 87 (2).

132 ibid arts 116–120, UNCLOS. Also see 1995 Agreement for the Implementation of the United Nations Convention on the Law of the Sea of 10 December 1982 Relating to the Conservation and Management of Straddling Fish Stocks and Highly Migratory Fish Stocks (adopted 4 August 1995, entered into force 11 December 2001) 34 ILM 1542.

133 BBNJ Agreement (n 125), Part II. The provisions of Part II do not apply to fishing regulated under relevant international law and fishing-related activities, art 8(2).

134 See, for example, Convention on Biological Diversity, Decision XI/20 'Climate-Related Geoengineering', UNEP/CBD/COP/DEC/XI/20, 5 December 2012.

1.2.3.4 Environmental Protection and Environmental Liability

UNCLOS establishes a relatively robust marine environmental protection regime in Part XII setting out general obligations relating to the prevention, reduction and control of marine pollution and specific obligations to address such pollution from a variety of sources.[135] Marine environmental protection obligations do not single out the high seas, but rather the approach is to treat the marine environment in an undifferentiated fashion, with the provisions of Part XII applying to all areas of the marine environment both inside national jurisdiction and beyond it.[136] There are, however, high seas specific obligations concerning the conservation and preservation of living resources.[137] Article 192 of UNCLOS sets out states' general obligation to protect and preserve the marine environment, and while simply stated, this obligation has been interpreted to place an obligation on states to protect the marine environment from future damage and to maintain or improve the existing condition of the marine environment as well as to take active measures to prevent the degradation of the marine environment.[138] States also have the obligation to ensure that activities that take place within their jurisdiction do not cause pollution to areas beyond national jurisdiction.[139]

Part XII of UNCLOS does contain a provision addressing liability, article 235, which reads as follows:

> 1. States are responsible for the fulfilment of their international obligations concerning the protection and preservation of the marine environment. They shall be liable in accordance with international law.
> 2. States shall ensure that recourse is available in accordance with their legal systems for prompt and adequate compensation or other relief in respect of damage caused by pollution of the marine environment by natural or juridical persons under their jurisdiction.
> 3. With the objective of assuring prompt and adequate compensation in respect of all damage caused by pollution of the marine environment, States shall cooperate in the implementation of existing international law and the further development of international law relating to responsibility and liability for the assessment of and compensation for damage

[135] Sections 1–4 of Part XI of UNCLOS set out general obligations to protect the marine environment while section 5 addresses six specific sources of pollution, namely from land-based sources, seabed activities subject to national jurisdiction, activities in the Area, dumping, vessels and pollution from or through the atmosphere.

[136] *The South China Sea Arbitration (The Republic of the Philippines v The People's Republic of China)* (Award) (2016) Oxford Reports on ICGJ 495 (PCA) (*South China Sea Arbitration*), para 940.

[137] UNCLOS (n 5) arts 116–120.

[138] *South China Sea Arbitration* (n 136) para 941.

[139] UNCLOS (n 5) art 193.

and the settlement of related disputes, as well as, where appropriate, development of criteria and procedures for payment of adequate compensation, such as compulsory insurance or compensation funds.

This provision, which is not specific to the high seas, does not so much elaborate on the liability rules as it restates the options available to states to address liability; namely, states themselves may attract liability under the rules of state responsibility, states are required to provide recourse for injured persons within their own legal systems and states may cooperatively develop new (civil liability) rules and procedures addressing liability.[140] Considerable progress has been made in the development of civil liability rules addressing oil and other hazardous releases in areas within national jurisdiction, but these regimes (for the most part) do not apply to environmental harm in the high seas and/or may not be in force.[141]

The 2023 BBNJ Agreement is designed to address the need for a more comprehensive global regime under UNCLOS to better address conservation and sustainable use of marine biodiversity of areas beyond national jurisdiction. The Agreement makes provision for the establishment of area-based management tools, including marine protected areas, in the high seas through the COP.[142] Indicative criteria for the identification of such areas are incorporated into Annex I of the Agreement. In the context of area-based management tools, the COP may also decide to adopt measures in ABNJ to be applied on an emergency basis if necessary 'if a natural phenomenon or human-caused disaster has caused, or is likely to cause, serious or irreversible harm to marine biological diversity of areas beyond national jurisdiction, to ensure that the serious or irreversible harm is not exacerbated'.[143] The COP is to adopt procedures and guidance for the establishment of such measures on the basis of recommendations to be elaborated by the Scientific and Technical Body.

The BBNJ Agreement also operationalizes the provisions of UNCLOS on environmental impact assessment for ABNJ.[144] There was much discussion during the negotiation of the Agreement as to who should be responsible for conducting an EIA and the threshold to trigger the EIA requirement. The Agreement sets out processes, thresholds and requirements for screening activities for the need for EIA,

140 A provision on the development of procedures for liability and dispute settlement was included in the London Convention for the Prevention of Marine Pollution by Dumping of Wastes and Other Matter (London Convention), (adopted 29 December 1972, entered into force 30 August 1975) 1046 UNTS 120 (1972), art X; article 15 of the 1996 Protocol to the London Convention (adopted 7 November 1996, entered into force 24 March 2006), 36 ILM 1 (1997) provides that '[i]n accordance with the principles of international law regarding State responsibility for damage to the environment of other States or to any other area of the environment, the Contracting Parties undertake to develop procedures regarding liability arising from the dumping or incineration at sea of wastes or other matter'.

141 See generally Gaskell (n 10).

142 BBNJ Agreement (n 125) Part III.

143 ibid art 19.

144 UNCLOS (n 5) art 206, and BBNJ Agreement (n 125), Part IV.

and for conducting and reporting EIAs, with further relevant guidelines to be developed by the Scientific and Technical Body for consideration and adoption by the COP.[145] The Agreement provides a role for the Scientific and Technical Body in aspects of the EIA process, but the responsibility for conducting EIAs lies with the party with jurisdiction or control over the planned activity. If, on the basis of screening, a party has reasonable grounds for believing that a proposed activity may cause substantial pollution of or significant and harmful changes to the marine environment, an EIA must be conducted. [146] Cumulative impacts, and uncertainties and gaps in knowledge, are amongst the factors that must be considered in the screening and EIA processes. A decision to authorize a planned activity under the jurisdiction or control of a party may only be made when 'taking into account mitigation or management measures, the Party has determined that it has made all reasonable efforts to ensure that the activity can be conducted in a manner consistent with the prevention of significant adverse impacts on the environment'.[147] Where activities in ABNJ are permitted by a party, it must monitor impacts of such activities and report on such impacts including through the BBNJ clearing house mechanism and the Scientific and Technical Body. Where significant adverse impacts that were either not foreseen in the EIA in terms of their nature or severity, or that arise from a breach of conditions in the authorization, the party must review its authorization decision and notify the COP, other parties and the public, and require that measures are proposed and implemented to prevent, mitigate and/or manage those impacts, or take any other necessary action including halting the activity as appropriate.[148] On the basis of its review of monitoring reports, the Scientific and Technical Body may also make recommendations to a party where it considers that an authorized activity may have significant adverse impacts that were unforeseen or that arise from a breach of authorization.

The negotiations of the BBNJ Agreement presented a further opportunity for the development of liability rules addressing environmental harm in areas beyond national jurisdiction. In the first phase of discussions in the Preparatory Committee from 2015 to 2017, responsibility and liability were discussed as a cross-cutting issue. At that time, the Chair included 'responsibility and liability' as one of the issues that the agreement should cover[149] and subsequently recognized that liability of states for damage to the marine environment and the 'polluter-pays' principle were amongst the principles and approaches that needed further discussion.[150] However,

[145] BBNJ Agreement (n 125), art 41 bis.
[146] ibid art 24.
[147] ibid art 38.
[148] ibid arts 40 and 41.
[149] Chair's Overview of the First Session of the Preparatory Committee, 28 March–8 April 2016, 18, 20.
[150] Chair's Overview of the Second Session of the Preparatory Committee, 26 August–9 September 2016, 6, 13; and see discussion of these proposed elements in Gaskell (n 10) 263–269.

the issue was not actively pursued throughout the negotiations, with the exception of a reference to the possibility of establishing a special rehabilitation and ecological restoration fund. In the final resumed negotiating session in February–March 2023, a renewed call was made for the inclusion of provisions on liability and compensation for damage or loss arising from activities in ABNJ.[151] However, there are no provisions on liability in the operative part of the Agreement. Instead a preambular provision reflects but does not replicate Article 235(1) UNCLOS stating that 'as set out in the Convention, States are responsible for the fulfilment of their international obligations concerning the protection and preservation of the marine environment and may be liable in accordance with international law'.[152] The Agreement provides that the COP may consider establishing additional funds as part of the financial mechanism, *inter alia*, to 'finance rehabilitation and ecological restoration of marine biological diversity of areas beyond national jurisdiction'.[153]

1.3 ENVIRONMENTAL HARM

The focus of this book is on environmental harm or damage (the terms environmental harm or damage are used interchangeably), as opposed to liability for harm to property and other economic interests. Our interest in environmental harm reflects what we view as the primary concern of the international community in promoting liability rules for the global commons (as signified in Principle 13 of the Rio Declaration). Given this focus, this book considers activities that take place in areas beyond national jurisdiction, but also those activities that may occur in areas under state jurisdiction but result in harm to the global commons.

The specific environmental risks in each of the global commons areas under discussion have been explored in Section 1.2. The different environmental risks highlight that environmental damage in areas beyond national jurisdiction is likely to occur in a range of different circumstances that could have an impact on the appropriate approach to reparation of harm. Damage could arise as a result of accidental discharges of oil or hazardous chemicals in the high seas or in Antarctica, comprising single catastrophic pollution incidents. In other scenarios, environmental damage might occur as a result of unlawful activities, such as illegal, unreported and unregulated fishing. Alternatively, environmental damage could arise from impacts of approved activities such as licensed fisheries or, prospectively, operational activities related to seabed mining in the Area. In these situations, it is likely that some impacts will have been foreseen in an environmental impact assessment prior to approval, and deemed acceptable provided specific risk management measures are applied. These raise the question whether there are

[151] See *Earth Negotiations Bulletin*, BBNJ IGC-5.2 No. 8, 2 March 2023, 2.
[152] BBNJ Agreement (n.125) preamble.
[153] BBNJ Agreement (n 125) art 52(4) bis ante.

circumstances in which damage arising from such activities should give rise to liability, for example where adverse effects occur that were unforeseen in nature and/or scale. Such impacts might be identified as scientific understanding of ecosystems in areas beyond national jurisdiction develops. Gaps in existing scientific knowledge, for example, on deep seabed ecosystems, prompt questions about inter-temporal aspects of any liability rules in the global commons – whether liability can or should be imposed in respect of activities that were not known to be harmful before evidence of damaging effects was available.[154]

Environmental damage in areas beyond national jurisdiction can occur over long periods of time, as a result of the combined or cumulative effects of diffuse drivers of damage, such as pollution of the marine environment by plastic, marine pollution by land-based sources or from the impacts of climate change, including ocean acidification. It can also result from the cumulative effects of specific activities, such as overfishing or destructive fishing practices. Diffuse and cumulative damage is trickier to address within the context of a liability regime as it gives rise to more intractable questions of causation, remoteness and attribution.

Based upon practice to date in international civil liability treaties and other relevant forums addressing environmental damage, the heads of damage that might be covered by the concept of 'environmental damage' in areas beyond national jurisdiction could encompass consequential loss to economic interests (loss of profit). This might include, for example, losses from reduced access to fisheries, mineral resources or marine genetic resources. They might also include the costs of measures to prevent or restore environmental damage, for example, where an accidental spill has occurred, as well as related monitoring and assessment costs. These types of damage, reflecting consequential loss, prevention or restoration costs incurred, may, in principle, be uncontroversial,[155] but in the global commons context there are unique issues respecting proportionality: how the reasonableness of restoration measures should be assessed in terms of, for example, cost, feasibility, likelihood of success and prospects for natural recovery. A second issue relates to situations of irreparable environmental harm, as well as to interim environmental losses incurred pending restoration. In this second category that is classed as pure environmental loss for our purposes, a central question is whether and how reparation can incorporate the provision of equivalent resources and ecosystem services.

[154] See Okowa (n 8) 312–315.

[155] See, for example, Edward Brans, *Liability for Damage to Public Natural Resources: Standing, Damage and Damage Assessment* (Kluwer Law International 2001); Peter Wetterstein (ed), *Harm to the Environment: The Right to Compensation and the Assessment of Damages* (OUP 1997); Michael Bowman and Alan Boyle (eds), *Environmental Damage in International and Comparative Law: Problems of Definition and Valuation* (OUP 2002); Günther Handl, 'Marine Environmental Damage: The Compensability of Ecosystem Service Loss in International Law' (2019) 34 IJMCL 602.

1.4 APPROACH AND STRUCTURE OF THE BOOK

Examinations of the international law concerning liability for environmental harm tend to be structured in relation to several key points of division. The first focuses on the potential subjects of liability: states – under the general law of state responsibility; and private operators – under civil liability treaties. As the risk associated with different activities is sector-specific and requires the participation of operators and, often their insurers, civil liability treaties are themselves sector-specific, with self-contained regimes governing areas such as oil transport, the movement of hazardous wastes and nuclear facilities. Consequently, descriptions of international liability rules are often presented on a regime-by-regime basis.

Our approach differs in that we are primarily interested in the unique legal issues associated with providing for a system of compensation for environmental harm to globally shared resources and ecosystems. Instead of structuring this book on a regime-by-regime basis, our approach is to organize the book around the central themes and issues that liability rules and processes need to address in order to comprehensively attend to compensation for environmental harm. Specifically, the book breaks down the topic of liability into the following constituent elements: the definition and valuation of environmental damage (Chapter 3); the allocation of liability, including channelling liability to different actors (Chapter 4); the standards of liability (Chapter 5); standing to bring claims (Chapter 6); access to remedies, addressing the forums in which claims may be brought (Chapter 7); and the issue of insurance and compensation funds (Chapter 8). In order to provide a more general framing for the chapters that follow, Chapter 2 introduces the topic of liability for environmental harm through a discussion of the purposes of liability regimes and the principal approaches that the international community has adopted to address liability. Chapter 9 sets out our conclusions, highlighting key developments as well as challenges and outlining some possible ways forward for addressing liability for environmental harm in areas beyond national jurisdiction.

The discussion within the chapters is oriented towards an examination of each issue in the context of environmental regulation of the commons generally. In particular, we are interested in how the key attributes of each commons regime shape the various elements of liability. Organizing the analysis in this way enables analysis across the commons regimes and informs a consideration of existing approaches to liability in international law upon which new rules for areas of global commons might draw. Abstracting and elaborating upon general approaches is particularly significant considering the relatively (vis-à-vis areas under state jurisdiction) underdeveloped approaches to liability in global commons areas.

We do, however, separate out the regime-specific rules in order to highlight their particular features where appropriate. As is evident from the preceding description of the three commons regimes addressed, the legal nature of the commons varies across each regime, with important implications for liability law. The rules are also influenced by the nature of the activities undertaken in each commons area, and the primary actors (state or non-state) involved.

The incomplete and very much evolving nature of the specific liability rules presents several challenges. First, the absence of specific liability rules, which is particularly the case in relation to the high seas, requires us to draw on more general rules, in both international and domestic law that structure liability. We examine the law on state responsibility, as it applies to the global commons, quite comprehensively. Our coverage of liability rules which apply to non-state actors (primarily operators), draws on civil liability treaties, and other harmonized approaches to liability that originate in international law – what the International Law Commission (ILC) refers to as 'loss allocation'. As these rules rely in some measure on domestic legal processes, we also draw on general approaches to liability found in domestic systems. Second, we are required to contend with rules that are not yet in force, in the case of the Antarctic Liability Annex, or are still under active negotiation, in the case of the deep seabed mining liability requirements. In relation to the former, we place considerable weight on the Antarctic Liability Annex, recognizing that it represents the position of the Antarctic parties, notwithstanding that it remains not in force. In connection with the deep seabed mining rules, we note, where appropriate, the approach under consideration (typically, in the form of draft regulations), but view these as simply indications of potential approaches to liability.

In addressing liability issues comprehensively and across several legal contexts, this book provides the first in-depth description and evaluation of current rules and possible avenues for future legal developments in an area that is attracting considerable attention from states, international organizations and commercial actors, in addition to legal and governance scholars. The book is predominantly descriptive and analytical in approach, with the intention of providing an authoritative account of current liability rules addressing areas beyond national jurisdiction and assessing trajectories for future legal developments. We do not adopt a particular theoretical perspective, but a central theme running throughout the book is the role and suitability of liability rules as tools for environmental harm prevention and remediation. It is hoped that the book will contribute to both policy and academic debates on the nature of environmental regulation of the commons, the role of liability in providing compensation for losses and for harm prevention, as well as the nature and implementation of rules on standing which recognize the right to bring claims on behalf of collective interests.

This book was completed at the end of October 2022. As far as possible, brief reference has also been made to significant relevant developments up to March 2023. References to the 2023 BBNJ Agreement, and provisions thereof, are to the agreed unedited text of 4 March 2023. The text of the Agreement was due to be edited with a view to adoption in June 2023.

2

Purposes of, and Approaches to, International Liability

2.1 INTRODUCTION

Much of the debate surrounding liability for environmental harm in international law has focused on the basic approach that states should adopt to best ensure that appropriate remedies are available to address environmental harms that have international dimensions. The central divide is concerned with whether liability rules ought to be directed at states, as the subjects of liability, or whether it is preferable to target operators of risky activities, with the primary function of states being to ensure recourse for injured parties within their national legal systems.[1] The debates about the most suitable approach have been strongly influenced by both conceptual and practical issues. In connection with the former, much ink has been spilt over whether states ought to be responsible for damages that arise from 'lawful' activities or whether liability ought to be restricted to harm that arises from a state's breach of international law. Extending liability to include damage from lawful activities leads to states potentially being held strictly liable for damages from risky or hazardous activities that occur within their territory or under their control.[2] Political opposition

[1] Much of this debate has unfolded within the work of the International Law Commission (ILC) on international liability for injurious consequences arising out of acts not prohibited by international law. For a brief summary of approaches in the ILC's work, see ILC, 'First Report on the Legal Regime for Allocation of Loss in the Case of Transboundary Harm Arising Out of Hazardous Activities, by Mr. Pemmaraju Sreenivasa Rao, Special Rapporteur' (2003) UN Doc A/CN.4/531. For general discussions of debate, see also Alan Boyle, 'State Responsibility and Liability for Injurious Consequences of Acts Not Prohibited by International Law: A Necessary Distinction?' (1990) 39 ICLQ 1; Jutta Brunnée, 'Of Sense and Sensibility: Reflections on Environmental Liability Regimes as Tools for Environmental Protection' (2004) 53 ICLQ 351.

[2] ILC, 'First Report on the Legal Regime' (n 1); see also ILC, 'Twelfth Report on International Liability for Injurious Consequences Arising Out of Acts Not Prohibited by International Law, by Mr. Julio Barboza, Special Rapporteur' (1996) UN Doc A/CN.4/475 & Corr.1 and Add.1 & Corr.1; but see Boyle (n 1).

from many states to strict liability has pushed legal developments on liability towards an approach that emphasizes allocation of loss amongst different (non-state) actors, and the development of mechanisms, such as insurance requirements and compensation funds, which facilitate recovery for victims of incidents.[3]

One consequence of the pragmatic turn in international rules of liability is that the rules tend to respond to contextual factors within particular issue areas or sectors involving risky activities, such that it is increasingly difficult to speak about a generalized law of liability.[4] Instead, there is a range of different approaches that have been adopted or proposed to address liability for environmental harm. As a starting point for this book, it is valuable to identify the different approaches that are available to address harm from activities that have transnational dimensions. The intention of this chapter is to consider how these approaches respond to the unique legal and practical issues associated with areas beyond national jurisdiction (ABNJ). As many of the specific questions respecting liability regimes are addressed in subsequent chapters, this chapter focuses primarily on the role of the state and the degree of institutionalization at the international level, but also seeks to situate the subsequent chapters in the context of these broader debates on how the international community ought to approach liability.

2.2 PURPOSES OF LIABILITY RULES

The choices that states and other international actors make respecting the different approaches to liability can be understood and analysed in light of the purposes for which liability rules are created. This is not to suggest that liability ought to be understood in purely instrumental terms,[5] but, as noted, much of the discussion of liability in international law has proceeded on pragmatic grounds. These purposes are not uniform across different activities or regimes, and will often reflect the underlying purposes of the governing treaties. While these purposes – compensation, environmental harm prevention and restoration, and the implementation of the polluter-pays principle – are consistently identified,[6] it remains important to tease out and elaborate upon these purposes, as they are of varying salience,

[3] These developments are examined in Robin Churchill, 'Facilitating (Transnational) Civil Liability Litigation for Environmental Damage by Means of Treaties: Progress, Problems, and Prospects' (2001) 12 Yrbk Intl Env L 3.

[4] In 1996, the ILC concluded that 'the trend of requiring compensation is pragmatic rather than grounded in a consistent concept of liability'. See ILC, 'Report of the Working Group on International Liability for Injurious Consequences Arising Out of Acts Not Prohibited by International Law' (1996) UN Doc A/CN.4/L.533 and Add.1, 116, para 32.

[5] See, for example, Ernest J Weinrib, *The Idea of Private Law* (rev edn, OUP 2012) (arguing in favour of a non-instrumental and formalist conceptualism of liability rooted in the relationship between 'doer' and 'sufferer' of harms).

[6] For a comprehensive discussion of the objectives associated with liability, see Lucas Bergkamp, *Liability and Environment: Private and Public Law Aspects of Civil Liability for Environmental Harm in an International Context* (Kluwer Law International 2001) ch 3.

depending on the context of their application. For present purposes, it is useful to consider which objectives are likely to be of greater importance in relation to activities in global commons areas.

2.2.1 *Adequate and Prompt Compensation*

The provision of compensation to those who have suffered as a result of environmental harm is a foundational purpose of virtually every liability regime, and reflects the intention to ensure that those that suffer harms at the hands of another are not left to bear the burden of the loss. Compensation is one of the stated objectives in nearly every international civil liability regime,[7] the 1982 United Nations Convention on the Law of the Sea (UNCLOS),[8] as well as the 2006 International Law Commission's (ILC) Draft Principles on Allocation of Loss in the Case of Transboundary Harm Arising Out of Hazardous Activities (Draft Principles).[9] The standard for compensation identified in these international instruments is 'prompt and adequate compensation'.[10] The purpose of 'adequate' compensation is not necessarily to provide full reparation to the victims of harm.[11] Instead, the standard of adequate compensation allows for a variety of factors to be considered in determining the quantum of compensation.

The degree of compensation may be linked to the level of wrongdoing but this is not necessarily always the case. For example, under the rules of state responsibility, which address the consequences of an internationally wrongful act, the rule of compensation (or reparation) is to 'as far as possible, wipe out all the consequences of the illegal act and reestablish the situation which would, in all probability, have

7 See, for example, International Convention on Civil Liability for Oil Pollution Damage (adopted 29 November 1969, entered into force 19 June 1975) 973 UNTS 3 (1969 Oil Pollution Liability Convention) amended by Protocol to Amend International Convention on Civil Liability for Oil Pollution Damage (adopted 27 November 1992, entered into force 30 May 1996) 1956 UNTS 255 (1992 Oil Pollution Liability Convention) preamble; Vienna Convention on Civil Liability for Nuclear Damage (adopted 21 May 1963, entered into force 12 November 1977) 1063 UNTS 265, amended by Protocol to Amend the Vienna Convention on Civil Liability for Nuclear Damage (adopted 12 September 1997, entered into force 4 October 2003) 2241 UNTS 270 (1997 Vienna Convention) preamble; Basel Protocol on Liability and Compensation for Damage Resulting from Transboundary Movement of Hazardous Wastes and Their Disposal (adopted 10 December 1999) UNEP/CHW.1/WG/1/9/2 (1999 Basel Liability Protocol) art 1.

8 United Nations Convention on the Law of the Sea (adopted 10 December 1982, entered into force 16 November 1994) 1833 UNTS 397 (UNCLOS) art 235.

9 ILC, 'Draft Principles on the Allocation of Loss in the Case of Transboundary Harm Arising Out of Hazardous Activities, with Commentaries' (2006) UN Doc A/61/10 (Draft Principles) principle 3, 72.

10 ibid.

11 ibid commentary to principle 4, 74, para 8.

existed if that act had not been committed'.[12] State responsibility addresses wrongful conduct (by definition).[13] As such, the goal of restitution is linked directly to the wrongful conduct. The approach is corrective in the sense that the remedy seeks to undo (or 'wipe out') the loss associated with the wrongful act. The importance of wrongdoing is reflected in the 1999 Protocol on Liability and Compensation to the Basel Convention on Transboundary Movements of Hazardous Wastes (1999 Basel Liability Protocol), which provides for an exception to the limitations on liability where the damage in question is a result of a lack of compliance with the Convention or 'wrongful intentional, reckless or negligent acts or omissions'.[14]

However, wrongfulness is not always a requirement for liability or compensation; as such, the goal of compensation is oriented less towards restitution and corrective justice, than addressing the losses suffered by those affected by risky activities. In this regard, the standard of 'adequacy' can be explained by the severing of the relationship between the remedy and wrong, since there is not a clear (moral) correspondence between the defendant's act and the victim's loss.[15] There is still an important moral element to the goal of compensation, but one which may be linked with the victim's lack of responsibility for the losses they have suffered, rather than the degree of wrongdoing of others. This is most plainly seen in provisions in civil liability treaties involving contributory negligence, whereby the responsible party is relieved of liability, wholly or partially, on the basis of the victim's own acts or omissions.[16]

The shift in focus from state responsibility to allocation of losses suggests a corresponding shift from corrective to distributive justice. The attention to distributive issues, particularly between an innocent victim and not-at-fault states or operators, was evident from the earliest discussions of this topic at the ILC, where the Commission explored the idea of 'equitable' balancing as a means to address the distributive consequences of accidents, and in particular, the concern that 'an innocent victim should not be left to bear loss or injury'.[17] The ILC's Draft Principles move away from a substantive version of distributive justice based on equitable balancing, and suggest a more procedurally oriented approach to justice, noting:

12 *Case Concerning the Factory at Chorzów (Germany v Poland)* (Merits) PCIJ Rep Series A No 17, 47.

13 ILC, 'Draft Articles on Responsibility of States for Internationally Wrongful Acts, with Commentaries' (2001) UN Doc A/56/10 (ASR) art 1 ('The present articles apply to activities not prohibited by international law which involve a risk of causing significant transboundary harm through their physical consequences.').

14 1999 Basel Liability Protocol (n 7) art 5.

15 Ernest J Weinrib, 'Corrective Justice in a Nutshell' (2002) 52 UTLJ 349.

16 See, eg 1969 Oil Pollution Liability Convention (n 7) art III (3).

17 ILC, 'Third Report on International Liability for Injurious Consequences Arising Out of Acts Not Prohibited by International Law, by Mr. Robert Q Quentin-Baxter, Special Rapporteur' (1982) UN Doc A/CN.4/360 and Corr.1, 63.

> It [compensation] is ipso facto adequate as long as the due process of the law requirements are met. As long as compensation given is not arbitrary, and grossly disproportionate to the damage actually suffered, even if it is less than full, it can be regarded as adequate. In other words, adequacy is not intended to denote 'sufficiency'.[18]

The need to balance compensation against other objectives is plainly seen in international civil liability structures where the parties have agreed to recovery caps and a range of exclusions.[19] Limits to recovery address the desire of the operators for commercial certainty associated with risks, including the facilitation of insurance and other risk pooling measures. Adequacy also captures the desirability of having readily accessible pools of funding that are available to satisfy successful claims. An award that provides for full (or partial) restitution of a claimant's losses cannot be viewed as adequate if it is not paid out due to impecuniosity or recalcitrance on the part of the responsible party. This aspect of adequacy similarly militates in favour of insurance, or other collective funds, that are available to satisfy claims.[20]

The extent to which compensation of private interests is likely to be a central objective of liability rules in areas beyond national jurisdiction depends on the density and nature of the activities in those areas. Certainly, there is potential for property and economic damages in areas beyond national jurisdiction. For example, cable infrastructure, established mining rights granted by the International Seabed Authority (ISA) under Part XI of UNCLOS or high seas fisheries activities may form the basis of an economic interest that may be protected from the wrongful conduct of others.[21] Emerging activities, such as the harvesting of marine genetic resources may also give rise to compensation claims.

A fundamental distinguishing feature of areas beyond national jurisdiction is the often collective and contingent nature of the rights in those areas, which complicates the rights to claim compensation, since the goal of compensation is premised on the presence of a victim, typically with clearly defined personal or property rights that have been abridged. Where those rights do not exist or are ill-defined, such as is often the case in global commons areas, the objective of compensation may be de-emphasized in favour of other objectives. For example, one could interpret the harm to fisheries resources as resources that may accrue to certain rights holders, such as recipients of allocations through international and state fisheries management regimes, or as harm to biological diversity that impacts the international community as a whole. It could, of course, be classified as both, but then it is less clear how the damages may be allocated. The relative absence of compensable

[18] Draft Principles (n 9) commentary to principle 4, 78, para 8.

[19] See, for example, 1969 Oil Pollution Liability Convention (n 7) art V.

[20] See discussion in Chapter 8.

[21] See, for example, UNCLOS (n 8) art 113 (injury to cables).

interests in the global commons explains, in part, the non-application of civil liability rules in areas beyond national jurisdiction.

Promptness requires that any procedures that are developed provide for efficient and accessible recourse for persons who have suffered damage. The goal of prompt compensation is responsive to concerns that the often-protracted nature of claims for compensation is unfairly burdensome on victims of harm, and may require specialized procedures to be developed to address access to compensation and ease of recovery.

2.2.2 *Environmental Harm Prevention and Restoration*

Liability rules and the compensation that flows from them are closely linked to the protection of the environment. The goal of environmental prevention and restoration has been central to the ILC's work on liability and is expressly identified as an objective (along with compensation) in its Draft Principles.[22] The role of liability rules as an economic incentive for less risky behaviour is central to the understanding of liability, and has animated the debates respecting the appropriate standard of liability for risky activities in domestic and international law.[23]

This objective is clearly identified in article 235 of UNCLOS, which links the obligation to ensure recourse is available to address liability and compensation in domestic legal systems to the obligation to protect and preserve the marine environment.[24] Under article 16 of the 1991 Antarctic Protocol,[25] environmental protection is the sole identified purpose for the elaboration of liability rules addressing damage arising from activities in the Antarctic Treaty area. In both cases, the rationale for privileging environmental protection reflects an understanding that the dominant form of loss is likely to be directly to the environment given the lower levels of economic activities in the Antarctic and marine areas beyond national jurisdiction.[26]

The underlying mechanism that links the imposition of liability to prevention is the deterrent effect of the consequences of liability, particularly awards of damages. Operators engaged in risky activities will be incentivized to avoid the imposition of

22 Draft Principles (n 9) principle 3, 72 ('The purposes of the present draft principles are: (a) to ensure prompt and adequate compensation to victims of transboundary damage; and (b) to preserve and protect the environment in the event of transboundary damage, especially with respect to mitigation of damage to the environment and its restoration or reinstatement.'). See also Lugano Convention on Civil Liability for Damage Resulting from Activities Dangerous to the Environment (adopted 21 June 1993) (1993) 32 ILM 1228 (Lugano Convention) art 1.

23 See Chapter 4.

24 UNCLOS (n 8) art 235(1).

25 Protocol on Environmental Protection to the Antarctic Treaty (adopted 4 October 1991, entered into force 14 January 1998) (1991) 30 ILM 1461 (1991 Antarctic Protocol).

26 ATCM, 'Liability – Report of the Group of Legal Experts' (1998) XXII ATCM/WP1.

liability awards where the costs associated with compensation exceed the costs of operating with the requisite level of care to avoid causing harm. In this regard, third party insurance may be viewed as presenting a moral hazard, in that it reduces the individual operator's costs associated with liability payments, and thereby reduces the incentives for care.[27] The effect of insurance on the risk behaviour of operators in international settings has not been the subject of any extended analysis. For present purposes, the key point here is that there is a potential for tension between compensation and prevention objectives.

The prevention goal may also justify recovery for actions taken to prevent further harm to the environment, as seen in a number of civil liability regimes.[28] Typically, in these cases, recovery is available where an accident has occurred and steps have been taken to prevent further harm, and recovery for those actions is allowable. The prevention goal also raises the possibility that legal obligations could be triggered by the presence of risk, as opposed to its manifestation in the form of actual harm. This latter approach to prevention is most clearly seen in the Liability Annex to the Antarctic Protocol, where the definition of 'environmental emergency' includes an accidental event that 'imminently threatens to result in, any significant and harmful impact'.[29] The availability of compensation for response actions also reflects the more general preference for harm avoidance over remediation in international environmental law.[30]

The restoration goal is distinct in that, unlike prevention, it is not prospective, but rather responds to damage already suffered. As an objective, restoration can be viewed as an element of restitution, in that it seeks to reinstate a previous condition, but the loss does not necessarily accrue to a specific person or entity and may also relate to losses to the environment *per se*. The ILC qualifies this purpose in functional terms:

> The aim is not to restore or return the environment to its original state but to enable it to maintain its permanent functions. In the process it is not expected that expenditures disproportionate to the results desired would be incurred and such costs should be reasonable. Where restoration or reinstatement of the environment is not possible, it is reasonable to introduce the equivalent of those components into the environment.[31]

[27] Christopher Parsons, 'Moral Hazard in Liability Insurance' (2003) 29 Geneva Papers on Risk and Insurance: Issues and Practice 448.

[28] See, for example, 1969 Oil Pollution Liability Convention (n 7) art I, which defines 'preventive measures' as 'reasonable measures taken by any person *after* an incident has occurred to prevent or minimize pollution damage' (emphasis added).

[29] Annex VI to the Protocol on Environmental Protection to the Antarctic Treaty on Liability Arising from Environmental Emergencies (adopted 17 June 2005) (2006) 45 ILM 5 (Liability Annex) art 2; see also Nagoya-Kuala Lumpur Supplementary Protocol on Liability and Redress to the Cartagena Protocol on Biosafety (adopted 15 October 2010, entered into force 5 March 2018) (2011) 50 ILM 105 (2010 Nagoya-Kuala Lumpur Supplementary Protocol).

[30] See Leslie-Anne Duvic-Paoli, *The Prevention Principle in International Environmental Law* (CUP 2018) ch 2.

[31] Draft Principles (n 9) commentary to principle 3, 73, para 7.

The Seabed Disputes Chamber (SDC), in its consideration of the responsibility of sponsoring states for activities in the Area, takes a similar view: '[i]t is the view of the Chamber that the form of reparation will depend on both the actual damage and the technical feasibility of restoring the situation to the *status quo ante*'.[32] The approach here is consistent with that taken in relation to compensation, in the sense that the goal is not a complete indemnification but rather an allocation of benefits and burdens associated with harmful incidents on the basis of fairness (proportionality) and feasibility. The attention being paid to feasibility and proportionality of response is likely to be salient in global commons settings, such as deep seabed mining, where restoration may be technically challenging or prohibitively expensive.[33]

2.2.3 *The Polluter-Pays Principle*

The polluter-pays principle tends to cut across the objectives discussed above, but given its prominence in international environmental governance institutions, including liability rules, it is helpful to discuss it separately. The polluter-pays principle focuses on which party ought to bear the burden of compensation requirements flowing from hazardous activities, favouring approaches that place liability with the operator, or more broadly, with the entity responsible for the creation of the risk.[34] In this latter regard, the polluter-pays principle is somewhat ambiguous about which entities are responsible as 'polluters',[35] and a number of civil liability regimes allocate responsibility amongst various actors involved in the chain of risky activities.[36] As a policy goal,[37] the polluter-pays principle seeks to internalize the cost of

[32] *Responsibilities and Obligations of States Sponsoring Persons and Entities with Respect to Activities in the Area* (Advisory Opinion of 1 February 2011) ITLOS Reports 2011 (*Activities in the Area* Advisory Opinion), para 197.

[33] Holly J Niner and others, 'Deep-Sea Mining with No Net Loss of Biodiversity – An Impossible Aim' (2018) 5 Front Mar Sci 53; see also Cindy Lee Van Dover and others, 'Biodiversity Loss from Deep Sea Mining' (2017) 10 Nat Geosci 464.

[34] Philippe Sands and Jacqueline Peel, *Principles of International Environmental Law* (4th edn, CUP 2018) 240.

[35] Patricia Birnie, Alan Boyle and Catherine Redgwell, *International Law and the Environment* (4th edn, OUP 2021) 559.

[36] 1969 Oil Pollution Liability Convention and 1999 Basel Liability Protocol (n 7).

[37] The legal status of the polluter-pays principle remains contested. It is referred to as 'a general principle of international environmental law' in the UNECE Protocol on Civil Liability and Compensation for Damage Caused by the Transboundary Effects of Industrial Accidents on Transboundary Waters (adopted 21 May 2003) (UNECE Convention on Liability for Industrial Accidents). The polluter-pays principle also finds expression in, *inter alia*, the International Convention on Oil Pollution Preparedness, Response and Cooperation (adopted 30 November 1990, entered into force 13 May 1995) 1891 UNTS 77; the Convention for the Protection of the Marine Environment of the North-East Atlantic (adopted 22 September 1992, entered into force 25 March 1998) 2354 UNTS 67 (1992 OSPAR Convention); and the Convention on the Protection and Use of Transboundary Watercourses and International Lakes (adopted 17 March 1992, 6 October 1996) 1936 UNTS 269 (1992 Watercourses and Lakes Convention). However, Birnie, Boyle and Redgwell question the extent and the

pollution, which should contribute to more economically efficient levels of pollution.[38] This links the polluter-pays principle to the goal of ensuring liability rules are not trade distorting by encouraging the internalization of environmental harm, as opposed to the state or international community subsidizing these costs by bearing them publicly.[39]

There is no reason to limit the application of the polluter-pays principle to areas under state jurisdiction. The principle is referenced in a number of oceans-based instruments, including the Convention for the Protection of the Marine Environment of the North-East Atlantic (1992 OSPAR Convention),[40] which includes some high seas areas.[41] The structure of the principle is not dependent upon the presence of sovereign jurisdiction, but rather the presence and impact of polluting activities.

The underlying economic goals of the polluter-pays principle, such as optimal resource allocation and minimizing trade distortions, may be particularly important in relation to resource development activities. However, insofar as a number of key forms of environmental harm in the global commons, such as ocean pollution from land-based sources or ocean acidification, may have diffused sources and cumulative impacts, the challenges with attribution may blunt the practical application of the polluter-pays principle.

2.2.4 *Economic Objectives*

The preambles to the 1992 Oil Pollution Liability Convention and the 1996 Hazardous and Noxious Substances Liability Convention (1996 HNS Convention) speak to another, perhaps, subsidiary, goal of liability regimes – the development of a level playing field amongst industry actors, in the form of 'uniform international rules and procedures for determining questions of liability and com-

capability to which the polluter-pays principle can be understood as an accepted legal principle, see Birnie, Boyle and Redgwell (n 35) 342 ('Principle 16 lacks the normative character of a rule of law'). But see Priscilla Schwartz, 'The Polluter-Pays Principle' in Ludwig Krämer and Emanuela Orlando (eds), *Principles of Environmental Law* (Edward Elgar 2018) 264.

38 OECD, 'The Polluter-Pays Principle' (1992) OECD/GD (92)81.

39 Draft Principles (n 9) principle 3, 74, para 11.

40 1992 OSPAR Convention (n 37).

41 Other regional seas treaties that include the polluter-pays principle are the Convention on the Protection of the Marine Environment of the Baltic Sea Area (adopted 9 April 1992, entered into force 17 January 2000) 2099 UNTS 195, and the Convention on the Protection of the Marine Environment of the Black Sea Against Pollution (adopted 21 April 1992, entered into force 15 January 1994) 1764 UNTS 4, as well as the UNEP, 'Guidelines for the Determination of Liability and Compensation for Damage Resulting from Pollution of the Marine Environment in the Mediterranean Sea Area' (2008) UNEP(DEPI)/MEDI G.17/10, Annex V.

pensation'.[42] Liability rules can potentially distort competitive positions if some operators are subject to higher degrees of exposure through stronger domestic liability requirements, and consequential requirements for insurance. Harmonization of liability laws is, therefore, a distinct purpose for international rules that serves the goal of trade competitiveness, and will therefore be of greater relevance to sectors that are highly globalized and exposed to trade competitiveness concerns.[43] For example, the emphasis in the deep seabed mining regime on non-discrimination reflects competitiveness concerns that are likely to push states towards common or harmonized liability rules.[44]

Liability rules and procedures may in some instances be structured so as to create viable operating conditions for risky activities by supplying pools of funds to supplement insurance or other industry funds and by the imposition of liability limits. This is most clearly evident in the nuclear industry where the civil liability schemes are backstopped by state funds and which shield operators and their suppliers from unlimited liability claims that might otherwise make the industry unviable.[45] Liability regimes may also serve operators' economic interests by creating conditions of greater social acceptability of risky activity (what we might now call a 'social license to operate')[46] by providing public assurances that losses from accidents can be addressed by sufficiently funded mechanisms. Again, this rationale is salient to risky novel activities, like deep seabed mining and marine geoengineering.

2.3 APPROACHES TO THE FORM OF LIABILITY SCHEMES

The starting point for a discussion on approaches to liability is what might be considered the two default approaches to addressing liability: state responsibility and unharmonized domestic liability rules. These are the default approaches in the sense that a body of rules and practices already exist, and will operate alongside other liability schemes (to the extent that these rules are not displaced by other approaches). The deficiencies with the default approaches provide a framing for the other approaches, which are responsive to the shortcomings of the default approaches. The other approaches considered are generalized requirements for

42 International Convention on Liability and Compensation for Damage in Connection with the Carriage of Hazardous and Noxious Substances by Sea (adopted 3 May 1996) (1996) 35 ILM 1415 (1996 HNS Convention) preamble; see also 1969 Oil Pollution Liability Convention (n 7).

43 Harmonization is also central to the European Council, Environmental Liability Directive 2004/35/CE (entered into force 30 April 2004) OJ L 143, 56.

44 UNCLOS (n 8) art 152(1).

45 See International Atomic Energy Agency, '1997 Vienna Convention on Civil Liability for Nuclear Damage and the 1997 Convention on Supplementary Compensation for Nuclear Damage: Explanatory Text' (2007) IAEA International Law Series No 3, 5; see also Birnie, Boyle and Redgwell (n 35) 439.

46 Michelle Voyer and Judith van Leeuwen, '"Social License to Operate" in the Blue Economy' (2019) 62 Resour Pol'y 102.

harmonization and minimum standards for domestic liability rules, and international civil liability schemes negotiated in connection with hazardous activities occurring within a specific sector, exemplified by the liability regimes respecting the carriage of oil by tankers or the operation of nuclear facilities. A further derivation on international civil liability rules are rules embedded directly within existing environmental treaty structures, which tie compensation more directly to the specific environmental goals of the treaty and may employ more regulatory-type mechanisms, such as administrative orders, that compel responsible parties to restore or otherwise address harm from hazardous activities. Finally, this chapter discusses 'loss and damage' as an alternative to liability, drawing on the collectivist approach to loss and damages from climate change.[47] This approach, at least as conceived under the Paris Agreement, expressly avoids any assignation of liability in favour of addressing losses through 'cooperative and facilitative' measures, such as risk pooling and insurance.[48]

2.3.1 *State Responsibility*

As an approach to liability, the rules of state responsibility flow from the requirement that breaches of international duties entail a corresponding obligation to make reparations to the state(s) to whom the duty was owed. The focus is, consequently, on states as the subjects of liability and as claimants. As a result, liability for harm occasioned by non-state entities must flow to states by attribution or, more likely, by virtue of a state's failure in its international obligations to oversee activities under its jurisdiction.[49] In a similar vein, non-state claimants are required to have states espouse their claims, and pursue them on their behalf.

Because state responsibility focuses on the behaviour of states and only indirectly on operators, its adequacy in addressing the goals of liability rules will depend on the presence of clearly defined primary obligations in international law that are likely to affect state behaviour and, indirectly, operator behaviour. The baseline rule that governs environmental responsibilities between states is the obligation of each state to 'ensure that activities within their jurisdiction or control do not cause damage to the environment of other states or of areas beyond the limits of national jurisdiction'.[50] As a rule governing transboundary interactions, the no-harm principle has

47 Paris Agreement (adopted 12 December 2015, entered into force 4 November 2016) UN Doc FCCC/CP/2015/10/Add.1, Annex, art 8.

48 ibid art 8(3).

49 See discussion in *Activities in the Area* Advisory Opinion (n 32), paras 107–116.

50 Declaration of the United Nations Conference on the Human Environment (1972) UN Doc A/Conf.48/14/Rev.1 (1972 Stockholm Declaration) principle 21; Report of the United Nations Conference on Environment and Development (1992) UN Doc A/Conf.151/26/Rev.1, Annex I (1992 Rio Declaration) principle 2. See also Louis Sohn, 'The Stockholm Declaration on the Human Environment' (1973) 14 Harv Int'l LJ 423.

been repeatedly recognized as a customary rule in international law.[51] The application of the no-harm principle to the global commons is supported by the wording of both the 1972 Stockholm Declaration and the 1992 Rio Declaration, as well as by treaty provisions requiring states to take harm prevention measures in relation to the marine environment,[52] deep seabed,[53] fisheries[54] and the Antarctic.[55] While the no-harm principle provides a general basis for pursuing liability in the global commons, its application presents numerous difficulties.

The ILC, for example, was of the view that the application of rules respecting environmental harm to the global commons was sufficiently unique to warrant their exclusion from the ILC's work on liability (and subsequently on transboundary harm). The central preoccupation of the ILC when it started its work on liability in 1978 was the management of transboundary environmental risk.[56] In particular, it was recognized that states might undertake a range of activities that they may view as being beneficial, but which posed risks to other states. The first Special Rapporteur on the topic, Quentin-Baxter, viewed the dynamic as one of mutual limitations to state sovereignty, as captured by the maxim *sic utere tuo ut alienum non laedas*. In this regard, the focus of the topic on 'acts not prohibited by international law' emphasized procedural obligations that facilitate inter-state negotiations over planned activities and equitable obligations to compensate those that suffer harm.[57] Instead of developing general rules governing the acceptability of risky activities, the approach recognized the inherently contextual nature of transboundary risks. Compensation was understood to be an element of the wider set of practices regulating hazardous transboundary activities, but not the sole or even dominant goal.

The exclusion of harm to the global commons from the ILC's work on liability flowed from the contextual approach that was premised on the presence of a source state and affected state.[58] Since the duty to prevent harm was a corollary to state

51 *Construction of a Road in Costa Rica along the San Juan River (Nicaragua v Costa Rica)* (Judgment) [2015] ICJ Rep 665 (Road Case); *Pulp Mills on the River Uruguay (Argentina v Uruguay)* (Judgment) [2010] ICJ Rep 14 (Pulp Mills); *Iron Rhine Arbitration (Belgium v Netherlands)* (Award) (2005) Oxford Reports on ICGJ 373.

52 UNCLOS (n 8) art 192.

53 ibid art 145.

54 *Request for an Advisory Opinion Submitted by the Sub-Regional Fisheries Commission (SRFC)* (Advisory Opinion of 2 April 2015) ITLOS Reports 2015 (SRFC Advisory Opinion), paras 104–112.

55 1991 Antarctic Protocol (n 25) art 3.

56 ILC, 'Report of the Working Group on International Liability for Injurious Consequences Arising Out of Acts Not Prohibited by International Law' (1978) UN Doc A/CN.4/L.284 and Corr.1, notion of risk.

57 ILC, 'Second Report on International Liability for Injurious Consequences Arising Out of Acts Not Prohibited by International Law, by Mr. Robert Q Quentin-Baxter, Special Rapporteur' (1981) UN Doc A/CN.4/346, Add.1 and Add.2.

58 See ILC, Yearbook of the International Law Commission (1998) vol I, 63, para 38.

sovereignty, it was traditionally invoked in connection with transboundary pollution between adjacent states. Since states have both a sovereign right to engage in economic activities (exploit their natural resources) within their territories, and the right to be free from harm to their territories, the harm principle was understood as being relational in character.[59] In the absence of clear sovereign rights in relation to the global commons, this relational character is absent, complicating the application of the harm principle in this context. In order to identify rights and obligations in relation to harm in the commons, the ILC felt it had to overcome the uncertain links between harm to the commons and individual state losses, or enter into an examination of collective rights, which it went beyond its mandate.[60]

In addition, the ILC characterized the principal forms of harm to the commons, which involved cumulative, multi-source impacts and harm to the environment *per se*, as being sufficiently distinct from those arising in transboundary contexts to further justify excluding areas beyond national jurisdiction from the scope of its work on liability.[61] As the topic evolved, and was divided into the subtopics of prevention of transboundary damage and allocation of loss, the exclusion of harm to the global commons environment was maintained.[62]

Despite the early reticence of the ILC to examine the primary obligations of states to protect areas beyond national jurisdiction, there is little reason to doubt that the fundamental obligation of states to prevent significant harm includes areas beyond national jurisdiction. This is, of course, reflected in the wording of both Principle 21 of the Stockholm Declaration and Principle 2 of the Rio Declaration.[63] The obligation is reflected in a number of instruments addressing state duties in relation to commons resources, including UNCLOS and the 1991 Antarctic Protocol.[64] The difficulty is not with the presence of the duty, but rather with the practicalities of its implementation, where the concerns raised by the ILC respecting causality, attribution and the quantification of damages remain significant barriers to implementing

59 The domestic analogy here is to the common law tort of nuisance, which makes unreasonable interferences with the use and enjoyment of another's property actionable. As the characterization of an activity as a nuisance affects the ability of both parties to use and enjoy their property, the test becomes a balancing of factors that seeks to protect the reasonable proprietary expectations of the parties. In international law, the move away from focusing on the acceptability of impacts towards defining standards of reasonable behaviour is analogous to moving from a nuisance-based system to one based on negligence. Discussed in ILC, 'Second Report on International Liability' (n 57) paras 41–52.

60 ILC, 'First Report on Prevention of Transboundary Damage from Hazardous Activities, by Mr. Pemmaraju Sreenivasa Rao, Special Rapporteur' (1998) UN Doc A/CN.4/487, paras 106–110; see also ILC, 'Report of the International Law Commission on the Work of Its Forty-Second Session' (1 May–20 July 1990) UN Doc A/45/10 (Report of the ILC), 104, para 527.

61 Report of the ILC (n 60) 104, para 527.

62 ILC, 'First Report on the Legal Regime' (n 1) para 37.

63 1972 Stockholm Declaration and 1992 Rio Declaration (n 50).

64 UNCLOS (n 8); 1991 Antarctic Protocol (n 25).

the duty.[65] The issue of standing for harms to commons resources, including environmental resources presents a further barrier.[66]

A further shortcoming of state responsibility as a basis for liability is the structure of the due diligence standard that governs the no-harm principle, which makes states responsible for their failures to take reasonable steps to prevent harm, either in carrying out activities or in their oversight functions.[67] The application of the due diligence standard to harm prevention in the commons is supported by treaty language. Notably, in relation to deep seabed mining, article 139 of UNCLOS identifies the obligations of states 'to ensure' activities under their jurisdiction or control are carried out in conformity with the requirements of Part XI of the Convention. Article 139 goes on to specify that while damages from the failure of states to carry their responsibilities entails liability, they will not be liable for damages arising from the failures of entities under their control if they have 'taken all necessary and appropriate measures to secure effective compliance' with the relevant rules.[68] The nature of the due diligence obligation under article 139 was characterized in the following terms by the Seabed Disputes Chamber of the ITLOS (SDC):

> The sponsoring State's obligation 'to ensure' is not an obligation to achieve, in each and every case, the result that the sponsored contractor complies with the aforementioned obligations. Rather, it is an obligation to deploy adequate means, to exercise best possible efforts, to do the utmost, to obtain this result.[69]

A similar approach is found under the 1991 Antarctic Protocol, whereby the liability of states is limited to oversight failures.[70] Proving a lack of due diligence, especially in the absence of clear behavioural standards, poses difficulties, as it requires the identification of what oversight steps ought to be considered reasonable across highly diverse contexts involving states with very different regulatory capabilities.[71]

Due diligence also leaves injured states (or parties whose claims they have espoused) without a remedy where the overseeing state has exercised reasonable care. In cases of accidental or unforeseeable harm, or in cases where harm arose due to operator faults, but not a result of oversight deficiencies, an innocent victim is left without recourse under the rules of state responsibility. The inability of the rules of

[65] ILC, 'Second Report on the Protection of the Atmosphere, by Shinya Murase, Special Rapporteur' (2015) UN Doc A/CN.4/681, para 57; see also Duvic-Paoli (n 30) 241; Catherine Redgwell, 'The Wrong Trousers: State Responsibility and International Environmental Law' in Malcolm Evans and Panos Koutrakos (eds), *The International Responsibility of the European Union: European and International Perspectives* (Hart Publishing 2013).

[66] See Chapter 6.

[67] Road Case (n 51); Pulp Mills (n 51); *Nuclear Tests Case (Australia v France)* (Judgment) [1974] ICJ Rep 253, and *Nuclear Tests Case (New Zealand v France)* (Judgment) [1974] ICJ Rep 457.

[68] UNCLOS (n 8) art 139; see also Annex III art 22.

[69] *Activities in the Area* Advisory Opinion (n 32) para 110.

[70] 1991 Antarctic Protocol (n 25) art 10.

[71] See Chapter 4.

state responsibility to address the full range of circumstances that may demand compensation is tacitly acknowledged in article 304 of UNCLOS, which contemplates the further development of liability rules.[72]

Addressing this liability gap goes to the heart of the debate respecting activities that pose risks to the international environment. Foster frames the debate in terms of public or private liability for harm arising from hazardous activities, noting,

> To base a general liability scheme on operator liability instead will denote the acceptability of States' abdication, in corresponding measure, as primary agents in relationships between their respective populations in relation to a core public function: protecting populations and the environment from physical harm.[73]

Viewed in light of states' due diligence obligations, the question is not so much one of abdication, as states maintain international legal obligations related to the direct activities and oversight, unless it is explicitly excluded (potentially through channelling of liability away from the state).[74] The concern of states, which was ultimately reflected in the ILC's work, was one of the extent to which states are to become the insurers of risky activities under their jurisdiction. States have shown no appetite to take on such a role.

At a state-to-state level, the preference has been for loss shifting only in the face of fault.[75] In a transboundary context, a fault-based approach is potentially disciplined by considerations of reciprocity: states that expose their neighbours to risks face the possibility of being exposed to the same risks from their neighbours, since it will be more difficult to require higher levels of risk protection from others than they are willing to provide themselves.[76] It is less clear that such a dynamic is present in relation to the global commons, since the risks are imposed on the commons as a whole. States may be incentivized to engage in risky activities in relation to the commons where they can externalize the risk, but they do not face the direct threats from other states, since similar risky activities of other states will likewise be imposed on the commons. In effect, states receive the benefit of their risky activities, but the burdens are shared, leading to a risk-based tragedy of the commons.

2.3.2 *Unharmonized Domestic Liability*

The other default approach to addressing liability is to rely on domestic liability law and domestic courts to address harms arising from activities in the global commons. Instead

72 UNCLOS (n 8) art 304; see also 1991 Antarctic Protocol (n 25) art 16.

73 Caroline Foster, 'The ILC Draft Principles on the Allocation of Loss in the Case of Transboundary Harm Arising out of Hazardous Activities: Privatizing Risk?' (2005) 14 RECIEL 265, 272.

74 See discussion in Section 2.3.3, and Chapter 4.

75 See discussions in Chapter 4.

76 Karin Mickelson, 'Rereading Trail Smelter' (1994) 31 Canadian YBIL 219.

of (or in addition to) being governed by international legal obligations, liability would flow from domestic legal requirements respecting private law obligations (in tort or delict), but also potentially from public law remedies, such as environmental statutes that provide for civil remedies.[77] The advantage of domestic legal processes (over the law of state responsibility) is that it does not require state intervention and espousal of claims to initiate proceedings, allowing those who suffer harm direct access to legal remedies. On the other hand, litigants face a variety of obstacles in pursuing claims for damage arising from activities in the global commons, such as inconsistent approaches to access to domestic courts, lack of standing in domestic courts for both state and non-state actors claiming harm to commons resources and complications regarding choice of law questions given that the governing law cannot be determined with reference to the place of injury or accident (*lex loci delicti*) where the place or injury or accident is in areas beyond national jurisdiction.

The fundamental difficulty, however, is that recovery for harm to areas beyond national jurisdiction will be determined by a patchwork of domestic law, which will vary in both its procedural and substantive requirements. Recovery under these circumstances will depend upon an alignment of these requirements, such that a domestic state has sufficient links to the subject matter of the litigation (for example, either the plaintiff or defendant is a national), its courts are willing to accept jurisdiction over the litigation, the applicable law extends to areas beyond national jurisdiction and, if it does, provides for suitable remedies. In the event of a suit in a jurisdiction where the defendant does not have assets, a further hurdle of recognition and enforcement of the judgment will arise. Under unharmonized conditions, recovery will be unpredictable at best, and simply unavailable, at worst, with likely implications for the environmental protection goals of liability rules, since the deterrent effect of liability rules on behaviour will be dependent upon the effectiveness of the rules.

2.3.3 *Harmonized Domestic Liability Rules*

One response to the shortcomings of domestic liability rules is for states to develop minimum standards or other harmonization requirements that seek to provide a more consistent approach across domestic legal systems. Harmonization is consistent with, and implements, the duty on states to provide recourse for victims of environmental harm in their domestic legal systems, found in article 235 on UNCLOS. A similar obligation forms the basis of the ILC's Draft Principles, which provide a set of minimum standards that domestic legal systems ought to reflect to meet their obligation to provide for 'prompt and adequate' compensation. The Draft

[77] See, generally Monika Hinteregger, 'Environmental Liability' in Emma Lees and Jorge E Viñuales (eds), *Oxford Handbook of Comparative Environmental Law* (OUP 2019) 1025; Comprehensive Environmental Response, Compensation, and Liability Act of 1980, 94 Stat 2767 (US) (CERCLA).

Principles identify minimum requirements for access to courts or other dispute settlement mechanisms for foreign claimants (on a non-discriminatory basis),[78] ensuring those bodies have the necessary jurisdiction to address transboundary claims,[79] indicating that rules should allow for no-fault recovery,[80] should provide for a full range of harms to be compensated, including damage to the environment itself, reinstatement measures and reasonable response measures[81] and should provide for national level insurance or compensation funds.[82] To a significant degree, the specifics of minimum standards identified by the ILC reflect the details of existing international civil liability treaties (discussed below), and are best understood as examples of how the general obligation to provide prompt and adequate compensation may be implemented.[83] Like civil liability treaties, and in keeping with the ILC's approach to prevention of transboundary harm, the ILC Draft Principles do not apply to areas beyond national jurisdiction.

Two important, and as yet unresolved, issues are the extent to which the lynchpin obligation of providing recourse to domestic courts for 'prompt and adequate compensation' is a customary rule of international law, and its application to areas beyond national jurisdiction. As noted, this obligation finds support in a number of general instruments addressing transboundary harm, such as the Nordic Convention,[84] and the UN Watercourses Convention,[85] but is framed in terms of non-discrimination, which does not provide a minimum standard, but only affords equal treatment. Principle 10 of the Rio Declaration contains a provision that guarantees '[e]ffective access to judicial and administrative proceedings, including redress and remedy'.[86] Principle 10 is reflected in the Aarhus Convention, which also includes provisions guaranteeing access to domestic courts, although, the requirements for access to justice appear to be more directed towards public law remedies than recourse for the purposes of pursuing compensation.[87] The one example of a treaty that provided for comprehensive obligations supporting this

[78] Draft Principles (n 9) commentary to principle 6(1), 86, para 2.

[79] ibid principle 6(1).

[80] ibid principle 4(2).

[81] ibid principle 2(a).

[82] ibid principle 4(3)–(5).

[83] Birnie, Boyle and Redgwell (n 35) 340–341('While the 2006 ILC Principles as a whole cannot be viewed as an exercise in codifying customary international law, they show how the Commission has made use of general principles of law as "an indication of policy and principle"').

[84] Convention on the Protection of the Environment (adopted 19 February 1974, entered into force 5 October 1976) 1092 UNTS 279 (1974 Nordic Convention) art 3.

[85] Convention on the Law of the Non-Navigational Uses of International Watercourses (adopted 21 May 1997, entered into force 17 August 2014) (1997) 36 ILM 700 (1997 Watercourses Convention) art 32.

[86] However, see 1992 Rio Declaration (n 50) principle 13.

[87] Convention on Access to Information, Public Participation in Decision-making and Access to Justice in Environmental Matters (adopted 25 June 1998, entered into force 30 October 2001) 2161 UNTS 447 (1998 Aarhus Convention) art 9.

duty, the Lugano Convention on Civil Liability for Damage Resulting from Activities Dangerous to the Environment, has failed to attract adherents.

There are numerous examples of courts awarding damages based on transboundary harms, but there is little evidence that the acceptance of these claims was based on a recognized general obligation to provide recourse to victims of environmental harms regardless of the location of the harm. The treaties on civil liability demonstrate a willingness to accept minimum standards, including access to domestic courts under certain conditions, such as channelling liability to operators (and away from the state) and implementation of risk pooling measures, but do not evince a general acceptance of the obligation to provide recourse. This points to a central difficulty associated with the development of a general obligation of recourse to pursue environmental compensation in domestic courts. In the absence of a more comprehensive set of common standards addressing issues such as standing, the basis and standard of liability, the scope of recoverable damages and recognition and enforcement of judgments, a general obligation is too vague to be of much practical value to victims of environmental harm.

The suggestion by the SDC that article 235 of UNCLOS is an aspect of a state's due diligence obligation raises the question of whether a general duty to provide recourse may flow from the customary due diligence obligation.[88] Understood as a preventive obligation, the argument draws on the deterrent effect that clear avenues of recourse would have on state behaviour; that is, since a state is required to take all reasonable steps that would prevent harm to another state or to areas beyond national jurisdiction, and providing recourse for harm occasioned is one such step, recourse ought to be viewed as an element of due diligence. The relationship between available avenues of recourse and reasonable standards of prudent behaviour respecting potentially environmentally harmful activities may be too attenuated to be generalized in such a manner. The alternative view of the SDC's characterization of article 235 as an element of due diligence is that in the very specific context of deep seabed mining, recourse is required to satisfy a sponsoring state's obligation to ensure contractor compliance with its obligations, which includes responsibility for damages occasioned by its wrongful acts (under Annex III, article 22).

Harmonized liability rules have taken two principal forms in international law: stand-alone, sector-specific civil liability regimes, and liability rules and procedures that are embedded within an existing multilateral environmental agreement.[89] The former are more activity-specific (i.e. transportation of oil by sea or operation of nuclear facilities), whereas the latter tend to address damages that relate to the particular environmental aims of the regime in question. That said, the approaches taken within these instruments draw on a common repertoire of mechanisms, such

[88] *Activities in the Area* Advisory Opinion (n 32) paras 139–140.

[89] See Brunnée (n 1).

as channelling liability, the use of a strict liability standard, limitations or caps on liability and the use of financial assurances.[90]

2.3.3.1 International Civil Liability Rules

International civil liability rules are a form of harmonization that is sector-specific, but are also facilitated by high degrees of international cooperation, particularly in relation to risk pooling measures. There are long standing civil liability schemes in relation to damages from nuclear facilities and transportation of oil by ship. More recently, civil liability treaties have been negotiated in relation to the transport of other hazardous substances.[91] The schemes have a number of common features that are intended to clarify responsibility, define the admissibility and extent of claims and provide a pool of resources to satisfy admissible claims. Liability, which is strict, is channelled to operators, who are required to hold a specified amount of insurance, and must contribute to compensation funds, whose purpose is to cover claims in excess of insured amounts. The particulars respecting the fund structure and contributions vary from regime to regime. Fund structures may involve a degree of risk sharing amongst parties beyond the frontline operator, such as including others who contribute to, or benefit from, the presence of the hazardous activity.[92] The amounts covered by the funds, which provide an upper limit to the available compensation, reflect the scale of potential claims, as well as pragmatic considerations respecting the willingness and ability of the contributors to provide funds.

Civil liability regimes respond quite directly to many of the shortcomings of unharmonized domestic liability rules by ensuring access to remedies, clear liability rules and other parameters affecting recovery, such as defining types of losses and damages covered by the scheme. Claims are brought and adjudicated within domestic courts, which contracting states are required to clothe with appropriate jurisdiction. The presence of an international organization, the International Oil Pollution Compensation Funds (IOPC Funds), facilitates the orderly management of claims through the negotiation of settlements and the conduct of litigation on behalf of the funds.

As an approach to addressing liability, international civil liability regimes direct responsibility, and consequently, deterrence, to private actors, and away from the state, which may obscure the state's oversight responsibilities from scrutiny in relation to incidents.[93] The exception is the nuclear facility regimes, where states

[90] See Sands and Peel (n 34) 772 (describing common features of international civil liability regimes).

[91] 1999 Basel Liability Protocol (n 7); 1996 HNS Convention (n 42).

[92] For example, the allocation of funding internationally between shipowners and receivers of oil under the oil transport liability regime, or between different parties in the chain of custody of hazardous waste under the 1999 Basel Liability Protocol (n 7).

[93] Foster (n 73).

have residual responsibilities to cover claims for compensation that exceed insurance and fund limits.[94] This reflects the higher degree of state involvement in nuclear facilities, and the inability of operators to acquire insurance or self-insure at the levels thought necessary to provide adequate compensation.

2.3.3.2 Liability Rules Contained in Existing Environmental Agreements

Beyond the nuclear, oil and hazardous substances sectors, there are a growing number of civil liability regimes that have been negotiated under the auspices of existing multilateral environmental agreements, notably the Basel Liability Protocol,[95] the Antarctic Protocol,[96] the UNECE Conventions on Transboundary Watercourses and Transboundary Effects of Industrial Accidents[97] and the 2010 Nagoya-Kuala Lumpur Supplementary Protocol.[98] The increased presence of liability rules as a further tool to address environmental aims responds to calls in the Stockholm Declaration, and then reiterated in the Rio Declaration, for the development of national and international rules governing 'liability and compensation for the victims of pollution and other environmental damage'.[99] The call for international cooperation on liability and compensation is echoed in the parent conventions of the instruments noted above,[100] as well as in UNCLOS and a number of regional seas conventions, indicating broad acceptance of the important role for liability in preventing and responding to environmental harm. The take-up by states of this call for cooperation has been mixed at best. Where liability rules have been developed, states have been slow to bring these instruments into force.[101]

94 1997 Vienna Convention (n 7) art VII (1).

95 1999 Basel Liability Protocol (n 7).

96 1991 Antarctic Protocol (n 25).

97 1997 Watercourses Convention (n 85); 1992 Watercourses and Lakes Convention (n 37); Convention on the Transboundary Effects of Industrial Accidents (adopted 17 March 1992, entered into force 19 April 2000) 2105 UNTS 457 (1992 Convention on Industrial Accidents).

98 2010 Nagoya-Kuala Lumpur Supplementary Protocol (n 29).

99 1992 Rio Declaration (n 50) principle 13; see also 1972 Stockholm Declaration (n 50) principle 22.

100 See, for example, Cartagena Protocol on Biosafety (adopted 29 January 2000, entered into force 11 September 2003) 2226 UNTS 208, art 27, the basis for the negotiation of the Nagoya-Kuala Lumpur Supplementary Protocol; see also 1996 Protocol to the Convention on the Prevention of Marine Pollution by Dumping of Wastes and Other Matter, 1972 (adopted 7 November 1996, entered into force 24 March 2006) (2006) ATS 11 (1996 Dumping Protocol) art 15, which has not yet led to the development of further procedures regarding liability arising from the dumping or incineration at sea of wastes or other matter.

101 Only the 2010 Nagoya-Kuala Lumpur Supplementary Protocol is in force. On the lack of action in relation to the liability provision in the regional seas agreements, see René Lefeber, 'The Liability Provisions of Regional Seas Conventions: Dead Letters in the Sea?' in Davor Vidas and Willy Østreng (eds), *Order for the Ocean at the Turn of the Century* (Kluwer Law International 1999) 507.

These agreements contain some of the same features found in the oil pollution liability schemes, such as the channelling of liability to the operator, the use of strict liability and liability caps and provisions for recourse within domestic legal systems, but they also reflect specific sectoral and regime conditions. Unlike the oil and nuclear liability conventions, the activities covered in these regimes are often more diffuse. For example, the UNECE Convention on Liability for Industrial Accidents addresses itself to transboundary water pollution from industrial accidents, and thus operates more like a general liability convention in relation to certain kinds of damages.[102] The 2010 Nagoya-Kuala Lumpur Supplementary Protocol, which addresses liability for damage 'resulting from living modified organisms which find their origin in a transboundary movement',[103] similarly addresses a potentially wide range of actors. However, this instrument provides states with high degrees of discretion in terms of the domestic rules they put in place.[104] The 2010 Nagoya-Kuala Lumpur Supplementary Protocol does not so much harmonize state approaches to liability than it provides guidance as to the acceptable approaches to domestic liability.[105]

One consequence of the diversity of potentially affected operators is that none of these agreements are supported by a compensation fund, which reflects the difficulty of risk pooling amongst diverse actors. Instead, the agreements provide for ad hoc insurance and financial security provisions. In the case of the Basel Liability Protocol, the parties agreed to use 'existing mechanisms' to address damages that exceeded coverage limitations,[106] which was ultimately determined to be the voluntarily funded Technical Cooperation Trust Fund. However, this body has none of the hallmarks of a compensation fund.[107]

These agreements reflect the environmental objectives of the parent agreements under which they have been negotiated, with greater attention paid to compensation for response measures, and damages associated with reinstatement. This is most clearly evident in the Liability Annex adopted under the 1991 Antarctic Protocol, which is focused entirely on the responsibilities of operators to respond to environmental emergencies and compensation for response measures taken by others.

Apart from the Liability Annex, none of the international civil liability regimes include damage to areas beyond national jurisdiction.

[102] UNECE Convention on Liability for Industrial Accidents (n 37) art 3.

[103] 2010 Nagoya-Kuala Lumpur Supplementary Protocol (n 29) art 3(1).

[104] ibid art 12.

[105] Sands and Peel (n 34) 797 (citing Anastasia Telesetsky, 'The 2010 Nagoya-Kuala Lumpur Supplementary Protocol: A New Treaty Assigning Transboundary Liability and Redress for Biodiversity Damage Caused by Genetically Modified Organisms' (2011) 14 ASIL Insight 2).

[106] 1999 Basel Liability Protocol (n 7) art 15(1). See Brunnée (n 1) 361.

[107] These structures are discussed in detail in Chapter 8.

2.3.4 *Administrative Approaches*

Given that environmental protection and remediation is a key objective of liability regimes, it should be recognized that these goals may be achieved through alternative measures that do not rely on liability rules *per se*, but rather respond to environmental harm through other collective mechanisms. Emergency or other administrative orders could be used to require actions that address environmental harm as a function of regulatory compliance, not civil liability. The domestic analogue would be statutory clean-up provisions and the associated ability of public authorities to take clean-up steps and recover funds from potentially responsible parties.[108] There is some limited potential for domestic administrative measures to be applied outside the territory of the issuing state,[109] but as discussed above, the need for a jurisdictional link limits the extraterritorial application of domestic laws to activities in the global commons.

The challenge in international law is that very few international organizations are endowed with direct regulatory authority over private actors, and as a consequence, civil liability regimes provide for recovery of reinstatement costs undertaken by domestic actors but do not provide a mechanism for direct regulatory action. The one exception to this is the ISA, which has direct oversight responsibilities in relation to deep seabed mining.[110] These powers include the authority to issue 'emergency orders'. This authority is limited to preventive action, but does provide that the executive organ of the ISA, the Council, may undertake actions on behalf of the contractor where the contractor fails to act, and may require financial security be posted to assure compliance.[111]

The Liability Annex adopted pursuant to the 1991 Antarctic Protocol obliges parties to require its operators to take 'prompt and effective response action to environmental emergencies'.[112] In the event such action is not taken, the party of the operator or other parties (where there is an imminent threat to the environment) may take steps themselves and seek recovery from the operator. The approach is quite narrow and prevention-oriented, in that it only addresses 'reasonable measures taken after an environmental emergency … to avoid, minimize or contain the impact' of that emergency, although these actions 'may include clean-up in appropriate circumstances'.[113] One interesting feature of the Antarctic Treaty system is

[108] CERCLA (n 77).

[109] See, for example, *Pakootas v Teck Cominco Metals, Ltd* (2006) 452 F.3d 1066 (9th Cir) (US), discussed in Jaye Ellis, 'Extraterritorial Excuse of Jurisdiction for Environmental Protection: Addressing Fairness Concerns' (2012) 25 LJIL 397.

[110] UNCLOS (n 8) art 161 (w); see also the International Seabed Authority's (ISA) Regulations on Prospecting and Exploration for Polymetallic Nodules in the Area (2013) ISBA/19/C/17 (PMN) reg 33.

[111] ibid.

[112] Liability Annex (n 29) art 5(1).

[113] ibid art 2.

that in the event appropriate response actions are not taken, the Liability Annex provides for recovery of an amount equal to the costs of the response action that should have been taken. In these circumstances, the recovered amount is paid into a fund created under the Annex that would be used to reimburse parties for response actions. The Annex does not empower a collective body, such as the Antarctic Treaty Consultative Meeting (ATCM), but rather permits individual states parties to seek recovery on behalf of the parties.

2.3.5 *Loss and Damage*

Loss and damage, as conceived by the parties to the 2015 Paris Agreement adopted under the auspices of the United Nations climate change regime,[114] is an alternative response to environmental damage that relies on collective responsibility to environmental harm, as opposed to individuated responsibility and liability. As an approach to losses resulting from environmental harm, the loss and damage provisions of the Paris Agreement are a product of the complicated political and legal circumstances surrounding climate change, where states vulnerable to climate change, particularly small island developing states threatened by sea-level rise, sought financial support from developed states to address the losses and damages suffered as a result of the adverse effects of climate change. These efforts were strongly resisted by developed states.[115] The resulting provision, article 8, in the Paris Agreement recognizes the importance of addressing loss and damage associated with climate change (although it does not define what that may be), and provides, in non-binding language, for future cooperation and facilitation to address loss and damage, including a permanent mechanism to coordinate these activities.[116] The specific areas of coordination include activities that address adaptation rather than losses *per se*, but also includes matters such as 'comprehensive risk assessment and management', 'risk insurance facilities, climate risk pooling and other insurance solutions' and 'non-economic losses' that respond more directly to conditions that might otherwise be addressed through liability rules. The parties in the decision adopting the Paris Agreement

[114] Paris Agreement (n 47) art 8.

[115] Discussed in Veera Pekkarinen, Patrick Toussaint and Harro van Asselt, 'Loss and Damage after Paris: Moving beyond Rhetoric' (2019) 13 CCLR 31; see also Linda Siegele, 'Loss and Damage (Article 8)' in Daniel Klein and others (eds), *The Paris Agreement on Climate Change: Analysis and Commentary* (Oxford University Press 2017) 224.

[116] The mechanism, the Warsaw International Mechanism for Loss and Damage (WIM), was created in 2013 under the 1992 UN Framework Convention on Climate Change (UNFCCC), 'Warsaw International Mechanism for Loss and Damage Associated with Climate Change Impacts' (31 January 2014) UN Doc FCCC/CP/2013/10/Add.1. The inclusion of the WIM in the Paris Agreement endowed a more permanent status on the WIM by embedding its role in a binding treaty. In 2022, the Parties to the Paris Agreement agreed to a funding mechanism that addresses loss and damage, Decision -CP. 27, -/CMA.4, 'Funding arrangements for responding to loss and damage associated with the adverse effects of climate change, including a focus on addressing loss and damage', 20 November 2022.

agreed 'that Article 8 of the Agreement does not involve or provide a basis for any liability and compensation'.[117]

Article 8 is of direct relevance to issues related to environmental harm in areas beyond national jurisdiction since it potentially contemplates within its scope harm to the oceans through acidification and warming of the oceans. It is doubtful that the effect of article 8, or the adopting decision, has the effect of displacing existing international or domestic law that governs the responsibility of states or private emitters for damages resulting from their greenhouse gas emissions.[118] But insofar as the loss and damage provision results in addressing harms that arise, these steps may best be seen as a form of mitigation of damages.

As an approach to addressing environmental harm, the loss and damage provision presents an alternative to liability by treating harm as a collective responsibility. In cases where the harm that arises is cumulative and may be difficult to attribute to specific polluters or responsible parties, whether states or private entities, collective measures may provide an alternative or supplementary pathway to address environmental harm. These conditions are certainly present in relation to environmental harms in areas beyond national jurisdiction and formed part of the ILC's justification for excluding global commons areas from their work on liability.[119] To be clear, loss and damage is not an approach to liability and should be viewed as an alternative as it lacks some of the key hallmarks of liability approaches, including the direct accountability of those who cause harm.

2.4 CONCLUSIONS

Approaches to liability are not mutually exclusive, nor are they watertight compartments. For example, state responsibility for environmental damages can, and often, will, operate alongside civil liability structures, and regulatory measures may operate alongside traditional forms of compensation. What emerges is a fairly complex landscape for the governance of compensation for environmental damage, whereby there is no best solution or easily transferable models. Instead, the approaches to liability are driven by a number of contextual factors that are themselves

[117] Paris Agreement (n 47) para 51.

[118] MJ Mace and Roda Verheyen, 'Loss, Damage and Responsibility after COP21: All Options Open for the Paris Agreement' (2016) 25 R ECIEL 197. Eight small island states made declarations upon signature or ratification of the Paris Agreement to the effect that acceptance of the Agreement did not constitute a renunciation of any rights under international law concerning state responsibility for the adverse effects of climate change and that no provision in the Agreement can be interpreted as derogating from principles of general international law or any claims or rights concerning compensation due to the impacts of climate change. United Nations, 'Paris Agreement' (*United Nations Treaty Collection*, 24 August 2022) <https://treaties.un.org/Pages/ViewDetails.aspx?src=IND&mtdsg_no=XXVII-7-d&chapter=27&clang=_en> accessed 24 August 2022.

[119] Report of the ILC (n 60).

interdependent. Amongst the key factors that are likely to influence the approach to liability are economic conditions relating to both the activities subject to potential liability and the interests affected by the harm caused; environmental conditions that influence questions such as attribution and the nature of the harm; the institutional context, including the presence of international organizations that can co-ordinate liability rules and the degree of state involvement; relatedly, the normative conditions that structure the purposes to which liability rules are directed; and last but not least, the political conditions, whether its popular demands for polluter to be held accountable or states seeking to preserve the position of powerful global or national actors. The alignment of these conditions within the global commons will vary between sectors and activities, and will be influenced by the existing rules and principles underlying commons environmental and economic regimes.

3

Definition and Valuation of Compensable Environmental Damage

3.1 INTRODUCTION

Principles and rules on liability and compensation need to define the nature and scope of losses that may be recoverable. This chapter examines issues related to the definition and valuation of environmental damage in areas beyond national jurisdiction (ABNJ), that is: what general principles govern reparation for environmental damage; what types of environmental damage should give rise to compensation or other measures of reparation; and how should such compensation or other measures be assessed in monetary terms. This chapter draws out the characteristics of, and considerations relating to, the global commons areas that might affect the approach taken to these questions, and how, if at all, compensation for environmental damage has been addressed in the existing regimes governing ABNJ under consideration in this study. To inform the discussion, the chapter examines other relevant international principles and rules that have been adopted or applied to address compensation for environmental damage at the international level.

As international concern for the environment and recognition of the significance and value of ecosystem services to humans has increased,[1] there has been some evolution in international legal approaches to compensability of environmental harm, both in international agreements addressing liability for damage arising from hazardous activities and in judicial forums. Approaches to defining compensable environmental damage remain, for the most part, incomplete, to the extent that they fail to adequately address irreparable environmental damage or interim losses pending restoration of the damaged environment. Legal approaches to defining compensable environmental damage, particularly in the more developed context of civil liability regimes, have usually been determined in light of concerns about

[1] ES Brondizio, J Settele, S Díaz and HT Ngo (eds), *Global Assessment Report on Biodiversity and Ecosystem Services of the Intergovernmental Science-Policy Platform on Biodiversity and Ecosystem Services* (IPBES 2019).

valuation methodologies, limits on liability and insurability of risks. There remains a lack of clarity about the elements of environmental damage that can be compensated, and the methods by which any monetary compensation should be assessed.[2] Most debate has concerned whether damage to environmental resources without a recognized commercial or market value[3] should be compensable, and, if so, how such losses should be quantified. This concept of pure environmental loss encompasses damage that is irreparable, or that may entail significant interim losses pending reinstatement or natural recovery of the damaged environment. On this point there are differences in the approaches that have been taken in different contexts and forums, but recent developments indicate that as a matter of principle such losses should be compensated notwithstanding difficulties in quantification.[4] These developments encompass a growing recognition of the importance of framing environmental damage not simply in terms of damage to components of the environment, but rather in the context of the loss of ecosystem services or functions: the provisioning, regulating, cultural and supporting services provided by environmental resources.[5]

As discussed further in Section 3.2.2, environmental damage in ABNJ could thus encompass various heads of damage, such as:

- Consequential loss as a result of impairment to the environment (loss of profit). This could include, for example, losses from reduced access to fisheries, mineral resources or marine genetic resources;
- The costs of measures to prevent environmental damage;
- The costs of measures of reinstatement taken to restore the damaged environment;

2 See generally, Louise de La Fayette, 'The Concept of Environmental Damage in International Liability Regimes' in Michael Bowman and Alan Boyle (eds), *Environmental Damage in International and Comparative Law: Problems of Definition and Valuation* (OUP 2002) 149; Edward Brans, *Liability for Damage to Public Natural Resources: Standing, Damage and Damage Assessment* (Kluwer Law International 2001); Peter Wetterstein (ed), *Harm to the Environment: The Right to Compensation and the Assessment of Damages* (OUP 1997); Jason Rudall, *Compensation for Environmental Damage under International Law* (Routledge 2020).

3 The International Court of Justice (ICJ) has referred to 'damage caused to the environment, in and of itself'. *Certain Activities Carried Out by Nicaragua in the Border Area (Costa Rica v Nicaragua), Compensation Owed by the Republic of Nicaragua to the Republic of Costa Rica* [2018] ICJ Rep 15, para 41 (*Certain Activities*). See further Section 3.2.1.3.

4 According to the International Law Commission (ILC), 'the earlier reluctance to accept liability for damage to the environment *per se*, without linking such damage to persons or property is gradually disappearing'. ILC, 'Draft Principles on the Allocation of Loss in the Case of Transboundary Harm Arising Out of Hazardous Activities, with Commentaries' (2006) UN Doc A/61/10 (Draft Principles), commentary to principle 3, 73, para 8.

5 See Brondizio and others (n 1); and on compensability of ecosystem service loss in the marine environment, see Günther Handl, 'Marine Environmental Damage: The Compensability of Ecosystem Service Loss in International Law' (2019) 34 IJMCL 602, arguing that '[ecosystem services] compensability is a touchstone for the robustness of contemporary international law and policy regarding the protection and conservation of the marine environment', at 611–612.

- Assessment and monitoring costs associated with identifying environmental damage and the effects of preventive or restoration measures; and
- Pure environmental damage that is incapable of restoration or that gives rise to interim losses pending restoration. Such losses would incorporate loss of ecosystem services, as well as components of biodiversity, and could incorporate provision of equivalent resources or services.

Environmental damage in ABNJ could occur in a range of different situations that impact on the appropriate approach to reparation and valuation of damage. For example, environmental damage could arise from impacts from approved activities, such as seabed mining in the Area. Such impacts may have been foreseen in the environmental impact assessment (EIA) prior to approval, and addressed in risk management measures, or they may comprise adverse effects unforeseen in nature and/or scale. Damage could also arise due to accidents, such as discharges of oil or chemicals in the high seas or in Antarctica. Environmental damage may arise from specific incidents, such as catastrophic pollution events, or it might arise as a result of the cumulative effects of certain activities, such as overfishing or destructive fishing practices. It may also result from more complex interactions between diffuse or cumulative sources, such as pollution of the marine environment by plastic, marine pollution by land-based sources or from the impacts of climate change including ocean acidification. Diffuse and cumulative damage raises complex questions around causation, remoteness and attribution. Beyond harm to components of the environment and ecosystem services as such, further consideration might also be given to environmental damage in the context of cultural harm, particularly in relation to indigenous peoples.[6]

Determining workable legal approaches to defining and valuing environmental damage also has to account for the significant technical and scientific challenges associated with assessing and monitoring damage to the environment in ABNJ, and with identifying and implementing any appropriate restoration or compensatory measures. Valuation methodologies have been a thorny issue in the international regime on oil pollution damage, and also in the context of national liability regimes.[7]

Section 3.2 of this chapter first outlines existing and emerging approaches to reparation for environmental damage in general international law, with Section 3.2.1 focusing on the rules of state responsibility and claims against states in respect of environmental damage made in international tribunals and the United Nations Compensation Commission (UNCC). These general rules and principles, as the

[6] Julian Aguon and Julie Hunter, 'Second Wave Due Diligence: The Case for Incorporating Free, Prior and Informed Consent into the Deep Seabed Mining Regulatory Regime' (2019) 38 Stan Envtl L J 3.

[7] See Rudall (n 2) 2, noting that 'there are many ways of calculating monetary compensation for environmental damage, and their outcomes vary significantly'.

default rules governing state liability, are applicable in ABNJ, and also provide the foundations for understanding how international law approaches the concept of environmental damage. Section 3.2.2 then examines elements of compensable environmental damage in various international instruments addressing civil liability for environmental harm. While not directly applicable to ABNJ,[8] these regimes provide further examples of the approaches to defining environmental damage in the context of specific hazardous activities that are likely to inform the development of rules in global commons areas. Section 3.3 then turns to the definition of environmental damage in relevant existing and emerging rules in ABNJ: in respect of Antarctica, the deep seabed and the high seas. Finally, Section 3.4 considers challenges associated with assessing or quantifying claims for environmental damage, and the ways in which such challenges might affect liability rules on environmental damage in ABNJ.

3.2 DEFINING COMPENSABLE ENVIRONMENTAL DAMAGE UNDER INTERNATIONAL LAW

3.2.1 *State Responsibility*

Under general international law, principles of state responsibility apply to reparation in respect of transboundary environmental damage arising from an internationally wrongful act of a state. States have the obligation to ensure that activities under their jurisdiction or control do not cause damage to the environment of ABNJ, or of other states.[9]

[8] Although note the provision for compensation in respect of preventive measures in, for example, International Convention on Civil Liability for Oil Pollution Damage (adopted 29 November 1969, entered into force 19 June 1975) 973 UNTS 3 (1969 Oil Pollution Liability Convention), amended by the 1992 Protocol to Amend the 1969 International Convention on Civil Liability for Oil Pollution Damage (adopted 27 November 1992, entered into force 30 May 1996) 1956 UNTS 255 (1992 Oil Pollution Liability Convention), art II(b); International Convention on Liability and Compensation for Damage in Connection with the Carriage of Hazardous and Noxious Substances by Sea (adopted 3 May 1996) (1996) 35 ILM 1415 (1996 HNS Convention), art 3(d) as amended by the International Convention on Liability and Compensation for Damage in Connection with the Carriage of Hazardous and Noxious Substances by Sea (adopted 30 April 2010) (2010 HNS Convention); and Basel Protocol on Liability and Compensation for Damage Resulting from Transboundary Movement of Hazardous Wastes and their Disposal (adopted 10 December 1999) UNEP/CHW.1/WG/1/9/2 (1999 Basel Liability Protocol), art 3(3)(c). On the high seas 'gap' in relation to pollution from tankers, see Nicholas Gaskell, 'Liability and Compensation Regimes: Pollution of the High Seas' in Robert C Beckman, Millicent McCreath, J Ashley Roach and Zhen Sun (eds), *High Seas Governance: Gaps and Challenges* (Brill Nijhoff 2018) 229–272, 236–237.

[9] Declaration of the United Nations Conference on the Human Environment (1972) UN Doc A/Conf.48/14/Rev.1 (1972 Stockholm Declaration) principle 21; Report of the United Nations Conference on Environment and Development (1992) UN Doc A/Conf.151/26/Rev.1, Annex I (1992 Rio Declaration) principle 2; *Legality of the Threat and Use of Nuclear Weapons*

3.2.1.1 General Principles of Reparation

Violations of international obligations by states constitute an internationally wrongful act, giving rise to an obligation to make reparation for the injury caused by the wrongful act.[10] While this principle is relatively straightforward, its application in the context of environmental damage raises a number of questions. In its work on state responsibility, the International Law Commission (ILC) touched upon some specific considerations concerning reparation for environmental harm, but, in light of the general scope of the Draft Articles on Responsibility of States for Internationally Wrongful Acts (ASR), left others unaddressed.[11] As the commission of an internationally wrongful act is the trigger for the application of rules of state responsibility, for these rules to come into play, states must either violate a rule of international environmental law directly or violate their obligations of due diligence in respect of the oversight of relevant activities.

The approach taken under article 31 of the ASR is that the wrongful act gives rise to a secondary obligation on the responsible state to make full reparation for the injury caused by the wrongful act.[12] The ILC notes that structuring reparation as an obligation of the responsible state, as opposed to being the right of the injured state, avoids difficulties where the obligation is owed simultaneously to several or many states, but only a few are specially affected by the breach. This is likely to be a recurring feature of harm to the global commons, and may facilitate a more inclusive approach to standing by allowing invocation of state responsibility by non-injured states.[13]

3.2.1.2 Causation and Remoteness

Article 31 makes references to the concept of causality, in that reparation must be made for injury 'caused by' the internationally wrongful act. This is addressed further in the commentary to article 31, which refers to various formulations concerning directness, proximity and remoteness of damage. While recognizing that no single formula can fully capture the question of remoteness, and that 'the

(Advisory Opinion) [1996] ICJ Rep 226, para 29; United Nations Convention on the Law of the Sea (adopted 10 December 1982, entered into force 16 November 1994) 1833 UNTS 397 (UNCLOS) arts 192 and 194(2); *The South China Sea Arbitration (The Republic of Philippines v The People's Republic of China)* (Award) (2016) Oxford Reports on ICGJ 495 (PCA) (*South China Sea Arbitration*), para 940.

10 ILC, 'Draft Articles on Responsibility of States for Internationally Wrongful Acts, with Commentaries' (2001) UN Doc A/56/10 (ASR) art 1, 32; art 31, 91.

11 See generally Alan Boyle, 'Reparation for Environmental Damage in International Law: Some Preliminary Problems' in Michael Bowman and Alan Boyle (eds), *Environmental Damage in International and Comparative Law: Problems of Definition and Valuation* (OUP 2002) 17.

12 ASR (n 10), art 31, 91.

13 ibid art 48, 126 (also discussed in Chapter 6).

requirement of a causal link is not necessarily the same in relation to every breach of an international obligation', article 31 reflects the need for a 'sufficient causal link which is not too remote'.[14] This is consistent with the approach to environmental damage in the *Trail Smelter* case, which noted that recovery may not be available for damage that is 'too indirect, remote and uncertain to be appraised'.[15]

Restricting recovery based on remoteness addresses two separate issues germane to damage in the commons. First, there is a policy question of the extent to which a responsible actor ought to bear the unforeseeable consequences of its breach. In complex ecosystems, such as oceans, the causal chains linking damage to specific (and attributable) actions are likely to be attenuated and subject to greater scientific uncertainty. A strict approach to remoteness or foreseeability may narrow the scope of recoverable damages, leaving indirect or unforeseeable harms unaddressed.

A second, related issue relates to the evidentiary challenges associated with proving damage. In the *Certain Activities* case, the International Court of Justice (ICJ) acknowledged that issues may arise as to the existence of damage and causation in cases of alleged environmental damage. It also noted in respect of valuation of such damage, that the absence of adequate evidence as to the extent of material damage would not, in all situations, preclude an award of compensation for that damage.[16] However, in a subsequent case, the ICJ did reject a claim in respect of damage to biodiversity through deforestation on the basis that the claimant did not provide evidence of the damage.[17] A liability claim related to environmental damage in an area beyond national jurisdiction would presumably impose an evidentiary burden on the claimant to prove the damage that has occurred as well as the causal link, which could give rise to challenges in terms of evidence-gathering. For example, the nature and accessibility of certain areas beyond national jurisdiction might mean that in practice only states with significant economic, technical and scientific capacity, or perhaps international organizations, could engage in gathering evidence upon which to found a claim for environmental damage, setting up a *de facto* barrier to access to justice.

Another issue with respect to causation is that while some incidents of environmental damage in ABNJ may be caused by a single identifiable event, conduct or source, there will be other situations in which such damage arises because of diffuse sources or of cumulative impacts over time – for example, impacts of marine

[14] ibid commentary to art 31, 93, para 10.

[15] *Trail Smelter Arbitration* (1949) III UNRIAA 1905, 1931. For a discussion of difficulties applying concepts of causation in the context of transboundary air pollution, see Phoebe Okowa, *State Responsibility for Transboundary Air Pollution in International Law* (OUP 2000) 184–190.

[16] *Certain Activities* (n 3), paras 34–35; see also para 86. See Section 3.4.

[17] *Armed Activities on the Territory of the Congo (Democratic Republic of the Congo v Uganda)* Judgment of 9 February 2022, General List No 116 [2022], para 350. The Court found that the claimant had not provided the Court with any basis for assessing damage to the environment, in particular to biodiversity, through deforestation.

pollution from land-based sources or of climate change. These challenge traditional concepts of causation for the purposes of establishing responsibility for harm and may operate to limit the potential for claims for environmental damage. Assessing responsibility in situations where there are multiple and cumulative sources of environmental damage will depend upon available evidence. However, in ABNJ, establishing a sufficient causal link in these circumstances may be complicated by factors such as deficient baseline data, scientific understanding of cause-and-effect relationships in complex ecosystems or the lack of monitoring to provide data on how and when environmental damage has occurred.

The ILC touched upon this scenario in its commentary to article 31 in the ASR noting that injury may be caused by a combination of factors,[18] but it did not directly consider the situation of environmental damage arising as a result of multiple drivers or impacts, focusing rather on the implications for allocation of responsibility. In its judgment on compensation in the *Certain Activities* case between Costa Rica and Nicaragua, the ICJ noted the need for a factual assessment of the evidence in addressing causation as follows:

> In cases of alleged environmental damage, particular issues may arise with respect to the existence of damage and causation. The damage may be due to several concurrent causes, or the state of science regarding the causal link between the wrongful act and the damage may be uncertain. These are difficulties that must be addressed as and when they arise in light of the facts of the case at hand and the evidence presented to the Court. Ultimately, it is for the Court to decide whether there is a sufficient causal nexus between the wrongful act and the injury suffered.[19]

The UNCC considered issues related to parallel or concurrent causes of harm in relation to environmental and natural resource claims, concluding that

> [w]here the evidence shows that damage resulted directly from Iraq's invasion and occupation of Kuwait but that other factors have contributed to the damage for which compensation is claimed, due account is taken of the contribution from such other factors in order to determine the level of compensation that is appropriate for the portion of the damage which is directly attributable to Iraq's invasion and occupation of Kuwait.[20]

International law allows for the invocation of state responsibility against a plurality of responsible states, allowing for actions to be brought against a group of states that are

[18] ibid paras 12–13.

[19] *Certain Activities* (n 3), para 34.

[20] United Nations Claims Commission (UNCC), 'Report and Recommendations made by the Panel of Commissioners concerning the Third Instalment of "F4" Claims' (2003) UN Doc S/AC.26/2003/31, para 39 (UNCC Third Instalment). See Vladyslav Lanovoy, 'Causation in the Law of State Responsibility' (2022) British Yearbook Intl L 1, 70–72, https://doi.org/10.1093/bybil/brab008, 27 January 2022.

jointly responsible for environmental harm.[21] The suggestion by the UNCC indicates that in relation to the calculation and allocation of damages, this may be done on a proportional basis.

3.2.1.3 Forms of Reparation

Chapter II of the ASR addresses forms of reparation for injury caused by an internationally wrongful act, namely restitution, compensation and satisfaction.

The basic approach in the ILC ASR is that of full reparation, reflecting the well-known dictum in the *Factory at Chorzów* case with its emphasis on restitution in kind or, if this is not possible, the payment of a sum corresponding to such restitution and the award, if necessary, of damages for loss sustained which would not be covered by restitution in kind or payment of such corresponding sum.[22] The notion of reparation to 'wipe out' the consequences of the illegal act and re-establish the *status quo ante* is inherently attractive in the environmental context, as it addresses the dual goals of compensation and environmental protection and restoration. There is no reason that the rationale for restitution hinges on individual rather than collective harm, as might be suffered in harm to the global commons. The wording of article 35 of the ASR, which addresses restitution, refers to an obligation 'to re-establish the situation which existed before the wrongful act was committed'.

One general concern in this regard is the question of proportionality: whether the requirement of full reparation might lead to 'disproportionate or crippling' requirements for the responsible state.[23] Rather than address the issue of proportionality as an aspect of the obligation to make full reparation, the ILC addresses it in respect of different forms of reparation.

In terms of the forms of reparation that may be appropriate, the starting point is restitution. Article 35 of the ASR recognizes that the obligation to make restitution is not unlimited. Restitution may be materially impossible or may impose a disproportionate burden compared to compensation.[24] Depending upon any preventive and remedial action taken in such scenarios, some costs incurred might be capable of calculation and recovery, but restoration in full may be impossible, or might only occur over long and/or uncertain timescales leaving significant interim losses, for example in terms of the physical environment, components of biodiversity and/or ecosystem functioning. As envisaged in article 35, the expected costs of such efforts might exceed anticipated benefits so that in some situations, the costs of restoration efforts may be deemed disproportionate to any potential benefits of restoration, even if feasible.[25] Determining when attempts at restoration are appropriate might in

[21] See Chapter 4, Section 4.3.4.
[22] *Chorzów Factory Case* (Indemnity) [1927] PCIJ Series A No 8/9.
[23] ASR (n 10) commentary to art 34, 96, para 5.
[24] ibid commentary to art 35, 98, para 7.
[25] ibid commentary to art 35, 98, para 11.

itself be a difficult task, and one that can only be resolved on a case-by-case basis. Relevant to proportionality, some civil liability conventions and other instruments discussed in Section 3.2.2 have made reference to recoverability of costs of 'reasonable measures' of reinstatement, which then requires that some criteria of reasonableness are established.

Compensation is the form of reparation envisaged where damage cannot be made good by reparation.[26] In terms of the standard of compensation, the implication in the ASR is that compensation should be full in that it should result in full reparation, including filling any reparation 'gap' where damage is not made good by restitution. In this regard it is noteworthy that article 235 of United Nations Convention on the Law of the Sea (UNCLOS) refers to the objective of assuring 'prompt and adequate' compensation in respect of all damage caused by pollution to the marine environment, and reference to 'prompt and adequate' compensation is also included in the ILC's Draft Principles on the Allocation of Loss (Draft Principles), principles 3 and 4.[27] However, the ILC notes that 'adequacy' here is not intended to denote 'sufficiency' but relates to a number of issues, including due process of law requirements, and that provided compensation given 'is not arbitrary, and grossly disproportionate to the damage actually suffered, even if it is less than full it can be regarded as adequate'.[28]

Compensation is not a straightforward solution for environmental damage.[29] Article 36 of the ASR provides that compensation shall cover 'financially assessable damage'. In accordance with article 31(2), both material and moral damage is covered by the obligation of reparation, but the commentary to article 36 clarifies that the term 'financially assessable' is intended to exclude moral damage (e.g. suffered by a state) which is to be reparable by way of satisfaction.[30] Compensation is not to be punitive, but is intended to ensure full reparation for damage suffered.[31] What constitutes financially assessable environmental damage, and how is such damage to be assessed? This requires a breakdown of the components of environmental damage that are compensable – the 'definition' of environmental damage – and then the assessment or valuation of such components in monetary terms. In light of the general applicability of the ASR, the ILC commentary to article 36 acknowledges that the appropriate heads of compensable damage and the principles of assessment to be applied in quantification will vary.[32] In

26 ibid art 36, 98.
27 Draft Principles (n 4) principle 3, 72.
28 ibid commentary to principle 4, 78, para 8.
29 See Section 3.4.
30 ASR (n 10) commentary to art 36, 99, para 1.
31 ibid paras 3–4. See also *Certain Activities* (n 3) para 31, 'compensation may be an appropriate form of reparation, particularly in those cases where restitution is materially impossible or unduly burdensome ... Compensation should not, however, have a punitive or exemplary character'.
32 ASR (n 10) commentary to art 36, 100, para 7.

relation to environmental damage, the ILC noted state practice in the context of Canada's Cosmos 954 claim, as well as the environmental claims in the UNCC, and referred to compensation payments relating to expenses reasonably incurred in preventing or remedying pollution, or providing compensation for a reduction in the value of polluted property.[33] The ILC's commentary also supports the view that pure environmental damage is compensable, acknowledging that

> environmental damage will often extend beyond that which can be readily quantified in terms of clean-up costs or property devaluation. Damage to such environmental values (biodiversity, amenity, etc. – sometimes referred to as 'non-use values') is, as a matter of principle, no less real and compensable than damage to property, though it may be difficult to quantify.[34]

While this supports compensation for pure environmental loss, in its work on state responsibility the ILC did not offer further guidance on such elements of environmental damage or on how they might be quantified.

In 2018, the ICJ handed down its judgment on compensation in the *Certain Activities* case, the first case in which the ICJ has made an order for compensation in respect of environmental damage caused by one state on the territory of another.[35] The ICJ affirmed that 'it is consistent with the principles of international law governing the consequences of internationally wrongful acts, including the principle of full reparation, to hold that compensation is due for damage caused to the environment in and of itself, in addition to expenses incurred by an injured state as a consequence of such damage'.[36] The ICJ took the view that 'damage to the environment, and the consequent impairment or loss of the ability of the environment to provide goods and services, is compensable under international law' and

33 ibid 101, paras 14–15.

34 ibid 101, para 15.

35 The ICJ has dealt with numerous disputes involving alleged violations of international law giving rise to actual or potential environmental harm. For example, in *Aerial Herbicide Spraying*, Ecuador detailed in its application to the Court the nature and extent of the environmental harm it claimed to have suffered, but did not address quantum of compensation. The case was settled before hearings on the merits commenced, *Case Concerning Aerial Herbicide Spraying (Ecuador v Colombia)* (Application Instituting Proceedings) General List No 138 [2008] ICJ Rep 4. In the *Gabčikovo-Nagymaros* case, Hungary referred in its Memorial to reparation for environmental damage, including compensation, and noted the difficulties associated with evaluating the costs of environmental damage. *Case Concerning the Gabčikovo-Nagymaros Project* (Hungary/Slovakia) Memorial of the Republic of Hungary, Volume 1, 2 May 1994, paras 8.22–8.48. However, the Court was not asked to address the question of quantum in the merits phase of the dispute. The ICJ has also addressed a case involving alleged violations of international environmental law taking place at least in part in areas beyond national jurisdiction in the *Whaling in the Antarctic* case. However, that case did not involve a claim for compensation and the Court's judgment was based solely on an analysis of the compatibility of Japan's activities with its obligations under the International Convention on the Regulation of Whaling. *Whaling in the Antarctic (Australia v Japan: New Zealand Intervening)* [2014] ICJ Rep 226, paras 39–40.

36 *Certain Activities* (n 3), para 41.

that '[s]uch compensation may include indemnification for the impairment or loss of environmental goods and services in the period prior to recovery and payment for the restoration of the damaged environment'.[37] While the judgment reflects challenges associated with the valuation of such claims,[38] the Court's approach reflects more contemporary approaches to address environmental damage 'in and of itself' not only in terms of damage to specific resources but also by reference to the services that those resources provide.

In establishing the UNCC, the UN Security Council had already determined that Iraq 'was liable under international law for any direct loss, damage, including environmental damage and the depletion of natural resources ... as a result of [its] unlawful invasion and occupation of Kuwait'.[39] Thus, the purpose of the UNCC was essentially to administer verifiable claims. Nonetheless, it was recognized that addressing claims for environmental damage and depletion of natural resources would pose special challenges. In this context, the UNCC had to develop criteria and methods to address such claims, and it received numerous claims under this head of damage.[40] As a first step, the UNCC Governing Council decided that compensation in respect of environmental damage or depletion of natural resources would *include* losses and expenses arising from:

(a) Abatement and prevention of environmental damage;
(b) Reasonable measures already taken to clean and restore the environment or future measures which can be documented as reasonably necessary to clean and restore the environment;
(c) Reasonable monitoring and assessment of the environmental damage for the purpose of evaluating and abating the harm and restoring the environment;
(d) Reasonable monitoring of public health and performing medical screening for the purposes of investigating and combating increased health risks as a result of the environmental damage; and
(e) Depletion of or damage to natural resources.[41]

The panel dealing with environmental damage and depletion of natural resources claim found that the criteria established by the Governing Council were not

[37] ibid para 42.
[38] See Section 3.4.
[39] UN Security Council Res 687 (1991) UN Doc S/RES/687, para 16.
[40] On environmental and natural resources claims in the UNCC, see Michael T Huguenin, Michael C Donlan, Alexandra E van Geel and Robert W Paterson, 'Assessment and Valuation of Damage to the Environment' in Cymie Payne and Peter Sand (eds), *Gulf War Reparations and the UN Compensation Commission: Environmental Claims* (OUP 2011) 67.
[41] UNCC, 'Criteria for Additional Categories of Claims' (1992) UN Doc S/AC 26/1991/7/Rev 1 (Governing Council Decision 7), para 35. The Governing Council decision did not address valuation of compensation for such damage.

exhaustive,[42] and that the term 'environmental damage' was not limited to damage to natural resources with a commercial value.[43] It also took the view that where loss or damage to the environment was temporary, this did not affect the question of compensability, although it might affect the nature and quantum of compensation deemed appropriate.[44] The panel found that there was 'no justification for the contention that general international law precludes compensation for pure environmental damage'.[45]

The UNCC also addressed claims in respect of monitoring and assessing environmental damage for the purpose of evaluating and abating the harm and restoring the environment.[46] Here, the UNCC found that environmental monitoring and assessment were justified even where it was not yet firmly established that environmental damage had occurred. Conclusive proof of environmental damage was not a prerequisite for a monitoring and assessment activity to be compensable.[47] However, the panel did not award compensation for monitoring and assessment activities that were 'purely theoretical and speculative'.[48]

The principles of state responsibility offer some valuable starting points in relation to defining and valuing compensable environmental damage, but they do not address all aspects. The approaches adopted in civil liability regimes provide a further indication of the international community's understanding of the scope of compensable damage. While liability under civil liability regimes is channelled to operators, often on a strict liability standard, the underlying theory of damage in civil liability regimes remains rooted in restitution and, as such, provides a fuller picture of how damage should be approached in specific commons regimes.

3.2.2 *Civil Liability*

The ILC has specifically addressed compensation for environmental damage in its Draft Principles on the Allocation of Loss. Principle 3 of the Draft Principles provides that '[t]he purpose of the present draft principles are: ... (b) to preserve and protect the environment in the event of transboundary damage, especially with

42 UNCC, 'Report and Recommendations Made by the Panel of Commissioners Concerning the Second Instalment of "F4" Claims' (2002) UN Doc S/AC 26/2002/26, paras 22–23.

43 UNCC, 'Report and Recommendations Made by the Panel of Commissioners Concerning the Fifth Instalment of "F4" Claims' (2005) UN Doc S/AC 26/2005/10, para 55.

44 ibid para 56.

45 ibid para 58. The panel added that '[i]n particular, the Panel does not consider that the exclusion of compensation for pure environmental damage in some international conventions on civil liability and compensation is a valid basis for asserting that international law, in general, prohibits compensation for such damage in all cases, even where the damage results from an internationally wrongful act' (footnote omitted).

46 Governing Council Decision 7 (n 41) para 35(c).

47 UNCC, 'Report and Recommendations on the First Instalment of "F4" Claims' (2001) UN Doc S/AC.26/2001/16, paras 29–30.

48 ibid para 31.

respect to mitigation of damage to the environment and its restoration or reinstatement'. In relation to the purposes of the Draft Principles, the ILC notes that Draft Principle 3(b) gives

> a prominent place to the protection and preservation of the environment and to the associated obligations to mitigate the damage and to restore or reinstate the same to its original condition to the extent possible. Thus it emphasizes the more recent concern of the international community to recognize protection of the environment *per se* as a value by itself without having to be seen only in the context of damage to persons and property. It reflects the policy to preserve the environment as a valuable resource not only for the benefit of the present generation but also for future generations. In view of its novelty and the common interest in its protection, it is important to emphasize that damage to the environment *per se* could constitute damage subject to prompt and adequate compensation, which includes reimbursement of reasonable costs of response and restoration and remediation measures undertaken.[49]

Principle 2 defines 'damage' as significant damage caused to persons, property or the environment, and including

i. loss of life or personal injury;
ii. loss of, or damage to, property, including property which forms part of the cultural heritage;
iii. loss or damage by impairment of the environment;
iv. the costs of reasonable measures of reinstatement of the property, or environment, including natural resources;
v. the costs of reasonable response measures.

'Environment' for the purpose of the Draft Principles includes natural resources, both abiotic and biotic, such as air, water, soil, fauna and flora and the interaction between the same factors, and the characteristic aspects of the landscape.[50]

The ILC's work on allocation of loss draws upon the approach taken in several of the civil liability instruments.[51] Each of these international agreements set out a scope and approaches tailored to the particular activity and/or environment that they address. They reflect the types of damage that might be caused by the activity or substances in question, and the degree of consensus amongst states about the nature and scope of risks posed and potential harm. The definition of compensable damage

49 Draft Principles (n 4) commentary to principle 3, 73, para 6.

50 ibid principle 2(b), 64.

51 For example, 1992 Oil Pollution Liability Convention (n 8); 1996 HNS Convention (n 8); Lugano Convention on Civil Liability for Damage Resulting from Activities Dangerous to the Environment (adopted 21 June 1993) 32 ILM 1228 (1993 Lugano Convention); 1999 Basel Liability Protocol (n 8); International Convention on Civil Liability for Bunker Oil Pollution Damage (adopted 23 March 2001, entered into force 21 November 2008) UNTS No 47 (2001 Bunker Oil Convention).

to the environment varies under the agreements,[52] and is generally incorporated into a wider definition of the 'damage' that is recoverable under the agreement. They typically define environmental damage in terms of reasonable preventive, response or reinstatement measures actually undertaken or to be undertaken, rather than by reference to impacts on the environment – that is, they are concerned with what type of costs might be recoverable under the arrangements established by the agreement. The approach to defining compensable damage in these regimes is influenced by considerations related to limits on liability and insurability of relevant activities.[53] Heads of environmental damage covered by some or all of the civil liability agreements are described below.

3.2.2.1 Loss of Profit Arising from Impairment to the Environment

This head of recoverable damage is included in most international civil liability regimes.[54] It does not compensate damage to the environment as such, but rather loss of income suffered by natural or legal persons derived from an economic interest in a use of the environment as a result of environmental impairment. Numerous claims for such loss have been addressed within the civil liability regime on oil pollution damage. The International Oil Pollution Compensation Funds' (IOPC Funds) 2016 Annual Report notes that, in addition to property damage, admissible claims include economic losses by fishers or those engaged in mariculture and economic losses in the tourism sector.[55]

It is conceivable that such losses from impairment to the environment might arise because of environmental damage in ABNJ. Such losses might be suffered by, for example, high seas fishing entities, tourism enterprises operating in Antarctica or operators with seabed mining licences impacted in some detrimental way by environmental harm. Claiming compensation for such losses in respect of environmental damage in ABNJ is more complicated in the context of non-exclusive rights based on high seas freedoms, but many of these high seas activities are subject to licensing regimes which arguably provide a legal basis for a claim and for quantifying losses.

3.2.2.2 Reasonable Preventive Measures

Reasonable costs relating to prevention of further environmental harm are also covered in most liability regimes. These are defined in the 1992 Oil Pollution Liability Convention as 'any reasonable measures taken by any person after an

52 See generally, de La Fayette, 'The Concept of Environmental Damage' (n 2); Brans (n 2).
53 See Chapter 8.
54 For example, 1992 Oil Pollution Liability Convention (n 8) art I(6)(a); 1996 HNS Convention (n 8) art 1(6)(c); 1993 Lugano Convention (n 51) art 2(7)(c); 1999 Basel Liability Protocol (n 8) art 2(2)(c)(iii); 2001 Bunker Oil Convention (n 51) art 1(9).
55 International Oil Pollution Compensation Funds (IOPC Funds), Annual Report 2016, 12.

incident has occurred to prevent or minimize pollution damage'.[56] The 1999 Basel Liability Protocol refers to measures to 'prevent, minimize, or mitigate loss or damage, or to effect environmental clean-up'.[57] Costs of preventive measures taken outside national jurisdiction may be recoverable where they are taken to avoid or minimize other environmental damage – within national jurisdiction – covered by the agreement in question.

As regards preventive measures to avoid or minimize environmental damage to ABNJ, a key issue, as described in relation to reinstatement costs below, would be who would have the requisite interest or entitlement to take such measures in ABNJ (discussed in Chapter 6). There is also a more general question of how the reasonableness of such preventive measures is to be determined as a matter of proportionality.[58]

3.2.2.3 Reasonable Measures of Reinstatement Actually Undertaken or to Be Undertaken

Reasonable measures of reinstatement reflect the approach to reparation in the work of the ILC on both state responsibility and allocation of loss. Such measures are incorporated into the definition of damage in most international civil liability regimes.[59] Some guidance as to what would constitute reasonable measures of reinstatement has also been provided, either within the treaties themselves or in subsequent guidance. The IOPC Funds Guidelines for presenting claims for environmental damage, published in 2018, address claims for costs of post-incident studies and reinstatement measures.[60] The Guidelines discuss, *inter alia*, specific criteria for reinstatement measures, which focus on accelerating and enhancing the recovery of the damaged components of the environment, and establish that the costs of reinstatement must be proportionate to the extent and duration of the damage and the benefits likely to be achieved.[61] Measures taken at some distance from the damaged area, but still within the general vicinity, may be acceptable as

[56] 1992 Oil Pollution Liability Convention (n 8) art I(7); similar provisions are found in the 1996 HNS Convention (n 8) art 1(7); 2001 Bunker Oil Convention (n 51) art 1(7); 1993 Lugano Convention (n 51) art 2(9).

[57] 1999 Basel Liability Protocol (n 8) art 2(2)(e).

[58] See Section 3.3 on existing and emerging approaches to this question in ABNJ-specific contexts.

[59] For example, 1992 Oil Pollution Liability Convention (n 8) art I(6)(a); 1996 HNS Convention (n 8) art 1(6)(c); 1993 Lugano Convention (n 51) arts 2(7)(c) and 8; 1999 Basel Liability Protocol (n 8) art 2(2)(c)(iv) and 2(2)(d); 2001 Bunker Oil Convention (n 51) art 1(9)(a). On the debates concerning the incorporation of such measures into the definition of 'pollution damage' in the oil pollution liability regime, see Wu Chao, *Pollution from the Carriage of Oil by Sea: Liability and Compensation* (Kluwer Law International 1996) 147–153.

[60] *Guidelines for Presenting Claims for Environmental Damage* (2018 edn, IOPC Funds 2018) (IOPC Guidelines).

[61] ibid para 4.3.

long as it can be demonstrated that they would actually enhance the recovery of the damaged components of the environment and the services those components provide.[62] However, the replacement of a damaged site by 'creating' an equivalent resource elsewhere may not satisfy the IOPC Funds' criteria.[63] The Guidelines acknowledge that there is little experience of admissible claims for reinstatement measures.[64]

It is evident that restoration measures will not always be feasible or effective. The determination of what constitutes reasonable measures of restoration might be challenging where there is no market value for the environmental resource, and the issue of proportionality of restoration measures is likely to arise given that quantifying both the damage and the benefits from reinstatement may be more challenging in ABNJ. The prospects for success of restoration measures in certain environments might also be open to question, and other potential environmental impacts of restoration measures need to be considered. In such situations, alternative methods for making good the environmental loss or loss of ecosystem services may be required.

In areas within national jurisdiction, coastal states have a right to undertake reinstatement actions, or to require or authorize others to do so. In ABNJ, it is less clear who might be entitled to recover as a result of taking such action. In the absence of clear authority to undertake reinstatement measures, a state or private entity may be viewed as acting voluntarily, and as such could be viewed as an 'officious intermeddler' since the claimant confers a benefit on the international community that was not necessarily asked for, and as such, the claimant may not be entitled to restitution.[65] The alternative view would be that states and their agents do have an interest in protecting the environment of the commons and should be able to recover their reasonable costs of reinstatement. This latter position is supported by the general approach in international law that the obligation to make reparation flows from the wrongful act and not from the right of an injured state.[66] There are also doctrines in both civil and common law jurisdictions that support the idea of necessitous intervention (*negotiorum gestio*) that permits recovery for interventions in support of community or public interests.[67] The point of law is far from clear, and the absence of a clear right of recovery acts as a disincentive for states to undertake reinstatement actions, notwithstanding the public benefit in such actions.

A final point in relation to reinstatement is that recovery is limited to the costs of measures 'actually undertaken or to be undertaken'.[68] Thus, reinstatement costs cannot be used as a proxy for calculating general damages.

62 ibid.
63 ibid para 5.22.
64 ibid para 5.11.
65 See, for example, C Mitchell and William Swadling (eds), *Restatement (Third) of Restitution and Unjust Enrichment* (Bloomsbury Publishing 2013) §§ 20–30.
66 ASR (n 10) art 31, 91.
67 Discussed in John McCamus, 'Necessitous Intervention: The Altruistic Intermeddler and the Law of Restitution' (1979) 11 Ottawa L Rev 297.
68 1992 Oil Pollution Liability Convention (n 8) art II; 1996 HNS Convention (n 8) art 1.

3.2.2.4 Monitoring and Assessment of Environmental Damage

Measures to prevent environmental damage and to reinstate damaged environments presuppose the assessment of damage, in order to understand the scope and nature of appropriate response measures. Monitoring the status and recovery of damaged environments, and impact of any reinstatement measures, will also be an important element of minimizing adverse effects on components of the environment and on ecosystem services. International liability instruments do not always make express reference to such costs, but as noted above, the IOPC Funds' 2018 Guidance makes reference to post-incident studies. The 1999 Basel Liability Protocol includes in the definition of 'measures of reinstatement', reasonable measures to 'assess' damaged or destroyed components of the environment.[69] Guidelines on liability adopted under the Barcelona Convention[70] also incorporate activities and studies to assess damage.[71]

In areas beyond national jurisdiction, questions as to who should be responsible for conducting assessment and monitoring of environmental damage arise. Depending upon the way in which any relevant rules are framed, responsibility might fall upon the entity responsible for causing the damage, upon a state or states or upon an international organization. In addition to identifying the most appropriate way to allocate such responsibility, capacity to conduct such activities in areas beyond national jurisdiction may limit the availability of assessment and monitoring.

3.2.2.5 'Pure Environmental Damage' and Ecosystem Services Loss

While the elements of environmental damage above relate to reasonable costs incurred in taking measures to prevent environmental damage or to reinstate damaged environments, it is evident that in some instances irreparable harm may occur, or that the affected environment or ecosystem services can only be restored over the long-term. While the concept of pure environmental damage can relate to notions of the intrinsic value of environmental resources, increasingly environmental loss is framed within the context of the ecosystem services provided by those resources. This type of damage is difficult to quantify in economic terms as the environmental resources and systems affected may well not have a commercial value. The compensation of pure environmental damage, or environmental damage

[69] 1999 Basel Liability Protocol (n 8) art 2(2)(d).

[70] Convention for the Protection of the Marine Environment and the Coastal Region of the Mediterranean, 16 February 1976, 15 ILM 290 (adopted 16 February 1976, entered into force 1 February 1979), as amended June 1995, UNEP(OCA)/MED IG.6/7 (entered into force 9 July 2004) (Barcelona Convention).

[71] Barcelona Convention, Decision IG 17/4 Guidelines for the Determination of Liability and Compensation resulting from Pollution of the Marine Environment of the Mediterranean Sea Area, UNEP(DEPI)MED IG.17/10 Annex V, 18 January 2008 (Barcelona Convention Guidelines) para 10.

per se, has been a matter of debate both in the context of international liability conventions and in other international forums.[72] In its commentary to principle 2, the ILC observed that

> [r]ecent trends are . . . encouraging in allowing compensation for loss of 'non-use value' of the environment. There is some support for this claim from the [International Law] Commission itself when it adopted its draft articles on State responsibility, even though it is admitted that such damage is difficult to quantify. The recent decisions of the United Nations Compensation Commission (UNCC) in opting for a broad interpretation of the term 'environmental damage' is a pointer of developments to come. In the case of F-4 category of environmental and public health claims, the F-4 Panel of the UNCC allowed claims for compensation for damage to natural resources without commercial value (so-called 'pure' environmental damage) and also claims where there was only a temporary loss of resource use during the period prior to full restoration.[73]

As yet, pure environmental damage is not generally incorporated into international civil liability regimes. Handl observes that

> [t]oday, both national legal systems and international law reflect a broad consensus that the compensation of environmental damage would cover the costs of any reasonable measures – already taken or to be taken – that aim to assess, reinstate or restore damaged or destroyed components of the environment, the principal goal of such measures being to return the affected environment to its pre-existing or baseline condition. However, as soon as in-kind, in-place restoration ('primary restoration', or 'primary remediation') is not possible and alternative measures might have to be contemplated, this consensus breaks down.[74]

Some commentators have observed that the unfortunate consequence of such an approach might be that minor, reparable damage might be subject to compensation through restoration costs, while more severe irreparable or long-term harm would not.[75] As is well known, the IOPC Funds have maintained that compensation for impairment to the environment is limited to financially assessable loss: loss of profit arising from impairment to the environment, and the costs of reasonable preventive measures and reasonable measures of reinstatement of the environment actually undertaken or to be undertaken. In the oil pollution regime, there has been a resistance to the idea of compensating non-economic loss associated with environmental damage. As discussed further below, such damage would require different means of assessment and valuation. In 1980, Resolution No. 3 of the 1971 IOPC Fund stated that assessment of compensation to be paid by the Fund would not be

72 Allan Rosas, 'Issues of State Liability for Transboundary Environmental Damage' (1991) 60 Nord J Intl L 29, 42.

73 Draft Principles (n 4) commentary to principle 2, 69, para 18 (footnotes omitted).

74 Handl (n 5) 607–608.

75 de La Fayette, 'The Concept of Environmental Damage' (n 2) 183.

made on the basis of an abstract quantification of damage calculated in accordance with theoretical models.[76] This position has been maintained, most recently in Guidelines for presenting claims for environmental damage published by the IOPC Funds in 2018.[77] Nonetheless, it has been the subject of growing critique and seems anachronistic in the face of evolving international environmental principles.[78]

Some liability instruments do incorporate ecosystem services within the definition of environmental damage. The 2010 Nagoya-Kuala Lumpur Supplementary Protocol on liability in the context of transboundary movement of genetically modified organisms refers to '[t]he reduction of the ability of components of biological diversity to provide goods and services' as a factor relevant to establishing a significant adverse effect for the purpose of establishing damage.[79] Other factors in determining a significant adverse effect under that Protocol include 'long-term or permanent change, to be understood as change that will not be redressed through natural recovery within a reasonable period of time' and 'the extent of the qualitative or quantitative changes that adversely affect the components of biological diversity'.[80]

Some international liability instruments include within the definition of covered damage the introduction of equivalent components of the environment, in the context of reinstatement measures, where reinstatement or restoration is not possible. The 2010 Nagoya-Kuala Lumpur Supplementary Protocol gives preference to restoration of biodiversity to the condition that existed before the damage occurred, or its nearest equivalent, but also provides for 'replacing the loss of biological diversity with other components of biological diversity for the same, or another type of use either at the same or, as appropriate at an alternative location'.[81] The 1993 Lugano Convention takes this approach, and leaves it to domestic law to determine who may take such measures.[82] The 2004 Protocol amending the

[76] IOPC Funds, *Resolutions of the 1971 Fund*, Resolution No. 3 Pollution Damage (October 1980), 5.

[77] IOPC Guidelines (n 60) 10, para 4.1.

[78] Handl observes that this 'categorical denial of [ecosystems services] loss … is at odds with international public policy'. Handl (n 5) 611. Wetterstein has also called for expansion of compensable environmental damage in the oil pollution liability regimes and other civil liability conventions, Peter Wetterstein 'Pure Environmental Damage' in Günther Handl and Kristoffer Svendsen (eds), *Managing the Risk of Offshore Oil and Gas Accidents* (Edward Elgar 2019), 305, 330.

[79] Nagoya-Kuala Lumpur Supplementary Protocol on Liability and Redress to the Cartagena Protocol on Biosafety (adopted 15 October 2010, entered into force 5 March 2018) (2011) 50 ILM 105 (2010 Nagoya-Kuala Lumpur Supplementary Protocol) art 2(3)(c). See Akiho Shibata (ed), *International Liability Regime for Biodiversity Damage: The Nagoya-Kuala Lumpur Supplementary Protocol* (Routledge 2014).

[80] 2010 Nagoya-Kuala Lumpur Supplementary Protocol (n 79) art 2(3)(a) and (b).

[81] ibid art 2(d). See also Barcelona Convention Guidelines (n 71) para 10 (e).

[82] 1993 Lugano Convention (n 51) art 2(8). See also 2003 Protocol on Strategic Environment Assessment to the Convention on Environmental Impact Assessment in a Transboundary

1960 Paris Convention on liability in the field of nuclear energy also provides for the introduction of equivalent components of the environment.[83]

Guidelines on liability adopted under the Barcelona Convention for the Protection of the Marine Environment and the Coastal Region of the Mediterranean[84] include within the scope of compensation for environmental damage 'diminution in value of natural or biological resources pending restoration' and 'compensation by equivalent if the impaired environment cannot return to its previous condition'.[85] The Guidelines note that where compensation is granted for these types of damage, it should be earmarked for intervention in the environmental field in the Mediterranean Sea Area.[86] The Guidelines are also to apply to damage caused by pollution of a diffuse character provided it is possible to establish a causal link between the damage and activities of individual operators.[87]

Given the challenges that reinstatement may pose in ABNJ, calculating losses with reference to the provision of offsets may be an attractive, even necessary, alternative.[88] The difficulty would be in determining suitable equivalents for losses to deep ocean ecosystems.

3.2.3 *Threshold of Harm*

A general issue that arises in terms of defining compensable environmental damage is the question whether there is a threshold of harm which must be met before any liability arises.[89]

The rationale for a threshold of severity to trigger both the obligation of prevention and corresponding liability is based on a recognition that lawful activities

Context (adopted 21 May 2003, entered into force 11 July 2010) 2865 UNTS 140 (2003 Kiev Protocol) art 2(2)(g).

83 Protocol to Amend the Convention on Third Party Liability in the Field of Nuclear Energy of 29 July 1960, as amended by the Additional Protocol of 29 January 1964 and by the Protocol of 16 November 1982 (adopted 12 February 2004, in force 1 January 2022), art I.B, www.oecd-nea.org/jcms/pl_20361/2004-protocol-to-amend-the-paris-convention, accessed 17 March 2023.

84 Barcelona Convention (n 70).

85 Barcelona Convention Guidelines (n 71) para 10(d) and (e). Para 10 also covers the types of environmental damage discussed above in relation to other agreements: activities and studies to assess damage; costs of preventive measures; and costs of measures taken or to be undertaken to clean up, restore and reinstate the impaired environment.

86 ibid para 13.

87 ibid para 15. See Tullio Scovazzi, 'The Mediterranean Guidelines for Determination of Environmental Liability and Compensation: The Negotiations of the Instrument and the Question of Damage that Can Be Compensated' (2009) 13 Max Planck UNYB 183.

88 HJ Niner and others, 'Deep-Sea Mining with No Net Loss of Biodiversity – An Impossible Aim' (2018) 5 Front Mar Sci 5(53).

89 See K Sachariew, 'The Definition of Thresholds of Tolerance for Transboundary Environmental Injury under International Law: Development and Present Status' (1990) XXXVII NILR 193; see also Okowa (n 15) 88–90; Philippe Sands and Jacqueline Peel, *Principles of International Environmental Law* (4th edn, CUP 2018) 743–745.

conducted within the jurisdiction of one state may well have impacts on other states in light of the ecological unity of the planet. Such mutual impacts are to be considered tolerable as long as they do not reach the 'significant' threshold.[90] Most notably the obligation of due diligence requires states to take reasonable steps to prevent significant environmental harm.[91] Such a threshold does not however seem to be of general application, but the degree of harm seems nonetheless to be relevant to the assessment of reparation. For example, in examining environmental claims, the UNCC rejected an argument by Iraq that only significant damage was compensable, finding that any direct loss or damage was covered. However, it did note that '[i]n considering the reasonableness of remediation measures, it is appropriate to have regard to the extent of the damage involved'.[92]

The question of whether environmental harm must exceed some minimum threshold is a function of the primary rule that defines the internationally wrongful act. In the UNCC claims, the wrongful act, the invasion of Kuwait by Iraq, is not connected to a threshold of harm. In the case of due diligence, where the wrongful conduct incorporates a threshold of significant harm, environmental harm below the threshold would not appear to result in a wrongful act. This situation may again be complicated by cumulative impacts, where the synergistic effects of multiple actions result in a harm that exceeds the significance threshold, but no one state's actions may amount to significant harm on their own.

In the Draft Principles, the ILC defined 'damage' as meaning 'significant damage', so that to be eligible for compensation, damage should meet a certain threshold.[93] To support this approach it cited existing case law, the *Trail Smelter* arbitration and the *Lake Lanoux* case, both of which referred to 'serious' injury, as well as international conventions imposing thresholds such as 'significant', 'serious' or 'substantial' harm.[94] The threshold of 'significant' damage in relation to allocation of loss reflected the scope of the ILC's related work on Prevention of Transboundary Harm which applies to 'activities not prohibited by international law which involve a risk of causing significant transboundary harm through their physical consequences'.[95] In its commentary to draft article 2 on Prevention of Transboundary Harm, the ILC explained that 'significant' '*is something more than "detectable" but need not be at the level of "serious" or "substantial"*'. The harm must lead to a real detrimental effect on matters such as ... environment' and 'such detrimental effects must be susceptible of being measured by factual and objective

[90] ILC, 'Draft Articles on Prevention of Transboundary Harm from Hazardous Activities, with Commentaries' (2001) UN Doc A/56/10 (Draft Articles on Prevention of Transboundary Harm) art 1, commentary to art 2, 152, para 5.

[91] See discussion in Chapter 5, Section 5.3.1.

[92] UNCC Third Instalment (n 20) para 36.

[93] Draft Principles (n 4) commentary to principle 2(a), 64, para 1.

[94] ibid para 1 and footnote 326.

[95] Draft Articles on Prevention of Transboundary Harm (n 90) art 1, 149.

standards'.[96] In the 2010 Nagoya-Kuala Lumpur Supplementary Protocol, damage must be 'significant'. A significant adverse effect for the purpose of the Protocol is to be determined based on factors such as:

(a) The long-term or permanent change, to be understood as change that will not be redressed through natural recovery within a reasonable period of time;
(b) The extent of the qualitative or quantitative changes that adversely affect the components of biological diversity;
(c) The reduction of the ability of components of biological diversity to provide goods and services;
(d) The extent of any adverse effects on human health in the context of the Protocol.[97]

The term 'significant' is one that requires determination on a case-by-case basis, and involves more factual considerations than legal determinations.[98] According to the ILC, it also incorporates value determinations depending upon the circumstances of the case and the period in which the determination is made, that might reflect available scientific knowledge and/or the value ascribed to particular resources.[99] Assessing whether a threshold of significant damage is met therefore is not an exact science, and might well give rise to different determinations in different international and domestic courts.[100]

To what extent is the threshold of 'significant' harm appropriate in the context of liability for environmental damage to the global commons, and, if so, how it is to be measured? In principle, the rationale put forward by the ILC for the threshold in relation to its Draft Principles on Allocation of Loss appears to apply equally in the context of areas beyond national jurisdiction: the recognition that lawful activities conducted within the jurisdiction of one state may have some impacts on areas

96 ibid, commentary to principle 2, 152, para 4; Draft Principles (n 4), commentary to principle 2 (a), 65, para 2.
97 2010 Nagoya-Kuala Lumpur Supplementary Protocol (n 79) art 2(3).
98 Draft Articles on Prevention of Transboundary Harm (n 90) commentary to art 2, 152, para 4.
99 ibid commentary to art 2, 153, para 7.
100 In this regard, it is notable that additional guidance has been published in the European Union on defining environmental damage and significant adverse effects for the purposes of the EU Environmental Liability Directive (Directive (CE) 2004/35 of the European Parliament and of the Council of 21 April 2004 on environmental liability with regard to the prevention and remedying of environmental damage [2004] OJ L143/56). A European Commission evaluation of implementation of the Directive in member states of the EU revealed that implementation was hampered by significant lack of uniform application of key concepts, in particular concepts related to environmental damage. European Commission, 'Guidelines providing a common understanding of the term "environmental damage" as defined in Article 2 of Directive 2004/35/EC of the European Parliament and of the Council on environmental liability with regard to the prevention and remedying of environmental damage' [2021] OJ C 118/01.

beyond national jurisdiction as well as on other states. At the same time, the need for factual and case-by-case assessment of significance of harm raises specific questions in the global commons context. As noted elsewhere, the factual assessment of damage and its significance may be challenging, in the light of current scientific knowledge including the availability of baseline data and sufficient understanding of ecosystem functioning. Moreover, any assessment of the significance of harm may depend upon the contemporary state of scientific knowledge, and complex equations relating to the value and need for particular resources of economic value as well as economic and non-economic values ascribed to ecosystem services and components of the environment. Such an assessment should also appropriately take account of the precautionary approach given gaps and uncertainties in relevant scientific knowledge.

3.3 DEFINING COMPENSABLE ENVIRONMENTAL DAMAGE IN ABNJ

The existing agreements on Antarctica, the deep seabed and the high seas begin to address the question of damage within their liability rules. However, the development of relevant rules in respect of environmental damage in the global commons has been slow and patchy. This makes it difficult to ascertain any common approach to defining compensable environmental damage because, for the most part, liability regimes establishing such definitions are not in place. Still the limited, and as yet untested, rules that have been adopted, and the difficulties in establishing such rules and securing their entry into force, offer some insights in relation to gaps and approaches for consideration in the future.

3.3.1 *Antarctic*

Article 3 of the 1991 Antarctic Protocol, which provides that activities in the Antarctic Treaty area are to be planned and conducted so as to limit adverse impacts on the Antarctic environment and dependent and associated ecosystems, identifies specific impacts to be avoided, including significant adverse effects on air and water quality, significant changes in the atmospheric, terrestrial, glacial or marine environments and detrimental changes in the distribution, abundance or productivity of fauna and flora.[101] It also reflects particular characteristics of the unique environment of Antarctica, including some features that may be relevant in other ABNJ, requiring that assessment of planned activities in the area, should take into account, *inter alia:* cumulative impacts of the activity, both by itself and in combination with other activities in the Antarctic Treaty area; capacity to monitor key environmental parameters and ecosystem components so as to identify and provide early warning of

[101] Protocol on Environmental Protection to the Antarctic Treaty (adopted 4 October 1991, entered into force 14 January 1998) (1991) 30 ILM 1461 (1991 Antarctic Protocol) art 3(2)(b).

any adverse effects; and whether there exists the capacity to respond promptly and effectively to accidents, particularly those with potential environmental effects.[102]

Activities taking place in the Antarctic comprise primarily scientific research and tourism, with ancillary activities including supply vessels, but exploitation activities, with the exception of fisheries, are limited.[103] Despite these limitations, the allowable activities entail environmental risks relating, for example, to waste and wastewater, and pollution from aircraft or ships, including fuel oil spills.[104] To address these risks, the parties adopted Annex VI to the Protocol (Liability Annex),[105] which establishes a liability regime applicable to environmental emergencies.[106] The Liability Annex is more limited in scope than the rules and procedures on liability envisaged in article 16 of the Antarctic Protocol in that it addresses only environmental emergencies and response measures thereto addressed in article 15 of the Protocol.[107]

The regime established in the Liability Annex is administrative in nature. Under the Liability Annex, each party must require its operators to undertake reasonable preventive measures that are designed to reduce the risk of environmental emergencies and their potential adverse impact,[108] and to take prompt and effective response action to environmental emergencies arising from the activities of that operator.[109] 'Response action' means 'reasonable measures taken after an environmental emergency has occurred to avoid, minimize or contain the impact of that environmental emergency, which to that end may include clean-up in appropriate circumstances, and includes determining the extent of that emergency and its impact'.[110] There is no reference to restoration measures. 'Reasonable', in relation to preventive measures and response action, means 'measures or actions which are appropriate, practicable, proportionate and based on the availability of objective criteria and information, including: (i) risks to the Antarctic environment, and the rate of its natural recovery; (ii) risks to human life and safety; and (iii) technological

[102] ibid art 3(2)(c).

[103] Mineral resource activities, other than scientific research, are prohibited under the 1991 Antarctic Protocol (n 101), art 7, and military activities are prohibited under the Antarctic Treaty (adopted 1 December 1959, entered into force 23 June 1961) 402 UNTS 71 art 1.

[104] See, for example, the Bahia Paraiso 1989 CEDRE, 'Bahia Paraiso – Spill report' online <wwz.cedre.fr/en/Resources/Spills/Spills/Bahia-Paraiso> accessed 13 October 2022.

[105] Annex VI to the Protocol on Environmental Protection to the Antarctic Treaty on Liability Arising from Environmental Emergencies (adopted 17 June 2005) (2006) 45 ILM 5 (Liability Annex). Not yet entered into force.

[106] These are defined as 'any accidental event that has occurred, having taken place after the entry into force of this Annex, and that results in, or imminently threatens to result in, any significant and harmful impact on the Antarctic environment': Liability Annex (n 105) art 2(b).

[107] Liability Annex (n 105) art 1; Alan D Hemmings, 'Liability Postponed: The Failure to Bring Annex VI of the Madrid Protocol into Force' (2018) 8(2) Polar J 315, 323.

[108] Liability Annex (n 105) art 3(1).

[109] ibid art 5(1).

[110] ibid art 2(e) and (f).

and economic feasibility'.[111] Beyond the definition of 'reasonable' noted above, no guidance is provided as to how costs of reasonable response measures should be assessed.

Article 9 does establish limits on liability of an operator in respect of an environmental emergency. Where an operator does not take prompt and effective response action, then the state party of that operator and other parties are encouraged to take such action,[112] and in such circumstances, the operator shall be liable to pay the costs of such response action. Where prompt and effective response action is not taken, and no response action is taken by any party, article 6 makes provisions for payments to a Fund established under article 12 of the Liability Annex of 'an amount of money that reflects as much as possible the costs of response action that should have been taken'.[113] Decisions on requests for reimbursement from the Fund of 'reasonable and justified costs' incurred by a party that has taken response action are to be decided by the Antarctic Treaty Consultative Meeting (ATCM), which may seek advice from the Committee for Environmental Protection. As the Liability Annex has not yet entered into force, further guidance remains unavailable.

The approach clarifies two key issues that arise in the commons. The first issue relates to who is entitled to effect response measures to environmental harm. By specifying that any party may take action and then seek their costs from the operator, the 1991 Antarctic Protocol addresses the uncertainty surrounding whether third party responders would be considered 'officious intermeddlers'.[114] The approach in the Antarctic is to recognize the collective right to address environmental harms and seek compensation from responsible parties. The second issue that is addressed is that the costs of a response action not undertaken may be used as a proxy for damages. This is in contrast to the approach under civil liability regimes, which only allow for compensation related to reinstatement measures actually taken or to be taken. Insofar as the rule under civil liability regimes is motivated by concerns over windfall awards, the presence of a Fund under the Antarctic Liability Annex ensures that damages collected are directed towards collective environmental interests.

Prior to the adoption of the 1991 Antarctic Protocol, the 1988 Convention on the Regulation of Antarctic Mineral Resources Activities (CRAMRA) would have put in place more extensive liability rules.[115] While not in force, nonetheless it is worth examining the relevant provisions of CRAMRA as it could provide a possible model

[111] ibid art 2(e).

[112] ibid art 5(2)–(5).

[113] ibid art 6(b) in respect of payments to the fund by non-state operators. Under art 6(1), a state operator which did not take required prompt and effective response action under art 5 is liable to pay 'the costs of the response action which should have been taken'.

[114] See discussion in Sections 3.2.2.3 and 3.2.2.4.

[115] Convention on the Regulation of Antarctic Mineral Resource Activity (adopted 2 June 1988, not yet entered into force) 27 ILM 868 (CRAMRA).

for developing new liability rules in areas beyond national jurisdiction under the 1991 Antarctic Protocol, in relation to deep seabed mining, or perhaps more widely. At the same time, caution is needed as CRAMRA addressed a specific economic activity involving a limited range of actors. Article 1(15) CRAMRA provides

> Damage to the Antarctic environment or dependent or associated ecosystems means any impact on the living or non-living components of that environment or those ecosystems, including harm to atmospheric, marine or terrestrial life, beyond that which is negligible, or which has been assessed and judged to be acceptable pursuant to this Convention.

This definition addresses both living and non-living components of the environment or ecosystems. The reference to damage 'which has been assessed and judged to be acceptable pursuant to this Convention' appears to relate to the regulatory objective to protect and preserve the Antarctic environment and to allow mineral resource activities only where it is judged, based upon assessment of possible impacts on the Antarctic environment and on dependent and associated ecosystems, that the activity in question would not cause significant adverse effects.[116] It is not linked to specific criteria or indicators that might define and revise acceptable levels of damage, and as the CRAMRA did not enter into force, no further elaboration of this definition was forthcoming. The definition suggests that damage arising out of authorized activities which have been subject to prior EIA would be non-compensable. This, in turn, raises the question whether and in what circumstances damage that is unforeseen in nature or scale prior to authorization might be compensable.

Article 8 of CRAMRA establishes certain rules and procedures for response action and liability. Under this provision, operators undertaking any Antarctic mineral resource activity would have to take necessary and timely response action, including prevention, containment, cleanup and removal measures, if that activity results in or threatens to result in damage to the Antarctic environment or dependent or associated ecosystems. Under article 8(2) an operator would be strictly liable for, *inter alia*, 'damage to the Antarctic environment or dependent or associated ecosystems arising from Antarctic mineral resource activities, including payment in the event that there has been no restoration to the *status quo ante*'.[117] This appears to provide for a compensatory payment where irreparable damage has occurred, rather than tying the obligation to compensate to reasonable response or restoration actions actually undertaken. The operator would also be liable for 'reimbursement of reasonable costs by whomsoever incurred relating to necessary response action, including prevention, containment, clean-up and removal measures, and action taken to restore the *status quo ante* where Antarctic mineral resource activities undertaken

[116] ibid art 4(2).

[117] ibid art 8(2) (emphasis added).

by that Operator result in or threaten to resulting damage to the Antarctic environment or dependent or associated ecosystems'.[118] Had CRAMRA entered into force, further liability rules and procedures were to be adopted through a separate protocol to enhance the protection of the Antarctic environment and dependent and associated ecosystems.[119]

3.3.2 *Deep Seabed*

The prospect of deep seabed mining in the Area gives rise to a range of potential environmental impacts.[120] While these activities and impacts relate to a distinct economic activity, they involve a range of actors, various mining techniques and diverse deep seabed ecosystems. In accordance with the relevant regulatory provisions, these activities will be subject to prior EIAs that should enable risks and risk mitigation measures to be identified before any approved exploitation activities commence. Nonetheless, it is possible that unforeseen impacts might arise, or that risks identified during the EIA have impacts of a scale beyond those envisaged. The possibility of cumulative impacts of deep seabed mining and other processes and activities on deep seabed ecosystems cannot be ruled out. Gaps and uncertainties in scientific knowledge about ecosystem functioning and services in the deep seabed must also be taken into account and, the precautionary approach constitutes an important element of the relevant regulatory framework.[121] Rates of recovery of deep seabed ecosystems raise potential issues of irreparable environmental damage or significant interim losses between damage and recovery.[122] In this context, defining environmental damage for the purpose of rules on liability and compensation poses particular challenges.

UNCLOS contains general obligations relating to protection of the marine environment, as well as more specific obligations in Part XI addressing protection of the marine environment from harmful effects which may arise from activities in the Area.[123] Article 1(4) defines pollution of the marine environment as the

> introduction by man, directly or indirectly, of substances or energy into the marine environment, including estuaries, which results or is likely to result in such

[118] ibid.
[119] ibid art 8(6).
[120] See discussion in Chapter 1.
[121] See, for example, International Seabed Authority's (ISA) Regulations on Prospecting and Exploration for Polymetallic Nodules in the Area (2013) ISBA/19/C/17 (PMN) reg 31 (2); ISA, 'Regulations on Prospecting and Exploration for Polymetallic Sulphides in the Area' (2010) ISBA/16/A/12/Rev.1 (PMS) reg 33 (2); ISA, 'Draft Regulations on Exploitation of Mineral Resources in the Area' (2019) ISBA/25/C/WP.1 (DER) reg 2 (e) (ii) and reg 44 (a).
[122] Lisa A Levin and others, 'Defining "Serious Harm" to the Marine Environment in the Context of Deep-Seabed Mining' (2016) 74 Mar Pol'y 245.
[123] UNCLOS (n 9) art 145; arts 192–206; arts 209 and 215.

> deleterious effects as harm to living resources and marine life, hazards to human health, hindrance to marine activities, including fishing and other legitimate uses of the sea, impairment of quality for use of sea water and reduction of amenities.

In relation to the activities in the Area, article 145 provides for the ISA to adopt rules for the prevention, reduction and control of pollution and other hazards to the marine environment, and to protect and conserve the natural resources of the Area and prevent damage to marine flora and fauna.

Part XI and Annex III of UNCLOS address responsibility and liability specifically in relation to damage arising from activities in the Area. Article 139(2) provides that damage caused by the failure of a *state party* or *international organization* to carry out its responsibilities under Part XI shall entail liability. Article 22 of Annex III provides that

> the contractor shall have responsibility or liability for any damage arising out of wrongful acts in the conduct of its operations, account being taken of contributory acts or omissions of the Authority. Similarly, the Authority shall have responsibility or liability for any damage arising out of wrongful acts in the exercise of its powers and functions … account being taken of contributory acts or omissions by the contractor. Liability in every case shall be for the actual amount of damage.[124]

In considering article 139 (2), the Seabed Disputes Chamber (SDC) in its 2011 Advisory Opinion noted that

> [n]either the Convention nor the relevant Regulations (regulation 30 of the Nodules Regulations and regulation 32 of the Sulphides Regulations) specifies what constitutes compensable damage, or which subjects may be entitled to claim compensation. It may be envisaged that the damage in question would include damage to the Area and its resources constituting the common heritage of mankind, and damage to the marine environment.[125]

The SDC also addressed the amount and form of compensation, by reference to Annex III of UNCLOS, article 22. Here the SDC was of the view that the provisions concerning liability of the contractor for the actual amount of damage under Annex III, article 22, were equally valid with regard to the liability of the sponsoring state.[126] The SDC suggested 'the form of reparation will depend on both the actual damage and the technical feasibility of restoring the situation to the *status quo ante*'.[127] While the SDC's Advisory Opinion makes reference on this point to article 31 of the ILC's ASR on reparation,[128] and to the material possibility (technical

[124] ibid Annex III, art 22.

[125] *Responsibilities and Obligations of States Sponsoring Persons and Entities with Respect to Activities in the Area* (Advisory Opinion of 1 February 2011) ITLOS Reports 2011 (*Activities in the Area* Advisory Opinion) para 179.

[126] ibid para 195.

[127] ibid para 197.

[128] ibid para 194.

feasibility) of restitution, it does not specifically address considerations of proportionality in respect of restitution. As noted above, the ILC subjects reparation by restitution to a proportionality test so that restitution would not be required where it involves a burden out of all proportion to the benefit deriving from restitution instead of compensation.[129] The SDC's Advisory Opinion falls short of defining when compensation might constitute a more appropriate form of reparation. The provisions of Part XI and Annex III of UNCLOS, and the SDC's Advisory Opinion, also leave open certain questions relating to the definition and valuation of environmental damage arising out of activities in the Area. These include how 'damage to the Area and its resources' and 'damage to the marine environment' might be defined; and how 'the actual amount of damage' might be quantified for the purposes of compensation.

Some of these issues are under discussion in the development of exploitation regulations by the ISA. The current version of the Draft Exploitation Regulations (DER) also envisages the establishment of an Environmental Compensation Fund (ECF) to finance, *inter alia*, the implementation of any necessary measures designed to prevent, limit or remediate any damage to the Area arising from activities therein, the costs of which cannot be recovered from a contractor or sponsoring state, and the restoration and rehabilitation of the Area when technically and economically feasible and supported by best available scientific evidence.[130] The DER do not currently contain a detailed definition of what types of costs might be recovered from, or met by, the proposed Fund. An ISA Technical Study on an Environmental Compensation Fund (ISA ECF Study), published in 2021, addressed, *inter alia*, the topic of compensable damage,[131] drawing upon a review of existing funds including the IOPC Funds. The study clarifies that only damage resulting from activities *in* the Area should be compensated from the proposed Fund – damage from other activities impacting the Area would in principle be excluded. It suggests that the Fund cover damage to the marine environment that cannot be recovered from a contractor or sponsoring State. On the basis of the provisions of article 145 of UNCLOS and the definition of pollution in article 1(4), the study suggests that the following elements may be considered as damage to the Area and the marine environment: interference with the ecological balance of the marine environment; damage to the flora and fauna of the marine environment; harm to living resources and marine life; hazards to human health; hindrance to marine activities, including fishing and other legitimate uses of the sea; impairment of quality for the use of sea water; and reduction of amenities.[132] The study further acknowledges that the DER allow for compensation of preventive measures, that is,

[129] ASR (n 10) commentary to art 35(3), 98, para 11.
[130] DER (n 121) regs 54–56.
[131] ISA, 'Study on an Environmental Compensation Fund for Activities in the Area' (2021) ISA Technical Study No. 27 (ISA ECF Study) 35–39.
[132] ibid 36.

measures intended to prevent or limit damage, as well as appropriate activities to study, monitor or assess damage. Under the DER, compensation would also be allowed for remediation measures aimed at cleaning up a contaminated area by removing or isolating contaminants, and for 'restoration and rehabilitation of the Area when technically and economically feasible and supported by best available scientific evidence'.[133]

The ISA ECF Study, referring to recent developments surveyed in Section 3.2, proposes following the model of the IOPC Funds in *excluding* pure environmental damage and limiting compensation to recovery for reasonable measures of reinstatement undertaken or to be undertaken and costs of post-incident studies (effectively excluding interim ecosystem services losses). Reasons given for excluding pure environmental damage include the challenges of quantifying such damage and the financial viability of the proposed ECF. The Study notes that the 'wider the notion of compensable damage, the higher the risk of dispute over the existence of an actual duty to compensate in any given circumstance', and that ambiguity in the notion of compensable damage should be avoided.[134] Mirroring the restricted IOPC Funds approach in respect of pure environmental damage seems problematic and out of step with more recent developments, particularly as the Study itself acknowledges that certain damage might not be capable of restoration. Of further note, the Study proposes that recovery of compensation from the Fund should not be subject to establishment of a threshold of harm – such as 'serious' or 'significant' harm, despite the fact that certain provisions of UNCLOS relating to activities in the Area, and certain provisions of the DER, refer to 'serious harm'. Instead compensation should be available for 'any damage' falling within the definition of compensable environmental damage, consistent with article 22 of Annex III UNCLOS, and the wording of the DER.[135]

The legal status of the Area and its mineral resources as common heritage of humankind generates additional questions concerning the definition and valuation of damage. As noted above, the SDC observed that 'the damage in question would include damage to the Area and its resources constituting the common heritage of mankind, and damage to the marine environment'.[136] This suggests that these elements may constitute separate heads of damage in some circumstances. On the one hand, it may be easier to determine when there has been an impact on mineral resources such that the extraction of such resources is affected in terms of volume, quality or cost. Given that the mineral resources of the Area have a commercial value, valuation of damage to such resources may be possible through more traditional commercial valuation methods. On the other hand, the mineral

[133] ibid.
[134] ibid 38.
[135] ibid 38–39.
[136] *Activities in the Area* Advisory Opinion (n 125) para 179.

resources of the Area, and the seabed itself, are at the same time important components of the deep seabed ecosystem.[137]

The authorization of mineral exploitation activities presupposes a level of acceptable interference in deep seabed ecosystems, in light of environmental impact assessment and the ISA decision-making process. However authorized activities could give rise to environmental impacts that are unforeseen in nature or extent, and that might be deemed to constitute environmental damage. The principle of common heritage of humankind also incorporates other considerations, such as intergenerational impacts, that might have a bearing on the definition of damage and questions of appropriate compensation.[138] Issues associated with impacts on marine genetic resources in the Area also require consideration. While such genetic resources fall within the concept of biodiversity, as a component of the environment that may be damaged, the legal status and terms of use of such resources have been addressed in negotiations outside the ISA (see Section 3.3.3). Conceivably, damage to marine genetic resources might be compensable as an aspect of damage to natural resources, where the recovery and exploitation of such resources is impacted by environmental damage arising out of activities in the Area. While loss or damage to such resources subject to existing recovery and use may be capable of economic valuation, any such valuation might pose challenges – for example if the resources are not unique to the damaged area or if they are not currently subject to commercial exploitation. Unlike mineral resources of the Area, marine genetic resources in the Area are not subject to exclusive rights in terms of access, and the legal status of such resources and issues relating to benefit-sharing, could raise questions of standing to claim.[139]

3.3.3 *High Seas*

As discussed in Chapter 1, there are a wide variety of processes and activities that impact on the environment and biodiversity of the high seas. This variety, and the physical nature of the high seas environment, poses particular challenges when it comes to identifying sources of specific environmental damage, and establishing causation. Where major pollution incidents occur, for example large spills of oil or other hazardous or noxious substances from vessels, it may be possible to establish

[137] The definition of 'Marine Environment' provided in the DER at the time of writing includes the physical, chemical, geological and biological components, conditions and factors which interact and determine the productivity, state, condition and quality and connectivity of the marine ecosystem(s), the waters of the seas and oceans and the airspace above those waters, as well as the seabed and ocean floor and subsoil thereof. DER (n 121), Schedule ('Use of terms and scope').

[138] See Aline Jaeckel, Kristina M Gjerde and Jeff A Ardron, 'Conserving the Common Heritage of Humankind – Options for the Deep-Seabed Mining Regime' (2017) 78 Mar Pol'y 150 (linking common heritage of mankind principle to intergenerational equity).

[139] See Section 3.3.3, and Chapter 6.

the source vessel. Yet in other instances this will not be the case. Many of the sources of marine pollution on the high seas are diffuse, and the impacts of certain activities and/or pollutants are cumulative and may become apparent only over the longer-term. Impacts may be direct, for example the impacts of an oil spill on marine mammals, fish or birds that come into contact with the oil. They may be indirect, such as the impact on fish stocks and dependent species of degradation or destruction of spawning grounds or nursery areas. Such factors pose difficulties for defining compensable environmental damage within any liability regime. Moreover, identifying appropriate measures for restoration of damaged and degraded marine ecosystems may pose particular challenges.

The approaches and trends in relation to compensable damage identified in connection with civil liability regimes (discussed above) may provide some guidance for approaches to reparation for environmental damage should the currently scant liability rules for environmental damage in ABNJ be enhanced. In relation to the high seas, however, it is notable that the geographic scope of the civil liability instruments does not generally extend to damage to areas beyond national jurisdiction, although the cost of certain preventive measures taken on the high seas to prevent or minimize pollution damage to areas under national jurisdiction may be recoverable.[140] On the possible expansion of existing civil liability regimes to the high seas, Gaskell has examined legal options and political will for such a move, and Leigh has noted that during the negotiation of the HNS Convention, Australia proposed that liability for damage caused by contamination of the environment beyond the 200 nautical miles exclusive economic zone be included, but this proposal was not taken up in the Convention.[141]

The 2023 draft agreement on marine biodiversity of ABNJ[142] does not address liability, but its provisions on, *inter alia*, area-based management tools and environmental impact assessment provide a basis for generating new information and understandings on some issues associated with addressing environmental damage in ABNJ. The draft agreement defines cumulative impacts, for example, and requires that these

[140] 1992 Oil Pollution Liability Convention (n 8) art II; 1971 International Convention on the Establishment of an International Fund for Compensation for Oil Pollution Damage (adopted 18 December 1971, entered into force 16 October 1978) 1110 UNTS 57 (amended by the 1992 Protocol on the International Convention on the Establishment of an International Fund for Compensation for Oil Pollution Damage, 27 November 1992) (1992 Fund Convention) art 3; 1996 HNS Convention (n 8) art 3; 1999 Basel Liability Protocol (n 8) art 3(3); 2001 Bunker Oil Convention (n 51) art 2.

[141] Gaskell (n 8); Kathy Leigh, 'Liability for Damage to the Global Commons' (1993) 14 Aust YBIL 129, 139. Leigh notes that Australia made a similar proposal in negotiations on the revision of the 1963 Vienna Convention on liability for nuclear damage, ibid. See also Robert S Schuda, 'The International Maritime Organization and the Draft Convention on Liability and Compensation in Connection with the Carriage of Hazardous and Noxious Substances by Sea: An Update on Recent Activity' (1992) 46 U Miami L Rev 1009, 1046.

[142] Draft agreement under the United Nations Convention on the Law of the Sea on the conservation and sustainable use of marine biological diversity of areas beyond national jurisdiction, Advance unedited text, 4 March 2023 ('BBNJ Agreement').

are considered in the context of environmental impact assessment.[143] Its requirements concerning proposals for marine protected areas and on environmental impact assessment require the provision of baseline data on the relevant marine environment and biodiversity,[144] and those on EIA require uncertainties and gaps in knowledge to be identified and considered.[145] The draft agreement also establishes thresholds for screening and for the conduct of environmental impact assessments in relation to planned activities in areas beyond national jurisdiction. In particular, parties must ensure that an EIA is conducted where a planned activity may cause 'substantial pollution of or significant and harmful changes to the marine environment' in ABNJ. The objectives of the provisions of the draft agreement on EIA are, *inter alia*, to ensure that relevant activities are assessed and conducted to prevent, mitigate and manage 'significant adverse impacts'.[146] While this language on threshold has been adopted in the context of prior assessment of activities, not in the context of liability rules, it might be germane to determining what is deemed an 'acceptable' impact beyond which liability for environmental damage could arise. The draft agreement further provides for monitoring and reporting of impacts of authorized activities, and where significant adverse impacts that were unforeseen in nature or severity or that arise from a breach of conditions in the authorization are identified, it requires the party with jurisdiction or control over the activity to require that measures are taken to prevent, mitigate and/or manage those impacts or take other necessary action or halt the activity. The Scientific and Technical Body is also given the power to make recommendations to the party concerned with regard to addressing such impacts.[147] Significantly, the Scientific and Technical Body also has a broader mandate to develop standards and/or guidelines related to the EIA thresholds and processes under the agreement.[148]

Two further aspects of the draft agreement appear pertinent in the context of advancing common understandings of environmental damage and appropriate response measures. First, in the context of area-based management measures, the agreement provides that under certain conditions the Conference of the Parties can adopt decisions on emergency measures in ABNJ where a natural phenomenon or human-caused disaster has caused or is likely to cause serious or irreversible harm to marine biodiversity of ABNJ to ensure that such harm is not exacerbated. Procedures

[143] These are defined as 'the combined and incremental impacts resulting from different activities, including known past and present and reasonably foreseeable activities, or from the repetition of similar activities over time, and the consequences of climate change, ocean acidification and related impacts', BBNJ Agreement (n 142), art 1(8); and on consideration in the context of EIA processes, see arts 21 bis (c), 24, 30(1), 35, and 41 bis (1).

[144] ibid art 17(4)(d), art 35(2); see also art 51(3)(e).

[145] ibid art 24(2)(f), art 35(2).

[146] ibid art 22(2) and art 21 bis (b). The obligation to screen a planned activity to assess whether an EIA is required arises where the planned activity may have 'more than a minor or transitory effect on the marine environment or the effects of the activity are unknown or poorly understood', art 24(1).

[147] ibid arts 39–41.

[148] ibid art 41 bis.

and guidance for the establishment of any such measures are to be elaborated after the agreement enters into force.[149] Second, the provisions on the financial mechanism refer to the possibility of the Conference of the Parties establishing a fund to finance rehabilitation and ecological restoration of marine biodiversity of ABNJ.[150] It remains to be seen whether these provisions and others in the BBNJ Agreement, once it enters into force, provide an impetus and legal framework for the further development of liability rules.[151]

3.4 VALUATION OF ENVIRONMENTAL DAMAGE

As suggested above, issues associated with valuing environmental damage have been invoked to limit the elements of environmental damage that are compensable within environmental liability regimes.[152] In particular, in the IOPC Funds, this consideration has proved a bar to broadening the scope of compensable damage, with the Funds maintaining the position that compensation for environmental damage should not be assessed on the basis of abstract quantification of damage calculated in accordance with theoretical models. By contrast, as discussed further below, the UNCC and the ICJ have demonstrated willingness to look into different valuation methods to compensate damage to components of the environment without a market value, as well as interim environmental losses pending restoration.

Developments in law and practice at the national and regional level have to some extent informed the more innovative, and arguably progressive, approaches to the definition and valuation of environmental damage. In particular, domestic law in the United States, under the Comprehensive Environmental Response, Compensation, and Liability Act (CERCLA) and the Oil Pollution Act 1990 have provided a forum for innovation in the assessment of natural resource damages, as well as for the evolution of an administrative approach to questions of assessing and restoring environmental damage.[153] The US approach has seen the utilization of a variety of valuation methods, such as contingent valuation methodology, travel cost method, hedonic pricing and habitat equivalency analysis (HEA), some of which were subsequently put forward to support claims in international forums.

[149] ibid art 20 ante.

[150] ibid art 52. See Chapter 8.

[151] Long suggested that the agreement should include an enabling provision for protocol on *sui generis* liability regime 'that is closely aligned with the rules on area-based management tools and environmental impact assessment' along similar lines to Annex VI of the Antarctic Protocol discussed above: R Long and Z Sun (eds), *Workshop Report: Biodiversity Beyond National Jurisdiction: Towards the Development of a Balanced, Effective and Universal International Agreement* (World Maritime University 2020) 6–7.

[152] Handl has noted that it is 'the valuation of ecosystem services that tends to pose a major obstacle to compensation'. Handl (n 5) 610.

[153] Emanuela Orlando, 'From Domestic to Global? Recent Trends in Environmental Liability from a Multilevel and Comparative Law Perspective' (2015) 24(3) RECIEL 289.

Contingent valuation is a stated preference model that bases valuation of damage upon a survey of people's willingness to pay to avoid such damage or maintain a level of environmental quality. The travel cost method assesses economic value of the quality and availability of environmental resources on the basis of willingness to pay to visit and use them; and hedonic pricing, an indirect valuation method, links changes in environmental quality to the market value of associated goods such as housing.[154] Decisions in other domestic jurisdictions have also supported the use of such methods, or the use of equitable considerations in quantifying environmental damage claims.[155] Amongst well-known cases in the context of civil liability for oil pollution damage are the *Patmos*[156] and *Haven*[157] cases in Italian courts, the *Erika*[158] case in France and the approach of the Soviet Union court in the *Antonio Gramsci*[159] incident (which prompted the IOPC Fund statement concerning abstract quantification methods). However, while these methods have faced an objection of principle in the IOPC Fund context, they also present more fundamental challenges in the context of quantifying environmental damage in areas beyond national jurisdiction. Applying contingent valuation based on willingness to pay seems difficult or impossible in relation to ABNJ; for the purpose of hedonic pricing, it is difficult to identify relevant marketed goods for the purpose of assessing changes in value; and travel cost methods face similar obstacles.

A more promising approach in relation to quantifying environmental damage by reference to ecosystem services loss is HEA, which assesses the nature and extent of the loss of ecological services from the damaged resources, determining the gain in ecological services anticipated from the compensatory projects, and calculating the cost of the compensatory projects. This method, and resource equivalency analysis, takes into account the biological, chemical and physical nature of the damage and remediation options. EU guidance on the Environmental Liability Directive explains that 'an equivalency analysis identifies which resources and services can be deemed to be "sufficiently similar" to the damaged resources and services and quantifies the amount to be remediated (credit) to be equal to the loss due to damage (debit)'.[160]

[154] See Nick Hanley, 'The Economic Valuation of Environmental Damage' in Michael Bowman and Alan Boyle (eds), *Environmental Damage in International and Comparative Law: Problems of Definition and Valuation* (OUP 2002) 27; and Tarcisio Hardman Reis, *Compensation for Environmental Damages under International Law: The Role of the International Judge* (Wolters Kluwer 2011) 138–141.

[155] See, for example, Rudall (n 2) 80–89.

[156] IOPC Funds, Annual Report 1994, 36–39.

[157] ibid 42–48.

[158] IOPC Funds, 'Incidents Concerning the IOPC Fund 2013', 6–11.

[159] IOPC Funds, Annual Report 1990, 27–30.

[160] European Commission, Environmental Liability Directive, Protecting Europe's Natural Resources (2013) 16. See also Annex II.

While the work of the UNCC and ICJ addresses damage arising out of wrongful acts of states, the approach to the definition and valuation of environmental damage has wider significance. The UNCC decided that where a resource had a commercial value, and was damaged for a period of time, compensation should be awarded on the basis of the market price for the period of time that the damage persisted, adjusted as appropriate to take into account the influence of other sources of damage.[161] For damage to resources that did *not* have a market reference price, the UNCC panel indicated that it would be willing to compensate natural resource losses by reference to the costs of other environmental projects that were put in place to compensate for the loss of ecological services that the natural resources would have provided had they not been damaged, so long as there was 'sufficient evidence that primary restoration will not fully compensate for any identified losses'.[162] Thus the emphasis was on primary remediation and restoration of services, but there appears to have been recognition that compensation for other restoration activities would be available where primary restoration was not possible or where there were interim losses.[163] Some claimants used HEA to determine the amount of compensation claimed. In considering approaches to valuation of damage, the panel expressed the view that 'international law does not prescribe any specific and exclusive methods of measurement for awards of damages for internationally wrongful acts by states. The general rule is to restore what has been damaged to integrity or, if this is not possible, to provide an equivalent for it'.[164] The panel recognized that

> there are inherent difficulties in attempting to place a monetary value on damaged natural resources, particularly resources that are not traded in the market. With specific regard to HEA, the Panel recognizes that it is a relatively novel methodology, and that it has had limited application at the national and international levels. The Panel is also aware that there are uncertainties in HEA calculations, especially for establishing a metric that appropriately accounts for different types of service losses and for determining the nature and scale of compensatory restoration measures that are appropriate for damage to particular resources. For these reasons, the Panel considers that claims presented on the basis of HEA or similar methodologies of resource valuation should be accepted only after the Panel has satisfied itself that the extent of damage and the quantification of compensation claimed are appropriate and reasonable in the circumstances of each claim. However, the Panel does not consider that these potential difficulties are a sufficient reason for a

[161] UNCC, 'Report on the Fifth Instalment of "F4" Claims' (n 43) paras 103–118, cited in Cymie Payne, 'UN Commission Awards Compensation for Environmental and Public Health Damage from 1990-91 Gulf War' (2005) 9(25) *ASIL Insights*.

[162] UNCC, 'Report on the Fifth Instalment of "F4" Claims' (n 43) para 82.

[163] José R Allen, 'Points of Law' in Cymie Payne and Peter Sand (eds), *Gulf War Reparations and the UN Compensation Commission: Environmental Claims* (OUP 2011) 141, 167.

[164] UNCC, 'Report on the Fifth Instalment of "F4" Claims' (n 43) para 80.

wholesale rejection of these methodologies, or for concluding that their use is contrary to international law principles.[165]

In the *Certain Activities* case between Costa Rica and Nicaragua, the ICJ made certain general observations about valuation of compensation and also addressed specific valuation methodologies put forward by the parties. As a general matter, in an earlier case, not involving environmental damage, the Court has observed that quantification of compensation for non-material injury rests on equitable considerations and awarded compensation on this basis.[166] The Court referred to this approach in its *Certain Activities* case reflecting that in respect of the valuation of damage, 'the absence of adequate evidence as to the extent of material damage will not, in all situations, preclude an award of compensation for that damage'.[167] It also cited the *Trail Smelter* award to the effect that 'it will be enough if the evidence show the extent of the damages as a matter of just and reasonable inference, although the result be only approximate'.[168] However, the Court also noted that compensation should not be punitive.[169] In terms of the specific arguments, the Court observed that the valuation methods put forward by the parties were not the only methods available, but that where certain elements of the proposed methods offered a reasonable basis for valuation, the Court would take them into account.[170] It noted that international law does not prescribe any specific method of valuation for the purposes of compensation for environmental damage, and that it was necessary to take into account the specific circumstances and characteristics of each case.[171] Costa Rica relied on an ecosystem service approach in evaluating its loss, referring to various categories of impaired goods and services including biodiversity, gas regulation and air quality services such as carbon sequestration, soil formation and erosion control. Nicaragua acknowledged Costa Rica's right to compensation for the ecosystem service replacement costs but challenged its valuation methodology. In the face of the competing valuation methodologies put forward by the parties, the Court's approach to the determination of compensation of environmental damage in this case was to assess the value to be assigned to the restoration of the damaged environment as well as to the impairment or loss of environmental goods and services prior to recovery.[172] Further, in the circumstances of the case, the Court considered it appropriate to approach the valuation of environmental damage

[165] ibid para 81.

[166] *Ahmadou Sadio Diallo (Republic of Guinea v Democratic Republic of the Congo)* (Compensation, Judgment) [2012] ICJ Rep 324, para 24.

[167] *Certain Activities* (n 3) para 35. See also Dissenting Opinion of Judge *ad hoc* Dugard on the Court's approach to valuation, and equitable considerations that the Court might properly have taken into account in quantification, para 29.

[168] ibid para 35.

[169] ibid para 31.

[170] ibid para 52.

[171] ibid.

[172] ibid para 53.

from the perspective of the ecosystem as a whole, by adopting an 'overall assessment' of the impairment of loss of environmental goods and services prior to recovery, rather than attributing values to specific categories of environmental goods and services and estimating recovery periods for each of them.[173] While in several respects, the Court's treatment of quantum remains unclear,[174] the judgment provides authoritative affirmation of the principle that damage to the environment *per se*, including interim losses pending full restoration, are compensable under international law.

In the reparations phase of *Armed Activities on the Territory of the Congo* in the ICJ,[175] Democratic Republic of the Congo (DRC) sought compensation for damage to natural resources including, in addition to claims for minerals, coffee and timber, damage to flora through deforestation and damage to fauna. In relation to deforestation, the Court noted that DRC had not offered evidence for the extent of environmental damage from deforestation, in particular loss of biodiversity, or a method for its valuation. The DRC did not address its environmental damage claim separately to that for unlawful exploitation of timber resources, and the Court-appointed expert had viewed the deforestation claim as referring to timber production.[176] The ICJ dismissed the claim for environmental damage resulting from deforestation as it had no basis upon which to assess it.[177] In relation to loss of fauna, the ICJ did make an award of compensation, but again found that the evidence adduced was not sufficient to determine a precise or approximate number of animal deaths. Finding that Uganda was nonetheless responsible for a significant amount of damage to fauna the Court awarded compensation for this damage as part of a 'global sum' for all damage to natural resources.[178] While the ICJ faced evidentiary obstacles in this case, the 'global sum' approach does little to clarify the approach to quantification of environmental damage, or other forms of damage addressed in the case.

A notable aspect of the *Certain Activities* case is that the ICJ approached the valuation of environmental damage without formally utilizing its power to appoint its own expert(s) to opine on the appropriate valuation methodology and its application. This bears noting as the Court has faced some criticism for aspects of its

[173] ibid para 78. For an analysis and critique of the Court's overall assessment approach, see Yoshifumi Tanaka, 'Temporal Elements in the Valuation of Environmental Damage: Reflections on the *Costa Rica v Nicaragua* Case before the International Court of Justice' (2021) 90 Nord J Intl L 257, 265–270.

[174] Kevine Kindje and Michael Faure, 'Assessing Reparation of Environmental Damage by the ICJ: A Lost Opportunity?' (2019) 57 QILJ 5, arguing that the ICJ took a narrow anthropocentric perspective on reparation of environmental damage and did not provide clear indications on how environmental damage would be assessed in future; see also Ronan Long, 'Restoring Marine Environmental Damage: Can the *Costa Rica v Nicaragua* Compensation Case Influence the BBNJ Negotiations?' (2019) 28 RECIEL 244; Rudall (n 2) 30.

[175] *Armed Activities on the Territory of the Congo* (n 17).

[176] ibid paras 345–347.

[177] ibid para 350.

[178] ibid para 363.

approach to expert evidence in environmental disputes.[179] In the *Pulp Mills* case, the joint dissenting opinion of Judges Al-Khasawneh and Simma highlighted questions and concerns about how the ICJ should approach issues of evidence in disputes that involve complex and voluminous scientific and technical evidence. The dissenting judges were highly critical of how the majority had approached the evaluation of evidence in the case, suggesting that the ICJ had approached the case 'in a way that will increase doubts in the international legal community whether it, as an institution, is well-placed to tackle complex scientific questions'.[180] In their view the ICJ was not, on its own, in a position adequately to assess and weigh complex scientific evidence of the types presented by Argentina and Uruguay in that case. By contrast, in the reparations phase of the *Armed Activities on the Territory of the Congo* case, the Court appointed experts to assist it, including in the assessment of damages related to natural resources.[181] In cases involving allegations of environmental harm, albeit not addressing compensation as such, other dispute settlement tribunals have also had recourse to tribunal-appointed independent experts to assess the existence and scale of damage.[182] The UNCC also made use of experts in its work on environmental damage claims.[183] In relation to ABNJ, such claims seem likely to involve complex issues of scientific evidence relating to baseline data, causation, the reasonableness or feasibility of any proposed restoration measures and consideration of alternative compensatory measures for ecosystem services loss. As such expert scientific input may be of particular importance.

3.5 CONCLUSIONS

How compensable damage is defined stands at the centre of liability for environmental harm in the global commons. If understood in narrow, economic terms, the ability of liability rules to protect the environment is severely constrained. On the

[179] On the *Certain Activities* case, see Tanaka (n 173) 282–287. See also Loretta Malintoppi, 'Fact-Finding and Evidence before the International Court of Justice (Notably in Scientific-Related Disputes)' (2016) 7 JIDS 421; Cymie Payne, 'Mastering the Evidence: Improving Fact Finding by International Courts' (2011) 41 Envtl L 1191; Caroline Foster, *Science and the Precautionary Principle in International Courts and Tribunals: Expert Evidence, Burden of Proof and Finality* (CUP 2011); Caroline Foster, 'New Clothes for the Emperor? Consultation of Experts by the International Court of Justice' (2014) 5 JIDS 139, 144.

[180] *Pulp Mills on the River Uruguay (Argentina v Uruguay)* [2010] ICJ Rep 14, Joint Dissenting Opinion of Judges Al-Khasawneh and Simma, para 3.

[181] *Armed Activities on the Territory of the Congo (Democratic Republic of the Congo v Uganda)* (Order of 8 September 2020) [2020] ICJ Rep 264 (Order of 12 October 2020) [2020] ICJ Rep 295; see also the appointment of an expert in *Corfu Channel Case (UK v Albania)* (Merits) [1949] ICJ Rep 4.

[182] *South China Sea Arbitration* (n 9) para 58; paras 978–983.

[183] See Huguenin and others (n 40). A further example, in the context of investor–state dispute settlement relating to an environmental claim, is the detailed account of the appointment and role of the tribunal-appointed independent expert in *Perenco Ecuador Limited and the Republic of Ecuador*, ICSID Case ARB/08/6 Award of 27 September 2019, paras 154–899.

other hand, if the legal definition of damage more closely reflects the evolving scientific understanding of environmental harm, then there is much greater scope for liability rules to play a more central role in protecting the commons environment. There is growing recognition in international law, including by the ILC and ICJ, of the need to provide for forms of compensation for loss of environmental resources and ecosystem services, including through restoration, and other measures such as the introduction of equivalent resources where primary restoration is not possible or gives rise to interim losses. However, as Handl has noted 'while there is evident and growing support for the compensability of ecosystem services losses in general, on the international legal plane the situation is fragmented'.[184] The concept of environmental damage ought to be seen in light of the evolving paradigm of international environmental policy-making in terms of the ecosystem approach and ecosystem services. Defining environmental damage in terms of lost ecosystem services, as well as lost or damaged components of the environment, better reflects contemporary understandings of ecosystem dynamics, even if it further complicates valuation exercises, particularly in ABNJ. This is already reflected in critiques of restricted definitions of environmental damage in civil liability conventions, and in the approach to assessment of environmental damage of the UNCC and the ICJ, albeit that neither body perhaps fully captured lost ecosystem services in their decisions on valuation.

Taking these developments in the compensability of environmental damage into the ABNJ environment poses a range of additional legal and other challenges. Cumulative environmental damage, a significant cause of concern in ABNJ, is difficult to address within existing liability approaches, both in terms of causation and attribution. In addition, potential claims in respect of preventive measures and reasonable measures of reinstatement for environmental damage in ABNJ are closely linked to challenges of establishing standing to bring a claim, and/or of incentives for states to take preventive or remedial action (discussed in Chapter 6). One possible avenue is to clarify the right of states or their agents to undertake response actions with the ability to seek compensation from responsible parties, as contemplated under the Antarctic Liability Annex. This might also imply the need for a role for international institutions in the provision of baseline data, and in assessing and determining appropriate responses to environmental damage in ABNJ – a feature that already appears to be evolving in the context of the role of ISA in a proposed Environmental Compensation Fund, and the role of the ATCM in the fund envisaged under Annex VI of the 1991 Antarctic Protocol.

Questions relating to the feasibility and likely success of restoration measures remain problematic, and, even where feasible, costs might prove disproportionate. The replacement of damaged components of the environment by 'equivalents' also poses potentially intractable challenges in the context of the high seas, deep seabed

[184] Handl (n 5) 609.

or Antarctica. Furthermore, baseline data on which to assess damage and ground restoration or offset efforts in ABNJ are likely to be incomplete or unreliable.

As to valuation of environmental damage in ABNJ, many of the existing valuation methods are poorly suited to the commons environment and pose significant evidentiary challenges. That said, these remain in a relatively early stage of development and the approach of UNCC and ICJ suggests methods such as HEA provide promising avenues for quantification and will likely evolve in concert with improved scientific understanding of ABNJ environments.

4

Allocation of Liability for Environmental Harm in Areas beyond National Jurisdiction

4.1 INTRODUCTION

A fundamental question that drafters of liability and compensation regimes for environmental harm must address is to whom and in what manner liability ought to be allocated. Questions of allocation raise two distinct types of issues. The first question is the extent to which the sufferer of harm ought to bear their loss themselves. This principally involves questions relating to the standard of liability, specifically whether an actor who causes harm will be required to provide compensation in the absence of fault – a determination of allocation between the victim and the perpetrator of harm. This question and related issues are addressed in Chapter 5. This chapter addresses a distinct set of issues that concern the allocation of liability amongst wrongdoers or other actors that may bear responsibility for the harm that has arisen.

Issues of allocation of liability are consequential for both the goals of ensuring prompt and adequate compensation and of environmental harm prevention. In relation to the former, allocation rules influence the availability of potential sources for compensation. Spreading legal responsibility amongst a range of actors can, for example, broaden the pool of available compensation for victims. Similarly, since the potential for liability impacts the incentives for actors to take steps to avoid environmental harm, the allocation of liability will influence standards of behaviour of both operational and oversight entities.

The allocation of liability for environmental harm in areas beyond national jurisdiction (ABNJ) is complicated by several factors relating to the nature of the activities undertaken and the nature of environmental harm itself. First, environmental harm in ABNJ can be the result of land-based or ocean-based activities (in any maritime zone) and may potentially involve a range of different actors. These include states, international organizations, corporations and individuals. Indeed, a typical maritime transportation operation can involve flag states, shipowners, parent companies, charterers, ship managers, cargo owners, shipbuilders, classification societies and other maritime service providers. Moreover, these actors are involved in different capacities – they are either directly engaged in these activities, have some form of control over the actors carrying out these activities (for example, parent corporations) or are responsible for regulating the actors that conduct these activities. This is not a simple division between states and international organizations, on the one hand, and private actors, on the other, as states or state-related entities may be operators themselves, in addition to having oversight responsibilities. States may also choose to adopt the role of insurer, covering losses that other responsible entities may be unwilling or unable to address.[1] States may also act through international organizations and such organizations may also play a supervisory or regulatory role, such as regional fisheries management organizations (for fisheries) or the International Seabed Authority (ISA) (for deep seabed mining). A single activity or event resulting in environmental damage may therefore involve both multiple 'wrongdoers' who have in some shape or form 'contributed' to the damage, as well as multiple overseers, leading to questions on the extent to which each actor should be held liable.

Second, allocation of liability is further complicated by the presence of environmental harms that have been contributed to by multiple actors. This may be single incidents of environmental harm in which there are multiple actors possibly responsible or cumulative environmental damage, arising over a course of time either out of a connected or unconnected set of activities involving multiple actors or from external natural causes (for example, ocean acidification or plastics pollution). Cumulative environmental damage poses challenges related to causation in identifying who should be held liable for environmental damage particularly when it is difficult to separate the different sources of damage.

The sources of rules concerning the allocation of liability in ABNJ are diffuse and inchoate, involving general rules and principles of state responsibility and the responsibility of international organizations, as well as regime specific treaty rules on the liability of operators, and the structuring of liability amongst multiple responsible parties. Because causation is central to the allocation of liability, Section 4.2 of this chapter begins with a discussion of legal approaches to causation and the challenges that complex causal pathways may present in ABNJ. Section 4.3 then discusses the general approach to allocating responsibility to states and international organizations under international law and national law, followed by a discussion of the allocation of liability amongst operational entities, which focuses on the practice of channelling of liability to operational entities, which is the principal approach in sector-specific civil liability regimes. Section 4.4 then turns to the rules that structure

[1] See, for example, the nuclear liability regime – the role of the state as an insurer is addressed in greater detail in Chapter 8.

the allocation of liability amongst these actors in relation to specific ABNJ regimes and activities.

4.2 CAUSATION

Causation, both under national law and international law, is an essential element in the imposition of liability and in assessment of compensation – there must be a link between the activity and the damage suffered. Causation difficulties in environmental damage claims include the existence of scientific uncertainty in identifying the source of damage; there may be several concurrent or diffuse causes of the damage which itself can be linked to several defendants; cumulative environmental damage is caused over a duration of time and can be linked to an even larger number of defendants coupled with the requirement that the burden of proof is on the claimant to establish the causal link between the harm, the activity and the defendant.[2] These issues are amplified in the context of environmental harm in ABNJ where multiple actors operating in either areas under national jurisdiction or in ABNJ may be factually responsible either for one-off incidents or cumulative environmental harm.

Under domestic approaches to liability, the most commonly used approach towards causal inquiries is the two-stage test on factual and legal causation.[3] Factual causation is determined using the '*but-for test*' or '*sine-qua-non*' test. It must be shown that the damage or harmful outcome would not have occurred without the act or omission of the defendant. Legal causation is intended to delimit factual causation 'by requiring that any factual cause is legally relevant to the consequence'.[4] Tort law has developed doctrines such as proximate cause and foreseeability to limit the scope of liability arising from a potentially unlimited set of claims.[5]

However, these orthodox rules on causation pose challenges to the identification of the actor liable for environmental harm given the lack of scientific certainty in identifying the cause of damage when there are several concurrent or diffuse causes of damage which can be linked to several actors. There are also difficulties posed by

2 Mark Wilde, *Civil Liability for Environmental Damage: A Comparative Analysis of Law and Policy in Europe and the United States* (Kluwer Law International 2004) 59–78. For issues related to scientific uncertainty in the context of climate change litigation, there is a growing field of science known as attribution science which analyses the relationship between anthropogenic emissions and specific extreme weather events which may be influential in evaluating causation issues in climate change litigation: See, for example, Sophie Marjanac and Lindene Patton, 'Extreme Weather Event Attribution Science and Climate Change Litigation: An Essential Step in the Causal Change' (2018) 36(3) J Energy Nat Resources Law 265–298.

3 See, for example, VH Harpwood, *Modern Tort Law* (7th edn, Routledge-Cavendish 2008) 161–185; Keith N Hylton, *Tort Law: A Modern Perspective* (CUP 2016) 195–226.

4 Martin Jarrett, *Contributory Fault and Investor Misconduct in Investment Arbitration* (CUP 2019) 45.

5 Hylton (n 3) 195–226.

the plaintiff's burden of proof in establishing a causal link between the harm and the wrongdoer.[6] To ameliorate issues related to causal uncertainty in environmental damage that occur within national territory, Anglo-American courts have eschewed the '*but-for test*' for other tests such as whether the defendant made a 'material contribution' to the loss, or whether the defendant's activity 'materially increased' the risk.[7] Other tests also seek to address the deficiencies of the '*but-for test*' such as the substantial factor test and the necessary element of a set of conditions sufficient to bring about the event (NESS test) but none are free from problems and still place a considerable burden of proof on the victim.[8]

The approach to causation in international law is less clear and has been described as 'mostly rudimentary' and subject to minimal systematic analysis.[9] Causation is often not explicitly discussed as a distinct element of state responsibility.[10] Moreover, there is no specific test of causation prescribed by international law, although it is relevant to several areas of the law of state responsibility, including determining whether the action or omission of a state has resulted in injury or damage (if required by the primary rule); whether one state may have been involved in the wrongful act of another; whether certain circumstances precluding wrongfulness exist; and in the determination of reparation under international law (discussed in Chapter 3).[11] The International Law Commission's (ILC) 2001 Draft Articles on Responsibility of States for Internationally Wrongful Acts (ASR) address causation perfunctorily, merely noting that the 'responsible State is under an obligation to make full reparation for the injury *caused by* the internationally wrongful act'.[12] As observed in Chapter 3, the ASR note that the tests applicable to causation must be determined on a case-by-case basis and in light of the primary rule, which was a pragmatic decision on the ILC's part considering the divergent views of ILC members in the long course of preparing

6 Michael Faure, 'Attribution of Liability: An Economic Analysis of Various Cases' (2016) 91(2) Chi-Kent L Rev 603, 623–624; Ilias Plakokefalos, 'Causation in the Law of State Responsibility and the Problem of Overdetermination: In Search of Clarity' (2015) 26(2) EJIL 471, 476.

7 See *Bonnington Castings v Wardlow* [1956] AC 613; *McGhee v National Coal Board* [1972] 3 All ER 1008.

8 The substantial factor test posits that a defendant can avoid liability for the plaintiff's injury if he can prove that his negligence was not a substantial factor: Hylton (n 3), 214. The NESS test posits that 'a particular condition is a cause of (contributed to) a specific result if and only if it was a necessary element of a set of antecedent actual conditions that was sufficient for the occurrence of the result': RW Wright, 'Causation, Responsibility, Risk, Probability, Naked Statistics and Proof: Pruning the Bramble Bush by Clarifying the Concepts' (1987–1988) 73 Iowa L Rev (1987–1988) 1001, 1019.

9 Plakokefalos (n 6); Vladyslav Lanovoy, 'Causation in the Law of State Responsibility' (2022) British Yearbook Intl L 1, 4.

10 Plakokefalos (n 6) 483–486.

11 André Nollkaemper and others, 'Guiding Principles on Shared Responsibility in International Law' (2020) 31 EJIL 15, 23; Lanovoy (n 9) 19–42.

12 International Law Commission (ILC), 'Draft Articles on the Responsibility of States for Internationally Wrongful Acts, with Commentaries' (53rd Session) (2001) UN Doc A/56/10 (ASR) art 31 (1), 91.

the ASR.[13] International courts and tribunals have employed varying standards of legal causation in the law of state responsibility including the standard of 'sufficiently direct and certain causal nexus' between the wrongful act and the injury suffered, and the standard of proximity, that is, whether the consequences are proximate or not too remote from the wrongful act.[14]

While it may be true that causation standards are necessarily dependent on the circumstances of the case and the nature of the breach, causation poses unique challenges in the context of environmental harm in ABNJ.[15] Reliance on the 'sufficiently direct and certain causal nexus' test, while ostensibly easy for the adjudicator, depends on a linear causal relationship and focuses on immediate harm which may not accurately reflect the true extent of environmental harm that may result.[16] The larger concern, beyond questions of doctrinal clarity, is that in ABNJ and in relation to environmental harm generally, the causal pathways may be complex and involve multiple parties whose acts singly may not result in significant (and therefore unlawful) harm, but their cumulative effect does result in such an effect. For example, a collapse in a fishing stock may not result from a single fishing operation but will occur due to multiple (poorly managed) fishery operations. The current focus of liability rules is on the harm from identifiable and often discrete pollution incidents, as opposed to long-term degradation from multiple actors and often multiple types of sources. On large-scale problems, such as marine plastics pollution or ocean acidification from greenhouse gas emissions, cumulative causation issues effectively insulate states and polluters from liability.

Issues associated with causation are by no means unique to ABNJ, and the approach to causation in the ABNJ context will be shaped by more general legal innovations. For example, national courts have grappled with the idea of probabilistic causation to address cases where a potential defendant has increased the risk of harm, but it is impossible to establish a factual connection between the defendant's behaviour and the plaintiff's harm.[17] This line of cases has relevance for circumstances like the impact of overfishing on stock collapse, since the act raises the risk of the environmental outcome, but the factual link between the wrongful act and the harm is difficult, if not impossible

[13] ibid commentary to art 31, 92, para 10; Lanovoy (n 9) 3–4.

[14] Lanovoy (n 9) 47.

[15] The International Court of Justice (ICJ), in relation to transboundary environmental harm, acknowledged that environmental damage may be due to several concurrent causes or the state of science regarding the causal link between the wrongful act and the damage may be uncertain but noted that these difficulties must be addressed as and when they arise in light of the facts of the case and evidence presented and that it was ultimately up to the Court to decide whether there is a sufficient causal nexus between the wrongful act and the injury suffered. See *Certain Activities Carried Out by Nicaragua in the Border Area (Costa Rica v Nicaragua), Compensation owed by the Republic of Nicaragua to the Republic of Costa Rica* [2018] ICJ Rep 15, para 34.

[16] Lanovoy (n 9) 53.

[17] See, for example, *McGhee v National Coal Board* [1973] 1 WLR 1 (QB). See also John G Fleming, 'Probabilistic Causation in Tort Law' (1989) 68(4) Can Bar Rev 661.

to establish. Similar legal innovations are being tested in a variety of climate litigation contexts drawing on scientific developments, such as probabilistic event attribution – which links the probability of climate-related events to emissions, which will shape cumulative harm issues in ABNJ.[18] The challenges here remain substantial, particularly in relation to large-scale problems, like marine plastics pollution, where contributions are so diffuse as to raise issues as to whether there are *de minimis* levels of contribution that are required to trigger legal responsibility.[19]

4.3 GENERAL APPROACHES TO THE ALLOCATION OF LIABILITY FOR ENVIRONMENTAL HARM

In considering the question of allocation, we are concerned with three distinct categories of actors: states, international organizations and operators usually tasked with the conduct of operations. Operators are the actors that are usually in direct control of an activity, consist of state-owned entities (such as state-owned enterprises carrying out commercial activities), as well as privately owned entities, and are typically subject to domestic law.[20] States and international organizations, on the other hand, are subject to international requirements relating to responsibility, and are less amenable to national laws. Consequently, the rules on allocation amongst these entities are somewhat fragmented between the law of state and international organization responsibility and requirements structuring liability amongst operators and may operate as parallel systems unless specifically addressed through treaties.

4.3.1 *State Responsibility*

4.3.1.1 International Law

Under the rules of state responsibility, states are responsible for damage arising out of their wrongful acts, that is, an act or omission that is attributable to that state under

[18] See, for example, Petra Minnerop and Otto Friederike, 'Climate Change and Causation: Joining Law and Climate Science on the Basis of Formal Logic' (2019) 27 Buff Env L J 49.

[19] For a discussion on potential liability and compensation regimes for marine plastics pollution that could be devised under current international efforts to address this problem, see Sandrine Maljean Dubois and Benoit Mayer, 'Liability and Compensation for Marine Plastic Pollution: Conceptual Issues and Possible Ways Forward' (2020) 114 AJIL Unbound 206.

[20] The ILC observes that while there is no general definition of 'operator' under international law, it is usually determined by a factual determination as to who has use, control and direction of the object at the relevant time: ILC, 'Draft Principles on the Allocation of Loss in the Case of Transboundary Harm Arising Out of Hazardous Activities, with Commentaries' (2006) UN Doc A/61/10 (Draft Principles), commentary to principle 2 (g), 71, paras 31–32. A state-owned entity or enterprise has been defined as 'any enterprise owned, controlled or specifically designated by any level of government to pursue financial objectives by commercial means' see Albert Badia, *Piercing the Veil of State Enterprises in International Arbitration* (Wolters Kluwer 2014) 2.

international law and that constitutes a breach of an international obligation.[21] The responsible state is then under an obligation to make full reparation for the injury caused to another state (included espoused claims) by the internationally wrongful act.[22]

Attribution refers to the 'process by which international law establishes whether the conduct of a natural person or other such intermediary can be considered an "act of state" and thus be capable of giving rise to state responsibility'.[23] The commentary in the ASR observes, '[W]hat is crucial is that a given event is sufficiently connected to the conduct (whether an act or omission) which is attributable to the State ...'.[24] The criteria determining the attribution of conduct to the state is based on international law and not on the mere recognition of a link of factual causality.[25] The need for a causal link is implicit in the attribution of conduct as there must be a causal link between the conduct and the consequences of the breach.[26] Given the potential for states to perform multiple roles in relation to activities affecting ABNJ and the fact that they may use a variety of direct and indirect means to perform those roles, attention must be paid to the conditions under which the resultant activities can be attributed to the state.

To the extent that states' activities in the oceans and in Antarctica are deemed the conduct of organs of government or of others who have acted under the direction, instigation or control of those organs as agents of the state and such conduct results in environmental harm in ABNJ, attribution of conduct to the state should not be difficult.[27] Determining whether an entity is an organ of the state will be determined by the status of the organ under the internal law of the state, and not by the nature of the activity in question.[28] For example, where a deep seabed mining entity is a state acting through a state organ, it is likely to be considered part of the state, notwithstanding that the activities have commercial purposes.[29] A state-owned entity, on the other hand, is likely to be considered distinct from the state.

The conduct of operators (i.e. state-owned entities or private entities) is only attributable to states in limited circumstances.[30] First, if a person or entity is empowered by a state's law to exercise elements of governmental authority, it is considered an act of the state under international law.[31] The commentary in the

21 ASR (n 12) arts 1 & 2.
22 ibid art 31.
23 James Crawford, *State Responsibility* (CUP 2013) 113.
24 ASR (n 12) commentary to art 2, 35, para 6.
25 ibid 38–39, para 4.
26 James D Fry, 'Attribution of Responsibility' in André Nollkaemper and Ilias Plakokefalos (eds), *Principles of Shared Responsibility in International Law* (CUP 2014) 98, 102.
27 ASR (n 12) 38, para 2.
28 ibid art 4 (2), 40.
29 ibid commentary to art 4, 40–41, para 6.
30 The ASR consider state-owned corporations or enterprises as separate from the state except where the 'corporate veil' is a mere device or a vehicle for fraud or evasion: ASR (n 12) commentary to art 8, 47–48, paras 1 and 6.
31 ibid art 5, 42.

ASR acknowledges that the term 'entity' may include 'public corporations, semi-public agencies of various kinds and even in special cases, private companies, provided that in each case, the entity is empowered by the law of the state to exercise functions of a public character normally exercised by state organs, and the conduct of the entity related to the exercise of the governmental authority concerned'.[32] However, 'governmental authority' is not defined and is a narrow concept.[33] It is limited to entities which are empowered by internal law to exercise governmental authority; that is, the internal law must specifically authorize the conduct as involving the exercise of public authority and it is not sufficient that the internal law simply 'permits activity as part of the general regulation of the affairs of the community'.[34] The 'mere exercise of public functions or of tasks in the public interest does not lead to attribution'.[35] Thus, the activities of state-owned entities engaging in activities such as marine scientific research or marine geoengineering which are ostensibly for 'public interest' would not automatically be attributed to the state.

The second circumstance is if the 'person or group of persons is in fact acting on the instructions of, or under the direction or control of, that state in carrying out the conduct'.[36] The ASR do not specify the level of control required for attribution, stating that it is dependent on the circumstances.[37] Generally, the jurisprudence of international courts and tribunals has vacillated between an 'effective control' test and an 'overall control' test,[38] with the former being perceived as imposing a higher threshold for attributing the conduct of private actors to states. The effective control test requires the state or a state organ to give the instructions or provide the direction pursuant to which the perpetrators of the wrongful act acted, or to have effective control over the action during which the wrong was committed.[39] In other words, the effective control test essentially requires evidence of factual control over specific conduct.[40] This idea of control was also endorsed in the ILC's 2006 Draft Principles on Allocation of Loss (Draft Principles).[41] The Draft Principles, which emphasized

32 ibid commentary to art 5, 43, para 2.
33 ibid commentary to art 5, 43, para 7.
34 ibid.
35 Alexander Kees, 'Responsibility of States for Private Actors' in Rüdiger Wolfrum (ed), *Max Planck Encyclopedia of International Law Online* (2011) para 13.
36 ASR (n 12) art 8, 47.
37 ibid commentary to art 8, 48, para 5.
38 For a discussion on the way the courts have utilized these two tests, please see Crawford (n 23) 147–150.
39 *Case Concerning the Application of the Convention on the Prevention and Punishment of the Crime of Genocide (Bosnia and Herzegovina v Serbia and Montenegro)* (Judgment) [2007] ICJ Rep 43 (Bosnian Genocide) 214, 257; see also *Military and Paramilitary Activities in and against Nicaragua (Nicaragua v the United States of America)* (Judgment) [1986] ICJ Rep 14.
40 Kristen E Boon, 'Are Control Tests Fit for the Future? The Spillage Problem in Attribution Doctrines' (2014) 15 MJIL 1, 9.
41 Draft Principles (n 20).

the liability of the operator, acknowledged that 'liability need not always be placed on the operator of a hazardous or a risk-bearing activity and other entities could equally be designated by agreement or by law', which could in principle include states provided they are 'functionally in command or control or directs or exercises overall supervision and hence, as the beneficiary of the activity, may be held liable'.[42]

Both the 'governmental authority' and 'instructions, direction and control' test impose high thresholds in the context of activities causing environmental harm in ABNJ. The fact that states have jurisdiction and control over activities by virtue of being a coastal state, flag state or sponsoring state would not be sufficient to attribute harmful conduct to that state under either of these tests. State-owned entities or private entities involved in the operation of vessels either in areas under national jurisdiction or in ABNJ are not acting under the direct governmental authority or instructions of flag states *per se*. Flag states, in most cases, will not have such factual control over the specific conduct undertaken by non-state actors involved in the operation of vessels used in ocean activities. Governmental authority and/or instructions, direction or control may be easier to establish if the vessel is a warship or a government ship operated for non-commercial purposes, but these vessels have sovereign immunity in respect of breaches of the marine environment protection provisions in the 1982 United Nations Convention on the Law of the Sea (UNCLOS).[43]

Similarly, coastal states, pursuant to their sovereignty over territorial waters and sovereign rights over their exclusive economic zones (EEZs) and continental shelves, will typically license activities of non-state actors in these maritime zones.[44] However, it cannot be automatically assumed that the actions of these non-state actors are attributable to the coastal state simply because they licensed such activities. It is still necessary to establish governmental authority, instructions, direction or control. For states that sponsor state-owned entities and private entities (sponsored contractors) to conduct activities in the Area, the Seabed Disputes Chamber (SDC) in its 2011 Advisory Opinion also noted that the liability regime established in Annex III of UNCLOS and related instruments do not provide for the attribution of activities of sponsored contractors to sponsoring states.[45]

42 ibid general commentary, 60, para 8.

43 United Nations Convention on the Law of the Sea (adopted 10 December 1982, entered into force 16 November 1994) 1833 UNTS 397 (UNCLOS) arts 29, 31, 236. However, note UNCLOS art 31 which states that the flag state shall bear international responsibility for any loss or damage resulting from the non-compliance by a warship or other government ship operated for non-commercial purposes with the provisions of UNCLOS or other rules of international law.

44 ibid arts 56, 77.

45 *Responsibilities and Obligations of States Sponsoring Persons and Entities with Respect to Activities in the Area* (Advisory Opinion of 1 February 2011) ITLOS Reports 2011, 10, para 182 (*Activities in the Area* Advisory Opinion).

Apart from the direct attribution of operators' conduct to states, the imposition of state responsibility for failure to prevent certain conduct resulting in environmental harm in ABNJ in contravention of its international obligations is also not straightforward.[46] The commentary to the ASR notes that a '[s]tate may be responsible for the effects of the conduct of private parties, if it failed to take necessary measures to prevent those effects'.[47] In the environmental context, the duty to prevent harm is reflected in states' obligations 'to ensure that activities within their jurisdiction and control respect the environment of other states, or of areas beyond national control' and is now part of the corpus of international law relating to the environment.[48] Obligations of prevention (in international environmental law or otherwise) are usually subject to 'best efforts obligations, requiring [s]tates to take all reasonable or necessary measures to prevent a given event from occurring but without warranting that the event will not occur',[49] commonly described as an obligation of due diligence. This is different from attribution of conduct where the state is being held liable for the conduct of private actors. In this case, the state is being held directly responsible for its own conduct. The specifics of due diligence are discussed in Chapter 5 on standards of liability.

4.3.1.2 National Law

States may be held liable under domestic law for environmental harm in ABNJ to which the state has contributed but allocating liability to them may face several obstacles.[50] Factors determining the likelihood of holding the state liable include whether domestic law automatically incorporates primary international law obligations relating to the environment in ABNJ, as well as the secondary obligations as reflected in the ASR, or needs specific implementing legislation, and whether national courts will decline to exercise jurisdiction on the basis of doctrines such as non-justiciability of the international legality of the conduct of a state before its

46 Boon (n 40) 34–35.

47 ASR (n 12) commentary to chapter II, 39, para 4. The example given in the commentary is as follows: '... a receiving State is not responsible, as such, for the acts of private individuals in seizing an embassy but it will be responsible, if it fails to take all necessary steps to protect the embassy from seizure or to regain control over it'.

48 *Legality of the Threat or Use of Nuclear Weapons* (Advisory Opinion) [1996] ICJ Rep 679, 226, para 29. *Gabčikovo-Nagymaros Project (Hungary v Slovakia)* (Judgment) [1997] ICJ Rep 7, para 140; *Pulp Mills on the River Uruguay (Argentina v Uruguay)* (Judgment) [2010] ICJ Rep 14, paras 101 and 185; See, for example, UNCLOS (n 43) arts 192 and 193.

49 ASR (n 12) commentary to art 14, 62, para 14. The ASR did not draw a distinction between obligations of conduct and obligations of result although it observed that the distinction may assist in ascertaining when a breach has occurred but that it is not exclusive and 'does not seem to bear specific or direct consequences as far as the present articles are concerned'. ASR, commentary to art 12, 56, para 11.

50 See Chapter 7 for further discussion.

own courts.[51] There are, of course, domestic doctrines of state liability for tortious acts but at the same time, there are doctrines on public authority liability that may provide immunity to public authorities for certain kinds of governmental actions.[52] For example, where the state is acting in its capacity as a sovereign (*jure imperii*), it has broad immunities from the jurisdictional competences of other states. Such immunity does not apply to state activities of a commercial nature (*jure gestionis*), although the boundaries of this more restrictive approach remain contested.[53] In considering the potential role of states in ABNJ, states would typically be immune from domestic jurisdiction for regulatory oversight failures, as this is clearly an exercise of sovereign authority. But in their more direct, operational capacity, states may be subject to the jurisdictional reach of another state's legal system, if the activity has a commercial character. The distinction between acts *jure imperii* and *jure gestionis* in these contexts will not necessarily be clear. For example, a state-owned entity conducting activities in the Area could be engaged in commercial activity, but it could also be acquiring critical minerals for national security purposes. While not applying directly to ABNJ, the approach under the 1992 Oil Pollution Liability Convention is to explicitly subject state-owned ships used for commercial purposes to the jurisdiction of the state where recovery actions are brought, including a waiver of all defences based on the status of the defendant shipowner as a sovereign state.[54] While the international rules respecting state immunity govern these matters, their determination is very much a function of the approach taken to immunity in the state in question.

4.3.2 *International Organizations Responsibility*

4.3.2.1 International Law

International organizations are international legal persons with personality separate from the states that established them and are subject to a regime of responsibility in

[51] See generally André Nollkaemper, 'Internationally Wrongful Acts in Domestic Courts' (2007) 101(4) AJIL 760; Francesco Messineo, 'The Invocation of Member State Responsibility before National and International Courts' (2015) 12 Int Org Law Rev 484.

[52] See, for example, *Anns v Merton London Borough Council* [1977] UKHL 4, [1978] AC 728, setting out immunity for activities that arise under public authorities policy (as opposed to operational) functions. This distinction has been much criticized, see, for example, SH Bailey and MJ Bowman, 'The Policy/Operational Dichotomy – A Cuckoo in the Nest' (1986) 45(3) CLJ 430; and Bruce Feldthusen, 'Public Authority Immunity from Negligence Liability: Uncertain, Unnecessary, and Unjustified' (2014) 92(2) Can Bar Rev 211.

[53] See, for example, Xiaodong Yang, *State Immunity in International Law* (CUP 2012) 75–131.

[54] International Convention on Civil Liability for Oil Pollution Damage (adopted 29 November 1969, entered into force 19 June 1975) 973 UNTS 3 (1969 Oil Pollution Liability Convention), amended by the 1992 Protocol to Amend the 1969 International Convention on Civil Liability for Oil Pollution Damage (adopted 27 November 1992, entered into force 30 May 1996) 1956 UNTS 255 (1992 Oil Pollution Liability Convention) art XI.

the international legal order.[55] Insofar as international organizations have direct oversight responsibilities, or may be directly involved in environmentally risky activities, they may be the subject of liability claims. While the ILC's attempt to set out the responsibility of international organizations in the 2011 Draft Articles on the Responsibility of International Organizations (DARIO) was not met with the same level of acceptance as the ASR, it still has relevance in setting out the 'normative framework' for the responsibility of international organizations.[56] Modelled on the ASR, the DARIO are intended to be a default regime applicable to the extent that the international organization concerned has not adopted specific rules to address responsibility.[57] Accordingly, like the ASR, the DARIO set out the general principle that every internationally wrongful act of an international organization engages the responsibility of that organization.[58] Breaches of international obligations are based on any customary rule of international law, by a treaty or by a general principle applicable within the international legal order,[59] and have to be binding on the international organization concerned.[60]

There are a multitude of institutional bodies and/or arrangements that have mandates that cover ABNJ, usually sectoral based and sometimes with overlapping mandates/responsibilities.[61] These institutional bodies/arrangements vary in structure, functions, objectives, powers and membership, and include typical intergovernmental organizations such as the International Maritime Organization (IMO), and the ISA to regional fisheries management organizations (RFMOs) or arrangements (RFMAs) to conferences of parties (for example, like the Antarctic Treaty Consultative Meeting (ATCM)), and also include operational entities, such as the Enterprise – the mining arm of the ISA.

There are challenges in holding international organizations responsible and liable for environmental harm in ABNJ under the rules of international organization responsibility, which dramatically reduces the likelihood of liability being allocated to international organizations. First, not all institutional bodies or arrangements will fall within the formal legal definition of an 'international organization' which the DARIO define as 'an organization established by a treaty or other instrument governed by international law and possessing its own international legal

55 Pierre Klein, 'Responsibility' in Jacob Katz Cogan, Ian Hurd and Ian Johnstone (eds), *The Oxford Handbook on International Organizations* (OUP 2016) 1026.

56 ibid.

57 ILC, 'Draft Articles on the Responsibility of International Organizations, with Commentaries' (2011) II (2) ILC Yearbook 1 (DARIO).

58 ibid art 3, 52.

59 ibid commentary to art 10, 63, para 2. Also see *Interpretation of the Agreement of 25 March 1951 between the WHO and Egypt* (Advisory Opinion) [1980] ICJ Rep 73, 89–90, para 37.

60 DARIO (n 57) art 11, 64.

61 See, for example, UNEP-WCMC, 'Governance of Areas beyond National Jurisdiction for Biodiversity Conservation and Sustainable Use: Institutional arrangements and cross-sectoral cooperation in the Western Indian Ocean and the Southeast Pacific' (UN Environment World Conservation Monitoring Centre 2017) 30–33.

personality'.[62] International legal personality is said to be a precondition to the attribution of responsibility to an international organization and whether they have international legal personality will depend on their constituent instrument.[63] To the extent that an RFMO has been established, it will usually have legal personality, although with limited powers and capacities.[64] Conferences or meetings of parties, such as those established under multilateral environmental agreements, are institutionalized but are generally not seen has having the requisite international legal personality.[65]

Second, except for the ISA (discussed in Section 4.4.2), international organizations, such as the IMO or RFMOs may not be directly engaging in activities they are supposed to regulate or conducting oversight activities and their main function is to establish rules and procedures intended to be implemented by member states. They may not have the requisite control to attract responsibility for lack of due diligence, where the standard of behaviour turns on the scope of their authority. This point lies at the heart of the policy question of under what conditions international organizations ought to be subject to liability rules, as it relates to the goal of ensuring that those entities that play an active role in environmental protection are held accountable where they fail to carry out their duties.

Third, establishing that an international organization has breached an international obligation to protect the environment in ABNJ requires that it is bound by that international obligation. Accordingly, a contentious issue in establishing international organization responsibility has been the applicability of international obligations to international organizations. It has been argued that 'the scope of the primary rules incumbent upon international organizations appears now to constitute the principal challenge to the implementation of a regime of international responsibility to international organizations'.[66] For example, international organizations can become party to UNCLOS, but presently only the European Union is a party (and its position is *sui generis*).[67] Prima facie, other international organizations are not bound by UNCLOS. International organizations may be bound by customary international law,[68] but it is not clear whether the marine environmental obligations in Part XII of UNCLOS in its

62 DARIO (n 57) art 2 (a).

63 ibid commentary to art 2, 49–50, paras 1–10. However, it has also been said that there is a 'strong presumption that once an organization is created, it will be a legal person for purposes of international law, but this presumption can be rebutted …' Jan Klabbers, 'Formal Intergovernmental Organizations' in Jacob Katz Cogan, Ian Hurd and Ian Johnstone (eds), *The Oxford Handbook on International Organizations* (OUP 2016) 142–143.

64 James Harrison, 'Key Challenges Relating to the Governance of Regional Fisheries' in Richard Caddell and Erik J Molenaar (eds), *Strengthening International Fisheries Law in an Era of Changing Oceans* (Hart Publishing 2019) 84.

65 Klabbers (n 63) 143.

66 Klein (n 55) 1026.

67 UNCLOS (n 43) art 305 (1)(f) and Annex XI.

68 For a general discussion on this issue, see Kristina Daugirdas, 'How and Why International Law Binds International Organizations' (2016) 57 Harv Intl L J 325.

entirety are customary international law.[69] As discussed below in connection with the ISA, treaties can specifically impose primary obligations on international organizations, the breach of which can form the basis of liability claims.

Fourth, a further obstacle is addressing how international organizations would pay for environmental harm if found liable. The DARIO provide that the responsible international organization is obliged to make full reparation for the injury caused by the internationally wrongful act, and this includes restitution, compensation and satisfaction.[70] While there have been instances where international organizations have compensated for damage caused to third parties, the DARIO acknowledge a reality that it may be difficult for an international organization to make the required reparation which is 'linked to the inadequacy of the financial resources that are generally available to international organizations for meeting this type of expense'.[71] Notwithstanding this, the DARIO state that 'this inadequacy cannot exempt a responsible organization from the legal consequences resulting from its responsibility under international law'.[72] The DARIO also lay down the rule that while there is no subsidiary obligation of member states towards the injured party when a responsible organization is not in a position to make reparation, an international organization shall take all appropriate measures to ensure that its members provide it with means for effectively fulfilling its obligations to compensate.[73] This implies 'that the members of the organization should be requested to provide the necessary means'.[74]

Finally, finding a suitable international forum to prosecute claims against international organizations may not be easy, as addressed further in Chapter 7. The constituent instruments of international organizations may set out mechanisms for internal review of certain acts, but these instances are rare. For external review of an international organization's acts by international courts and tribunals, there must be a specific agreement either in the constitutive instrument of the international organization (for example, UNCLOS expressly recognizes that certain disputes to which the ISA is a party can be brought before UNCLOS courts and tribunals) or in the procedural rules of the international court or tribunal itself.[75]

69 Some clearly have been found to be part of customary international law by international courts and tribunals or scholars, such as art 192 on the obligation to protect the marine environment; art 194 (2) on the obligation on states to ensure that activities under their jurisdiction or control respect the environment or areas beyond national control; and art 206 on the need to conduct environmental impact assessments, but others are not so clear-cut.

70 DARIO (n 57) arts 31 and 34, 77, 79.

71 ibid commentary to art 31, 77, para 4. Compensation has been paid by the United Nations, for example, to nations of Belgium, Greece, Italy, Luxembourg and Switzerland, arising out of UN operations in Congo: See discussion in DARIO (n 57) commentary to art 36, 79–80, paras 1–3.

72 ibid commentary to art 31, 77, para 4.

73 ibid commentary to art 40, 81–82, paras 2–3.

74 ibid commentary to art 40, 82, para 3.

75 See generally, Jan Wouters and Jed Odermatt, 'Assessing the Legality of Decisions' in Jacob Katz Cogan, Ian Hurd and Ian Johnstone (eds), *The Oxford Handbook on International Organizations* (OUP 2016) 1006–1025.

4.3.2.2 National Law

International organizations are generally granted privileges and immunities from state jurisdiction to the extent that such immunities are required for the international organizations' effective functioning.[76] Some international organizations are also granted absolute immunity except to the extent they have waived such immunity.[77] Justifications for such immunity include the need to preserve operational autonomy of international organizations by minimizing the interference or undue influence of member states, or arguments that they flow from the sovereignty of the organization's members.[78] However, certain national courts have restricted immunities of international organizations on various grounds, including on the basis that an international organization's acts did not fall within its functions; or due to the *jure gestionis–jure imperii* distinction borrowed from state immunity; or more recently on the basis that granting immunity to international organizations could violate the right to access to remedies in the event the applicant has no access to an alternative remedy.[79]

4.3.3 *Operator Responsibility*

The key issue for non-state actors such as state-owned entities or private entities, which for present purposes, will be described as 'operators', is not whether they can be made subject to liability rules, but rather how liability is allocated amongst the complex array of actors that may be involved in environmentally risky activities. International rules generally adopt two approaches to allocation of liability to operators, either (1) the channelling of legal liability exclusively to the operator or (2) the allocation of liability to a range of other actors engaged directly or indirectly in connected activities. An operational entity is most often a privately owned one, but states, whether directly or through state agencies or state-owned enterprises, may themselves be operators. The approach that is ultimately chosen will depend on a variety of factors including the number of actors involved in the activity, the nature

[76] See, for example, Charter of the United Nations (adopted 26 June 1945, entered into force 24 October 1945) 1 UNTS XVI art 105; see also General Convention on the Privileges and Immunities of the United Nations (adopted 13 February 1946, entered into force 17 September 1946) 1 UNTS 15, 90 UNTS 327 and the Convention on Privileges and Immunities of Specialized Agencies (adopted 21 November 1947, entered into force 2 December 1948) 33 UNTS 261; Niels Blokker, 'International Organizations: The Untouchables?' (2013) 10 Int Organ Law Rev 259.

[77] August Reinisch, 'Privileges and Immunities' in Jacob Katz Cogan, Ian Hurd and Ian Johnstone (eds), *The Oxford Handbook on International Organizations* (OUP 2016) 1048.

[78] Luca Pasquet, 'Litigating the Immunities of International Organizations in Europe: The "Alternative Remedy" Approach and Its Humanizing Function' (2021) 36(2) Utrecht J Int Eur Law 192.

[79] Reinisch (n 77) 1058–1059.

of the activity, the availability of insurance, as well as the availability of compensation funds.

The channelling of legal liability is where responsibility is ascribed to a particular person or enterprise 'who is deemed by the legal rule to be the origin of damage, independently of any proof of intentional conduct or of his or her fault'.[80] In typical tort cases in national courts (not brought pursuant to a civil liability regime), causation and the necessary evidence to establish a causal link is a complex undertaking for claimants and rules vary from jurisdiction to jurisdiction (see discussion in Section 4.2).[81] Channelling liability (coupled with strict liability) minimizes the issues related to establishing causation. The person or enterprise is usually the operator of that activity that has use, control and direction of the object at the relevant time or the 'one in actual, legal or economic control of the polluting activity'.[82] The ILC observed that control 'denotes power or authority to manage, direct, regulate, administer or oversee'[83] and this could cover a range of persons including persons with decisive power over technical functioning of an activity, the holder of a permit or authorization for such an activity or person registering or notifying such an activity, or a parent company, particularly if that company has actual control of the operation.[84]

Channelling of liability to the operator has been adopted in relation to nuclear liability,[85] maritime transport of oil,[86] the carriage of hazardous and noxious

80 Guido Fernando Silva Soares and Everton Vieira Vargas, 'The Basel Liability Protocol on Liability and Compensation for Damage Resulting from Transboundary Movements of Hazardous Wastes and Their Disposal' (2001) 12(1) Yearbk Int Environ Law 69, 74.

81 Draft Principles (n 20) commentary to principle 4, 79, para 16.

82 ibid commentary to principle 2, 72, paras 32, 33.

83 ibid commentary to principle 2, 72, para 33.

84 ibid.

85 The production of nuclear energy from the 1960s prompted the development of a specific legal framework for liability consisting of a series of conventions established under two different organizations, namely the Organization for Economic Co-operation and Development Nuclear Energy Agency (NEA) and the International Atomic Energy Agency (IAEA). The 1960 Paris Convention was adopted under the auspices of the NEA: 1960 Convention on Third Party Liability in the Field of Nuclear Energy (adopted 29 July 1960, entered into force 1 April 1968) 956 UNTS 251. The 1963 Vienna Convention on the Civil Liability for Nuclear Damage was adopted under the auspices of the IAEA: Vienna Convention on the Civil Liability for Nuclear Damage (adopted 21 May 1963, entered into force 12 November 1977) 1063 UNTS 265 (1963 Vienna Convention). Both set out the basic principles on nuclear liability law, supplemented by subsequent conventions. For a detailed history of nuclear liability law, see Michael Faure, Jing Liu and Hui Wang, 'Analysis of Existing Regimes' in Michael Faure (ed), *Civil Liability and Financial Security for Offshore Oil and Gas Activities* (CUP 2016) 170–190.

86 The civil liability regime for vessel-based cargo oil pollution damage currently consists of the (1) 1992 Oil Pollution Liability Convention (n 54); (2) 1971 International Convention on the Establishment of an International Fund for Compensation for Oil Pollution Damage (adopted 18 December 1971, entered into force 16 October 1978) 110 UNTS 57 amended by the 1992 Protocol on the International Convention on the Establishment of an International Fund for Compensation for Oil Pollution Damage (adopted 27 November 1992, entered into force

substances,[87] removal of ship wrecks[88] and the carriage of passengers and luggage.[89] Channelling of liability is usually accompanied by the following elements: (1) liability of the operator is strict, that is, it is not necessary to establish the fault of the operator; (2) the operator may rely on certain exceptions to the imposition of strict liability such as armed conflict, civil war, natural disasters and so forth; (3) the operator may or may not have rights of recourse against third parties responsible for the damage; (4) the operator is usually allowed to limit its liability; (5) the operator is usually obliged to take out insurance or financial security, at least to the limits of its liability; (6) if limits are insufficient to provide adequate compensation, supplementary funds are established to complement compensation, which can either be funded by industry or states. Thus, while in principle, legal liability is channelled to one actor, in reality, the payment of compensation is shared amongst a number of actors, namely the operator, the insurance company, the industry supporting the supplementary funds and in certain cases, the state.[90]

The first-generation nuclear liability conventions initiated the trend of channelling liability back to the operator 'no matter how long the chain of causation, nor how novel the intervening factors (other than a very limited number of exculpatory ones)'.[91] While the formal justifications for channelling legal liability was to avoid the difficulties in identifying liable parties and to allow a concentration of insurance capacity, it was largely a result of interest group politics and particularly the unwillingness of American fuel suppliers to bear liability for potential nuclear accidents in Europe, and the desire of Western European governments to promote the peaceful use of nuclear energy.[92] 'Hold-harmless' clauses were adopted in bilateral contracts

30 May 1996) 1953 UNTS 330 (1992 Fund Convention); Protocol of 2003 to the International Convention on the Establishment of an International Fund for Compensation for Oil (adopted 16 May 2003, entered into force 3 March 2005) 92FUND/A.8/4 Annex 1 (2003 Supplementary Fund Convention).

[87] International Convention on Liability and Compensation for Damage in Connection with the Carriage of Hazardous and Noxious Substances by Sea, (adopted 3 May 1996, not yet entered into force) 35 ILM 1415 (1996 HNS Convention), as amended by the Protocol of 2010 to the International Convention on Liability and Compensation for Damage in Connection with the Carriage of Hazardous and Noxious Substances by Sea (adopted 30 April 2010, not yet entered into force) (2010 HNS Convention).

[88] Nairobi International Convention on the Removal of Wrecks (adopted 18 May 2007, entered into force 14 April 2015) 46 ILM 2007.

[89] Protocol to the Athens Convention relating to the Carriage of Passengers and Their Luggage by Sea, Consolidated text of the 1974 Athens Convention relating to the Carriage of Passengers and their Luggage by Sea and the 2002 Protocol to the Convention (adopted 1 November 2002, entered into force 23 April 2014) Cmnd 8760.

[90] This is the case in the nuclear liability regime – for a more comprehensive discussion on this, see Chapter 8.

[91] LFE Goldie, 'Concepts of Strict and Absolute Liability and the Ranking of Liability in Terms of Relative Exposure to Risk' (1985) 16 NYIL 175, 196.

[92] Tom Vanden Borre, 'Shifts in Governance in Compensation for Nuclear Damage 20 Years after Chernobyl' in Michael Faure and Albert Verheij (eds), *Compensation for Environmental Damage* (Springer 2007) 262; Faure, 'Attribution of Liability' (n 6) 623–624.

between the United States and Europe which required European nuclear operators to indemnify American suppliers for all claims resulting from their activities.[93] The exclusive channelling of liability to the nuclear operators (coupled with a limitation of liability and compulsory insurance) was incorporated in a draft nuclear liability treaty.[94] The intention was to minimize the unpredictability of multiple claims against suppliers, builders, designers, carriers, operators and states.[95] The nuclear installation operator is exclusively liable for damage resulting from accidents at its installation or during the transport of nuclear substances to and from that installation.[96] No other party may be held liable for the damage, although several operators can be held joint and severally liable.[97] The operator, in principle, does not have any right of recourse against other parties, including nuclear suppliers.[98] The absence of a right of recourse is to prevent the need for suppliers to seek insurance thereby avoiding costly duplication of insurance.[99] Supplementary funds after liability limits are exceeded are provided by the installation states and/or the contracting state.[100]

Similarly, the channelling of liability for cargo oil pollution was shaped by shipping and oil interests. After the 1967 Torrey Canyon incident in the English Channel, the British government was faced with expensive clean-up costs. Discussions at the predecessor to the IMO on which actor should provide compensation focused on either the shipowner or the cargo owner being liable, and whether it should be based on strict liability or fault.[101] Imposing liability on the flag state of the oil-polluting vessel was not seriously discussed.[102] The impasse was resolved when the Belgian delegation proposed that an additional layer of compensation be contributed by the oil industry, and this was to be coupled with channelling and

93 Faure, 'Attribution of Liability' (n 6) 623.

94 Günther Doeker and Thomas Gehring, 'Private or International Liability for Transnational Environmental Damage – The Precedent of Conventional Liability Regimes' (1990) 2(1) JEL 1, 8–9.

95 Patricia Birnie, Alan Boyle and Catherine Redgwell, *International Law and the Environment* (4th edn, OUP 2021) 439.

96 1960 Paris Convention (n 85) arts 3, 4 and 6; 1963 Vienna Convention (n 85) arts II and IV.

97 See, for example, 1963 Vienna Convention (n 85) arts II (3) and (4).

98 Both the 1960 Paris Convention and 1963 Vienna Conventions acknowledge that the installation operator shall have a right of recourse only if the damage results from an act or omission done with intent to cause damage against the individual acting or omitting to act with such intent or if it is expressly provided for in contract: 1960 Paris Convention (n 85) art 6 (f); 1963 Vienna Convention (n 85) art X.

99 Exposes des Motifs, of the 1960 Paris Convention of Third-Party Liability in the Field of Nuclear Energy (n 85).

100 For a more detailed discussion, see Chapter 8, Section 8.3.

101 Faure and others, 'Analysis of Existing Regimes' (n 85) 74.

102 Doeker and Gehring note that Liberia (a flag of convenience State) had requested that states should consider the possibility of multilateral governmental relief action instead of putting the burden on the shipping industry and that national relief funds be established but these proposals were ultimately unsuccessful: Doeker and Gehring (n 94) 5.

strict liability of the shipowner.[103] States did not consider that they should 'underwrite a guarantee of the financial contributions of the respective national oil industries under their control', in contrast to the position of states in the nuclear liability regime.[104]

The 1969 Oil Pollution Liability Convention imposes strict liability on the shipowner for incidents resulting in any oil pollution damage.[105] Channelling is exclusive, as no claims can be brought against the servants or agents of the owner.[106] The 1992 Oil Pollution Liability Convention (which amended the 1969 Oil Pollution Liability Convention) strengthened the channelling of liability to the shipowners in that it also excludes liability of not only the servants and agents of the owner, but also the pilot, or any other person who is not a crew member and performs services for the ship, any charterer, any person performing salvage with the consent of the owner or on the instructions of a competent public authority, any person taking preventive measures and their agents or servants.[107] The extension of the benefit of channelling to these actors was prompted by litigation in US courts after the *Amoco Cadiz* oil spill off the coast of France which found that the 1969 Oil Pollution Liability Convention channelling provisions would not bar proceedings against the registered shipowners' parent company as they were not the 'agents or servants' of the shipowner.[108] Unlike the nuclear liability conventions, the 1992 Oil Pollution Liability Convention does not prejudice any right of recourse of the owner against third parties.[109]

Civil liability regimes that have not adopted exclusive channelling provisions have taken this approach for a variety of reasons. For example, in the 1999 Protocol on Liability and Compensation for Damage Resulting from the Transboundary Movement of Hazardous Wastes and Their Disposal (1999 Basel Liability Protocol)[110] to the 1989 Basel Convention on Transboundary Movements of Hazardous Wastes and Their Disposal (1989 Basel Convention),[111] waste

[103] Faure and others, 'Analysis of Existing Regimes' (n 85) 74. Oil companies had previously already agreed on a private 'Contract Regarding an Interim Supplement to Tanker Liability for Oil Pollution': See Doeker and Gehring (n 94).

[104] Doeker and Gehring (n 94) 6.

[105] 1969 Oil Pollution Liability Convention (n 54) art III.

[106] ibid art III (4).

[107] 1992 Oil Pollution Liability Convention (n 54) art III (4). However, if it can be shown that the damage resulted from their personal act or omission, committed with the intent to cause such damage, or recklessly and with knowledge that such damage would result, these actors will be held liable.

[108] Sarah Gahlen, *Civil Liability for Accidents at Sea* (Springer-Verlag 2015) 108–110.

[109] 1992 Oil Pollution Liability Convention (n 54) art III (5).

[110] Basel Protocol on Liability and Compensation for Damage Resulting from Transboundary Movements of Hazardous Wastes and their Disposal (adopted 9 December 1999, not yet entered into force, UNTS 120 2005) art 4 (1999 Basel Liability Protocol).

[111] Basel Convention on Transboundary Movements of Hazardous Wastes and Their Disposal (adopted 22 March 1989, entered into force 5 May 1992, 28 ILM No. 657) (1989 Basel Convention).

generators, exporters, importers and disposers are potentially liable at different stages in the transit of waste. One single operation of a transboundary movement of hazardous waste and its disposal could involve several different entities and the 'determination of an individual or of an enterprise to whom liability could be channeled is not an easy task'.[112] Channelling liability to only one person would create 'a disincentive in the other persons involved to exercise the best possible care in order to prevent the occurrence of damage'.[113] Each occurrence of damage can be attributed to the sphere of responsibility of one person, depending on which stage the damage occurs.

Another reason for not adopting exclusive channelling provisions is the lack of availability of supplementary funding from industry or states. For example, the 2001 Bunker Oil Convention is modelled on the 1992 Oil Pollution Liability Convention for cargo oil pollution but adopts a different approach to exclusive channelling of liability.[114] Unlike the 1992 Oil Pollution Liability Convention where the shipowner is confined to the registered owner, the 2001 Bunker Oil Convention defines the shipowner as 'the owner, including the registered owner, bareboat charterer, manager and operator of the ship'.[115] Liability is attributed not only to the person formally registered as the owner of the ship but also to persons typically having control over the operation of the ship, that is, the bareboat charterer, manager and operator of the ship.[116] However, only the registered owner is required to carry compulsory insurance or financial security.[117] There is no secondary tier of compensation, as there is no other industry other than the shipowners which could contribute to compensation – by 'providing a vast number of defendants to possible victims, the negotiating parties apparently hoped to mitigate this shortcoming in material compensation'.[118]

There are advantages and disadvantages to exclusive channelling of liability. First, channelling of legal liability (coupled with strict liability) facilitates adequate and prompt compensation to the victim. Victims do not have to identify the person liable (and the evidentiary complexities that entails) and it avoids uncertainties in cases where there is more than one party at fault. This limits the potential problems arising from the concurrence of lawsuits and decreases administrative costs.[119] This

[112] Soares and Vargas (n 80) 86.
[113] ibid.
[114] International Convention on Civil Liability for Bunker Oil Pollution Damage (adopted 23 March 2001, entered into force 21 November 2008) IMO LEG/CONF.12/19, OJ L 256/7 (2001 Bunker Oil Convention).
[115] ibid art 1 (3).
[116] Gahlen (n 108) 179.
[117] 2001 Bunker Oil Convention (n 114) art 7.
[118] Gahlen (n 108) 180.
[119] Michael Faure and Tom Vanden Borre, 'Compensating Nuclear Damage: A Comparative Economic Analysis of the US and International Liability Schemes' (2008) 33 Wm & Mary Envtl L & Pol'y Rev 219, 264.

is a non-trivial factor in ABNJ, where responsible parties could arise in multiple jurisdictions, all with varying rules affecting recovery. Second, channelling may facilitate the availability of insurance as it reduces the number of persons required to obtain insurance coverage and avoids overlapping insurance coverage.[120] That said, it has also been argued that the insurability justification often used to rationalize exclusive channelling to the operator is 'simplistic and to some extent even incorrect'. The existence of several potentially liable parties that need insurance coverage does not necessarily mean that total insurance costs will increase.[121] Further, because the insurer will also have to cover losses in cases where the losses may not have been theoretically caused by the insured but by a third party, channelling actually creates a greater risk exposure and, consequently, uncertainty for the insurer.[122] Third, it is said that channelling liability to the operator is appropriate because the operator is usually in the best position to exercise effective control over the activity.[123] However, the event that may have led to the damage could have occurred before the operator exercised control over the activity. Fourth, another related rationale for channelling of liability is that the operator is the one 'who created high risks seeking economic benefit' and 'must bear the burden any adverse consequences of controlling the activity'.[124] Most activities both in areas under jurisdiction and in ABNJ involve a complex web of actors, all of whom could be said to create the risk and reap the benefit. Thus, channelling of liability to one party is inefficient from an economic point of view as it 'negatively affects the incentives to take care more particularly by all other parties who could have equally influenced the accident risk',[125] thus undermining the deterrence goals of liability regimes.

Finally, it is argued that to concentrate liability on an actor that may not have caused the damage is a deviation from ordinary rules on liability and hence unjust.[126] Indeed, it is questionable whether channelling of liability is an implementation of the 'polluter-pays' principle. In most civil liability regimes that adopt channelling to the operator (or shipowner), loss is borne by the operator and the industry or state concerned, so there is some form of shared responsibility for cost of

[120] Jan Albers, *Responsibility and Liability in the Context of Transboundary Movements of Hazardous Wastes by Sea* (Springer-Verlag 2015) 200; Faure, 'Attribution of Liability' (n 6) 623; Kristel de Smedt, Hui Wang and Michael Faure, 'Towards Optimal Liability and Compensation for Offshore Oil and Gas Activities' in Michael Faure (ed), *Civil Liability and Financial Security for Offshore Oil and Gas Activities* (CUP 2016) 313–314.

[121] Faure, 'Attribution of Liability' (n 6) 629.

[122] ibid.

[123] Birnie and others (n 95) 443.

[124] Draft Principles (n 20) commentary to art 4, 78, para 11.

[125] de Smedt and others (n 120) 314.

[126] Evelyne M Ameye, 'United States and India: Two Nuclear States with Legislation that Truly Holds Responsible Parties Liable in Case of a Nuclear Accident' (2015) 18(8) J Risk Res 1070, 1073–1074.

pollution damage, and they are arguably jointly treated as polluters.[127] However, the contributors of the funds may not have any direct responsibility for the pollution and 'there is no forensic analysis of responsibility and the allocation of liability and the activation of the secondary layer of compensation are based purely on pre-prescribed formulae'.[128] Thus, channelling of liability does not implement the polluter-pays principle *per se*. National courts deciding on oil pollution claims have occasionally rejected channelling provisions and found other entities apart from the registered shipowner liable because they have contributed to the risk of the incident, reflecting a desire to hold responsible parties excluded by the international regime accountable for exposing the marine environment to risk.[129]

The upshot of this discussion is that there is no general overarching rule or approach that necessitates the adoption of channelling of liability to the operator, although there is an increasing trend to do so in many civil liability regimes. Channelling is usually a policy choice dictated by extra-legal considerations, including the specific industry and the availability of insurance and supplementary funding. If there is a discernible pattern, it is towards limiting the exposure of the state through restricted attribution rules, due diligence and channelling of liability to operators, a trend that is likely to also characterize allocation of liability in ABNJ, as demonstrated by the lack of appetite to extend the civil liability regimes to the high seas.

4.3.4 *Allocating Liability amongst Several Responsible Actors*

There are several scenarios in which environmental harm is the result of the actions of multiple actors and/or causes. In a one-off incident or series of connected activities leading to environmental harm, multiple international actors (states and international organizations) and private entities may have contributed to environmental harm. Such environmental harm may also be worsened by natural causes or cumulative environmental harm that has occurred over a period. In another scenario, cumulative environmental harm can arise over a course of time either out of a connected or unconnected set of activities involving multiple actors or from external natural causes. In the absence of channelling which directs responsibility to one actor, liability rules need to address the allocation of liability when there are potentially multiple responsible actors.

Under general rules of tort, tortfeasors are presumptively liable in equal shares, unless the court allocates liability based on some other criterion such as relative fault – an approach referred to as *several liability*.[130] Under *joint and several liability*,

[127] Birnie and others (n 95) 344.

[128] Julie Adshead, 'The Application and Development of the Polluter-Pays Principle across Jurisdictions in Liability for Marine Oil Pollution: The Tales of the "Erika" and the "Prestige"' (2018) 30 JEL 425, 435.

[129] ibid 443–451.

[130] Hylton (n 3) 180.

any one of the tortfeasors may be held liable for the entire damage vis-à-vis the victim.[131] Joint and several liability usually arises when various tortfeasors have knowingly acted in concert to produce the injury.[132] If the tortfeasors acted independently of each other, joint and several liability is found if it can be demonstrated that each defendant contributed to the injury or if it can be demonstrated that each defendant contributed to part of the injury and it is impossible to allocate respective fault.[133] The primary advantage of joint and several liability is that it relieves the burden on the victim to demonstrate how responsibility amongst multiple tortfeasors should be allocated, as victims can collect the entire damage from one of the contributing tortfeasors who, in turn, could claim recourse against the other liable tortfeasors in proportion to their comparative responsibility for the loss based on relative causal contribution and fault.[134] It places the risk of insolvency on the defendants rather than the victim, gives the victim incentive to sue and reduces administrative costs.[135] It is also said to provide incentives for mutual monitoring between tortfeasors and to promote the exercise of reasonable care.[136] Accordingly, civil liability rules regimes generally recognize that when more than one operator/owner is liable and damage is not reasonably separable, liability will be joint and severable.[137] However, joint and several liability has also been critiqued as unfair to insurers and the defendant with deeper pockets who may only be responsible for a small proportion of damage in comparison to the other defendant.[138] This is particularly problematic when one of the defendants is insolvent resulting in a situation where only the solvent tortfeasor is held liable for damage, encouraging litigation against tortfeasors or insurers with the most funds.[139] In response to this, certain jurisdictions have adopted *proportionate liability* whereby liability for damage is apportioned between all the concurrent tortfeasors according to their respective responsibility.[140]

The rules of state and international organization responsibility start from the premise that states and international organizations are individually and independently responsible for their own conduct that is attributable to them (known as individual responsibility).[141] The ASR explicitly address the 'plurality of responsible states', that is, the situation where there are multiple wrongdoing states and stipulates

[131] ibid.

[132] Faure, 'Attribution of Liability' (n 6) 607.

[133] ibid; Hylton (n 3) 183–185.

[134] de Smedt and others (n 120) 316.

[135] Faure, 'Attribution of Liability' (n 6) 609–615.

[136] ibid 614.

[137] Paris Convention (n 85) art 5 (b); Vienna Convention (n 85) art II (3); 1992 Oil Pollution Liability Convention (n 54) art IV; 2001 Bunker Oil Convention (n 114) art V.

[138] See, for example, *AWA Ltd v Daniels t/as Deloitte, Haskins and Sells* (1992) 7 ACSR 759 at 877.

[139] Faure, 'Attribution of Liability' (n 6) 617.

[140] ibid 608.

[141] ASR (n 12) art 1, 32.

that where multiple states are responsible for the same internationally wrongful act, each state is separately responsible for the conduct attributable to it.[142] In the DARIO, it states that 'when an international organization and one or more States or other international organizations are responsible for the same internationally wrongful act, the responsibility of each State or international organization may be invoked in relation to that act'.[143] However, the current framework on state and international organization responsibility is said to, in principle at least, accommodate multiple actors in that the same conduct can be attributed to more than one subject of international law at the same time and multiple states and/or international organizations can therefore be found independently responsible and liable for the same damage.[144]

That said, there are limitations to independent responsibility, particularly in complicated situations of multiple wrongdoers, including the fact that it provides no basis for the apportionment of responsibility and reparation. This is also linked to the complexities in developing appropriate causation tests in cases of 'causal overdetermination'.[145] The ASR conclude, 'international practice and the decisions of international tribunals do not support the reduction or attenuation of reparation for concurrent causes except in cases of contributory fault' and a state will be held responsible for all consequences (not being too remote) of its wrongful conduct unless the injury can be shown to be severable in causal terms from that attributed to the responsible state.[146] The ASR 'neither recognizes a general rule of joint and several responsibility nor does it exclude the possibility that two or more States will be responsible for the internationally wrongful act'.[147] International courts and tribunals have also taken different approaches.[148] For example, in the *Certain Phosphate Lands in Nauru Case*, the International Court of Justice (ICJ) found that the conduct of the Administering Authority of Nauru that damaged phosphate lands was attributable to each of the states that had established the Administering Authority, namely, Australia, New Zealand and the United Kingdom, even though Nauru had only brought a claim against Australia.[149] The United Nations Claims

[142] ibid art 47, 124.

[143] DARIO (n 57) art 48 (1), 88.

[144] André Nollkaemper and Dov Jacobs, 'Shared Responsibility in International Law: A Conceptual Framework' (2013) 34 Mich J Intl L 359, 389–393.

[145] Plakokefalos has defined overdetermination as 'the existence of multiple causes [multiple wrongdoers, external natural causes, contribution to the injury by the victim and so on] contributing to a harmful outcome': See Plakokefalos (n 6) 472.

[146] ASR (n 12) commentary to art 31, 93–94, paras 12 and 13.

[147] ibid commentary to art 47, 125, para 6. The Special Rapporteur, James Crawford, has cautioned against drawing from private law analogies such as the doctrine of joint and several liability and has argued that there is no evidence that joint and several liability has been accepted in international law: Crawford (n 23) 328–332.

[148] Lanovoy (n 9) 69–74.

[149] *Certain Phosphate Lands in Nauru (Nauru v Australia)*, Preliminary Objections, [1992] ICJ Rep 240, paras 45–47.

Commission (UNCC) also considered concurrent causes of harm and found that where damage directly resulted from an act but that other factors have contributed to the damage, 'due account is taken of the contribution from such other factors in order to determine the level of compensation that is appropriate for the portion of damage which is directly attributable' to the act for which compensation is being claimed.[150]

In situations where two or more *international actors* are responsible for environmental harm in ABNJ the question will arise as to what portion of the harm caused to a third party the actors are responsible for and lack of clarity on this issue may result in too much or too little responsibility for a given individual state or international organization.[151] As observed by some scholars, it could also result in blame shifting between the actors involved.[152] The upshot is that there is no satisfactory solution to issues of causation and shared responsibility under international law.[153]

4.4 SPECIFIC RULES ON ALLOCATION OF LIABILITY IN ABNJ

4.4.1 *Antarctic*

The activities taking place in Antarctica consist mostly of fishing, scientific research and tourism.[154] The actors conducting such activities consist of state operators and non-state operators. There is presently no liability regime in force and allocation for liability for environmental harm, the primary obligations of which are found in the 1959 Antarctic Treaty and the 1991 Protocol on Environmental Protection to the Antarctic Treaty (1991 Antarctic Protocol), will be determined by the default rules on state responsibility discussed in Section 4.3.1.[155] There are no international organizations specific to the Antarctic that possess the requisite legal personality to be subject to legal actions. The ATCM is *prima facie* a conference of parties, and while it has been argued that it is functionally equivalent to an international organization, its status has been intentionally ambiguous and is not considered an actor to which international responsibility can be attributed.[156]

[150] UNCC S/AC.26/20003/31, 18 Dec 2003, para 39; Lanovoy (n 9) 70–72.

[151] Nollkaemper and Jacobs, 'Shared Responsibility in International Law' (n 144) 391.

[152] ibid 392.

[153] See generally Nollkaemper and others, 'Guiding Principles' (n 11).

[154] See discussion in Chapter 1.

[155] Antarctic Treaty (adopted 1 December 1959, entered into force 23 June 1961) 402 UNTS 71; Protocol on Environmental Protection to the Antarctic Treaty (adopted 4 October 1991, entered into force 14 January 1998) (1991) 30 ILM 1461 (1991 Antarctic Protocol).

[156] During the negotiations for the Secretariat in 2002–2003, there had been debate on whether the Antarctic Treaty Consultative Meeting (ATCM) is an international organization–some ATCPs considered it to be an international organization while others did not. Ultimately, the Secretariat was created with legal personality and capacity only under Argentine domestic law, and the exact status of the ATCM was left intentionally ambiguous. On the other hand, the Chair of the ATCM signed the Headquarters Agreement for the Secretariat on behalf of the

However, it is instructive to examine how allocation of liability is addressed in instruments which have been negotiated but are currently not in force, namely the 1988 Convention on the Regulation of Antarctic Mineral Resource Activities (CRAMRA)[157] and the 2005 Annex VI to the Environmental Protocol on Liability Arising from Environmental Emergencies (Liability Annex).[158] Both allocate liability to the 'operator' which includes state operators and non-state operators and envisage some form of liability for states parties.

Although CRAMRA did not contain a complete liability scheme and is unlikely to ever come into force given the moratorium on exploitation activities in Antarctica, it contains provisions on liability which are worth examining.[159] The basic structure of the CRAMRA liability regime mirrors the central features of civil liability treaties, with operators being strictly liable for several categories of damages, including failure to take 'necessary and timely response action, including prevention, containment, clean-up and removal measures, if the activity results or threatens to result in damage to the Antarctic environment or dependent or associated ecosystems' (similar to administrative approaches to liability),[160] and the establishment of a Fund when the operator is financially incapable of meeting its obligations in full or when damage exceeds limitation of liability or where the damage is of an undetermined origin.[161] However, unlike traditional civil liability regimes, there is a role for states by providing for a limited form of residual state liability. While this approach was met with strong opposition,[162] CRAMRA ultimately recognized that the sponsoring state was responsible and consequently liable for damage which would not have occurred or continued if the sponsoring state had carried out its obligations under the Convention and that state was only liable for that portion of liability not satisfied by the operator.[163] The approach, while linking state liability to unsatisfied damages, still requires a breach and causal connection to

ATCM which has led some scholars to suggest that it is an entity separate from its members: Jill Barrett, 'The Antarctic Treaty System' in Karen N Scott and David L VanderZwaag (eds), *Research Handbook on Polar Law* (Edward Elgar 2020) 40, 53–54.

157 Convention on the Regulation of Antarctic Mineral Resource Activity, 2 June 1988 27 ILM 868 (not yet entered into force) (CRAMRA).

158 Annex VI to Protocol on Environmental Protection to the Antarctic Treaty on Liability Arising from Environmental Emergencies (adopted 17 June 2005, not yet entered into force) 45 ILM 5 (Liability Annex).

159 Art VIII of CRAMRA set out the liability scheme, although it was not complete.

160 Liability Annex (n 158) art 8(1).

161 The issue of whether there should be limits to liability for environmental damage to the Antarctic was contentious and it was therefore decided to defer the issue to the prospective Protocol and art VIII(7) provides that the Protocol may contain appropriate limits on liability, where such limits can be justified.

162 Henry C Burmester, 'Liability for Damage from Antarctic Mineral Resource Activities' (1989) 29 Va J Int'l L 621, 649.

163 CRAMRA (n 157) art VIII (3)(a). The 'sponsoring state' of a juridical has been defined in art XII of CRAMRA.

the loss.[164] CRAMRA also envisages the establishment of a Fund which would first be financed by operators but which may also require states to ensure 'permanent liquidity and mandatory supplementation thereof in the event of insufficiency',[165] although the ultimate means of financing a Fund would be left to the negotiations of a protocol. This latter requirement signals an intention to address liability gaps, and the potential responsibility of states to ensure sufficiency of coverage.

The Liability Annex combines elements of civil liability and administrative approaches. The objectives of the Liability Annex are quite different from CRAMRA, which was intended to regulate the liability of corporations engaged in mineral extraction and was based on the assumption that these corporations would finance any liability arising out of their activities.[166] In contrast, the Liability Annex was negotiated against the overarching objective to comprehensively 'protect the Antarctic environment and dependent and associated ecosystems'.[167] Further, the most common activity in the Antarctic Treaty area is scientific research or small-scale tourist activities which were presumed not to pose the same level of environmental risk as mineral extraction activities.[168] It was also implicitly understood that scientific research should not be unduly restrained by onerous liability provisions.[169]

The Liability Annex defines 'operator' as 'any natural or juridical person, whether governmental or non-governmental, which organizes activities to be carried out in the Antarctic Treaty Area', and includes both non-state operators and state operators.[170] Unlike traditional civil liability regimes and even CRAMRA, the Liability Annex adopts a regulatory or administrative approach by obliging states parties to require its operators to take prompt and effective response action to environmental emergencies if the emergencies arise from the activities of those operators. If an operator fails to do so, states parties of that operator or other states parties are encouraged to take such action. Article 6 states that if an operator fails to take prompt and effective response action to environmental emergencies, it shall be liable to pay the costs of response action taken by parties.[171] However, the Liability Annex differentiates between the liability of state operators and non-state operators.

When a state operator fails to take prompt and effective response action and no response action was taken by any state party, the state operator is liable to *pay the costs of the response action* which should have been undertaken into a fund to be

164 In this regard the approach follows a state responsibility model, but recovery is not limited to other states, as it is under customary international law.

165 CRAMRA (n 157) art 8(7).

166 Alan D Hemmings, 'Liability Postponed: The Failure to Bring Annex VI of the Madrid Protocol into Force' (2018) 8(2) Polar J 315, 322.

167 1991 Antarctic Protocol (n 155), art 2, 16.

168 Hemmings (n 166) 322.

169 ibid.

170 Liability Annex (n 158) art 1(c),

171 ibid art 6(1).

administered by the Secretariat.[172] The amount to be paid is to be determined by the ATCM by means of a decision.[173] However, decisions can only be adopted if there are no objections by a consultative party, which means that a consultative party who is also a state operator can determine or veto the amount.[174] Further, the liability of state operators shall be resolved only by the ATCM and if the question is unresolved, it is to be resolved by the dispute settlement procedure of the Protocol (articles 18, 19, 20), that is, by negotiation, inquiry, mediation, conciliation and lastly arbitration.[175] Unlike, the deep seabed mining regime in UNCLOS (Section 4.4.2) or CRAMRA, state operators are afforded much greater protection from liability claims, notwithstanding the operational nature of the activity.

When a non-state operator fails to take prompt and effective response action and no response action was taken by any state party, the non-state operator shall be liable to pay an *amount of money that reflects as much as possible the costs of the response action* that should have been taken.[176] This amount of money should be paid directly to the fund, or to the state party of that operator or to the party that is obliged to establish that there is a mechanism in place under its domestic law for enforcement against the non-state operator.[177] A state party receiving such money shall *make best efforts* to make a contribution to the fund which at least equals the money received by the operator. An action can be brought against the non-state operator in the courts of a party where the operator is incorporated or has its principal place of business or his habitual place of residence.[178]

With regard to state liability for the failure of non-state operators to undertake emergency response actions (separate from a state operator's liability), there is no sponsoring state liability *per se* but activities by non-state actors must either be subject to the authorization of states parties or if there is no formal authorization process, non-state operator's activities are subject to a comparable regulatory process by that state party.[179] The Liability Annex does not impose residual liability on states if non-state operators fail to take response action, and only encourages states parties of the operator and other states parties to take action.[180] Article 10 provides, however, that a state party shall not be liable for the failure of a non-state operator

[172] ibid art 6(2) (a), read with art 12.

[173] ibid art 7(5).

[174] This clause was highly debated with some states suggesting that the state party of the operator should be excluded from the decision-making process, but no consensus could be reached on this. See Silja Vönecky, 'The Liability Annex to the Protocol on Environmental Protection to the Antarctic Treaty' in Doris König, Peter-Tobias Stoll, Volker Röben and Nele Matz-Lück (eds), *International Law Today: New Challenges and the Need for Reform?* (Springer 2007) 186.

[175] Liability Annex (n 158) art 7(4).

[176] ibid art 6(2)(b).

[177] ibid.

[178] ibid art 7(1).

[179] ibid art 1(d).

[180] ibid art 5(2).

to take response action except to the extent that the state party did not take appropriate measures within its competence (i.e. adoption of laws and regulations, administrative actions and enforcement measures) to ensure compliance with the Annex, that is, in effect a due diligence obligation.[181]

4.4.2 *Deep Seabed*

There are potentially a range of actors whose actions may result in damage to the marine environment, including the contractor, the ISA, the sponsoring state, the Enterprise (currently non-operational), manufacturers of equipment, the owner or operator of vessels, installations and equipment used for deep seabed mining, the flag state of the vessel engaged in deep seabed mining (to the extent a vessel is used and not an installation), the parent companies of non-state contractors and the home states of parent companies.

UNCLOS allocates liability for damage arising out of activities in the Area (including damage to the marine environment) to the contractor (i.e. either the state, the state-owned entity or the private entity provided the latter two are sponsored by a sponsoring state), the ISA and the sponsoring state.[182] During the negotiations of UNCLOS, the Group of 77, which represented the interests of developing states, proposed that liability and risk arising out of the conduct of operations would lie solely with the contractor but it was eventually recognized that both the contractor and the ISA would be responsible for damage arising out of their wrongful conduct.[183] Moreover, state responsibility for activities carried out by governmental agencies and non-governmental entities or persons acting under its jurisdiction was always contemplated even as early as the 1970 Declaration of Principles.[184] It is clear the intention was to place responsibility on all three actors either because they were directly conducting activities or had supervisory responsibilities over the contractors.

Accordingly, article 22 of Annex III of UNCLOS provides that the contractor and the ISA shall have responsibility or liability for any damage arising out of its wrongful acts in the conduct of its operations and exercise of its powers and functions

[181] This was inspired by UNCLOS (n 43) art 139, read with Annex III, art 4(4).

[182] UNCLOS (n 43) art 139; Annex III, art 22.

[183] Third United Nations Conference on the Law of the Sea, *Text on Conditions of Exploration and Exploitation Prepared by the Group of Seventy-Seven*, A/CONF.62/C.1/L.7, vol 3; the text prepared in 1974 stated, 'Any responsibility, liability or risk arising out of the conduct of operations shall lie only with the person, natural or juridical, entering into a contract with the Authority' (ibid at para 13). The records do not reveal detailed reasons as to why the ISA was also added as a potentially liable party: Satya N Nandan, Michael W Lodge and Shabtai Rosenne (eds), *United Nations Convention on the Law of the Sea 1982: A Commentary*, vol VI (Brill 2002) 753.

[184] Declaration of Principles Governing the Sea-Bed and Ocean Floor and the Subsoil Thereof, Beyond the Limits of National Jurisdiction, UNGA Res 2749 (XXV) (17 December 1970).

respectively, account being taken of contributory acts or omissions by the contractor or the ISA, as the case may be. The Exploration Regulations build upon the distribution of responsibility and liability between the contractor and the ISA which is also mirrored in the latest version (as of writing) of the Draft Exploitation Regulations (DER).[185] The liability of the sponsoring state is set out in article 139. This distribution of liability (as opposed to exclusively placing liability on the contractors) may have also been motivated by the fact that contractors were not just confined to privately owned corporations (which was what initially pushed for by the industrialized countries), but also states and their state-owned entities which are traditionally reluctant to accept liability. This allocation of liability between the contractors, the ISA and the sponsoring state and the SDC's elaboration on this allocation in its 2011 Advisory Opinion raises several interesting issues.

With the exception of the exclusive channelling of liability to contractors, which is not present under the deep seabed regime, both the existing liability framework and developing liability framework for activities in the Area contain elements commonly found in civil liability regimes. For example, the contractor is liable for the wrongful acts or omissions of its employees, subcontractors, agents and all persons engaged in, working or acting for them in the conduct of its operations under the contract.[186] Both the Exploration Regulations and DER place obligations on the contractors to take out insurance.[187] The SDC's Advisory Opinion suggested the establishment of a trust fund to compensate for damage that was not caused by any of the actors or that exceeded what the contractor was able to compensate. Funds are a key element of civil liability regimes and the DER envisages the establishment of an Environmental Compensation Fund, with funding coming out of fees and penalties paid to the ISA, amounts received as a result of legal proceedings arising out of a violation of the terms of the exploitation contract, any monies paid into the Fund at the direction of the Council and any income received by the Fund from the investment of monies belonging to the Fund.[188]

Further, there are also signs that under the existing framework, liability for damage will be placed on the contractors if not *de jure*, at least *de facto*. For example, several sponsoring states' national legislation provide that a sponsored contractor shall at all times keep the sponsoring state indemnified against all actions,

[185] See, for example, International Seabed Authority's (ISA) Regulations on Prospecting and Exploration for Polymetallic Nodules in the Area (2013) ISBA/19/C/17 (PMN), Annex IV, s 16; 'Draft Regulations on Exploitation of Mineral Resources in the Area, prepared by the Legal and Technical Commission' (2019), ISBA/25/C/WP.1 (LTC), Annex X, s 12 (DER).

[186] See, for example, PMN (n 185) Annex IV, s 16(1). The extent to which other actors engaged in deep seabed mining such as the flag states, the vessel owner/operator, the manufacturer, the parent companies of non-state contractors will fall within the definition of 'employees, subcontractors, agents and all persons engaged in, working or acting for them in the conduct of its operations under the contract' is not clear.

[187] PMN (n 185) Annex IV, s 16(5); DER (n 185) reg 36.

[188] DER (n 185) reg 56; see also discussion in Chapter 8.

proceedings, costs, charges, claims and demands which may be or brought by any third party in relation to activities in the Area.[189] Similarly, the current version of the DER also requires the contractors to include the ISA as an additional assured and oblige the underwriters to waive any rights of recourse including subrogation rights against the ISA in relation to exploitation.[190] This would suggest that in the event that damage is caused by some failure of due diligence on either part of the ISA and the sponsoring state, they could escape liability through contractual means.

Channelling legal liability to the contractor, to the exclusion of sponsoring states and the ISA, appears to derogate from the intention of the negotiators of UNCLOS on the allocation of liability and may undermine the incentive of the sponsoring state and the ISA to exercise reasonable care in the exercise of their obligations. It is also not clear whether the ISA has the authority to fundamentally change the allocation of liability set out in UNCLOS.[191] While an indemnity under domestic law cannot alter the international legal obligations of sponsoring states, the effect is to allow the sponsoring state to contract out of their responsibilities under UNCLOS.

There are several scenarios where the conduct of the ISA could cause damage, including failing to ensure sufficient supervision of activities in the Area or even in the conduct of its inspections.[192] Article 22 of Annex III provides that along with the contractor, the ISA shall 'have responsibility or liability for any damage arising out of wrongful acts in the exercise of its powers and functions, including violations under article 168, paragraph 2, account being taken of contributory acts or omissions by the contractor. Liability in every case shall be for the actual amount of damage'.[193] The Exploration Regulations build upon this. UNCLOS, the Exploration Regulations and the DER place obligations on the ISA and its organs in relation to the exercise of its powers and functions, and failure to exercise due diligence that results in damage to the marine environment will incur liability. This is consistent with the responsibility of international organizations under the DARIO.

[189] Kiribati's Seabed Minerals Act 2017 s 92(3); also see 'Code Project: Template National Sponsorship Law for Seabed Mining beyond National Jurisdiction', (Pew Charitable Trusts, October 2020) s 27 available at <www.pewtrusts.org/-/media/assets/2020/09/seabed_mining_white_paper.pdf>.

[190] DER (n 185) reg 36.

[191] The ISA has express powers under UNCLOS as well as 'such incidental powers … as are implicit in and necessary for the exercise of those powers and functions with respect to activities in the Area': UNCLOS (n 43) art 157(2). The SDC noted that the ISA Regulations are instruments subordinate to UNCLOS and if not in conformity, should be interpreted to ensure consistency with its provisions but at the same time acknowledged that further rules could be developed in the context of deep seabed mining: *Activities in the Area* Advisory Opinion (n 45) paras 93 and 211.

[192] UNCLOS (n 43) art 153(5).

[193] UNCLOS (n 43) Annex III, art 22. art 168 (2) mandates that the Secretary-General and the staff shall have no financial interest in any activity relating to activities in the Area and are subject to confidentiality requirements in respect of industrial secrets, proprietary data and other confidential information.

However, several issues remain. First, while article 22 of UNCLOS does not limit the type of damage for which the ISA can be held liable for, the Exploration Regulations provide that the ISA shall be liable for the 'actual amount of any damage *to the Contractor*' which appears to assume that the ISA will only be held liable for damage suffered by the contractor. This is in contrast to the contractor's liability in the Exploration Regulations which states that the contractor is liable for 'the actual amount of any damage, *including damage to the marine environment*, arising out of its wrongful acts or omissions ...'.[194] The Exploration Regulations suggest that the only claimant that can bring a claim against the ISA is the contractor, who may seek to bring a contributory claim against the ISA. UNCLOS states parties are the only other entities that could bring a claim against the ISA. The ISA will also most likely have immunity in national courts.[195]

Second, from a practical perspective, it is also not clear how the ISA, if it were held liable, would be able to pay for any compensation given that its operations are funded by assessed contributions from states and from the fees paid by the contractors. As acknowledged in the DARIO, the member states of the ISA may be required to step in if the ISA is unable to compensate. This may also be why the DER requires the contractors to include the ISA as an additional assured and that the underwriters waive any rights of recourse including subrogation rights against the ISA in relation to exploitation.[196]

Other issues concern the liability of the sponsoring state. The SDC found that the sponsoring state would only be found liable if (1) its sponsored contractor's actions resulted in damage; (2) the sponsored contractor failed to pay the actual amount of damage; (3) the sponsoring state failed to carry out its responsibilities under UNCLOS and the failure to carry out these responsibilities was causally linked to the damage caused by the sponsored Contractor.[197] The SDC observed that under article 153 (4) of UNCLOS, the sponsoring state has the obligation to 'assist' the ISA in ensuring compliance with UNCLOS and related instruments and that the 'subordinate role of the sponsoring State is reflected in Annex III, Article 22 of the Convention, in which the liability of the contractor and the Authority is mentioned while that of the sponsoring State is not'.[198] In this connection, the SDC went on to say that the 'main liability for a wrongful act committed in the conduct of the contractor's operations or in the exercise of the Authority's powers and functions rests with the contractor and the Authority, respectively, rather than with the sponsoring State'. This 'reflects the distribution of responsibilities for deep seabed mining activities between the contractor, the Authority and the sponsoring State'.[199]

[194] PMN (n 185) s 16.1.
[195] UNCLOS (n 43) arts 177, 178; see also discussion in Section 4.3.2.2.
[196] DER (n 185) reg 36.
[197] *Activities in the Area* Advisory Opinion (n 45) paras 181–182, 202.
[198] ibid para 102.
[199] ibid para 200.

Accordingly, the SDC found that the liability of the sponsoring state and the contractor exists in parallel and that UNCLOS and related instruments leave no room for residual liability.[200]

While non-residual liability of states is arguably consistent with general trends in international law, the SDC's reasoning as to why deserves further examination.[201] 'Subordinate' suggests a less important position or role and could imply that the sponsoring state's role is secondary or subsidiary to that of the ISA in terms of regulating the contractor. A plain reading of the text does not support this. The absence of reference to the sponsoring state in article 22 of Annex III does not warrant a description of the sponsoring state's role as 'subordinate' given that article 139 of UNCLOS specifically mentions state responsibility and liability. The fact that the sponsoring state is to assist the ISA in ensuring the contractor's compliance with UNCLOS and relevant instruments also seems like a weak justification for imposing a 'subordinate' role on the sponsoring state. The obligation of the sponsoring state to 'assist' the ISA in ensuring that activities in the Area are carried out in conformity with UNCLOS and related instruments are manifested in its obligation to adopt necessary measures within its national legal system – it does not necessarily mean that greater responsibility is placed on the ISA in regulating the contractor. Indeed, the subordinate role of the sponsoring state seems at odds with the overarching purpose of the sponsoring state laid out by the SDC which is to contribute 'to the realization of the common interest of all States in the proper application of the principle of the common heritage of mankind which requires faithful compliance with the obligations set out in Part XI'.[202] It also does not make sense, considering that both the ISA and the sponsoring state have similar supervisory roles vis-à-vis the contractors and this creates uncertainty in the allocation of primary obligations between the ISA and the sponsoring state.

The issue of shared responsibility, that is, instances where a multiplicity of actors contribute to a single harmful outcome by breaching either the same or different obligations is not explicitly addressed in UNCLOS or the Exploration Regulations.[203] There are various permutations where several of the actors identified above may be responsible for damage arising from activities in the Area, that is, either multiple contractors; multiple sponsoring states; the contractor and the ISA; the contractor and the sponsoring state; and the ISA and the sponsoring state.

200 ibid para 204.

201 For arguments on why the sponsoring state should have residual liability, please see Donald Anton, 'The Principle of Residual Liability in the Seabed Disputes Chamber of the International Tribunal for the Law of the Sea: The Advisory Opinion on Responsibility and Liability for International Seabed Mining (ITLOS Case No. 17)' (2012) 7 (2) JSDLP-RDPDD 241.

202 *Activities in the Area* Advisory Opinion (n 45) para 76.

203 Ilias Plakokefalos, 'Environmental Protection of the Deep Seabed' in André Nollkaemper and Ilias Plakokefalos (eds), *The Practice of Shared Responsibility in International Law* (CUP 2017) 380, 380–381.

The SDC only addressed two scenarios where multiple actors may be responsible. First, where there are multiple sponsoring states, the SDC observed that neither article 139(2) nor article 4(4) of Annex III indicates how sponsoring states are to share their liability, and do not differentiate between single and multiple sponsorship. Accordingly, the SDC opined that 'in the event of multiple sponsorship, liability is joint and several unless otherwise provided in the Regulations issued by the Authority'.[204] Second, where both the sponsoring state and contractor have contributed to the same damage, the SDC held that the sponsoring state and the contractor are not to be held joint and severally liable. This is because 'the liability of the sponsoring State arises from its own failure to carry out its responsibilities, whereas the contractor's liability arises from its own non-compliance' and as a result, both 'forms of liability exist in parallel'.[205] The sponsoring state is not responsible for the damage caused by the sponsored contractor. Thus, the SDC suggests that if the contractor has compensated for the actual amount of damage, claims cannot be brought against the sponsoring state. However, separating fault and corresponding compensation due to the sponsoring state's lack of due diligence from those arising from the contractor's misfeasance would be a challenge.

The wording of article 139 has given rise to questions about the potential liability of parent companies and the home state of parent companies. Specifically, article 139 states that parties have oversight responsibilities for activities in the Area carried by state entities and 'natural or juridical persons who possess the nationality of States Parties or are *effectively controlled* by them or their nationals'.[206] The term effective control could be interpreted as having a narrow regulatory meaning, which would restrict responsibility to the sponsoring state. Alternatively, if effective control is interpreted as having an economic element, through corporate ownership, then the home state of the parent company may bear some responsibility, which in turn influences the allocation of liability. The economic approach reflects the realities of corporate decision-making and has support in some national and international approaches to parent company and home state responsibility for environmental and social issues.[207] In the deep seabed mining context, there is no definitive approach, although the issue has been the subject of analysis by the ISA Secretariat, which favoured the narrow, regulatory approach.[208]

Finally, the Enterprise, as an organ of the ISA that would carry out activities in the Area, would also be subject to liability. While the activities of the Enterprise are

[204] *Activities in the Area* Advisory Opinion (n 45) paras 190–192.

[205] ibid para 201.

[206] UNCLOS (n 43) art 139(1) (emphasis added).

[207] For an overview, see Andrés Sebastián Rojas and Freedom-Kai Philips, 'Effective Control and Deep Seabed Mining: Toward a Definition' Centre for International Governance Innovation, Liability Issues for Deep Seabed Mining Series, Paper No. 7, February 2019.

[208] ISA Legal and Technical Commission, Note by the Secretariat: Analysis of Regulation 11.2 of the Regulations on Prospecting and Exploration for Polymetallic Nodules and Polymetallic Sulphides in the Area. 20th Sess, ISBA/20/LTC/10 (2014).

currently in abeyance, the statute of the Enterprise clearly contemplates the ability for persons harmed by the Enterprise's activities to be able to bring actions in domestic courts.[209]

4.4.3 *High Seas*

There are no specific provisions in either UNCLOS or the newly agreed upon agreement on the conservation and sustainable use of marine biological diversity of areas beyond national jurisdiction (2023 BBNJ Agreement) on the allocation of liability. State liability for activities resulting in environmental harm in the high seas will be determined by the default rules on state responsibility discussed in Section 4.3.1.[210] However, as already discussed, to the extent that such activities are carried out by non-state actors, that is, state-owned entities or private entities, the wrongful conduct will only be attributed to states if the state concerned exercised some form of 'governmental authority' or issued 'instructions, directions or control' over the non-state actor's conduct or activity that led to the damage. Such conduct must have been specifically authorized by the state in question or that the state had actual factual control over the specific conduct which led to the damage. This is a high threshold, and typical commercial activities on the oceans conducted by vessels cannot be attributed to flag states. The fact that flag states, coastal states or sponsoring states exercise supervisory jurisdiction over non-state actors is not sufficient to warrant a finding that the conduct of non-state actors can be attributed to those states. However, it remains available for victims of harm to use the failure of states to exercise due diligence over non-state actors under their jurisdiction and control to establish the responsibility and liability of states (provided that the resultant environmental harm was caused by this failure to exercise due diligence).

With regard to international organizations, as mentioned in Section 4.3.2, there are a multitude of international organizations that have mandates that may cover the high seas but allocating responsibility and consequent liability to them may be an uphill task that is dependent on various factors, including whether the international organization has the requisite legal personality to be allocated responsibility; the nature of its role or authority in relation to the activity potentially resulting in harm (supervisory versus standard setting); whether they are bound by primary obligations to protect the marine environment, the breach of which would incur responsibility and liability; how such international organizations would fund any compensation; and last, in which forum would they be held liable given that international courts and tribunals may not have personal jurisdiction over them and their immunities in national courts. In this regard, it is noteworthy that the 2023 BBNJ Agreement has adopted similar institutional mechanisms found in multilateral environmental

[209] UNCLOS (n 43) Annex IV, art 13(3).

[210] See generally Chapter 1, Section 1.2.3.4.

agreements, consisting of a conference of parties, a scientific and technical body, clearing-house mechanisms and a secretariat,[211] and are unlikely to have the requisite international legal personality to attract responsibility and liability.

Apart from allocating liability to states and international organizations, and given that there is presently no civil liability regime that covers environmental harm in the high seas, non-state actors can potentially be held liable for environmental damage that occurs in the high seas in national courts. Article 235 (2) of UNCLOS obliges states to ensure that recourse is available in accordance with their legal systems for prompt and adequate compensation or other relief in respect of damage caused by pollution of the marine environment by natural or juridical persons under their jurisdiction. There is thus a primary obligation on states parties to UNCLOS to ensure adequate recourse in national systems for pollution to the marine environment by non-state actors under their jurisdiction, which would at least apply to companies registered in that state party. However, as explained in Chapters 2 and 7, litigants may face a range of obstacles in pursuing claims for damage to the marine environment of the high seas including a lack of access to national procedures; a lack of clear jurisdictional provisions that allow courts to hear claims that occur outside of territory; and choice of law issues.

As previously mentioned, one response to the patchwork approach to liability claims for environmental harm in the high seas under unharmonized domestic liability approaches is to develop harmonized rules and procedures through civil liability regimes. There have been proposals to extend the application of existing civil liability regimes to the high seas through a high seas protocol but, as noted by some scholars, this would not be a holistic approach and could result in damage from certain activities being compensated and others not.[212] Channelling of liability to an operator would not work in a single multilateral civil liability regime that covers all activities resulting to damage in the high seas as it would be impossible to treat all operators potentially undertaking activities (i.e. shipowners, rig operators, etc.) equally, particularly if separate insurance rules for different types of activities were needed.[213] The more likely scenario is the development of sector-specific regimes, with potential recourse to channelling as activities in ABNJ develop, but much will depend on the character of the sector.

[211] Draft agreement under the United Nations Convention on the Law of the Sea on the conservation and sustainable use of marine biological diversity of areas beyond national jurisdiction, Advance, Unedited text, 4 March 2023 ('BBNJ Agreement'), Part VI; David S Berry, 'Unity or Fragmentation in the Deep Blue: Choices in Institutional Design for Marine Biological Diversity in Areas beyond National Jurisdiction' (2021) 8 Front Mar Sci 1, 7–11.

[212] Nicholas Gaskell, 'Liability and Compensation Regimes: Pollution of the High Seas' in Robert Beckman, Millicent McCreath, J Ashley Roach and Zhen Sun (eds), *High Seas Governance: Gaps and Challenges* (Brill 2019) 229, 248.

[213] ibid 249.

4.5 CONCLUSIONS

The central questions raised in this chapter concern which actors should bear the losses associated with risky activities. The approach taken up in connection with many of the existing civil liability regimes is to focus liability on the operators. Channelling liability in this manner simplifies claims for potential harm sufferers by relieving them of the burden of identifying defendants and having to pursue multiple parties, and in this regard can be viewed as supporting the goal of prompt and adequate compensation. Channelling also reflects the lack of willingness of states to share in the burdens of risky activities, preferring instead to focus responsibility for harms on those actors most directly involved – an approach that is arguably in line with the polluter-pays principle. The channelling of liability runs the risk of reducing the range of available actors that can provide compensation if the primary responsible party is unable to do so. However, this risk is mitigated by the presence of robust insurance and compensation fund requirements. Relieving potentially responsible actors of liability (through channelling) may have indirect effects on the incentives of these actors to maintain high standards of care. Thus, for activities, such as the movement of hazardous waste, involving multiple phases and different risk creating actors, liability is more diffusely allocated. These concerns over incentives ought to be seen as being germane to regulatory actors, with attention being paid to conditions that will best promote high standards of regulatory oversight.

In the ABNJ context, there is no overarching approach to the allocation of liability. The approach under the Antarctic Liability Annex focuses on operators and de-emphasizes the responsibility of states in their capacity as regulators of Antarctic activities. The deep seabed mining regime must contend with the relative responsibilities of contractors, sponsoring states and the ISA, all of whom are identified in Part XI of UNCLOS as having key roles in protecting the marine environment and responding to incidents. The ISA's position is singular in international law and, as such, raises unique legal, political and practical questions concerning its position as a subject of liability. The SDC in its analysis confirmed the oversight responsibility of both the ISA and sponsoring states and connected these responsibilities to potential liability for harms arising from failures of due diligence. It is perhaps noteworthy that under the CRAMRA liability structure, states of mining entities bore some responsibility to ensure the compensation fund system was sufficient. No such role for sponsoring states of sponsored contractors under the deep seabed mining regime has been identified.

The allocation of liability will, of course, be strongly influenced by questions of causation. The approach to causation in international law has not received much attention from jurists and remains ambiguous on points that have been the source of contention in domestic environmental litigation. The larger concern, beyond questions of doctrinal clarity, is that in ABNJ and in relation to environmental harm generally, the causal pathways are often complex and involve multiple parties whose acts singly may not result in significant (and therefore unlawful) harm, but their cumulative effect does result in such an effect. The current focus of liability rules is on the harm from identifiable and often discrete pollution incidents, as opposed to long-term degradation from multiple actors and often multiple types of sources.

On very large-scale problems, such as ocean plastics pollution or ocean acidification from greenhouse gas emissions, the inability of legal doctrine to address cumulative causation issues effectively insulates states, international organizations and operators from liability. Loss and damage approaches may provide an alternative to cumulative causation problems as they do not focus on allocating liability to an identifiable actor but instead recognize that there is collective responsibility for certain environmental harms like climate change. Loss and damage approaches may still identify responsible parties, but could shift liability towards a looser coupling of specific wrongful acts and remedies.[214] For example, extreme weather events and slow onset events, identified in article 8 of the Paris Agreement, may be analogous to some of the diffuse and cumulative harms affecting the marine environment, such as oceans plastics pollution.[215]

214 Meinhard Doelle and Sara Seck, 'Introducing Loss and Damage' in Meinhard Doelle and Sara Seck (eds), *Research Handbook on Climate Change Loss and Damage* (Edward Elgar 2021) 1.

215 Maljean Dubois and Mayer (n 19).

5

Standards of Liability

5.1 INTRODUCTION

A threshold question for designing liability rules in any legal system is the degree of fault required to impose liability. At the core of this question are both moral and distributive considerations in determining when a loss that is suffered by one person – or in the case of environmental harm, by the community as a whole – ought to be shifted to another, usually to the person who caused the harm. The moral dimensions concern the characterization and degree of blameworthy conduct that is required to justify shifting the loss. The distributive dimensions carry with them a range of policy implications concerning the relative utility of the activity posing a risk of harm as compared to the harm itself, the ability of parties involved to bear a particular loss and practical concerns respecting the efficient and effective implementation of loss allocation measures.

One result of the complex array of considerations at play in addressing the appropriate standard of liability is that any consideration of this question is necessarily influenced by the context of its application. Where attempts have been made to develop generalized rules of international law concerning the approach to liability for environmental harm, the result has been a degree of conceptual confusion and no shortage of debate.[1] As a consequence, the rules respecting environmental liability have not developed as a unitary body of law common to all activities, but rather on a regime by regime basis with different approaches to the standard and scope of liability that respond to the regulatory setting of the activity.

With this diversity in mind, this chapter identifies the policy considerations that underlie different approaches to the standard of liability before examining the rules

[1] See Alan E Boyle, 'State Responsibility and Liability for Injurious Consequences of Acts Not Prohibited by International Law: A Necessary Distinction?' (1990) 39 ICLQ 1; Günther Handl, 'Liability as an Obligation Established by a Primary Rule of International Law: Some Basic Reflections on the International Law Commission's Work' (1985) 16 NYIL 49.

currently in place within the various global commons contexts. The approach to which entities are the main focus of liability is important to the issue of the standard chosen, as states and operators perform distinct functions in relation to the risk that bears on the justification for requiring fault, which has influenced state practice in this area.[2] As both approaches are used in the global commons contexts examined here, this chapter considers the rules that have developed in relation to both state responsibility and where liability is channelled to operators. Finally, this chapter examines the specific rules governing the standard of liability in the global commons.

In discussing the approach to liability, most legal systems distinguish between two main forms of liability: negligence, or fault-based liability, on the one hand, and strict liability, on the other.[3] Negligence regimes are defined as requiring a degree of fault, usually a breach of an identified standard of care, as well as a causal link between the activities undertaken by the subject of liability and the harm, in order to impose liability for environmental harm. The standard of care for negligence can be defined variably, but it is often identified as reasonably prudent or duly diligent behaviour, as evidenced by accepted standards of behaviour in the relevant area of activity. Extensive consideration is given in this chapter to the application of the due diligence standard to environmental harm prevention obligations on states. Strict liability, on the other hand, requires no proof of fault for a finding of liability in relation to harm, but does require causation. Strict liability may still allow certain defences or exceptions to the imposition of liability, such as acts of God, acts of war, necessity and third party or contributory negligence. Where there are no exceptions or very limited exceptions, the liability is often classified as being absolute in nature.[4] Given the limited application of absolute liability in international law,[5] this chapter focuses on the more binary distinction between fault and no-fault (strict) liability.

2 For general discussions of standards of liability in international environmental law, see Louise de La Fayette, 'International Liability for Damage to the Environment' in Malgosia Fitzmaurice, David M Ong and Panos Merkouris (eds), *Research Handbook on International Environmental Law* (Edward Elgar 2010) 320; Alan Boyle, 'Globalising Environmental Liability: The Interplay of National and International Law' (2005) 17 JEL 3; Philippe Sands and Jacqueline Peel, *Principles of International Environmental Law* (4th edn, CUP 2018) 746–748.

3 For a general discussion on liability approaches, see International Law Commission (ILC), 'Survey on Liability Regimes Relevant to the Topic International Liability for Injurious Consequences Arising Out of Acts Not Prohibited by International Law: Study Prepared by the Secretariat' (1995) II(1) ILC Yearbook 61.

4 See LFE Goldie, 'Concepts of Strict and Absolute Liability and the Ranking of Liability in Terms of Relative Exposure to Risk' (1985) 16 NYIL 175.

5 The Vienna Convention on Civil Liability for Nuclear Damage (adopted 21 May 1963, entered into force 12 November 1977) 1063 UNTS 265, amended by Protocol to Amend the Vienna Convention on Civil Liability for Nuclear Damage (adopted 12 September 1997, entered into force 4 October 2003) 2241 UNTS 270 (1997 Vienna Convention) art IV, is the only treaty that uses the term 'absolute', although the approach might better be described as strict, since it does allow for some limited exceptions.

5.2 POLICY CONSIDERATIONS UNDERLYING STANDARDS OF LIABILITY

The basic theory behind requiring fault as an element of attributing liability is an ethical or justice-based idea that a person who causes harm should only be compelled to compensate the person who suffers an associated loss where the person who causes the harm has acted wrongly in some fashion.[6] Where the incident in question is purely accidental, there is no moral reason for loss shifting. The requirement for fault is not punitive, since the goal is not to make the defendant worse off than they were before the incident, but rather corrective in the sense that compensation is tied to the plaintiff's loss.[7] Wrongfulness, of course, lies at the heart of the law of state responsibility, but only in the thin sense of arising by virtue of a breach of an international obligation.[8] However, the requirement for fault in a subjective sense is a function of the obligation in question.[9]

The difficulty with subjective fault requirements, such as negligence, is that, in the absence of fault, there is no liability, but the victim remains harmed through no fault of their own. Thus, in the absence of fault, the policy question that arises is who should bear the loss as between two potentially non-culpable actors. Creation of risk is most often raised as a basis for imposing liability without a requirement of proof of fault.[10] As a consequence, activities with higher degrees of risk are often subjected to strict forms of liability in both international and domestic law.[11] The presence of risk underlies the law of strict liability in common law tort regimes,[12] as well as

[6] Xue notes that the requirement for subjective fault as a basis for liability was noted by Grotius: 'Pure misfortunes do not deserve punishment, nor do they obligate anyone to make good the damage. Wrong acts do both'. Hanqin Xue, *Transboundary Damage in International Law* (CUP 2003) 297.

[7] Ernest J Weinrib, 'Corrective Justice in a Nutshell' (2002) 52 UTLJ 349.

[8] ILC, 'Draft Articles on Responsibility of States for Internationally Wrongful Acts, with Commentaries' (2001) UN Doc A/56/10 (ASR) art 2.

[9] ibid commentary to art 2, 34, para 3 (the ILC refers to art II of the Genocide Convention, which requires 'intent to destroy, in whole or in part, a national, ethnical, racial or religious group, as such . . .' as a necessary element of the wrongful act, as an example of subjective fault; that is, the breach depends upon the intention or knowledge of the state organ or agent).

[10] de La Fayette (n 2) 3; ILC, 'Draft Principles on the Allocation of Loss in the Case of Transboundary Harm Arising Out of Hazardous Activities, with Commentaries' (2006) UN Doc A/61/10 (Draft Principles) commentary to principle 4, 78, para 13.

[11] For a comparative analysis on domestic legal practices, see Elspeth Reid, 'Liability for Dangerous Activities: A Comparative Analysis' (1999) 48 ICLQ 731; ILC, 'Survey on Liability Regimes' (n 3); Monika Hinteregger, 'Environmental Liability' in Emma Lees and Jorge E Viñuales (eds), *Oxford Handbook of Comparative Environmental Law* (OUP 2019) 1025.

[12] See, for example, *Rylands v Fletcher* (1868) LR 3 HL 330 (UK) but see *Cambridge Water Co Ltd v Eastern Countries Leather plc* [1994] 1 All ER 53 (UK). In the United States, the approach is captured in the American Law Institute, *Restatement (Second) of Torts* § 46 (1965).

influencing liability in civil law jurisdictions.[13] Risk has also been raised as a basis for imposing strict liability on states where they engage in or authorize hazardous or 'ultra-hazardous' activities.[14]

Subjecting nuclear power, marine transport of oil and hazardous substances and the movement of living modified organisms to strict liability regimes reflects the risk concerns associated with those activities.[15] Risk in this context is a function of both the probability of harm and the severity of harm. Goldie further expands on the concept of risk by linking it to concerns respecting the unforeseeability of harm associated with certain activities, and related difficulties in determining acceptable standards of due diligence.[16] Goldie was thinking specifically about the harms arising from new technologies such as nuclear power and outer space activities. In such instances, it may be impossible for operators to reduce risks to acceptable levels through the exercise of due care, but it may nevertheless be desirable for the activities to be pursued. Thus, for Goldie, strict liability has a facilitative function, insofar as it creates conditions (indemnification of those harmed) that allow for the undertaking of activities that might otherwise not be permitted. Moreover, in the event of harm from technologically advanced and complex activities, proving negligence imposes a high evidentiary burden on injured parties.

What is less clear is the degree of risk that is required to justify applying a standard of strict liability. Should, for example, no-fault liability be restricted to 'ultra-hazardous' activities only? [17] And, if so, what differentiates these activities from more

[13] Hinteregger notes that Germanic countries draw a clear distinction between fault and strict liability based on risk, but the distinction is less clear in some other civil law jurisdictions, such as France, which uses a notion of 'presumptive' fault for certain identified activities; see Hinteregger (n 11) 1029; see also Reid (n 11) 743 et seq.

[14] C Wilfred Jenks, 'The Scope and Nature of Ultra-Hazardous Liability in International Law' (1968) 117 Recueil de Cours 99; LFE Goldie, 'Liability for Damage and the Progressive Development of International Law' (1965) 14(4) ICLQ 1189; Kerryn Brent, 'Solar Radiation Management Geoengineering and Strict Liability for Ultrahazardous Activities' in Neil Craik, Cameron SG Jefferies, Sara L Seck and Tim Stephens (eds), *Global Environmental Change and Innovation in International Law* (CUP 2018) 161.

[15] 1997 Vienna Convention (n 5); International Convention on Civil Liability for Oil Pollution Damage (adopted 29 November 1969, entered into force 19 June 1975) 973 UNTS 3 (1969 Oil Pollution Liability Convention), amended by the 1992 Protocol to Amend the 1969 International Convention on Civil Liability for Oil Pollution Damage (adopted 27 November 1992, entered into force 30 May 1996) 1956 UNTS 255 (1992 Oil Pollution Liability Convention); International Convention on Liability and Compensation for Damage in Connection with the Carriage of Hazardous and Noxious Substances by Sea (adopted 3 May 1996) (1996) 35 International Legal Materials (ILM) 1415 (1996 HNS Convention); Nagoya-Kuala Lumpur Supplementary Protocol on Liability and Redress to the Cartagena Protocol on Biosafety (adopted 15 October 2010, entered into force 5 March 2018) (2011) 50 ILM 105 (2010 Nagoya-Kuala Lumpur Supplementary Protocol).

[16] Goldie, 'Liability for Damage' (n 14) 1196–1197. See also Joni Charme, 'Transnational Injury and Ultra-hazardous Activity: An Emerging Norm of International Strict Liability' (1989) 4 J L & Tech 75.

[17] There is a degree of circularity in the definitions of ultrahazardous risk. Consider, for example, the following comment respect risk from the *Restatement (Second) of Torts*:

pedestrian forms of risk? The approach of imposing strict liability for ultrahazardous activities is found across different municipal law systems, with a high degree of variance as to what activities attract strict liability.[18] The US Restatement on the Law of Torts (Second) identifies the following factors:

> § 520: In determining whether an activity is abnormally dangerous, the following factors are to be considered: (a) existence of a high degree of risk of some harm to the person, land, or chattels of others; (b) likelihood that the harm that results from it will be great; (c) inability to eliminate the risk by the exercise of reasonable care; (d) extent to which the activity is not a matter of common usage; (e) inappropriateness of the activity to the place where it is carried on; and (f) extent to which its value to the community is outweighed by its dangerous attributes.[19]

While these factors may have some purchase in explaining the adoption of strict liability approaches within civil liability treaties, there is no generalizable approach in international law. Indeed, sub-paragraph (f), above, indicates a contextual approach where risk must be weighed against wider considerations of social utility. Thus, the determination of the approach to liability within sector-specific international regimes is more a function of state and industry policy preferences, and less a principled consideration of risk.

There is a further aspect to imposing liability on the basis of risk exposure that relates to sovereign equality and consent: the act of exposing others to risk that they cannot be presumed to have accepted justifies the imposition of liability without fault. Goldie notes that, unlike municipal legal systems that have sufficient authority to prohibit excessively risky activities, international law 'is still largely a system of permissive and facultative norms', which in turn justifies the imposition of strict or absolute liability.[20] The reasoning here is that states should not be able to unilaterally impose high levels of risk on other (equally sovereign) states without their consent. Strict liability apportions that risk by making the source state or operator responsible for the harm occasioned by its choice. Goldie's approach is also influenced by distributive questions, particularly the degree to which the benefits from the activity are shared amongst states. Where activities involve socially beneficial outcomes, the utility structure favours the imposition of a fault-based, or at least a less stringent, approach, since there is a more balanced distribution of risks and

The essential question is whether the risk created is so unusual, either because of its magnitude or because of circumstances surrounding it, as to justify the imposition of strict liability for the harm that results from it, even though it is carried on with all reasonable care. In other words, are its dangers and inappropriateness for the locality so great that, despite any usefulness it may have for the community, it should be required as a matter of law to pay for any harm it causes, without the need of a finding of negligence. (cited by Charme at 78) (American Law Institute, *Restatement (Second) of Torts* (1965)).

[18] For an overview of civil and common law approaches, see Hinteregger (n 11) 1025.

[19] *Restatement (Second) of Torts* (n 17).

[20] Goldie, 'Liability for Damage' (n 14) 1221.

benefits.[21] Goldie analogizes the imposition of risk to a form of expropriation, suggesting the standard of liability is influenced by the nature of sovereign interests that affected states have in the impacted environment.[22] The preferred approach is a liability rule that allows the activity to be carried out, but with payment of compensation in the event that another state's sovereign interests are interfered with, as opposed to a rule that would prevent invasion of the interest without consent.[23]

These concerns permeated the approach taken by Quentin-Baxter and Barboza in their roles as special rapporteurs in the International Law Commission's (ILC) work on liability, where the approach was to impose liability without proof of fault, but to subject the allocation of losses to a form of equitable balancing.[24] In effect, the sovereign rights of both the source state – to engage in lawful but risky activities – and the affected state – to not be subjected to risk of harm without its consent – had to be reconciled, which in turn gives rise to the introduction of equity as a means of apportioning liability. While the approach was ultimately rejected as flawed and not supported by state practice, the concerns respecting exposure to risk and consent remain an important factor.

Considerations of the degree to which states may consent to activities and may benefit from those activities have some clear application to commons activities. Arguably, the sovereign interests affected in areas beyond national jurisdiction (ABNJ) are more attenuated and depend upon the characterization of the legal interest of states in the area or resource in question. In relation to activities on the high seas, which may be undertaken by states unilaterally, and the benefit of which accrues entirely to the state undertaking or authorizing the activity, the structure looks similar to transboundary harm, particularly if the interests of states in the global commons are viewed as sovereign amenities. For example, cable-laying is undertaken with little international oversight and is an activity that any state may engage in, subject to the due regard of other high seas freedoms and activities, yet may impose risks on states or on the international community as a whole, on which they have little say. Similarly, states have a wide margin of freedom to undertake scientific and tourism activities in the Antarctic, but in doing so impose risks of the

[21] Concern over the distributive tensions between socially desirable (or at least legally permissible) activities and the harmful consequences of those activities informed much of the earlier work on liability by the ILC, particularly the approach of Special Rapporteur Quentin-Baxter.

[22] Goldie, 'Liability for Damage' (n 14) 206–213.

[23] While Goldie does not frame it in quite these terms, the approach captures the distinction between types of entitlement rules (liability versus property) introduced by law and economic scholars, Guido Calabresi and A Douglas Melamed, 'Property Rules, Liability Rules, and Inalienability: One View of the Cathedral' (1972) 85 Harv L Rev 1089. (Goldie does not cite this paper but cites Calabresi throughout his 1985 paper on international liability.)

[24] These approaches are summarized by ILC, 'First Report on the Legal Regime for Allocation of Loss in the Case of Transboundary Harm Arising Out of Hazardous Activities, by Mr. Pemmaraju Sreenivasa Rao, Special Rapporteur' (2003) II(1) ILC Yearbook 71, paras 6–14 (describing the reliance by both Quentin-Baxter and Barboza on negotiation and a balancing of interests as a means to settle compensation arising from environmental harm).

international community from those activities. The ILC notes, with reference to a survey undertaken on national liability regimes, that '[t]he case for strict liability is strengthened when the risk has been introduced unilaterally by the defendant'.[25]

The role of consent further complicates matters. For example, deep seabed mining is structured as a communally regulated activity, in which all parties to the 1982 United Nations Convention on the Law of the Sea (UNCLOS) have a degree of control over through their participation in the organs of the International Seabed Authority (ISA).[26] Not only are the risks of deep seabed mining not imposed unilaterally, but a portion of the benefits of the activity are to be equitably shared.[27] In this regard, the structure of the deep seabed mining regime may militate against the imposition of strict liability – at least on the basis that the allocation of risks and benefits justify shifting losses to the sponsoring state or operators under the sponsoring state's jurisdiction.

Risk is not only a function of the nature of the activity but is also affected by the nature of the receiving environment. Where the potentially affected environment is fragile or less resilient, the risks of harm posed by activities carried out in those areas are heightened. The absence of scientific knowledge respecting impacts may also be viewed as a source of risk since the environmental outcomes are more challenging to predict. In these circumstances, reasonable steps may be difficult to determine *ex ante*, providing further justification for strict liability approaches in environmental sensitive ecosystems or receiving environments characterized by high levels of uncertainty. Such concerns have been raised in connection with the deep seabed and the Antarctic environment.[28]

There is also an intergenerational element to risk allocation insofar as future generations neither consent to nor benefit (directly) from risky activities, but where unforeseeable or non-negligent environmental harm arises, the costs of addressing that harm is often borne by future generations through unremedied harm.[29] This may particularly be the case in relation to commons resources where the victim of

[25] Draft Principles (n 10) commentary to principle 4, 78, para 13.

[26] See Agreement Relating to the Implementation of Part XI of the United Nations Convention on the Law of the Sea (adopted 28 July 1994, entered into force 28 July 1996) 1836 UNTS 3 (1994 Implementation Agreement) Annex, s 3(11)(a) (requiring the ISA Council to authorize of Plans of Work for activities in the Area). See also discussion in Chapter 1.

[27] United Nations Convention on the Law of the Sea (adopted 10 December 1982, entered into force 16 November 1994) 1833 UNTS 397 (UNCLOS) art 140.

[28] See, for example, Lisa Levin and others, 'Defining "Serious Harm" to the Marine Environment in the Context of Deep-Seabed Mining' (2016) 74 Mar Pol'y 245; Peter Convey and Lloyd S Peck, 'Antarctic Environmental Change and Biological Responses' (2019) 5 Science Advances 11.

[29] Resolution on Responsibility and Liability under International Law for Environmental Damage (adopted 4 September 1997) (1998) 67(2) Annuaire de l'Institut de Droit International 486 art 25.

the harm is the international community. The intergenerational dimensions of liability have been an emerging trend in atmospheric trust litigation.[30]

Standards of liability may also respond to other shared objectives in international law. Viewed in light of an environmental harm prevention objective, strict liability may be justified as a means to promote deterrence of risky behaviour by providing greater incentives for operators to take steps to prevent accidental damage. This rationale applies equally, if not more, to fault-based liability, since what is sought to be deterred most often is intentional, reckless or negligent behaviour. In a no-fault context, the rationale of deterrence focuses on the imposition of a higher standard of care than mere non-negligence in order to avoid harms that are viewed as socially undesirable. In the case of pollution, deterrence also reflects the notion that harm prevention is preferred to compensation, given that some environmental harms may be difficult or impossible to restore, and that the full measure of harm is not easily quantifiable. As a regulatory matter, operators are much better positioned to take risk minimization measures, and therefore placing a higher standard facilitates greater care, as the law requires that the operator take all steps to prevent harm, not just those that are reasonable. In the absence of strict liability, operators are able to externalize the costs of measures taken to protect the environment that go beyond mere negligence.

In relation to states in their oversight role, it may be argued that strict liability might result in more vigilant oversight of operators. However, accidents that are causally connected to weak oversight would likely result in liability under a due diligence standard, and a higher standard would not prevent unforeseen or purely accidental harm. Strict liability for states has some potential to make more funds available for addressing harm since the responsible state effectively becomes the insurer of the operator, but this would depend on the financial capabilities of the state in question, and there may be more effective ways, such as pooled insurance and compensation funds, to achieve that goal.[31]

As a matter of environmental protection, and as a reflection of economic efficiency, cost internalization is often cited as a desirable policy goal.[32] Cost internalization may promote more efficient methods of loss sharing through insurance or compensation schemes, which spread the risk amongst operators and better protect

[30] Described in Mary C Wood and Charles W Woodward IV, 'Atmospheric Trust Litigation and the Constitutional Right to a Healthy Climate System: Judicial Recognition at Last' (2016) 6 Wash J Envtl L & Pol'y 634.

[31] On the other hand, where the state is the operator, as may be the case in Antarctic research activities or where the state is undertaking seabed mining activities, the deterrence rationale may militate in favour of the imposition of a strict standard, particularly where non-state actors are subject to strict liability.

[32] See Organization for Economic Co-operation and Development (OECD), 'The Polluter-Pays Principle' (1992) OECD/GD(92)81. The appropriate standard of liability from an efficiency standpoint has been the subject of much attention by law and economics scholars, see Steven Shavell, 'Strict Liability versus Negligence' (1980) 9 JLS 1.

against unfunded harm due to insufficient funds. No-fault regimes may also provide for simplified dispute settlement processes, since the claimant is relieved of the burden of proving fault and may therefore be preferred on efficiency grounds; a goal that might be seen as being present under international law in the requirement for 'prompt' compensation.[33]

Cost internalization is reflected in the inclusion of the polluter-pays principle in international declarations and treaties.[34] The polluter-pays principle has some clear purchase in the area of marine pollution,[35] and is identified as a relevant principle in relation to marine pollution from oil transport.[36] Outside the marine pollution area, it has been linked to strict liability under the Lugano Convention on Civil Liability for Damage Resulting from Activities Dangerous to the Environment.[37] The polluter-pays principle has been referenced as a core principle in both the deep seabed mining regime and the negotiations of a new international legally binding instrument (ILBI) on marine biodiversity beyond national jurisdiction.[38] As an allocation rule, the polluter-pays principle favours placing costs associated with environmental harm on the operator, not the victim, and in this regard favours strict liability.[39] The principle reflects the goal of deterrence and harm prevention, as well as recognizing that responsibility should follow those actors who benefit from activity. The principle is not without qualification and provides room for policy choices respecting exceptions and limitations on liability.[40]

33 UNCLOS (n 27) art 235(2).

34 United Nations General Assembly 'Report of the United Nations Conference on Environment and Development' (3–14 June 1992) UN Doc A/Conf.151/26/Rev.1 (1992) Annex I (1992 Rio Declaration) principle 16. See also Priscilla Schwartz, 'Principle 16: The Polluter Pays Principle' in Jorge E Viñuales (ed), *The Rio Declaration on Environment and Development: A Commentary* (OUP 2015) 429; ILC, 'Third Report on the Legal Regime for the Allocation of Loss in the Case of Transboundary Harm Arising Out of Hazardous Activities, by Mr. Pemmaraju Sreenivasa Rao, Special Rapporteur' (2006) II(1) ILC Yearbook 71, paras 27–30.

35 Convention for the Protection of the Marine Environment of the North-East Atlantic (adopted 22 September 1992, entered into force 25 March 1998) 2354 UNTS 67 art 2(2)(b); Convention on the Protection of the Marine Environment of the Baltic Sea Area (adopted 9 April 1992, entered into force 17 January 2000) 2099 UNTS 195 art 3(4).

36 Patricia Birnie, Alan Boyle and Catherine Redgwell, *International Law and the Environment* (4th edn, OUP 2021) 341–342.

37 Lugano Convention on Civil Liability for Damage resulting from Activities Dangerous to the Environment (adopted 21 June 1993) (1993) 32 ILM 1228 preamble ('Having regard to the desirability of providing for strict liability in this field taking into account the "Polluter-Pays Principle"').

38 International Seabed Authority (ISA), 'Draft Regulations on Exploitation of Mineral Resources in the Area' (2019) ISBA/25/C/WP.1 (DER) reg 2; Further revised draft text of an agreement under the United Nations Convention on the Law of the Sea on the conservation and sustainable use of marine biological diversity of areas beyond national jurisdiction, Note by the President UN Doc A/CONF.232/2022/5, 1 June 2022 (2022 Draft ILBI Text) art 5.

39 Birnie and others (n 36) 343.

40 ILC, 'Third Report on the Legal Regime for the Allocation of Loss in the Case of Transboundary Harm Arising Out of Hazardous Activities' (n 34) para 30.

5.3 APPROACHES TO STANDARDS OF LIABILITY IN INTERNATIONAL LAW

The two principal approaches to addressing liability for environmental harm in international law involve leaving states as the primary subjects of liability through rules of state responsibility, or by channelling liability directly to operators.[41] The approaches are not mutually exclusive. Where states opt to develop a civil liability regime, they may not necessarily divest themselves of responsibility, but rather make operators liable in the first instance.[42] The policy choice regarding which party shall be primarily responsible is severable from the decision respecting the standard of liability, but in practice, states have opted to couple strict liability with civil liability regimes that channel liability to the operator, while maintaining a requirement for wrongful activity (fault-based liability, at least in the sense of a breach of international obligation) in relation to state responsibility for environmental harm.

5.3.1 *State Responsibility*

The default rules for state liability for environmental harm combine two fundamental rules. The first establishes the primary obligation on states to prevent transboundary harm. This obligation applies to activities under state control and includes harm to both the territory of other states, as well as harm to areas or resources beyond national jurisdiction. The crucial feature of the no-harm rule for current purposes is that it is a rule of due diligence; that is, the standard of liability is negligence-based, not strict. The second is the basic rule of state responsibility that maintains that states are responsible for the harm that flows from breaches of their international obligations. Thus, this rule requires the responsible state to make reparations for the injury caused by wrongful acts that are attributable to the state.[43] Reparations include restitution and compensation by way of damages.[44]

The due diligence obligation to prevent harm is well established in international law. The rule has been recognized in numerous decisions of international courts and tribunals,[45] and finds expression in numerous treaties,[46] as well as in Principle

41 Discussed in Chapter 2.

42 See discussion in Chapter 3. Although, the effect of channelling liability may foreclose the ability of victims of harm to pursue claims against third parties, including states.

43 ASR (n 8) art 31, 91.

44 ibid art 34, 95.

45 *Legality of the Threat or Use of Nuclear Weapons* (Advisory Opinion) [1996] ICJ Rep 226, 241–242, para 29; *Pulp Mills on the River Uruguay (Argentina v Uruguay)* (Judgment) [2010] ICJ Rep 14; *Certain Activities Carried Out by Nicaragua in the Border Area (Costa Rica v Nicaragua) and Construction of a Road in Costa Rica along the San Juan River (Nicaragua v Costa Rica)* (Judgment) [2015] ICJ Rep 665; *Iron Rhine Arbitration (Belgium v Netherlands)* (Award) Oxford Reports on ICGJ 373 (PCA 2005) para 222.

46 Convention on Biological Diversity (adopted 5 June 1992, entered into force 29 December 1993) 1760 UNTS 79 art 3; United Nations Framework Convention on Climate Change

21 of the 1972 Stockholm Declaration and Principle 2 of the 1992 Rio Declaration.[47] Ultimately, after consideration of state practice, the ILC adopted a due diligence standard in relation to the obligation of states to prevent transboundary harm,[48] while leaving the precise contours of liability to be determined in accordance with the obligation to provide recourse for victims of harm through domestic or other agreed upon mechanisms.[49]

The extension of the no harm principle to areas beyond national jurisdiction is explicitly recognized in Principle 21 and Principle 2, and is reflected in treaty commitments concerning commons resources, such as the deep seabed,[50] the high seas,[51] as well as the Antarctic environment.[52] The Seabed Disputes Chamber (SDC) considered the nature of the due diligence obligations owed by sponsoring states in the context of mining activities in the Area. The SDC described the nature of the sponsoring states obligations flowing from the specific provisions within Part XI of UNCLOS as follows:

> The sponsoring State's obligation 'to ensure' is not an obligation to achieve, in each and every case, the result that the sponsored contractor complies with the aforementioned obligations. Rather, it is an obligation to deploy adequate means, to exercise best possible efforts, to do the utmost, to obtain this result. To utilize the terminology current in international law, this obligation may be characterized as an obligation 'of conduct' and not 'of result', and as an obligation of 'due diligence'.[53]

The reasoning of the SDC concerning due diligence was subsequently adopted by the International Tribunal for the Law of the Sea (ITLOS) and applied to the obligations of flag states in relation to fisheries activities in the exclusive economic zone, and more broadly to obligations to conserve living resources with the marine environment.[54]

(adopted 9 May 1992, entered into force 21 March 1994) 1771 UNTS 107 preamble, para 8; Convention on the Law of the Non-Navigational Uses of International Watercourses (adopted 21 May 1997, entered into force 17 August 2014) (1997) 36 ILM 700 art 7; Convention on Environmental Impact Assessment in a Transboundary Context (adopted 25 February 1991, entered into force 10 September 1997) 1989 UNTS 309 art 2.

47 Declaration of the United Nations Conference on the Human Environment (1972) UN Doc A/Conf.48/14/Rev.1 (1972 Stockholm Declaration); 1992 Rio Declaration (n 34).

48 ILC, Draft Articles on Prevention of Transboundary Harm from Hazardous Activities, with Commentaries, UN Doc a/56/10 (Draft Articles on Prevention of Transboundary Harm) art 3.

49 Draft Principles (n 10) principle 4, 76.

50 UNCLOS (n 27) art 145.

51 ibid arts 192 and 117 (duty to take measures to conserve living resources of the high seas).

52 Protocol on Environmental Protection to the Antarctic Treaty (adopted 4 October 1991, entered into force 14 January 1998) (1991) 30 ILM 1461 (1991 Antarctic Protocol) arts 2–3.

53 *Responsibilities and Obligations of States Sponsoring Persons and Entities with Respect to Activities in the Area* (Advisory Opinion of 1 February 2011) International Tribunal for the Law of the Sea (ITLOS) Reports 2011, 10 (*Activities in the Area* Advisory Opinion) para 110.

54 *Request for an Advisory Opinion Submitted by the Sub-Regional Fisheries Commission (SRFC)* (Advisory Opinion of 2 April 2015) ITLOS Reports 2015, 4 (SRFC Advisory Opinion) paras 125–139.

As discussed earlier, a number of commentators, inside and outside the ILC's work on 'international liability for injurious consequences arising out of acts not prohibited by international law', have argued in favour of imposing a no-fault standard in relation to those activities that can be classed as ultrahazardous in nature.[55] The principal justification relates to the role of the source state in authorizing the risk. In such circumstances, the source state voluntarily creates a risk, which is involuntarily borne by the affected state. Despite the broad acceptance of the underlying logic, the support for such a principle in international law is weak. The regimes respecting nuclear facilities, oil pollution and other hazardous activities have all channelled liability to the operator, and thus, do not speak to state liability. The only example of strict liability imposed directly on states is the 1972 Convention on International Liability for Damage Caused by Space Objects,[56] and the Cosmos 954 claim that was filed under that treaty.[57]

The approach taken in relation to space objects can be distinguished from other state activities in the commons on the basis of the role of the state in the activity in question. Unlike the placement of space objects, which may be understood as an activity (at least until recently) requiring direct state involvement, in other commons activities, such as fisheries or deep seabed mining, the sponsoring state is only involved in the activity in its oversight role. Thus, the issue of control, which is fundamental to the deterrence justification,[58] is indirect. Liability for oversight activities is unquestionably fault-based. Where states are acting as operators, for example as contractors in relation to activities in the Area, they will typically be subject to the same liability requirements applicable to other (non-state) operators. This is also evident in the Liability Annex adopted under the Antarctic Treaty system, where state and non-state operators are subject to strict requirements to respond to environmental emergencies, albeit with each subject to different procedural requirements.[59]

The issue of risk was addressed by the 2011 *Activities in the Area* Advisory Opinion, where in the context of considering the content of due diligence, the SDC notes:

> The content of 'due diligence' obligations may not easily be described in precise terms. . . . It may change over time as measures considered sufficiently diligent at a

[55] See Jenks (n 14); Goldie, 'Liability for Damage' (n 14); See also the Resolution on Responsibility and Liability under International Law for Environmental Damage (n 29) art 4.

[56] Convention on International Liability for Damage Caused by Space Objects (adopted 29 March 1972, entered into force 1 September 1972) 961 UNTS 187 art II.

[57] Protocol between the Government of Canada and the Government of the USSR (entered into force 2 April 1981) (1981) 20 ILM 689.

[58] de La Fayette (n 2) 327.

[59] 2005 Annex VI to the Environmental Protocol on Environmental Protection to the Antarctic Treaty on Liability Arising from Environmental Emergencies (adopted 17 June 2005, not yet entered into force) (2006) 45 ILM 5 (Liability Annex) art 6.

> certain moment may become not diligent enough in light, for instance, of new scientific or technological knowledge. It may also change in relation to the risks involved in the activity. As regards activities in the Area, it seems reasonable to state that prospecting is, generally speaking, less risky than exploration activities which, in turn, entail less risk than exploitation. . . . The standard of due diligence has to be more severe for the riskier activities.[60]

The approach to risk, therefore, is not to alter the standard of liability, but to vary the content of due diligence. States may be held to a high standard of vigilance in relation to riskier activities, but the basis of liability will be the failure of the state to meet the standards of conduct that the particular context requires, and not causation alone. The SDC also considers the relationship between due diligence and the precautionary principle,[61] noting that precaution is 'an integral part of the general obligation of due diligence'.[62] This then requires that the sponsoring state incorporates prudential risk assessment in exercising due diligence. Consistent with the approach cited above, the precaution does not operate to alter the standard of liability, but rather informs the content of the standard of care.

5.3.2 *Civil Liability*

5.3.2.1 Approach to Liability

While international law does not support strict liability for states in connection with transboundary (including impacts to areas beyond national jurisdiction) environmental harm, states are under an obligation to take measures to ensure prompt and adequate compensation in the event of harm occurring.[63] These measures may be taken in their domestic legal systems or through collective measures, such as sector-specific civil liability regimes.[64] The current sectors where civil liability regimes have been negotiated include nuclear facilities,[65] oil pollution, carriage of

60 *Activities in the Area* Advisory Opinion (n 53) 117.

61 The Exploration Regulations for Nodules and Sulphides both require the sponsoring state and the Authority to 'apply the precautionary principle, as reflected in Principle 15 of the Rio Declaration'; ISA, 'Regulations on Prospecting and Exploration for Polymetallic Nodules in the Area' (2013) ISBA/19/C/17 (PMN) reg 31(2); ISA, 'Regulations on Prospecting and Exploration for Polymetallic Sulphides in the Area' (2010) ISBA/16/A/12/Rev.1 (PMS) reg 33(2).

62 *Activities in the Area* Advisory Opinion (n 53) para 131.

63 Draft Principles (n 10) principle 4, 76.

64 See discussion in Chapter 2.

65 Convention on Third Party Liability in the Field of Nuclear Energy (adopted 29 July 1960, entered into force 1 April 1968) 956 UNTS 251 (amended by 1964 and 1982 Protocols) (Convention on Third Party Liability); 1997 Vienna Convention (n 5); Convention on Supplementary Compensation for Nuclear Damage (adopted 12 September 1997, in force 15 April 2015) (1997) 36 ILM 1473.

hazardous and noxious substances by sea,[66] bunker oil,[67] hazardous waste,[68] transboundary movement of living modified organisms[69] and Antarctic activities.[70] The standard of liability for operators under these civil liability regimes is strict but not absolute.[71] The standard of strict liability is implemented through a provision that indicates that the responsible party 'shall be liable for any pollution damage' caused by the activity in question.[72] In order to recover damages, the claimant need only prove a causal link between the activity and the damage.

The policy justifications for imposing strict liability, as discussed above, include the objective to ensure prompt and adequate compensation, including available compensation for remediation and reinstatement of environmental harm; the desire to encourage a high standard of care and deter pollution; the polluter-pays principle; the recognition of the fairness of having the creator of risks (as opposed to the victim) bear losses associated with that activity; and the greater efficiency of providing for compensation without proof of fault. As the entity that directly controls the activity, the policy justification for a strict standard is stronger for operators than for states. Similarly, the polluter-pays principle is more clearly applicable to operators (who are directly causally responsible for harm).

The exclusion of environmental damage to areas beyond national jurisdiction under civil liability regimes is a reflection of the uncertainty of standing to recover for harm in areas beyond national jurisdiction, but also points to the incompleteness of civil liability regimes in responding to the preventive and remedial aims of compensation.[73] The 2001 Bunker Oil Convention, for example, cites both articles 194 and 235 of UNCLOS in its preamble, indicating an intent to address 'all damage caused by pollution of the marine environment', but goes on to exclude damages in areas beyond national jurisdiction.[74]

While states have adopted a consistent approach to operator liability in international civil liability regimes, it remains an open question whether the duty to take measures to ensure prompt and adequate compensation requires the adoption of a strict liability standard in all cases involving hazardous or ultrahazardous activities.

66 Basel Protocol on Liability and Compensation for Damage Resulting from Transboundary Movement of Hazardous Wastes and their Disposal (adopted 10 December 1999) UNEP/CHW.1/WG/1/9/2 (1999 Basel Liability Protocol).

67 International Convention on Civil Liability for Bunker Oil Pollution Damage (adopted 23 March 2001, entered into force 21 November 2008) UNTS No 47 (2012) (2001 Bunker Oil Convention).

68 1999 Basel Liability Protocol (n 66).

69 2010 Nagoya-Kuala Lumpur Supplementary Protocol (n 15).

70 Liability Annex (n 59).

71 But see 1997 Vienna Convention (n 5).

72 1992 Oil Pollution Liability Convention (n 15) art III(1); see also 1996 HNS Convention (n 15) art 7; Convention on Third Party Liability (n 65) art 3.

73 1992 Oil Pollution Liability Convention (n 15) art II; 1996 HNS Convention (n 15) art 3; 1999 Basel Liability Protocol (n 66) art 3(a).

74 2001 Bunker Oil Convention (n 67) preamble and art 2.

The argument is different from the discussion above on whether states are themselves strictly liable for ultrahazardous activities under their jurisdiction or control, as the subject of liability here is the operator not the state itself, and therefore flows indirectly from the obligation to provide prompt and adequate compensation. This is the approach of the ILC in the Draft Principles,[75] although the ILC's position appears to reflect more of a policy preference than a recognition of an established or emerging requirement in international law.[76]

Generalizing from the practice derived from civil liability regimes is challenging because each regime reflects the particular constellation of interests amongst the states, operators and providers of financial assurance, as reflected in a variety of approaches to exceptions and liability caps. Nonetheless, the consistent imposition of strict liability on operators indicates a high degree of consensus amongst states that strict liability best serves the multiple objectives of liability regimes, and, as such, creates a high burden of justification on states that seek to use a fault-based approach. While the civil liability conventions tend to exclude harm to the commons as compensable damage, the considerations that have informed the preference for strict liability approaches apply equally to harm in areas beyond national jurisdiction.

5.3.2.2 Exceptions to Liability

Liability is said to be strict, not absolute, because each civil liability regime contains exceptions to the imposition of liability, which range in their breadth.[77] Even the 1997 Vienna Convention, which identifies the imposed standard as 'absolute',[78] contains a narrow set of exonerating circumstances, namely incidents due to armed conflict and 'a grave natural disaster of an exceptional character'.[79] More typically, treaties contain a longer list of exceptions,[80] which include:

75 Draft Principles (n 10) principle 4(2). The Resolution on Responsibility and Liability under International Law for Environmental Damage (n 29) adopts a similar position.

76 Methodologically, the ILC does not review state practice, but rather notes the approach taken towards liability for environmental harm in different legal systems and emphasizes the consistency of strict liability with the underlying purposes of compensation set out in principle 3. See Draft Principles (n 10) commentary to principle 3, 74–76, paras 12–18.

77 1992 Oil Pollution Liability Convention (n 15) art III(2); 1971 International Convention on the Establishment of an International Fund for Compensation for Oil Pollution Damage (adopted 18 December 1971, entered into force 16 October 1978) 1110 UNTS 57 (amended by the 1992 Protocol on the International Convention on the Establishment of an International Fund for Compensation for Oil Pollution Damage, 27 November 1992) (1992 Fund Convention) art 4(2); 1991 Antarctic Protocol (n 52) Annex VI art 8; 2010 Nagoya-Kuala Lumpur Supplementary Protocol (n 15) art 6; 1996 HNS Convention (n 15) art 4(2)(3); 1999 Basel Liability Protocol (n 66) art 4(5).

78 1997 Vienna Convention (n 5) art IV(1).

79 ibid art IV(3).

80 For example, 1992 Oil Pollution Liability Convention (n 15) art III(2); 1996 HNS Convention (n 15) art 7(2).

- Armed conflict;
- Intentional damage by a third party;
- Contributory negligence (the incident resulted from the intentional or negligent actions of the claimant);
- Damage caused by government negligence;
- The result of 'a natural phenomena of exceptional, inevitable, unforeseeable and irresistible character'; or[81]
- Damage caused as a result of compliance with a compulsory measure of a public authority.[82]

The presence of exceptions moves away from a rigid application of polluter-pays and appears to be largely driven by issues of fairness and control. For example, exonerations based on governmental contributory negligence or compliance with governmental measures respond to the inequities of imposing liability on an operator where the fault lies elsewhere. The natural phenomena exception can be justified on the basis that the exonerating circumstances are limited to those instances where the event is unforeseeable and the resulting damage cannot be guarded against. Given that the liabilities are typically insured against as part of the scheme, the exceptions may also reflect the unwillingness of insurers to cover wholly unforeseeable events.

5.3.2.3 Liability Caps under Civil Liability Regimes

The other common feature of civil liability regimes is the practice of limiting liability to identified compensation caps on a per incident basis. The presence of liability caps responds to the practicality of insurance and pooled compensation funds, since insurers and funds cannot take on limitless liability.[83] The approach is a further derogation from the application of the polluter-pays principle, as it may result in victims of environmental harms having to bear some of the losses themselves. Coupling liability caps with strict liability approaches reflects the greater acceptability from an ethical standpoint of relieving a non-negligent, but causally responsible, party from the obligation to provide full compensation. Of course, the absence of a fault requirement does not necessarily mean that the responsible party did not act without requisite care. However, the efficiencies associated with a more simple, strict liability approach counterbalance the desirability of holding negligent parties fully responsible. However, the 1999 Basel Liability Protocol provides for unlimited liability where the harm is a result of 'wrongful intentional, reckless or

81 1999 Basel Liability Protocol (n 66) art 4(5).
82 ibid.
83 Discussed in Chapter 8.

negligent acts or omissions',[84] which is consistent with imposing a higher degree of responsibility (in terms of compensation) for morally wrongful acts.

The amount and structure of the caps is highly variable, but there are some evident attempts to match the amounts to reasonably anticipated claims. For example, where the maximum liability amounts in the nuclear regime appeared insufficient following the Chernobyl incident, the amounts were raised.[85] A similar reaction has been seen in the oil pollution regime where severe incidents led to concerns about unfunded damages, which in turn led to higher overall ceilings. Thus, despite the practical considerations surrounding insurability, there remains an evident desire to prevent loss shifting to victims of harm.

5.4 STANDARDS OF LIABILITY IN ABNJ

5.4.1 *Antarctic*

While not in force, the Convention on the Regulation of Antarctic Mineral Resource Activities (CRAMRA) provides a useful example of the structure of liability rules in the Antarctic in the face of risky activities. CRAMRA, which sets out the rules and procedures governing mineral resource exploitation in the Antarctic, contains specific liability rules that impose strict liability on the operator for broadly defined environmental harms and economic losses arising from its resource activities.[86] The operator's liability is subject to very narrow exceptions, namely damage caused by 'a natural disaster of an exceptional character' and armed conflict.[87] The liability rules are incomplete, and a further protocol was contemplated (but never negotiated), which may have contained further provisions placing limits on liability, in conjunction with financial assurances and the establishment of a fund.[88] The liability provision of CRAMRA also addresses state liability in article 8(3) which provides for sponsoring state liability, where the sponsoring state's failure to carry out its oversight obligations under the Convention contributed (from a causation standpoint) to compensable damage.[89] The distinction between operators and sponsoring states is functional in that states, when involved directly as resource operators, will be subject to the strict standard of liability. Fault-based liability will apply to states in their oversight capacity.

84 1999 Basel Liability Protocol (n 66) art 5.

85 See the amendments made by the Protocol to Amend the Vienna Convention on Civil Liability for Nuclear Damage (adopted 12 September 1997, entered into force 4 October 2003) 2241 UNTS 270 (n 5).

86 Convention on the Regulation of Antarctic Mineral Resource Activities (adopted 2 June 1988, not yet entered into force) (1988) 27 ILM 868 (CRAMRA).

87 ibid art 8(4).

88 ibid art 8(6).

89 ibid art 8(3). Liability is residual, in the sense that the state is only liable for that portion of the damages not satisfied by the operator.

The subsequent negotiation of the 1991 Protocol on Environmental Protection to the Antarctic Treaty (1991 Antarctic Protocol) prohibits extractive activities in the Antarctic in accordance with the objective to prioritize the conservation and protection of the Antarctic environment, effectively denouncing the objectives of the CRAMRA.[90] The structure of the principal obligations respecting environmental protection under the 1991 Antarctic Protocol are conduct, not result, based.[91] Liability rules and procedures are governed by a separate Annex, the negotiation of which was anticipated under the 1991 Antarctic Protocol.[92] As discussed in Chapter 2, the approach has an administrative posture in that the primary obligation in the face of an environmental emergency is a 'response action'. Liability flows from the failure to take appropriate response actions, and damages are related to the costs actually incurred or estimated for the response action.[93] Operator liability is strict but subject to exceptions and liability caps.[94] Although, the liability caps do not apply to damage arising from acts that are committed with intention to cause an emergency or recklessness.[95] The state liability provision adopts a fault-based standard, with states only being held liable for the failure of an operator to take response actions where the state failed to take 'appropriate measures within its competence, including the adoption of law and regulations, administrative actions and enforcement measures, to ensure compliance with the Annex'.[96] The content of due diligence will reflect the obligations on states to protect the Antarctic environment as specified in the 1991 Antarctic Protocol such as carrying out environmental assessments, and monitoring activities,[97] but also reflects general customary legal requirements respecting harm prevention.

5.4.2 *Deep Seabed*

The rules governing liability from activities in the Area are a combination of general provisions within UNCLOS, provisions dealing with deep seabed mining specifically found within Part XI and Annex III of UNCLOS, and requirements found within the regulations enacted by the ISA. There is no special liability regime that has been developed by the ISA to date, although the need for such rules has been

[90] 1991 Antarctic Protocol (n 52) art 7.
[91] ibid art 3.
[92] ibid art 16.
[93] Liability Annex (n 59) art 6 (where no response action is taken, the operator is liable for the estimated costs of the response action that should have been taken. The money is paid into a fund created under the Liability Annex.)
[94] ibid arts 8–9.
[95] ibid art 9(3).
[96] ibid art 10.
[97] 1991 Antarctic Protocol (n 52) art 8 and Annex I (setting out specific requirements for environmental impact assessments, including monitoring; see Annex I, art 5).

acknowledged by the ISA.[98] In keeping with other sector-specific liability regimes, the liability rules for deep seabed mining distinguish between the liability of contractors (operators) and of sponsoring states. UNCLOS also recognizes that the ISA, which shares oversight duties with sponsoring states, may also be liable for damages arising from its own activities.[99]

For contractors, liability for damage arising from their activities in the Area is addressed in Annex III, article 22, which provides that 'contractors shall have responsibility or liability for any damages arising out of wrongful acts in the conduct of its operations . . .'.[100] The phrase 'wrongful act' should not be interpreted as requiring fault-based liability. 'Wrongful' in this context should be taken to mean that liability will flow from a breach of legal requirements to which the contractor is subjected to. Article 22 of Annex III is analogous to the basic rule of state responsibility that recognizes that liability flows from breaches of international law attributable to the state.[101] The requirements for fault will be determined by the specific requirements imposed on contractors by UNCLOS and the rules enacted by the ISA.

The obligation on contractors to prevent environmental harm in relation to exploration activities is set out in the ISA's regulations. As it stands under the Exploration Regulations,[102] the standard of liability imposed on contractors requires a failure of due diligence. Regulation 31(5) of the Regulations on Prospecting and Exploration for Polymetallic Nodules in the Area (PMN) is framed as a duty of conduct to take 'necessary measures to prevent, reduce and control pollution and other hazards to the marine environment arising from its activities in the area *as far as reasonably possible*, applying a precautionary approach and best environmental practices'.[103] Accidental damages that arise despite all reasonable measures being taken or damages that are unforeseen are not currently 'wrongful', and therefore, not compensable under the ISA's rules. Although, where the failure to comply with a direct, primary obligation results in harm – for example, failing to comply with an emergency order – non-compliance ought to be viewed as wrongful, with liability consequences flowing from the non-compliance.[104] It is open for the ISA to impose a strict liability standard on contractors through the enactment of further rules that entail obligations of result. The potential for the development of rules further specifying compensation obligations is expressly contemplated in UNCLOS.[105] The ISA's Draft Exploitation Regulations (DER) takes a similar administratively

98 ISA, 'Report of the Chair of the Legal and Technical Commission' (22nd Session, 11–22 July 2016) (2016) ISBA/22/C/17.

99 UNCLOS (n 27) Annex III art 22.

100 ibid.

101 ASR (n 8) commentary to art 2, 35, para 7.

102 PMN (n 61) reg 31(5).

103 ibid reg 31(5) (emphasis added).

104 ibid reg 30 and Annex IV s 16.

105 UNCLOS (n 27) arts 235(3) and 304.

oriented approach, whereby contractor liability flows from its wrongful acts, which could include obligations of conduct and result.[106]

The liability of sponsoring states was addressed comprehensively by the SDC in its 2011 Advisory Opinion.[107] The principal obligations on sponsoring states are contained in article 139(1) and article 4(4) of Annex III of UNCLOS, both of which impose a 'responsibility to ensure' that mining activities are carried out in accordance with the requirements of Part XI.[108] The focus of these provisions is on the oversight functions of the sponsoring states; although to be clear, the wording of article 139 is directed towards all states parties, not just sponsoring states. These obligations were characterized by the SDC as being those requiring adherence to standards of conduct, namely 'due diligence'.[109]

The content of due diligence is driven by the treaty language and context, but also appears to be influenced by more general customary rules governing state obligations to prevent environmental harm. The primary requirements of due diligence require states to adopt 'reasonably appropriate' laws and regulations and to take measures to secure compliance.[110] The SDC enumerates a set of further obligations that must be complied with as a measure of due diligence:

- The obligation to assist the Authority in the exercise of control over activities in the Area;
- The obligation to apply a precautionary approach;
- The obligation to apply best environmental practices;
- The obligation to take measures to ensure the provision of guarantees in the event of an emergency order by the Authority for protection of the marine environment;
- The obligation to ensure the availability of recourse for compensation in respect of damage caused by pollution; and
- The obligation to conduct environmental impact assessments.[111]

The relationship between these obligations and due diligence is complex. As noted, they are constituent factors that contribute to the state's general obligation to take reasonable steps to prevent harm to the marine environment. However, these obligations are separate or direct obligations on the sponsoring state (each of which is identified under the rules applicable to deep seabed mining), and as such, states

[106] At the time of writing, the Legal and Technical Commission (LTC) has prepared a set of Draft Exploitation Regulations: ISA, DER (n 38).
[107] *Activities in the Area* Advisory Opinion (n 53).
[108] ibid para 105 ('rules, regulations and procedures of the Authority, and the contracts').
[109] ibid para 110.
[110] ibid paras 117–118, relying on Annex III art 4(4).
[111] ibid para 122.

are required to comply with each of these obligations independently from their general obligation to ensure contractor compliance.[112]

The SDC also considered the question of whether the development status of the sponsoring state is a relevant factor in determining the reasonableness of the oversight steps taken by the sponsoring state. In holding that the obligations apply equally to all states regardless of development status, the SDC relies on the specific wording of Part XI, which discloses no intent to differentiate oversight obligations on the basis of development status.[113] The SDC also observes that, were responsibilities to be differentiated between developing states and developed states, there may be incentives for contractors to seek sponsorship from states that are subject to a lesser set of oversight obligations, linking the uniform content of due diligence to 'the highest standards of protection of the marine environment, the safe development of activities in the Area and the protection of the common heritage of mankind'.[114]

The obligation on sponsoring states to provide recourse for victims of harm within their domestic legal systems under article 235 is also viewed as part of that state's due diligence obligations. This obligation requires states assure 'prompt and adequate compensation'. As discussed above, the standard of 'prompt and adequate compensation' supports, but does not require, the imposition of strict liability. The SDC points out that article 235(2) ensures that the contractor can live up to its obligation to provide reparation for damages caused by its wrongful acts. It appears open for the sponsoring state to impose domestic rules that provide for strict liability, regardless of the approach taken by the ISA, although this may turn on whether imposing a strict standard is seen as being 'inconsistent with Part XI'.[115] This provision does allow sponsoring states to adopt rules that are 'more stringent' than those adopted by the Authority, which may provide greater latitude for sponsoring states to impose a strict liability standard.[116] Article 235(3) recognizes that states may also address this objective through the development of a specialized international (civil) liability regime, which could include compulsory insurance or compensation funds.[117]

As the first of the enumerated direct obligations indicates, sponsoring states do not have sole responsibility for oversight of mining operators. These responsibilities are

[112] See *Certain Activities* (n 45) (debating whether an environmental impact assessment is a distinct customary obligation from due diligence), but in the context of deep seabed mining, these constituent elements are independently identified obligations contained in UNCLOS and the ISA Exploration Regulations and the DER. Moreover, due diligence, or reasonableness is likely the measure by which these distinct obligations will be assessed.

[113] *Activities in the Area* Advisory Opinion (n 53) para 158.

[114] ibid para 159.

[115] UNCLOS (n 27) Annex III art 21(3).

[116] ibid art 209 frames the duty to adopt laws and regulations 'no less effective than international rules' to control pollution from activities in the Area under a state's jurisdiction as a requirement.

[117] UNCLOS (n 27) art 235(3); the important role that such funds could play in avoiding gaps in liability coverage was noted by the SDC in its Advisory Opinion: *Activities in the Area* Advisory Opinion (n 53) paras 205 and 208.

shared with the ISA. Consequently, the ISA is also liable for damages arising out of its own wrongful conduct.[118] The standard of liability for the ISA is not addressed in the SDC's 2011 Advisory Opinion, but flows from its obligations in article 153 to 'exercise such control over Activities in the Area as is necessary for the purpose of securing compliance with the provisions of this Part'.[119] While the wording of the obligations of the ISA does not match with that of sponsoring states ('responsibility to ensure'), the thrust of the obligation to oversee is the same, and, ought, therefore, to be understood as requiring due diligence.

5.4.3 *High Seas*

The standard of liability for activities causing harm within the high seas area will again be a function of the specific obligations to prevent harm. The nature of the commitments within UNCLOS to protect the marine environment and its resources was the subject of the *Sub-Regional Fisheries Commission Advisory Opinion* (SRFC Advisory Opinion) issued by the ITLOS in 2015,[120] as well as the *South China Sea Arbitration*.[121] The SRFC Advisory Opinion was concerned with the obligations of flag states to prevent illegal, unreported and unregulated fishing activity in the exclusive economic zones of other states, but the reasoning of the ITLOS applies equally to activities in the high seas.[122] In reviewing these obligations,[123] the ITLOS notes that flag states are required to exercise 'effective jurisdiction and control in administrative matters' over fishing vessels subject to their jurisdiction.[124] This requires flag states to adopt appropriate laws and to take measures to ensure compliance with those laws.[125] As a set of oversight obligations, the standard of liability is due diligence.[126] The ITLOS adopts the reasoning of the SDC in its 2011 *Activities in the Area* Advisory Opinion as to the variable and contextual nature of due diligence. Due diligence obligations extend to international organizations, such as the European Union, that exercise jurisdiction over aspects of the activities in question.

One important clarification respecting the nature of due diligence provided in the *SRFC* Advisory Opinion relates to the relationship between harm and due

[118] UNCLOS (n 27) Annex III art 22.
[119] ibid art 153(4).
[120] SRFC Advisory Opinion (n 54).
[121] *The South China Sea Arbitration (The Republic of Philippines v The People's Republic of China)* (Award) (2016) Oxford Reports on ICGJ 495 (PCA) (*South China Sea Arbitration*).
[122] SRFC Advisory Opinion (n 54) para 120 (noting the application of UNCLOS art 192 to all maritime zones).
[123] Throughout the SRFC Advisory Opinion (n 54) ITLOS identifies UNCLOS arts 91, 92, 94, 192, 193, as well as arts 58(3) and 62(4), as principal sources of flag state obligations.
[124] ibid para 119.
[125] ibid paras 134–139.
[126] SRFC Advisory Opinion (n 54) para 125.

diligence. The issue was framed in terms of whether flag states could be found to have breached their due diligence obligations in the event of isolated illegalities or whether a breach required a more sustained pattern of illegality. In holding that the frequency of illegal fishing activity is not a relevant consideration, the ITLOS centres the analysis of due diligence on the adequacy of the measures taken, not the frequency of the illegal activity.[127] In principle, the reasoning is sound; liability will flow where a causal relationship between environmental harm and insufficient oversight can be demonstrated. In practice, however, determining the reasonableness of the oversight will be influenced by the degree of compliance that the measures are likely to bring about.

The *SRFC* Advisory Opinion does not address the issue of the relative capabilities of states in relation to their due diligence obligations, but there may be reasons to consider whether the approach of the SDC on this issue is generalizable to activities in the high seas. There are provisions within UNCLOS that may be relevant to the determination of the standard of oversight required. For example, article 194(1) requires states to take measures to prevent marine pollution 'in accordance with their capabilities'. The 1996 London Protocol to the Convention on the Prevention of Marine Pollution by Dumping qualifies the obligation to protect and preserve the marine environment in a similar fashion.[128] Notably, however, the recognition of the relevance of differentiation capabilities is not present in other key provisions on oversight obligations in the high seas, including the obligation to conserve living resources,[129] and the provisions requiring states to 'take all necessary measures to ensure activities under their jurisdiction' are conducted so as not to cause pollution in areas outside of their jurisdiction.[130] In this regard, the approach of the SDC is more important than the result. What is required is a careful consideration of the specific obligations and the context of their application, as well as the minimal reasonable requirements for 'vigilance, employment of infrastructure and monitoring of hazardous activities' that are expected.[131] Given that developed states are under obligations to share technologies and contribute to the capacities of developing states, the availability of such mechanisms and support to developing states is a further salient consideration.[132]

[127] SRFC Advisory Opinion (n 54) para 150.

[128] Protocol to the Convention on the Prevention of Marine Pollution by Dumping of Wastes and Other Matter (adopted 17 November 1996, entered into force 24 March 2006) (1997) 36 ILM 1 art 2 ('according to their scientific, technical and economic capabilities').

[129] UNCLOS (n 27) art 117.

[130] ibid art 194(2).

[131] ILC, Draft Articles on Prevention of Transboundary Harm (n 48), commentary to art 3, 155, para 17 (also noting 'it is, however, understood that the degree of care expected of a State with a well-developed economy and human and material resources and with highly evolved systems and structures of governance is different from States which are not so well placed').

[132] Contained in UNCLOS (n 27), arts 202 and 203, Part XIV.

As with fisheries, there is no specialized regime for liability for environmental harm arising from shipping activities in the high seas. The result is that the default standard of liability will reflect general obligations of due diligence for states and domestic negligence standards for operators. States have the ability to impose strict liability on ships operating (flagged) under their jurisdiction, but the incentives to do so are minimal in the absence of international cooperation to impose a uniform standard. The *SRFC Advisory Opinion* has relevance for the standard of conduct that applies to flag states, including those states that maintain open registries, in relation to oversight of shipping activities. Article 94 requires any state to 'exercise its jurisdiction and control in administrative, technical and social matters over ships flying its flag'.[133] A failure to exercise due diligence exposes the flag state to liability for environmental harm that is causally connected to oversight failures.

Standard limitations of liability under the Convention on Limitation of Liability for Maritime Claims (1976 LLMC) may still serve to limit liability regardless of the standard imposed.[134] While the 1996 Protocol to amend the 1976 LLMC (1996 LLMC Protocol) exempts claims arising under the oil pollution liability regime, the non-application of the oil pollution liability rules to areas beyond national jurisdiction means that the 1976 LLMC limits will have broad application to environmental claims in the high seas.[135] The one exception to the fault-based standard is the transportation of nuclear materials by sea that is covered under the 1997 Vienna Convention, which applies to damage 'wherever suffered', including the high seas.[136]

Due diligence, as a standard of required state behaviour, has a broad application to other high seas activities or to matters affecting the high seas, with implications for the development of new liability rules for emerging ocean activities and concerns, including marine genetic resources,[137] ocean acidification[138] and ocean fertilization.[139] The difficulty is not with extending the general obligation to emerging circumstances, but rather with identifying the content of the standard of care. In relation to state responsibility, what amounts to reasonable oversight steps will depend upon the surrounding normative environment. In the deep seabed mining

[133] ibid art 94.

[134] Convention on Limitation of Liability for Maritime Claims (adopted 19 November 1976, entered into force 1 December 1986) 1456 UNTS 221 (1976 LLMC), and Protocol of 1996 to Amend the Convention on Limitation of Liability for Maritime Claims, 1976 (adopted 2 May 1996, entered into force 13 May 2004) Can TS 2008 No 18 (1996 LLMC Protocol).

[135] 1976 LLMC (n 134) art 3.

[136] 1997 Vienna Convention (n 5) art 1A.

[137] Hua Zhang, 'The Obligation of Due Diligence in Regulating the Marine Genetic Resources in Areas beyond National Jurisdiction' in Keyuan Zou (ed), *Global Commons and the Law of the Sea* (Brill Nijhoff 2018) 286.

[138] Karen Scott, 'Ocean Acidification: A Due Diligence Obligation under the LOSC' (2020) 35 IJMCL 382.

[139] Karen Scott, 'Geoengineering and the Marine Environment' in Rosemary Rayfuse (ed), *Research Handbook on International Marine Environmental Law* (Edward Elgar 2015) 451.

context, the SDC draws on the regulatory framework with Part XI, as elaborated upon in the ISA's regulations. While the SDC focused on the application of due diligence to sponsoring states, it is equally clear that the contractor's standard of care will be assessed in light of the regulatory requirements of the regime. Similarly, state oversight of ocean fertilization activities is likely to be assessed in light of the requirements of the 1996 London Protocol.[140] Generally accepted international rules and standards (GAIRS) will also play an important role in defining the standard of care, although the lower density of regulations and guidance in the high seas that could structure the content of state and private actor due diligence will pose some challenges in determining applicable standards of conduct with precision.

5.5 CONCLUSIONS

At the heart of the policy question concerning standards of liability is the distribution of losses following an event which causes harm to third parties, be they states or individuals. The prevailing approach within the law of state responsibility is not to impose a strict standard on states in relation to activities under their jurisdiction or control. States are simply unwilling to become the insurers of environmentally risky activities, preferring instead to oversee these activities with due diligence. It is unsurprising that in relation to activities affecting the commons environment that states have not been more open to moving towards a strict standard. The distributive calculus of risk in the commons does not favour a strict standard since states are not required to bear the full risk of environmental harm themselves, but are to share that risk with all states, and in many cases, with future generations. Restricting loss-shifting to failures of state due diligence subjects the international community to risks that they neither consent to nor control, although states can influence the content of the standard of care through their own oversight actions and through the development of international standards of duly diligent conduct. The concerns, first raised by Goldie, with foreseeability of harm for emerging activities and where there is an absence of clear standards of behaviour, have ongoing purchase in commons activities, where the risks to the environment are often less well understood.

The shifting of losses to third parties and to the international community as a whole can, however, be substantially mitigated through the imposition of strict liability standards on operators. The greater willingness to use strict liability standards in civil liability regimes is again a reflection of risk distribution, where the victims of environmental harm, which often include states themselves, are less diffuse. There is a growing association between the obligation on states to provide

[140] See art 6 bis and Annex 4 addressing marine geoengineering in the 2013 amendments to the 1996 Protocol to the 1972 Convention on the Prevention of Marine Pollution by Dumping of Wastes and Other Matter: Amendment to the London Protocol to Regulate the Placement of Matter for Ocean Fertilization and Other Marine Geoengineering Activities, Resolution LP.4 (8) (adopted 18 October 2013).

prompt and adequate compensation and the imposition of strict liability on operators. This association reflects a policy preference, as opposed to being an obligation. However, the consistent adoption of strict liability standards for activities that pose clear transboundary risks, including risks to commons resources, raises a strong presumption in favour of strict operator liability, albeit accompanied by liability caps. Insofar as strict liability incentivizes higher standards of care and reduces the risk of environmental harm that is not remediated, the rationale supporting no-fault liability applies with equal force to the global commons.

6

Standing to Bring Claims for Environmental Harm in Areas beyond National Jurisdiction

6.1 INTRODUCTION

Standing requires a particular claimant to have a sufficient *legal* interest to make a claim, as opposed to *access* to a particular court or tribunal (which is discussed in Chapter 7).[1] Most legal systems, including international law, locate this right in the injury to a material interest protected by law; which is to say an interest that relates to the personal integrity, property or economic interests of the potential claimant. Environmental harm claims often raise collective legal interests due to the shared benefits that environmental resources confer, and legal systems must develop rules determining under what conditions these legal interests may be protected by individual members of the group or collectively by rights holders. Environmental harm claims in areas beyond national jurisdiction (ABNJ) raise paradigmatic issues of standing because of the collective nature of environmental interests in these areas, including who has the right (or obligation) to take the necessary response action to address environmental harm.

Notwithstanding these difficulties, both international law and national law recognize that certain actors have sufficient legal interest to bring claims for environmental damage despite not directly suffering injury or loss.[2] These developments reflect an increasing recognition of the intrinsic value of the environment and shifting conceptions of the environment as a collective good subject to community interests. However, the parameters of the concepts that affirm collective interests in

[1] Standing is an aspect of admissibility of a claim and is separate from the jurisdiction of a court or tribunal to hear the claim. Pok Yin S Chow, 'On Obligations Erga Omnes Partes' (2021) 52 Geo J Int'l L 469, 498.

[2] There is scholarly literature as well as practice that recognizes that 'nature' has rights of standing. See, for example, Christopher D Stone, 'Should Trees Have Standing – Toward Legal Rights for Natural Objects' (1972) 45 S Cal L Rev 450; Peter Burdon and Claire Williams, 'Rights of Nature: A Constructive Analysis' in Douglas Fisher (ed), *Research Handbook on Fundamental Concepts of Environmental Law* (Edward Elgar 2016) 196.

the protection of the environment are nebulous and the scenarios in which they would apply are likely to be contested.

In considering the application of the rules of standing in ABNJ, this chapter explores trends in standing in relation to the environment under international law, civil liability regimes and national law before turning to how the specific regimes governing areas beyond national jurisdiction address the issue of standing. The interest in domestic legal approaches is more conceptual but may inform international practice by analogy and at the level of general principles of law.

6.2 GENERAL APPROACHES TO STANDING FOR ENVIRONMENTAL HARM

6.2.1 *Standing under International Law*

6.2.1.1 States

The rules on standing are closely connected to the nature of the relief sought and are consequently influenced by evolving understandings of the types of harms recognized as compensable by international law.[3] Here it is useful to consider three distinct types of harm in ABNJ that will each trigger unique considerations for standing. First, states or their nationals may suffer direct harm to economic interests in ABNJ. For example, environmental harm could affect the ability of an actor to pursue living or non-living resource exploitation activities in ABNJ for which they have a right to access, for example, when fishing in the high seas is suspended in response to a pollution incident. Such harm relates less to the environment and more to the effects of environmental harm on an activity or resource for which a potential claimant has a property or economic interest. Second, states or actors under their jurisdiction may incur losses from undertaking preventive or reinstatement measures to protect or preserve the environment in ABNJ. These actions may be undertaken where a state feels these measures are necessary to protect maritime zones under their jurisdiction or other sovereign interests or a state or international organization could potentially undertake such actions where the sole purpose is to protect and preserve the environment in ABNJ. In this case, some loss is sustained by the actor taking these preventive or reinstatement measures. Could, for example, a non-state actor that seeks to remove oceans plastics seek damages from states or other actors that are the principal source of that form of pollution?[4] Finally, there are cases where a state or other actors seek compensation for unrestored (and often interim)

[3] For a more detailed discussion on the definition of environmental damage, see Chapter 3.

[4] This is not an abstract scenario as the non-profit organization registered in the Netherlands, The Ocean Cleanup, has been attempting to utilize huge booms to collect plastic in accumulation zones such as the Great Pacific Garbage Patch in ABNJ: see <https://theoceancleanup.com/about/> accessed 1 September 2022.

harm to the environment, what is often described as 'pure environmental loss' or 'environmental damage *per se*'. In this scenario, there is no identifiable actor that has suffered quantifiable harm or loss.[5] This section considers how international law may address the standing of states, international organizations and non-state actors to pursue liability claims for environmental harm in these different contexts.

Standing to bring environmental harm claims against states is generally confined to 'injured states', as reflected in article 42 of the International Law Commission's (ILC) 2001 Draft Articles on the Responsibility of States for Internationally Wrongful Acts (ASR).[6] The 'injured state' is the 'state whose individual right has been denied or impaired by the internationally wrongful act or which has otherwise been particularly affected by that act'.[7] Article 42 stipulates that a state is entitled 'as an injured state' to invoke the responsibility of another state if the obligation breached is owed to

> (a) that State individually; or
> (b) a group of States including that State, or the international community as a whole, and the breach of the obligation
>   (i) specially affects that State; or
>   (ii) is of such a character as radically to change the position of all the other States to which the obligation is owed with respect to the further performance of the obligation.[8]

The ASR do not define 'injured state', but specify that an injury 'includes any damages, whether material or moral, caused by the internationally wrongfully act'.[9] The distinction between the circumstances outlined in subparagraphs (a) and (b) relate to the nature of the obligation owed, but both fundamentally require that the invoking state suffer an injury that arises due to the breach of obligation. The more likely situation in ABNJ are breaches of obligations that are owed to a group of states, as most international rules governing aspects of ABNJ tend to be communal not bilateral. However, where a state suffers direct material injury to its interests as a result of environmental harm in ABNJ, it will satisfy the requirements of being specially affected. For example, the commentary to article 42 observes that 'a specially affected state' may arise in the 'case of pollution of the high seas in breach of article 194' of the 1982 UN Convention on the Law of the Sea (UNCLOS) as this 'may particularly impact on one of several States whose beaches may be polluted by

5 International Law Commission (ILC), 'Draft Principles on the Allocation of Loss in the Case of Transboundary Harm Arising Out of Hazardous Activities, with Commentaries' (2006) UN Doc A/61/10 (Draft Principles) commentary to principle 2, 67–68, para 14.

6 ILC, 'Draft Articles on Responsibility of States for Internationally Wrongful Acts, with Commentaries' (2001) UN Doc A/56/10 (ASR) art 42, 117.

7 ibid commentary to principle 42, 116, para 2.

8 ibid art 42(b)(ii), 117.

9 ibid art 31(2), 92.

toxic residues or whose coastal fisheries may be closed'.[10] Accordingly, 'independently of any general interest of the States parties to [UNCLOS] in the preservation of the marine environment, those coastal States parties should be considered as injured by the breach'.[11] Injury to the coastal state here is simply an example of a material injury to the legally protected interests of the injured state. Such interests could include rights or interests exercisable in ABNJ, such as damage to a submarine cable or interference with established fishing rights.[12] Article 42 does not require that the harm be suffered exclusively by the injured state, but rather that the nature of the harm is distinct from any communal harm.

The more difficult legal question is how broadly or narrowly the notion of 'specially affected' is to be interpreted. One could conceive of circumstances – for example, an incident of pollution leading to damage to a high seas fish stock which a particular state had traditionally fished, or a state having to take specific response measures to mitigate an incident of pollution on the high seas – that could warrant the designation of a specially affected injured state under the rules of state responsibility.[13] However, this characterization is contingent on the claimant state showing some form of specific loss or damage. Fisheries, for example, are *res communis* and are subject to the freedom of the high seas – a state must establish that even though it did not have sovereign rights over the fisheries resource *per se*, it had a sufficient connection with it in that its loss directly or indirectly harmed it. This may be demonstrated by having a right to harvest certain fishery resources under a fisheries management agreement or acceptance by states of historic reliance on the fishery in question. The acceptance of a claim for standing will, thus, be context dependent and contingent upon the surrounding rights.

The case of a state seeking compensation for undertaking a response action deserves particular attention. The argument is that undertaking a response action, even though it is not required to do so, results in the state suffering damages that are unique. Under the Liability Annex to the 1991 Antarctic Protocol (discussed in Section 6.3.1), states are empowered to take response actions to protect resources in the Antarctic Treaty Area, and there are specific rules that provide for recovery in

[10] United Nations Convention on the Law of the Sea (adopted 10 December 1982, entered into force 16 November 1994) 1833 UNTS 397 (UNCLOS).

[11] ASR (n 6) commentary to art 42, 119, para 12.

[12] UNCLOS (n 10) art 87 which specifically mentions the freedom of fishing and the freedom to lay submarine cables as high seas freedoms exercisable by all states.

[13] International Convention Relating to Intervention on the High Seas in Cases of Oil Pollution Casualties (adopted 29 November 1969, entered into force 6 May 1975) 970 UNTS 211 (Intervention Convention) affirms the right of a coastal state to take such measures on the high seas necessary to prevent, mitigate or eliminate danger to its coastline or related interests from oil pollution or the threat thereof after a maritime casualty but only provides that the coastal state is liable to pay compensation for any damage caused by such measures that go beyond what is permitted by the Convention. This has been reflected in UNCLOS (n 10) art 221.

those circumstances.[14] States are not specifically authorized to take response actions in connection with high seas pollution, but a state could potentially rely on articles 192 and 194 of UNCLOS to argue that states are entitled to take positive steps to protect and preserve the environment, including response measures. If the response action is to prevent harm to the acting state's own environment, there is a stronger argument that the state is specially affected and entitled to take reasonable steps to protect harm to its territorial interests.[15] The correct approach is far from clear, and raises issues concerning what have been called 'officious intermeddlers' in domestic legal settings – that is, actors who voluntarily undertake actions for the benefit of others and then seek compensation.[16] The distinction between 'officious' and 'necessitous' intermeddlers has not arisen in international law and some care must be taken to import such concepts. Nonetheless, a robust doctrine of necessitous intervention is consistent with calls by legal scholars to approach the question of 'specially affected' states from a remedial standpoint: Peel, for example, has suggested a liberal approach along the following lines:

> [o]ne possible solution to the difficulties posed in attempting to fit breaches of collective environmental obligations ... within the framework of the category of specially affected States, is to interpret the specially affected requirement broadly to include States with some reasonable nexus to the damage suffered, over and above a general interest in the protection of the environmental resource damaged.[17]

The above discussion focused on when there is some form of material injury but there are also situations where there is no 'injured state' *per se*. In this case, article 48 (1) of the ASR states:

> [a]ny State other than an injured State is entitled to invoke the responsibility of another State ... if (a) the obligation breached is owed to a group of States including that State, and is established for the protection of a collective interest of the group; or (b) the obligation breached is owed to the international community as a whole.[18]

The ILC's intention was to address those obligations where there may be no injured states to invoke responsibility for a breach, but felt it 'highly desirable' that states

[14] Annex VI to the Protocol on Environmental Protection to the Antarctic Treaty on Liability Arising from Environmental Emergencies (adopted 17 June 2005) (2006) 45 ILM 5 (Liability Annex).

[15] See Intervention Convention (n 13).

[16] John McCamus, 'Necessitous Intervention: The Altruistic Intermeddler and the Law of Restitution' (1979) 11 Ottawa L Rev 297.

[17] Jacqueline Peel, 'New State Responsibility Rules and Compliance with Multilateral Environmental Obligations: Some Case Studies of How the New Rules Might Apply in the International Environmental Context' (2001) 10(1) RECIEL 82, 86. But see Kevin Jon Heller, 'Specially-Affected States and the Formation of Custom' (2018) 112(2) AJIL 191, 223.

[18] ASR (n 6) art 48, 126.

other than an injured state be entitled to take some measures in order 'to protect the community or collective interest at stake'.[19]

Article 48 (1) (a) refers to what has been described in the commentary to this article in the ASR as obligations *erga omnes partes*, that is, obligations owed between a group of states derived from multilateral treaties or customary international law, and established for the protection of a collective interest of the group.[20] It is based on the SS *Wimbledon* case brought by the United Kingdom, France, Italy and Japan for Germany's breach of its obligations under the 1919 Treaty of Versailles when it denied the passage of the United Kingdom registered vessel (chartered by a French company) through the Kiel Canal.[21] The Permanent Court of International Justice (PCIJ) affirmed that both Italy and Japan 'had a clear interest in the execution of the provisions relating to the Kiel Canal, since they all possessed fleets and merchant vessels flying their respective flags'.[22] Notwithstanding the fact that they had not suffered any interference in their pecuniary interests, the Court recognized that they were an 'Interested Power' under article 368 (1) of the Treaty which gave them the right to institute proceedings before it.[23] In effect, the doctrine recognizes that states do not need to wait until they are harmed by a breach of an obligation that is owed to them in order to take legal steps to address the breach.

Article 48 (1) (b) reflects the concept of general obligations *erga omnes* or obligations of a state towards the international community as a whole, as articulated in the *obiter* statement of the International Court of Justice (ICJ) in *Barcelona Traction*:

> ... an essential distinction should be drawn between the obligations of a State towards the international community as a whole, and those arising vis-à-vis another State in the field of diplomatic protection. By their very nature, the former are the concern of all States. In view of the importance of the rights involved, all States can be held to have a legal interest in their protection; they are *erga omnes*.
>
> Such obligations derive, for example, in contemporary international law, from the outlawing of acts of aggression, and of genocide, as also from the principles and rules concerning the basic rights of the human person, including protection from slavery and racial discrimination. Some of the corresponding rights of protection have entered into the body of general international law (Reservations to the Convention on the Prevention and Punishment of the Crime of Genocide,

19 Priya Urs, 'Obligations *Erga Omnes* and the Question of Standing before the International Court of Justice' (2021) 34(2) LJIL 505, 508; ASR (n 6) commentary to art 48, 127, para 12.

20 For obligations *erga omnes partes*, two conditions must be met: first, the obligation whose breach has given rise to responsibility must have been owed to a group to which the state invoking responsibility belongs; second, the obligation must have been established for the protection of a collective interest established by a treaty or customary international law: see ASR (n 6) commentary to art 48, 126, para 6.

21 ibid commentary to art 48, 126, para 7.

22 SS *Wimbledon* [1923] Permanent Court of International Justice Reports Series A No 1, 15.

23 ibid.

Advisory Opinion, ICJ Reports 1951, p. 23); others are conferred by international instruments of a universal or quasi-universal character.[24]

The ASR do not identify which primary obligations are obligations *erga omnes* or *erga omnes partes* under article 48, and there are differing views on what type of obligations are *erga omnes partes* or *erga omnes* owed to the international community as a whole.[25] The lack of consensus surrounding the nature of *erga omnes* has led some to argue that the concept of *erga omnes* remains shrouded in uncertainty.[26] That said, international courts and tribunals have explicitly recognized several examples of *erga omnes* obligations such as prohibitions against aggression, slavery, racial discrimination, genocide,[27] the right to self-determination[28] and the rules of international humanitarian law embodying 'elementary considerations of humanity'.[29] At the same time, these courts and tribunals have not elucidated why these obligations should be considered *erga omnes*, meaning that the identification of such obligations remains opaque.[30] For *erga omnes partes* obligations, the ASR cite examples such as the environment or security of a region and note that they are not limited to arrangements established only in the interests of member states but would

[24] *Barcelona Traction, Light and Power Company, Limited (Belgium v Spain); Second Phase* [1970] ICJ Rep 3 (*Barcelona Traction*) paras 33–34. For references to *erga omnes* obligations prior to *Barcelona Traction*, please see Maurizio Ragazzi, *The Concept of International Obligations Erga Omnes* (Clarendon Press 1997) 7–12.

[25] Christian J Tams, *Enforcing Obligations Erga Omnes in International Law* (CUP 2005) 119. A case in point is the debate that occurred in the ILC on whether the obligation of states to protect the atmosphere is an obligation *erga omnes*. The commentary to Draft Guideline 3 which set out the due diligence obligation of states to protect the atmosphere noted that it was 'without prejudice to whether or not the obligation to protect the atmosphere is an *erga omnes* obligation in the sense of' article 48 of the ASR (n 6) as it was subject to different views. The commentary went on to note '[w]hile there is support for recognizing that the obligations pertaining to the protection of the atmosphere from transboundary atmospheric pollution of global significance and global atmospheric degradation are obligations erga omnes, there is also support for the view that the legal consequences of such a recognition are not yet fully clear in the context of the present topic'. See ILC, 'Report of the International Law Commission' (70th Session, 30 April–1 June and 2 July–10 August 2018) UN Doc A/73/10, 175.

[26] For a discussion on the uncertainty of the concept of *erga omnes* obligations, please see Tams (n 25) 99–116.

[27] *Barcelona Traction* (n 24) para 34; *Case Concerning Armed Activities on the Territory of the Congo (Democratic Republic of the Congo v Rwanda)* (Jurisdiction and Admissibility) [2006] ICJ Rep 6, para 71; *Application of the Convention on the Prevention and Punishment of the Crime of Genocide (The Gambia v Myanmar)* (Order for Provisional Measures) [2020] ICJ Rep 3 (*The Gambia v Myanmar* case 2020) para 41.

[28] *Case Concerning East Timor (Portugal v Australia)* [1995] ICJ Rep 90, para 29; *Legal Consequences of the Separation of the Chagos Archipelago from Mauritius in 1965* (Advisory Opinion) [2019] ICJ Rep 95, para 180.

[29] *Legal Consequences of the Construction of a Wall in the Occupied Palestinian Territory* (Advisory Opinion) [2004] ICJ Rep 136, paras 155 and 157.

[30] Tams (n 25) 118–119. Arguably, the *Barcelona Traction* case provides some guidance. The court emphasized that to be *erga omnes*, it must protect important values, suggested by the statement 'in view of the importance of the rights involved, all States can be held to have a legal interest of obligations … *erga omnes*': *Barcelona Traction* (n 24) para 33.

extend to agreements established by a group of states in some wider common interest, transcending the sphere of bilateral relations of states parties.[31] The commentary does not elaborate on what was meant by collective interest except to say that the principal purpose would be to foster a 'common interest, over and above any interests of the States concerned individually'.[32]

The question of the *erga omnes* status of norms has arisen in relation to ABNJ resources and/or the environment. For example, in the 2014 *Whaling in the Antarctic* case, Australia alleged that Japan had violated the International Convention for the Regulation of Whaling (ICRW) although it had not suffered any direct injury.[33] The Court, without expressly saying so, 'accepted the position that Australia had purported to act in the collective interest and on that basis engaged Japan's responsibility for the breach of obligations *erga omnes partes*'.[34] Similarly, the recognition that the preservation of the marine environment of the high seas was an obligation *erga omnes partes* was implicitly reaffirmed in the 2016 *South China Sea Arbitration*.[35] The Philippines brought, *inter alia*, a claim against China for breaches of its environmental protection obligations under UNCLOS as a result of its island-building activities on features that were located both within the Philippines' exclusive economic zone (EEZ) and in ABNJ.[36] The Tribunal did not question that the Philippines had standing to mount claims under UNCLOS for environmental harm that occurred in ABNJ although *erga omnes* / *erga omnes partes* obligations were not raised in the pleadings or acknowledged by the Tribunal.[37] The Tribunal found that Part XII obligations on marine environmental protection apply to all maritime areas, both within national jurisdiction and beyond.[38]

More explicitly, the Seabed Disputes Chamber (SDC) of the International Tribunal for the Law of the Sea (ITLOS) in its 2011 Advisory Opinion observed

[31] ASR (n 6) commentary to art 48, 126, para 7.

[32] ibid.

[33] *Whaling in the Antarctic (Australia v Japan: New Zealand intervening)* (Judgment) [2014] ICJ Rep 226 (*Whaling in the Antarctic*). During oral proceedings, Australia clarified that it was seeking to 'uphold its collective interest, an interest it shares with all other parties'. Verbatim Record (9 July 2013) CR2013/18, 28, para 19.

[34] Urs (n 19) 514.

[35] *The South China Sea Arbitration (The Republic of Philippines v The People's Republic of China)* (Award) (2016) Oxford Reports on ICGJ 495 (PCA) (*South China Sea Arbitration*).

[36] Cuarteron Reef, Fiery Cross Reef, Gaven Reef (North) and Subi Reef are located beyond the 200 nautical miles EEZ of the Philippines.

[37] Nilüfer Oral, 'The South China Sea Arbitral Award, Part XII of UNCLOS and the Protection and Preservation of the Marine Environment' in S Jayakumar, Tommy Koh, Robert Beckman, Tara Davenport and Hao Duy Phan (eds), *The South China Sea Arbitration: The Legal Dimension* (Edward Elgar 2018) 223, 242–245. Also see discussion in Yoshifumi Tanaka, 'Reflections on *Locus Standi* in Response to a Breach of Obligations *Erga Omnes Partes*: A Comparative Analysis of the *Whaling in the Antarctic* and *South China Sea* Cases' (2018) 17 LPICT 527, 545–553.

[38] *South China Sea Arbitration* (n 35) para 940.

in the context of damage arising from activities in the Area, that '[e]ach State Party [to UNCLOS] may also be entitled to claim compensation in light of the *erga omnes* character of the obligations relating to the preservation of the environment of the high seas and in the Area'.[39] It did not distinguish between *erga omnes partes* and *erga omnes*, although they specified that *states parties* were the only actors that could bring a claim on the basis of *erga omnes*, which suggests that obligations to protect the marine environment in UNCLOS are, at minimum, *erga omnes partes* applicable between UNCLOS parties.

There is accordingly a strong argument that the obligations in UNCLOS Part XII are obligations *erga omnes partes* that can be invoked by all UNCLOS states parties without having to demonstrate that they have been specially harmed by that breach.[40] UNCLOS obligations on the protection of the marine environment can certainly be said to be established for the protection of collective interests of UNCLOS states parties.[41] Consistent with the ICJ's finding on *erga omnes partes* in the *Belgium v Senegal* case and *The Gambia v Myanmar* case, many of Part XII's marine environmental obligations can be said to be owed by any state party to all other UNCLOS states parties.[42] Article 192 provides that states have the obligation to protect and preserve the marine environment, which is an obligation owed (at the very minimum) to other UNCLOS states parties. As observed by the *South China Sea* award, Part XII obligations apply to states irrespective of where the alleged harmful activities take place.[43] Moreover, it is salient that UNCLOS gives port states certain enforcement jurisdiction powers over vessel discharge violations that occur outside zones of national jurisdiction which have been said to be 'complementary to and enhancing the *erga omnes* effect of general obligations'.[44] Article 286, which triggers the jurisdiction of an UNCLOS court or tribunal, is drafted in general terms and only requires a dispute concerning the interpretation or application of UNCLOS 'without requiring that the applicant should demonstrate a special

[39] *Responsibilities and Obligations of States Sponsoring Persons and Entities with Respect to Activities in the Area* (Advisory Opinion of 1 February 2011) International Tribunal for the Law of the Sea (ITLOS) Reports 2011, 10 (*Activities in the Area* Advisory Opinion) para 180.

[40] P Chandrasekhara Rao and Philippe Gautier, *The International Tribunal for the Law of the Sea: Law, Practice and Procedure* (Edward Elgar 2018) 327. See also Rüdiger Wolfrum, 'Purposes and Principles of International Environmental Law' (1990) 33 GYIL 308, 325–326; Patricia Birnie, Alan Boyle and Catherine Redgwell, *International Law and the Environment* (4th edn, OUP 2021) 145–146, 244; Kathy Leigh, 'Liability for Damage to the Global Commons' (1992) 14 Aust YBIL 129, 147–148; Eirini-Erasmia Fasia, 'No Provision Left Behind – Law of the Sea Convention's Dispute Settlement System and Obligations *Erga Omnes*' (2021) 20 LPICT 519, 530–533; Tanaka, 'Reflections on *Locus Standi*' (n 37) 551; Hanqin Xue, *Transboundary Damage in International Law* (CUP 2003) 237–250.

[41] UNCLOS (n 10) preamble.

[42] *Questions Relating to the Obligation to Prosecute or Extradite (Belgium v Senegal)* [2012] ICJ Rep 422 (*Belgium v Senegal*); *The Gambia v Myanmar* case (n 27).

[43] *South China Sea Arbitration* (n 35) para 548.

[44] Fasia (n 40) 531.

interest'.[45] In addition, also consistent with the *Belgium v Senegal* case and *The Gambia v Myanmar* case, all UNCLOS states parties have a common interest in compliance with the marine environmental obligations under UNCLOS, given the interrelated nature of the oceans, and the critical role that the oceans play in supporting a myriad of ecosystem services.

Notwithstanding the *erga omnes partes* nature of UNCLOS marine environmental obligations, there remains a lack of clarity on the implications of the designation of UNCLOS marine environmental obligations as *erga omnes partes*. *Barcelona Traction* only acknowledged that every state had a legal interest in the protection of *erga omnes* obligations but did not elaborate on the consequences of this legal interest including whether it amounted to a right of standing. For example, it has been contended that the simple identification of a category of collective interests does not necessarily confer a right of standing on states individually to invoke responsibility for that breach.[46] However, this argument is undermined by ICJ jurisprudence in the *Belgium v Senegal* case, the *Whaling in the Antarctic* case and *The Gambia v Myanmar* case, where the ICJ has either explicitly or implicitly recognized a broad right of standing to enforce obligations *erga omnes partes* arising under multilateral treaties.[47] For example, in its judgment on preliminary objections in *The Gambia v Myanmar* case, the ICJ concluded that due to the 'common interest in compliance with the relevant obligations under the Genocide Convention', any state party is entitled to invoke the responsibility of another state party for an alleged breach of its obligations *erga omnes partes* 'regardless of whether a special interest can be demonstrated'.[48] Moreover, the SDC has also stated that each UNCLOS state party was 'entitled to claim compensation' in the event of damage to the marine environment resulting from activities in the Area which presumes a sufficient legal interest to substantiate standing for such claims.[49]

[45] Tanaka, 'Reflections on *Locus Standi*' (n 37) 551.

[46] See, for example, Judge Xue's dissenting opinion in *Belgium v Senegal* where she noted 'it is one thing that each State party has an interest in the compliance with these obligations, and it is another that every State party has standing to bring a claim against another State for the breach of such obligations in the Court'. She also did not accept the position of the majority that the concept of *erga omnes partes* was necessary in cases where no state would be in the position to make a claim and argued that the non-adjudicatory accountability mechanisms specified in the Convention, such as the Committee against Torture 'are designed to exactly to serve the common interest of the States parties in the compliance with the obligations under the Convention'. See *Belgium v Senegal* (n 42), Judge Xue, Dissenting Opinion, paras 15–17, 19. Judge Xue made similar arguments in *The Gambia v Myanmar* case: See *The Gambia v Myanmar* case (2020) (n 27), Separate Opinion of Judge Xue; and *Application of the Convention on the Prevention and Punishment of the Crime of Genocide (The Gambia v Myanmar)* (Judgment on Preliminary Objections) (2022) GL No 178, Dissenting Opinion of Judge Xue (*The Gambia v Myanmar* case 2022).

[47] Urs (n 19) 516.

[48] The *Gambia v Myanmar Case* 2022 (n 46) para 108.

[49] *Activities in the Area* Advisory Opinion (n 39) para 180.

Obligations *erga omnes partes* are unlikely to confer sufficient legal interest on states that are not parties to UNCLOS to ground a claim for environmental harm. While it has been suggested that peremptory norms of international law (*jus cogens*) establish obligations *erga omnes*, the breach of which concerns all states,[50] environmental obligations have not as yet been recognized as non-derogable peremptory norms by the international community.[51] On the other hand, other scholars have said that 'certain rules relating to common spaces, in particular common heritage regimes, may produce *erga omnes* obligations independent of whether they have peremptory status'[52] and that the scope of obligations *erga omnes* is wider than *jus cogens*.[53] Another argument that may give some basis for non-states parties to UNCLOS to have standing to bring claims for environmental harm in ABNJ is grounded in the notion that the obligation to protect and preserve the marine environment in article 192 reflects a rule of customary international law and the environmental obligation under article 192 should be regarded as an obligation *erga omnes*.[54] However, the ICJ has only so far affirmed a right of standing in respect of breaches of *obligations erga omnes partes* under multilateral treaties and this 'cannot necessarily be taken to represent the endorsement of a broader right of standing also in respect of obligations *erga omnes* under customary international law'.[55]

Even accepting the characterization of the protection of the marine environment as an *erga omnes partes* obligation that gives rise to rights of standing, there remain several potential obstacles. First, questions arise as to the remedy available to a non-injured state that has standing to bring a claim for environmental harm in ABNJ. Under article 48 (2) of the ASR, a state entitled to invoke responsibility based on *erga omnes* or *erga omnes partes* obligations may claim from the responsible state (a) a cessation of the wrongful act and assurances and guarantees of non-repetition; and (b) performance of the obligation of the reparation in the interest of the injured state or of the beneficiaries of the obligation breached. The remedies for breaches of *erga omnes* obligations under article 48 are more limited than those available to an 'injured state' under article 42 (which include countermeasures). The availability of reparation for a non-injured state will usually depend upon 'the circumstances of the breach, the extent to which the claimant's interests are affected and the nature of the risk to community interests'.[56] The ASR note that the non-injured state is not claiming compensation on its own account and that a claim must be made in the

[50] ILC, 'Report of the International Law Commission' (68th Session, 2 May–10 June and 4 July–12 August 2016) UN Doc A/71/10, paras 103–111.

[51] Birnie and others (n 40) 245.

[52] James Crawford, *The International Law Commission's Articles on State Responsibility: Introduction, Text and Commentaries* (CUP 2002) 192, para 3.

[53] Yoshifumi Tanaka, 'The Legal Consequences of Obligations *Erga Omnes* in International Law' (2021) 68(1) NILR 1, 10–11.

[54] ibid 5.

[55] Urs (n 19) 518.

[56] Birnie and others (n 40) 244.

interest of the injured state, if any, or the beneficiaries of the obligation breached.[57] It acknowledges that this aspect 'involves a measure of progressive development, which is justified since it provides a means of protecting the community or collective interest at stake',[58] but that cases where the non-injured state is acting not on behalf of the injured state but on behalf of beneficiaries of the obligations presents greater difficulties which the ASR cannot resolve.[59] For example, if a non-injured state claims compensation for environmental damage to a collective interest, how should this compensation be used? It would not be fair for the non-injured state to use compensation for its own purposes, resulting in a potential windfall gain. This highlights the utility of institutional mechanisms that enable such compensation to be directed into a fund whose purpose is to address environmental harm as is contemplated for both activities in the Area and activities in the Antarctic.[60]

Second, the characterization of an obligation as *erga omnes partes* is not sufficient to overcome jurisdictional rules of an international court or tribunal,[61] thus the state bringing the claim must have access to a particular court or tribunal to enforce claims for environmental harm in the global commons. Tanaka rightly observes 'the availability of a procedure is key in effectuating obligations *erga omnes*'.[62]

Finally, it should be recognized that even if UNCLOS states parties are entitled to bring a claim for environmental harm, there may be disincentives for states to exercise this option. States appear to be more willing to engage in litigation when their individual interests are being impacted.[63] Litigation proceedings can be costly; and may be perceived as too confrontational, risking damage in bilateral relations, particularly if the initiating state has not suffered direct injury and there is no guaranteed outcome. Decisions by governments to initiate proceedings before courts and tribunals 'are influenced by a range of factors, including diplomatic, security and economic concerns; the applicable law; the operation of relevant international organizations; and the level of domestic public interest'.[64] For

57 ASR (n 6) commentary to art 48, 127, para 11.

58 ibid commentary to art 48, 127, para 12.

59 ibid.

60 See discussion in Section 8.3 and in Chapter 8.

61 See Chapter 7. In the *East Timor* case between Portugal and Australia, the ICJ recognized that the right to self-determination had *erga omnes* status, but that it could not rule on the lawfulness of the conduct of a state when its judgment would necessitate an evaluation of the lawfulness of the conduct of another state that is not a party to the case, that is, Indonesia. As the ICJ explained, 'the *erga omnes* character of a norm and the rule of consent to jurisdiction are two different things'. *East Timor Case* (n 28) para 29; *Armed Activities Case* (n 27) paras 64, 125 where the ICJ acknowledged that the principles underlying the Genocide Convention have the status of *jus cogens* or create rights and obligations *erga omnes*, but this cannot in itself constitute an exception to the principle that its jurisdiction always depends on the consent of the parties.

62 Tanaka, 'The Legal Consequences of Obligations' (n 53) 23.

63 Fasia (n 40) 534.

64 Tim Stephens, 'Environmental Litigation by Asia Pacific States at the International Court of Justice' (2021) 21 MJIL 653, 668.

example, civil society groups are said to have played a role in the decision by Australia to bring proceedings against Japan before the ICJ for the latter's whaling activities, coupled with strong domestic political pressure.[65] The initiation of The Gambia's claim against Myanmar was reportedly driven by the Organisation of Islamic Cooperation (OIC), an intergovernmental organization.[66] Having a right of standing does not automatically mean that states will exercise it.

6.2.1.2 International Organizations

There are a variety of international organizations that have mandates that cover areas or activities in ABNJ, for example, various regional fisheries management organizations (RFMOs), regional seas organizations and sectoral organizations, including the International Seabed Authority (ISA).[67] It is conceivable that environmental harm in ABNJ could impact the interests of such international organizations and fall under their relevant mandate. In some cases, international organizations may in principle be better positioned than individual states to pursue a claim, where they have a broad mandate to take steps to protect the commons environment. For example, the windfall concern discussed in Section 6.2.1.1 where non-injured states claim compensation for environmental damage to a collective interest and questions on what can be done with that compensation, may be less problematic for international organizations. The question is whether they would have the capacity and recognized legal interests to bring claims against the responsible parties.

The question of capacity relates to whether the international organization has legal personality and legal capacity to bring claims. Capacity does not necessarily follow from legal personality since international organizations will have unique powers provided for in its constitutive instrument. Where there is no express authority to bring claims, the ability to bring a claim could be justified on the basis of the implied powers doctrine,[68] subject to the caveat that careful attention must be paid to the purposes of the international organization.

[65] Shirley V Scott, 'Australia's Decision to Initiate Whaling in the Antarctic: Winning the Case versus Resolving the Dispute' (2014) 68(1) Aust J Int'l Aff 1.

[66] 'Myanmar Hits Out at Top UN Court over Rohingya Genocide Case' *France 24* (Paris, 21 February 2022) <www.france24.com/en/asia-pacific/20220221-myanmar-hits-out-at-top-un-court-over-rohingya-genocide-case> accessed 1 September 2022.

[67] See, for example, 'Mapping Governance Gaps on the High Seas' (The Pew Charitable Trusts, March 2017) available at <www.pewtrusts.org/-/media/assets/2017/04/highseas_mapping_governance_gaps_on_the_high_seas.pdf> accessed 1 September 2022.

[68] Implied powers refer to powers which are not mentioned explicitly in the constituent instrument but are said to come with explicit powers described in the constituent instrument to give effect to the functions of the international organization. The rationale for implied powers is that it is impossible to spell out in detail in the constituent instrument each and every specific power an international organization will need to perform their functions either now or in the future: See generally, Niels M Blokker, 'International Organizations or Institutions, Implied

The 2011 Draft Articles on the Responsibility of International Organizations (DARIO), (which largely mirror the ASR), affirm that an international organization could invoke the responsibility of another international organization if the obligation breached is owed to that international organization or the international community as a whole and that breach specially affects that international organization.[69] Article 49 of the DARIO entitles

> a State or an international organization other than an injured State or international organization … to invoke the responsibility of another international organization … if the obligation breached is (1) owed to a group of States or international organizations, including the State or organization that invokes responsibility, and is established for the protection of a collective interest of the group; (2) owed to the international community as a whole; and (3) owed to the international community as a whole and safeguarding the interest of the international community as a whole underlying the obligation breached is within the functions of the international organization invoking responsibility.[70]

While the DARIO are confined to the right of a state or international organization to invoke the responsibility of another international organization, in principle, an international organization could also invoke the responsibility of a state, where the obligations are owed to the international organization. In the 1949 ICJ Advisory Opinion on *Reparation for Injuries Suffered In the Service of the United Nations*, the ICJ found that, although the United Nations Charter does not expressly confer upon the UN the capacity to include damage to the victim in its claim for reparation, the United Nations has the capacity to bring an international claim against a state (whether a member or non-member) for damage resulting from a breach by that state of its obligations towards the organization as well as to the victim on the basis of its implied powers necessary for the performance of its duties.[71] The commentary in the DARIO notes that legal writings have acknowledged the entitlement of international organizations to invoke responsibility in case of a breach of an obligation owed to the international community *as a whole* by a state but that practice is not very indicative. It goes on to say that '[w]hen international organizations respond to breaches committed by their members, they often act only on the basis of their

Powers' (last updated December 2021) in Anne Peters and Rüdiger Wolfrum (eds), *The Max Planck Encyclopedia of Public International Law* (OUP 2008). Also see the 1949 ICJ Advisory Opinion on *Reparation for Injuries Suffered in the Service of the United Nations* which made the classic observation: '[u]nder international law, the Organization must be deemed to have those powers which, though not expressly provided in the Charter, are conferred upon it by necessary implication as being essential to the performance of its duties'. *Reparation for Injuries Suffered in the Service of the United Nations* (Advisory Opinion) [1949] ICJ Rep 174 (ICJ Advisory Opinion on Reparations) para 182.

69 ILC, 'Draft Articles on the Responsibility of International Organizations, with Commentaries' (2011) II(2) ILC Yearbook 46 (DARIO).

70 ibid arts 49(1), (2) and (3), 88–89.

71 ICJ Advisory Opinion on Reparations (n 68) para 182.

respective rules', and 'it would be difficult to infer from this practice the existence of a general entitlement of international organizations to invoke responsibility' of states.[72]

As a result, to determine whether an international organization has sufficient legal interest to bring claims for environmental harm to specific areas beyond national jurisdiction or resources that fall within their respective mandates, attention must be paid to the specific obligations owed to the international organization and its legal responsibilities. For example, article 137 UNCLOS specifies that the ISA shall act on behalf of 'mankind as a whole', while article 145 places specific obligations on the ISA to ensure effective protection for the marine environment. These provisions indicate that the ISA may have an express legal mandate to pursue certain forms of damage, including reparations for reinstatement.[73] In addition, international organizations that seek compensation for environmental harm will also have to demonstrate how the loss accrues to its own interests, as opposed to those of its members. In this regard, an international organization may be better placed to ensure that any compensation received is used for collective benefit. While international organizations may have the right to mount such claims (subject to rules on access to international courts and tribunals discussed in Chapter 7), they may be unwilling to. Most international organizations are driven by the interests of their member states and any decision to bring a claim against its own member states or non-member states may be limited by procedural rules on decision-making, as well as the broader politics inherent in an international organization.

6.2.1.3 Non-state Actors

Non-state actors (which include corporate entities, non-governmental organizations and individuals), while not traditional subjects of international law, are increasingly playing a critical role in international law. They are, *inter alia*, often granted observer status in intergovernmental organizations, they are consulted during the formation of international regulations, they lobby governments and they serve as *amici curiae* in international litigation.[74] In certain treaty regimes, some non-state actors are recognized as having international legal personality capable of asserting rights against states and international organizations, for example, in international human rights law and international investment law.[75] This possibility is explicitly

[72] DARIO (n 69) commentary to art 49, 90, paras 8–9.

[73] The unique position of the ISA is considered in greater detail in Section 6.3.2.1.

[74] Cymie R Payne, 'Negotiation and Dispute Prevention in Global Cooperative Institutions: International Community Interests, IUU Fishing and the Biodiversity beyond National Jurisdiction Negotiation' (2020) 22 Int C L Rev 428, 436.

[75] Luisa Vierucci, 'NGOs before International Courts and Tribunals' in Pierre-Marie Dupuy and Luisa Vierucci (eds), *NGOs in International Law: Efficiency in Flexibility?* (Edward Elgar 2008) 160. Vierucci notes in the 2008 study that only the European Court of Human Rights, the Inter-American Commission of Human Rights, the African Commission for Human and

contemplated under article 33(2) of the ASR.[76] Thus, it is certainly within the competence of states to confer limited international legal status on non-state actors – the most salient example in ABNJ being the ability conferred on contractors under Part XI of the UNCLOS to bring claims against the ISA under UNCLOS.[77] Apart from certain treaty regimes, however, the ability of non-state actors to bring claims before international courts and tribunals is limited, particularly in connection with claims for environmental harm in ABNJ.

There is, of course, the possibility that states can espouse the claims of non-state actors. Thus, one avenue for claims against states or international organizations whose actions harm the interests of non-state actors in ABNJ – for example in fisheries related claims – is through espousal. There are examples of states espousing claims of non-state actors (including NGOs) although this has been confined to situations where these non-state actors had suffered direct losses.[78]

Undoubtedly, there are policy reasons to recognize the rights of standing of certain non-state actors. Payne observes that it would serve the interests of states to agree that civil society entities should be granted standing so as to 'overcome the problem that although humanity may need the oceans to be protected, individual states may be constrained or merely uninterested in taking action'.[79] One only has to look at the exponential growth in climate change and other environmental-related litigation in national courts, driven in part by frustration at legal and policy failures of governments coupled with recognition in some domestic jurisdictions of broad rights of standing of NGOs and public interest groups, to see that such actors can play a useful role in 'representing' the public interest of present and future generations.[80] The shadow of possible litigation by non-state actors may provide a much-needed impetus to states and international organizations to take steps to ensure that environmental harm in ABNJ is prosecuted and compensated to the extent possible. When victims cannot be identified because damage is to the environment *per se* in ABNJ (for example), NGOs could bring claims for such environmental harm, overcoming the issue of the lack of an 'injured party' and increasing the possibility that damage is compensated. Indeed, the issue of standing for NGOs has been part of the rationale for calls for the establishment of a specialized international court for the environment discussed further in Chapter 7.

At the same time, questions inevitably arise as to which non-state actors, particularly NGOs, may be entitled to represent the interests of the international

Peoples' Rights, the African Court and the European Court of Justice grant legal standing to NGOs to varying degrees (Vierucci, 158).

76 ASR (n 6) art 33(2), 94; commentary to art 33(2), 95, para 4.

77 UNCLOS (n 10), art 187 read with art 22 of Annex III.

78 Payne (n 74) 436 citing *Elettronica Sicula, S.p.A (ELSI) (United States of America v Italy)* (Judgment) [1989] ICJ Rep 15; *Arctic Sunrise Arbitration (Netherlands v Russia)* (Provisional Measures) ITLOS Case No 22 (2013).

79 Payne (n 74) 437.

80 See discussion in Section 6.2.3.

community (particularly when that term itself is one that is contested).[81] There would need to be rules in place to ensure that such litigation is genuine and not vexatious and that it does not slow down the administration of claims as has been seen in certain national jurisdictions where broad rights of standing have led to 'immobility and inefficiency in administration as well as the clogging of cases before courts'.[82] In addition, any rules providing standing in such cases would need to address the uses to which any monetary compensation might be put in order to avoid concerns relating to 'windfall' compensation identified above.

6.2.2 *Civil Liability*

Civil liability regimes have generally taken a traditional approach to standing and entitlement to bring claims is contingent on loss or injury being sustained – in other words, the victims must have suffered damage. For example, the 2006 Draft Principles on Allocation of Loss (Draft Principles), which reflects civil liability principles, has defined 'victim' as any natural or legal person or state that suffers damage.[83] Under the civil liability regime established for marine pollution from cargo oil, hazardous and noxious substances and bunker oil, the phrase 'person suffering damage' is used and defines person as 'any individual or partnership or any public or private body, whether corporate or not, including a State or any of its constituent subdivisions'.[84] As indicated, victims can include states or governments that have suffered damage or loss or taken reasonable response or preventive measures.[85] The right of states or other sub-state entities to claim for reasonable reinstatement is broadly accepted in civil liability regimes and is reflected in the International Oil Pollution Compensation Funds (IOPC Funds) Claims Manual,

81 Isabel Feichtner, 'Community Interests' (last updated February 2007) in Anne Peters and Rüdiger Wolfrum (eds), *Max Planck Encyclopedia of Public International Law* (OUP 2008) paras 39–55.

82 Draft Principles (n 5) commentary to principle 2(f), 71, para 30, footnote 373.

83 ibid, principle 2(f), 64.

84 International Convention on Civil Liability for Oil Pollution Damage (adopted 29 November 1969, entered into force 19 June 1975) 973 UNTS 3 (1969 Oil Pollution Liability Convention), amended by the 1992 Protocol to Amend the 1969 International Convention on Civil Liability for Oil Pollution Damage (adopted 27 November 1992, entered into force 30 May 1996) 1956 UNTS 255 (1992 Oil Pollution Liability Convention) art I(2); International Convention on Liability and Compensation for Damage in Connection with the Carriage of Hazardous and Noxious Substances by Sea (adopted 3 May 1996) (1996) 35 ILM 1415 (1996 HNS Convention), as amended by the Protocol of 2010 to the International Convention on Liability and Compensation for Damage in Connection with the Carriage of Hazardous and Noxious Substances by Sea (adopted 30 April 2010) (2010 HNS Convention) art I(2); International Convention on Civil Liability for Bunker Oil Pollution Damage (adopted 23 March 2001, entered into force 21 November 2008) 40 ILM 1493 art 1(2).

85 The Draft Principles noted that after the *Amoco Cadiz* oil spill off the coast of France, the French government also laid claims for recovery of pollution damages and clean-up costs. See Draft Principles (n 5) commentary to principle 2(f), 70, para 29.

which also recognizes the capacity of 'private organizations and public bodies' to bring claims.[86] Some civil liability regimes also recognize that states or competent authorities can bring claims on behalf of individuals that have suffered damage.[87]

Under the 1992 Oil Pollution Liability Convention, claims may be brought for preventive actions in ABNJ, where the preventive measures are taken to prevent or minimize harm to areas subject to state jurisdiction.[88] This limitation indicates the close relationship that the international community currently requires between sovereign interests and standing, and the unwillingness, at this time, to confer on states a right to damages in connection with commons resources.

Were civil liability regimes to be extended to cover environmental harm in ABNJ, their structure makes for an uneasy fit for claims being brought on behalf of the collective interest. Claims of direct economic losses suffered because of environmental damage in ABNJ, whether made by private or public parties, are analogous to the losses suffered in territorial areas. However, the recognition of the right of states to claim reasonable reinstatement costs under existing rules is rooted in the state's interests in the coastal environment in maritime zones under sovereignty or national jurisdiction. The state's more attenuated claims to have legal rights in, and responsibilities for, the environment in ABNJ would require clarity on the nature of these uncertain rights. The close connection between standing and damage presents further obstacles to the extension of civil liability regimes to the environment of ABNJ, given the current non-recognition of pure environmental losses in those regimes. Even the notion of 'reasonable' reinstatement, which anchors the right to claim for clean-up is highly uncertain given the lack of clear standards for reasonable actions in response to pollution incidents in ABNJ. From the perspective of insurers as well as the administrators of compensation funds, focusing on parties that have actually suffered damage avoids the uncertainty of complex questions of assessing and quantifying pure environmental damage, as well as a potential slew of claims from governments, environmental organizations and individuals all claiming to act on behalf of 'the environment'.[89]

6.2.3 *National Law*

Most jurisdictions generally require that claimants have a sufficient direct interest in the outcome of the action to confer standing. Claims for environmental harm

86 International Oil Pollution Compensation Funds (IOPC Funds), *Claims Manual* (IOPC Funds 2019) para 2.1.2.

87 See, for example, the Convention on Third Party Liability in the Field of Nuclear Energy (adopted 29 July 1960, entered into force 1 April 1968) 956 UNTS 251 art 13(g) which recognizes that 'any State may bring an action on behalf of persons who have suffered nuclear damage, who are nationals of that State or have their domicile or residence in its territory, and who have consented thereto'.

88 1992 Oil Pollution Liability Convention (n 84) art II(b).

89 Emanuela Orlando, 'From Domestic to Global? Recent Trends in Environmental Liability from a Multi-level and Comparative Law Perspective' (2015) 24 RECIEL 289, 296.

within national borders have traditionally been based on the private law of the tort or delict and were limited by the requirement that the private plaintiff suffered damage or injury.[90] While there may be other obstacles relating to jurisdiction or choice of law questions for claims brought in domestic courts for harms suffered in ABNJ, where the harm relates to a direct, private interest of the type usually recognized by national courts, standing is not likely to be an obstacle. A private property or economic interest retains its essential character regardless of its location inside or outside the state. As with the international law on standing, the more vexing cases relate to claims identified as being rooted in collective rights, such as environmental reinstatement and prevention measures and pure environmental losses.

Standing in these latter types of claims is typically linked to questions of resource ownership and to the state's regulatory authority over the environment. In the case of publicly owned lands or resources, the state's basic rights of standing follow the foundational rule that entities who have suffered material injury to a legally protected interest will have standing to sue. This basic rule, however, raises questions about the precise nature of the state's interest in natural resources. Does ownership only provide the state with the right to protect its economic interests or do its rights include the ability to secure remedies for the loss of non-economic elements, the benefit of which accrue to the public generally?

Certain doctrines developed in the national context affirm that states or their competent authorities have standing to bring claims for environmental harm that encompasses both economic and non-economic interests. For example, the doctrine of *parens patriae* suggests that the state should act to protect common resources because of its ownership over the resources and its role as protector of these common interests.[91] The state has standing to bring a suit on behalf of its citizens in order to protect its quasi-sovereign interests, provided that it has an interest of its own, separate and distinct from the interests of particular private parties, and that a significant number of the state's inhabitants are threatened or will be adversely impacted by the acts of the defendants.[92] While the majority of *parens patriae* suits seek injunctive relief, such suits could also cover a claim for damages, based on either the state's role as guardian of the entity or the state's quasi-sovereign interest in the general welfare of its residents.[93] States have also successfully used the *parens patriae* doctrine to bring claims for cross-border pollution on the basis that the state has articulated an interest apart from the interest of private parties; the state has

90 Monique Evans, '*Parens Patriae* and Public Trust: Litigating Environmental Harm *Per Se*' (2016) 12(1) MJSDL 1, 6.

91 Deborah G Musiker, Tom France and Lisa A Hallenbeck, 'The Public Trust and *Parens Patriae* Doctrines: Protecting Wildlife in Uncertain Political Times' (1995) 16 Pub Land L Rev 87, 101.

92 Edward HP Brans, *Liability for Damage to Public Natural Resources: Standing, Damage and Damage Assessment* (Kluwer Law 2001) 55.

93 *British Columbia v Canadian Forest Products Ltd* 2004 SCC 38, para 63. See also Musiker and others (n 91) 102; Brans (n 92) 56–57.

expressed a quasi-sovereign interest; and the state has alleged an injury to a sufficiently substantial segment of the population.[94]

A related concept is the public trust doctrine.[95] While it has been interpreted differently by various courts (principally in the United States) and given both narrow and expansive interpretations,[96] the doctrine essentially posits that it is the government or state that holds the resource interest (which covers navigable waters, tidelands, the land beneath these waters and the living resources therein) on behalf of beneficiaries, which are usually the public at large (including present and future generations).[97] The designation of resources as public trust resources may place certain obligations on the state or government as trustee, including the obligation to act in the best interest of the beneficiaries, to take into account the public trust nature of the resource when allocating or using such resources, to continually supervise the use of such resource and revisit decisions in light of changing knowledge and needs.[98] While the public trust doctrine has been typically used to challenge the decisions of public authorities, courts in the United States have recognized the state 'has not only the right but also the affirmative fiduciary obligation to … seek compensation for any diminution in that trust corpus'.[99] In certain instances, courts have utilized the public trust doctrine to find that the state had standing to bring suit as *parens patriae*, which have led some scholars to argue that 'parens patriae doctrine essentially provides a mechanism for the state to fulfil its public trust obligations'.[100] The public trust doctrine is not explicitly a right of

[94] *Alfred L Snapp & Son, Inc v Puerto Rico ex rel Barez* (1982) 458 US 592. See also Evans (n 90) 9. For civil law approach to *parens patriae*, see the French Civil Code, art 538.

[95] While the public trust doctrine was said to have first been articulated in the 1892 US Supreme Court decision of *Illinois Central Railroad v Illinois* where the court acknowledged that the state had title to land under Lake Michigan but that it is title held in trust for the people of the state, it became entrenched in United States through the publication of Joseph Sax's seminal article in the Michigan Law Review in 1969 (Joseph L Sax, 'The Public Trust Doctrine in Natural Resource Law: Effective Judicial Intervention' (1969) 68 Mich L Rev 571). See also Michael C Blumm and Rachel D Guthrie, 'Internationalizing the Public Trust Doctrine: Natural Law and Constitutional and Statutory Approaches to Fulfilling the Saxion Vision' (2012) 45 UC Davis L Rev 741, 750.

[96] Derek Tarver, '"Hunnuh Mus Tek Cyare da Root fa Heal da Tree": Saving the South Carolina Lowcountry from Overdevelopment through Judicial Application of a Modern Public Trust' (2017) 68 S C L Rev 1047, 1054.

[97] Mary Turnipseed, Raphael Sagarin, Peter Barnes, Michael C Blumm, Patrick Parenteau and Peter H Sand, 'Reinvigorating the Public Trust Doctrine: Expert Opinion on the Potential of Public Trust Mandate in US and International Environmental Law' (2010) 52(5) Environment: Science and Policy for Sustainable Development 7, 7; Catherine Redgwell, *Intergenerational Trusts and Environmental Protection* (Manchester UP 1999) 47.

[98] See, for example, *National Audubon Society v Superior Court of Alpine County* (1983) 33 Cal 3d 419; *Re Water Use Permit Applications* (2002) 9 P 3d 409, 450.

[99] See, for example, *Selma Pressure Treating Co v Osmose Wood Preserving Co* 271 Cal Rptr 596, 606 (Cal Ct App 1990), citing *State v Jersey Central Power & Light Co* (1975) 336 1A 2d 750, 759 (NJ App Div 1975).

[100] Musiker and others (n 91) 107.

standing (as opposed to *parens patriae*) but provides legal justification for a state's pursuit of claims for harm to the environment and natural resources.

Given the reliance on ownership or regulatory authority to ground public authority standing, it is questionable whether doctrines such as *parens patriae* and the public trust can provide the legal justification for standing of states to initiate claims in their national courts or foreign national courts for environmental harm in ABNJ. The doctrines have their foundations in notions of state sovereignty that are antithetical to the 'commons' status of ABNJ. Moreover, while there have been attempts to declare certain global resources in ABNJ as subject to trustee obligations, it is still far from established that states have general trustee obligations in relation to the environment in ABNJ.[101] Nonetheless, the ideas that animate the notion of public trusteeship may provide a useful leverage point to expand the ability of individual states and domestic courts to hold polluters responsible. In particular, the idea that states have specific responsibilities to preserve and protect the marine environment is well-established and may fortify claims, for example, of necessitous interventions in response to marine pollution.[102] A state could argue in some instances that reinstatement measures taken in ABNJ are not voluntary, but are based on legal duties, entitling states to recover those costs from responsible parties.[103] In this regard, an UNCLOS state party is unlikely to be able to rely upon the *erga omnes partes* nature of marine environmental obligations to bring a claim for environmental harm in ABNJ in its own national courts. The doctrine of *erga omnes* operates between states in relation to the invocation of state responsibility, which is distinct from the question before a domestic court concerning liability in tort or delict.

Apart from states having standing for environmental harm claims under national law, a recent trend in national jurisdiction has been the recognition of standing of non-state actors such as NGOs and public interest groups for environmental damage in national courts. Underlying this conferral of standing is the notion that a public trust in environmental resources confers both rights and responsibilities on states. As a public trustee, the state has both the ability to pursue remedies on behalf of the broader community of interest holders, but also may be understood to owe obligations to manage environmental resources in the interests of beneficiaries. This latter argument has been prominent in climate change litigation in both the Global North and South and has become an essential component of strategic climate change

[101] There have been multiple proposals to apply the public trust doctrine and/or trusteeship to Antarctica; the Amazon rainforest, to all genetic resources or biological resources, to regional seas, to oceans in general, to the atmosphere as a whole, to the global commons or the global environment: See generally Peter H Sand, 'The Rise of Public Trusteeship in International Environmental Law' (2014) 44(1) EPL 210.

[102] See discussion in Section 6.2.1.

[103] For a fuller examination of the potential role of the doctrine of public trusteeship, see Klaus Bosselmann, *Earth Governance: Trusteeship of the Global Commons* (Edward Elgar 2015).

action by certain NGOs to highlight the failure of governments and private actors to live up to their climate change obligations under relevant national and international climate change legal frameworks.[104] For example, in *Juliana v United States*, the plaintiffs sought a declaration that their constitutional and public trust rights were violated by governmental non-action on climate and an order requiring the federal government to develop a plan to reduce its greenhouse gas emissions. The court of first instance refused to dismiss the claim and relied in part on the climate impacts in the ocean and its status as a trust resource.[105] The *Juliana* case echoes some of the successful arguments made in the *Urgenda* case, where the Dutch government was required to take further steps to address climate change, based in part on the duty of the Dutch government to protect rights under the European Convention on Human Rights.[106] The reasoning behind this ruling was subsequently extended to Royal Dutch Shell, on the basis that as a large emitter, it too owed obligations to mitigate its emissions in line with global commitments.[107]

It is important to note that these cases draw on the potential for *government inaction* to contravene fundamental rights held by the claimants. As such, the cases can rely on a broader basis for standing that goes to the ability of litigants to pursue legal actions in vindication of their human rights. Where the claims are pursued by public interest groups on behalf of a class of claimants, the claimants take advantage of national jurisdictions that have broad rights of standing either embedded in their constitutions or civil procedures or a climate conscious judiciary that is broadly interpreting rights of standing to include NGOs and public interest groups.[108] In other jurisdictions, the applicable rules on standing afforded to individuals, NGOs and other public interest groups may be carefully circumscribed in national legislation[109] and will be subject to more intense scrutiny by courts.[110]

[104] See, for example, Joseph Regalia, 'The Public Trust Doctrine and the Climate Crisis: Panacea or Platitude?' (2021) 11(1) MJEAL 1; Jacqueline Peel and Jolene Lin, 'Transnational Climate Litigation: The Contribution of the Global South' (2019) 113(4) AJIL 679.

[105] *Juliana v United States* 217 F Supp 3d 1224 (D Or 2016), overruled on standing grounds, *Juliana v United States* 947 F 3d 1159 (9th Cir 2020).

[106] *Urgenda Foundation v State of the Netherlands*, The Hague Court of Appeal (Decision of 9 October 2018) Case No 200.178.245/01.

[107] *Friends of the Earth Netherlands (Milieudefensie) v Royal Dutch Shell*, District Court The Hague (Judgment of 26 May 2021) Case No C/09/571932.

[108] United Nations Environment Programme, 'Environmental Courts and Tribunals 2021: A Guide for Policymakers' (2021) 34–35 <www.unep.org/resources/publication/environmental-courts-and-tribunals-2021-guide-policy-makers> accessed 11 October 2022.

[109] See discussion in Brans (n 92) 35–62 and 358–360. Also see Blumm and Guthrie which highlight various jurisdictions which confer standing on NGOs on the basis of the public trust doctrine: Blumm and Guthrie (n 95).

[110] For example, standing has been a central issue in climate change litigation in certain jurisdictions, with courts interpreting and applying relevant statutes to determine whether a particular plaintiff has standing. In *Urgenda Foundation v State of Netherlands*, the Hague District Court held that Urgenda had standing on its own behalf, due to Dutch law which allows non-governmental organizations to bring a court action to protect the general interests or collective

The remedies sought in these cases tend to be public law remedies, typically seeking government actions in line with climate commitments, not compensation for harm. Claims for compensation in the climate context raise complex issues concerning attribution, but also potentially raise questions regarding the standing of litigants to pursue compensation for harm to collective legal interests.[111] There are examples of jurisdictions that have specific environmental regulations which recognize the right of NGOs to bring civil claims directly against polluters for liability for environmental damage, either for direct damage they have suffered in terms of actual clean-up costs they have taken, or for pure ecological damage. In France, NGOs can claim direct damages covering 'material damages' incurred in clean-up and restorative costs and 'moral damages' on the basis that failure to respect environmental legislation by operators undermines the efforts made by NGOs to protect the environment.[112] NGOs can also claim for 'purely ecological damage' even though they have not suffered damage.[113] Similarly in Portugal, NGOs can sue the operator directly through the civil *actio popularis* to obtain the restoration of the environment, including compensation for direct costs incurred for clean-up.[114]

While no state has extended these rights to ABNJ, these domestic legal developments signal the emergence of a greater judicial willingness to allow the beneficiaries of common resources to hold those who threaten them to account. The legal interests being recognized in these cases are often connected to abridgement of human rights, which are located with the litigants. Analogous arguments could potentially be made in light of recognition of the critical role of oceans and the potential for irreversible and large-scale damage. While the approaches to date have been centred on public law remedies, compensation claims have a clear public

interests for other person but, partly for practical reasons, the 886 individual claimants involved in the suit were not granted standing separate from that of Urgenda. Michael Burger and Justin Gundlach, 'The Status of Climate Change Litigation: A Global Review' (Report, United Nations Environment Programme, May 2017) <https://climate.law.columbia.edu/content/climate-change-litigation> 28–29, accessed 1 September 2022.

111 Much of the climate change litigation has been confined to pure mitigation and adaptation cases. There are relatively few cases that concern the remediation or compensation for harm caused by climate change and the outcome of these cases is either unsuccessful or still pending, although there have been calls for more efforts to use climate change litigation to pursue loss and damage: See generally Patrick Toussaint, 'Loss and Damage and Climate Litigation: The Case for Greater Interlinkage' (2022) 30(1) RECIEL 16.

112 Ordonnance n° 2000-914 du 18 septembre 2000 relative à la partie Législative du code de l'environnement. See also discussion in Elena Fasoli, 'The Possibilities for Nongovernmental Organizations Promoting Environmental Protection to Claim Damages in Relation to the Environment in France, Italy, the Netherlands and Portugal' (2017) 26(1) RECIEL 30, 34; Pierre Bentata and Michael Faure, 'The Role of ENGOs in Environmental Litigation: A French Case Study' (2015) 25 EPG 459, 461.

113 For example, in one case, an NGO was able to claim a sum of money for dead birds caused by an oil spill equivalent to the necessary costs for the nesting and breeding of replacement birds: Cour de cassation, criminelle, Chambre criminelle, 25 septembre 2012, n° 10-82.938.

114 See discussion in Fasoli (n 112) 35–36.

purpose, in protecting and restoring the environment, that makes the extension of these types of legal claims in ABNJ a logical direction.

A final approach to standing to make environmental claims that is gaining greater traction in domestic legal systems is conferring rights of standing on the environment or features of the environment directly. The idea, mapped out by Christopher Stone in his seminal paper, 'Should Trees Have Standing – Toward Legal Rights For Natural Objects',[115] challenges the legal orthodoxy that rights holders are a limited class (noting the expansion of entities that have been accepted as having legal rights), and arguing that natural features are worthy as being considered rights holders. In an advisory opinion, the Inter-American Court of Human Rights has also stated that the right to a healthy environment protects components of the environment as legal interests in their own right even in the absence of a risk to humans.[116] The idea of rights of nature has been taken up in recent years by a number of domestic jurisdictions in relation to specific natural features, such as rivers and forests,[117] or nature writ large.[118] The approach to date has focused on public law approaches that provide representatives of natural features to implement protective measures and in some cases to provide access to courts to uphold the rights of natural entities.[119] The extension of rights of nature to ABNJ is consistent with the ecocentric ethos that these laws capture, and is to some degree reflected in existing international legal instruments, such as the Convention on Biological Diversity that, although fundamentally anthropocentric in approach, recognizes the 'intrinsic

[115] Stone (n 2).

[116] *The Environment and Human Rights*, Advisory Opinion OC-23/17, Inter-American Court of Human Rights Series A No 23 (15 November 2017) para 62 ('The Court considers it important to stress that, as an autonomous right, the right to a healthy environment, unlike other rights, protects the components of the environment, such as forests, rivers and seas, as legal interests in themselves, even in the absence of the certainty or evidence of a risk to individuals. This means that it protects nature and the environment, not only because of the benefits they provide to humanity or the effects that their degradation may have on other human rights, such as health, life or personal integrity, but because of their importance to the other living organisms with which we share the planet that also merit protection in their own right. In this regard, the Court notes a tendency, not only in court judgments, but also in Constitutions, to recognize legal personality and, consequently, rights to nature').

[117] For example, see Te Awa Tupua (Whanganui River Claims Settlement) Act 2017 (NZ) <www.legislation.govt.nz/act/public/2017/0007/latest/whole.html> accessed 1 September 2022; and Te Urewera Act 2014 (NZ) <www.legislation.govt.nz/act/public/2014/0051/latest/whole.html> accessed 1 September 2022.

[118] Ley de Derechos de la Madre Tierra, Ley Nº 071, Ley de 21 de Diciembre de 2010 (Bolivia) <https://bolivia.infoleyes.com/norma/2689/ley-de-derecho%20s-de-la-madre-tierra-071> accessed 1 September 2022, and also <www.worldfuturefund.org/Projects/Indicators/motherearthbolivia.html> accessed 1 September 2022.

[119] Harriet Harden-Davies, Fran Humphries, Michelle Maloney, Glen Wright, Kristina Gjerde and Marjo Vierros, 'Rights of Nature: Perspectives for Global Ocean Stewardship' (2020) 122 Mar Pol'y 104059 (noting over twenty cases have been taken in Ecuador's courts that have asserted the rights of nature).

value' of ecological features.[120] There would be legal challenges in extending this approach, including defining the boundaries of natural features that may be right holders and identifying the appropriate entity to represent the interests of ABNJ natural features.[121] However, like the emerging approaches in trusteeship, the rights of nature may push states to develop approaches to standing that provide greater emphasis on the non-instrumental values of ABNJ resources.

6.3 RULES OF STANDING IN SPECIFIC REGIMES IN ABNJ

6.3.1 *Antarctic*

6.3.1.1 States

Any attempt to bring a claim for environmental harm in the Antarctic Treaty area by the seven states (Argentina, Australia, Chile, France, New Zealand, Norway and the United Kingdom) that have made claims to the Antarctic continent, including maritime claims, may face objections on the basis that these claims have not been accepted by the international community and are held in abeyance by the 1959 Antarctic Treaty.[122] In the *Whaling in the Antarctic* case, even though Australia acknowledged that some of Japan's whaling activities fell in waters over which Australia claims sovereign rights and jurisdiction, it maintained that it brought the claim under the 1946 International Convention for the Regulation of Whaling in order to 'uphold its collective interest, an interest it shares with all other parties'.[123] Australia deliberately avoided any mention of its Antarctic Treaty claim. These states may feel that to assert a claim may have political consequences or be a de facto breach of 'sovereign neutrality' in article IV of the Antarctic Treaty.[124]

A stronger claim as an injured state may be made by the Antarctic Treaty Consultative Parties (ATCPs), whose activities are directly impacted by environmental harm.[125] For example, were an incident to adversely affect a state's tourism

[120] Convention on Biological Diversity (adopted 5 June 1992, entered into force 29 December 1993) 1760 UNTS 79, 31 ILM 818 (1992) preamble.

[121] See Harden-Davies and others (n 119) discussing a proposal to create a representative council that could advocate for the interests of the ocean.

[122] Both France and Australia have proclaimed an exclusive economic zone (EEZ) off their Antarctic territories and all seven states have either submitted preliminary information, partial submissions or full submissions on the outer limits of their continental shelves beyond 200 nautical miles before the Commission on the Limits of the Continental Shelf (CLCS): See Karen Scott and David VanderZwaag, 'Polar Oceans and Law of the Sea' in Donald Rothwell, Alex Oude Elferink, Karen Scott and Tim Stephens (eds), *The Oxford Handbook of the Law of the Sea* (OUP 2015) 724, 738–739.

[123] Presentation by Henry Burmester, Verbatim Record, CR 2013/18, 9 July 2013, 28, para 19.

[124] Martijn Wilder, 'The Settlement of Disputes under the Protocol on Environmental Protection to the Antarctic Treaty' (1995) 31(179) Polar Rec 399, 405.

[125] See Chapter 1 for an overview of the arrangements in the Antarctic.

or research activities in the Antarctic, these interests would be sufficient to support standing to make a claim against the responsible state or private actor. As the obligations are owed to a group of states, the argument here is that they are specially affected by the environmental harm in question.[126] A further possibility would include claims for damage that arise where a state undertakes response measures. Such a claim is supported by article 15 of the 1991 Antarctic Protocol, where each state party has agreed to respond to environmental emergencies in the Antarctic Treaty Area by providing for prompt and effective response action to such emergencies, even if they or their operators did not cause it. It is anticipated that these types of claims will be addressed through the Liability Annex, discussed below, but claims can still be made outside the procedures under the Liability Annex. It should be noted, however, that at the Final Act of the Eleventh Antarctic Treaty Special Consultative Meeting where the 1991 Antarctic Protocol was adopted, the ATCPs agreed that the arbitral tribunal established under the Protocol would not make determinations on damages relating to liability arising from activities taking place in the Antarctic Treaty area until a binding legal regime had entered into force through an Annex pursuant to article 16 of the 1991 Antarctic Protocol (while the Liability Annex has been concluded, it has not entered into force yet).[127]

The more complex question is whether parties to the 1959 Antarctic Treaty and 1991 Antarctic Protocol can bring a claim for environmental harm based on *erga omnes partes* even if they have not suffered harm directly. The obligations under the 1959 Antarctic Treaty and 1991 Antarctic Protocol clearly meet the characteristics of obligations *erga omnes partes* set out in the ASR of 'agreements established by a group of states in some wider common interest and which transcend the sphere of bilateral relations of States parties'.[128] Both the 1959 Antarctic Treaty and 1991 Antarctic Protocol have been established to 'foster a common interest, over and above any interests of the States concerned individually'.[129] Both instruments recognize the need to protect Antarctica in the interest of mankind as a whole, and article 15 of the Antarctic Protocol requires each party to respond to environmental emergencies even if their operators did not cause it.[130] The challenges in relying on *erga omnes partes* outlined in Section 6.2.1.1 would apply equally to environmental

[126] See discussion in Section 6.2.1.1.

[127] Final Session of the Eleventh Antarctic Treaty Special Consultative Meeting, 32.

[128] ASR (n 6) commentary to art 48, 126, para 7.

[129] ibid.

[130] The Antarctic Treaty (adopted 1 December 1959, entered into force 23 June 1961) 402 UNTS 71 (1959 Antarctic Treaty), preamble; Protocol on Environmental Protection to the Antarctic Treaty (adopted 4 October 1991, entered into force 14 January 1998) (1991) 30 ILM 1461 (1991 Antarctic Protocol) preamble. An example (although prior to the 1991 Protocol) is the *Bahia Paraiso* incident where an Argentine government ship caused extensive oil pollution. The Argentine government initially refused to accept any responsibility but contracted a Netherlands team to clean-up the oil pollution and the United States, which had the closest base to the spill, was the first state to act to limit the spill. Wilder (n 124) 404.

harm claims in Antarctica, including overcoming the limitations in remedies and concerns about windfall gains in the absence of a fund or other mechanism.

The Liability Annex, which is not in force, addresses liability only arising from environmental emergencies.[131] It requires both state operators and non-state operators to take prompt and effective response action to environmental emergencies arising from the activities of that operator and allows other states parties to step in if the state and non-state operator fail to take action, provided certain conditions are met, including notification to the party of the operator and the Antarctic Secretariat that such response action will be undertaken.[132] The Liability Annex addresses a number of ambiguities surrounding who may bring claims and under what conditions.

There is a distinction between which parties have standing to bring claims depending on the status of the actor that is responsible for the environmental emergency. If the state operator fails to take such response action, it is either strictly liable to the state party that did take the response action under article 6 (1) of the Liability Annex ('liability for reimbursement costs'), or if no other party took action, the state operator is strictly liable to pay the costs of the response action into a fund established under the Liability Annex under article 6 (2) ('liability for payment of costs of response action into fund').[133] The determination of liability of the state for reimbursement costs to another state party for response action undertaken by it is decided by state-to state dispute settlement mechanisms including any enquiry procedures and the dispute settlement procedures provided for in articles 18, 19 and 20 of the 1991 Antarctic Protocol. The only actors which have 'standing' in this regard are other states parties who have incurred costs, consistent with traditional understandings of standing being based on the 'injured party'.

Regarding liability of state operators for payment of the costs of response action into the fund, the identification of the state which has the requisite standing to initiate proceedings is less straightforward. There is no injured state *per se* and the negotiating states 'thought it undesirable to allow all other [States] Parties the simultaneous ability to bring dispute settlement actions against the responsible State operator'.[134] Therefore, rather than identifying the state who could invoke dispute settlement procedures, the Liability Annex leaves the settlement of disputes to the Antarctic Treaty Consultative Meeting (ATCMs).[135] The amount of the costs of the response action is to be approved by a decision of the ATCM with advice of the Committee on Environmental Protection where appropriate.[136] Given the

131 Liability Annex (n 14).
132 ibid art 5.
133 ibid art 6(2)(a).
134 Michael Johnson, 'Liability for Environmental Damage in Antarctica: The Adoption of Annex VI to the Antarctic Environmental Protocol' (2006) 19(1) Geo Int'l Envtl L Rev 33, 48.
135 See Chapter 1 for an overview of the governance arrangements in the Antarctic.
136 Liability Annex (n 14) art 7(5)(b).

voting rules of the ATCM, there is the possibility that an ATCP can block a decision related to its own liability.[137] However, if a dispute remains unresolved, the dispute can go to the dispute settlement mechanism in articles 18, 19 and 20 of the 1991 Antarctic Protocol, although the Liability Annex still does not identify which state would have standing to invoke the dispute settlement mechanism.[138]

Regarding claims against non-state operators, the issue of which actor has standing to bring an action depends on whether it is an action for liability for reimbursement costs or if it is an action for liability for payment of costs of response action into the fund. With regard to liability for reimbursement costs, the only actor that can bring a claim against the non-state operator is the state party which has taken response action.[139] The forum where such action could be taken was subject to debate and ultimately, two options were given.[140] First, a state party can bring an action in the country where the non-state operator is incorporated or has its principal place of business or his habitual place of residence.[141] Second, if this fails, then states parties can bring an action in the courts of the state party that authorized the activity.[142]

With regard to actions for payment of the costs of response actions into the fund, it was also not immediately clear which actor would be the plaintiff to bring a claim and therefore the issue of standing is not explicitly addressed.[143] Instead, states parties only have an obligation to ensure that there is a domestic law mechanism that exists for the enforcement of the liability of the non-state operator to ensure that it pays the costs of response actions into the fund (either directly or via the party of the non-state operator).[144] It leaves it to the domestic mechanism to determine which actor has standing, but appears to imply that only states parties would be able to bring claims.[145] To avoid the issue of multiplicity of proceedings, a consultation process was included which obliged states parties to consult amongst themselves as to which party should take enforcement action.[146]

[137] ibid art 7(5)(a).
[138] ibid art 7(5)(a). Johnson notes that dispute settlement mechanisms in the 1991 Antarctic Protocol were included late in negotiations, and this may be why the issue of the state which could invoke dispute settlement mechanisms was not elaborated on, but that it should be possible for the ATCM to determine how the mechanism will be invoked. See Johnson (n 134) 49.
[139] Liability Annex (n 14) art 7(1).
[140] This will be discussed further in Chapter 7.
[141] Liability Annex (n 14) art 7(1).
[142] ibid art 7(2).
[143] Johnson (n 134) 48.
[144] Liability Annex (n 14) art 7(3).
[145] Johnson (n 134) 48. See art 7(3) of the Liability Annex (n 14) which states 'where there are multiple *Parties* that are capable of enforcing Article 7(2)(b)' against non-state operators.
[146] Liability Annex (n 14) art 7(3).

6.3.1.2 International Organizations

Institutional governance under the 1959 Antarctic Treaty System is carried out primarily through the ATCPs via the ATCMs.[147] The ATCM is a treaty body with responsibilities to define the general policy for the comprehensive protection of the Antarctic environment and dependent and associated ecosystems under the 1991 Antarctic Protocol.[148] While the ATCM clearly has a strong mandate to protect and preserve the environment of Antarctica, including ensuring that environmental harm is addressed, it lacks international legal personality to make legal claims. The ATCM would not fall within the definition of an international organization under the DARIO,[149] and there is nothing in either the 1959 Antarctic Treaty or the 1991 Antarctic Protocol that suggests the parties intended the ATCM to be able to bring claims on behalf of the parties. For example, the dispute settlement procedures in the 1959 Antarctic Treaty and 1991 Antarctic Protocol are confined to states parties to these instruments and the ATCM has no role in deciding officially whether or not claims are brought pursuant to these instruments.[150] The Committee on Environmental Protection, (established under the 1991 Antarctic Protocol) provides recommendations to the ATCM on the implementation of the Protocol and has a range of functions related to the protection of the environment but is similarly constrained.[151] Thus, neither the ATCM nor the Committee on Environmental Protection would be able to initiate claims for environmental harm suffered in the Antarctic Treaty Area.

The only institutional body with legal personality and legal capacity is the Commission on the Conservation of Antarctic Marine Living Resources (CCAMLR Commission), an international organization created under the Convention on the Conservation of Antarctic Marine Living Resources (CCAMLR), whose mandate includes 'prevention of changes or minimization of the risk of changes in the marine ecosystem which are not potentially reversible'.[152] Its legal capacity is limited to actions 'as may be necessary to perform its function and achieve the purposes of the Convention'.[153] However, the functions of the Commission are administrative and do not disclose any explicit or implied powers to pursue claims on behalf of the parties nor does it have the authority to respond directly to environmental incidents.[154] Dispute settlement procedures in CCAMLR

[147] See Chapter 1 for an overview of the governance arrangements in the Antarctic.

[148] 1991 Antarctic Protocol (n 130) art 10.

[149] DARIO (n 69) art 2.

[150] 1959 Antarctic Treaty (n 130) art XI; 1991 Antarctic Protocol (n 130) arts 18, 19 and 20.

[151] 1991 Antarctic Protocol (n 130) arts 11 and 12.

[152] Convention on the Conservation of Antarctic Marine Living Resources (adopted 20 May 1980, entered into force 7 April 1982) 1329 UNTS 47 (CCAMLR) arts II(3)(a) and (c).

[153] ibid art VIII.

[154] ibid art IX.

are confined to states parties and based on consent of both parties, limiting the ability of the CCAMLR Commission to bring claims for environmental harm.

Regarding the Liability Annex, as mentioned in Section 6.3.1.1, while the ATCM is not empowered to initiate claims against state or non-state operators for liability relating to environmental emergencies, it does have a role to play in relation to the liability of state operators for payment of the costs of the response action into the fund. The amount of the costs of the response action is to be approved by a decision of the ATCM with advice of the Committee on Environmental Protection where appropriate,[155] and while an ATCP can block a decision related to its own liability,[156] unresolved disputes will be subject to the dispute settlement mechanism in articles 18, 19 and 20 of the 1991 Antarctic Protocol.[157]

6.3.1.3 Non-state Actors

Non-state actors (including non-state operators or NGOs) are not conferred explicit rights of standing under the 1991 Antarctic Protocol or the Liability Annex to bring claims either for direct harm/losses they have suffered or for environmental harm. While the Liability Annex envisages that there is a mechanism in place under the domestic law of the party for the enforcement of the liability of non-state operators for the costs of response action that they failed to take, it appears that only states are entitled to bring claims against non-state operators.[158]

6.3.2 *Deep Seabed*

The issue of standing for environmental harm caused by activities in the Area was addressed by the SDC in its Advisory Opinion, where it noted:

> Neither the Convention nor the relevant Regulations (regulation 30 of the Nodules Regulations and regulation 30 of the Sulphides Regulations) specifies what constitutes compensable damage, or which subject may be entitled to claim compensation. It may be envisaged that the damage in question would include damage to the Area and its resources constituting the common heritage of mankind and damage to the marine environment. Subjects entitled to claim compensation may include the Authority, entities engaged in deep seabed mining, other users of the sea, and coastal States.
>
> No provision of the Convention can be read explicitly entitling the Authority to make such a claim. It may, however, be argued that such entitlement is implicit in article 137, paragraph 2 of the Convention, which States that the Authority shall act

[155] Liability Annex (n 14) art 7(5)(b).
[156] ibid art 7(5)(a).
[157] ibid art 7(5)(a).
[158] Johnson (n 134) 48 and accompanying text to (n 145).

> on "on behalf" of mankind. Each State Party may also be entitled to claim compensation in light of the *erga omnes* character of the obligations relating to the preservation of the environment of the high seas and in the Area. In support of this view, reference may be made to article 48 of the ILC Articles on State Responsibility ...[159]

The SDC uses somewhat equivocal language, suggesting there is still some uncertainty as to which actors will have the requisite standing to bring a claim for harm to the marine environment in the Area. As such, it may be helpful to address the basis of standing for both the ISA, states and non-state actors, including contractors.

6.3.2.1 The ISA

Unlike the ATCM, the ISA has international legal personality and 'such legal capacity as may be necessary for the exercise of its functions and the fulfilment of its purposes'.[160] The ISA has extensive explicit powers to administer the resources of the Area, as well as implied powers that are necessary for the ISA to carry out its functions.[161] Express powers include the ability of the ISA Council to initiate proceedings on behalf of the ISA.[162]

The SDC identified the source of the ISA's standing as article 137(2) of UNCLOS, which provides that 'all rights in the resources of the Area are vested in mankind as a whole, on whose behalf the Authority shall act'. This provision, which is unique in international law, establishes the *res communis* nature of the resources of the Area, and vests those rights in 'mankind as a whole'. The term 'vests' has a proprietary connotation, and the structure of the provision creates a trust-like relationship. The legal interest created in article 137 is not unlike the *parens patriae* powers of a state, whereby the state has the authority to represent the communal interests of its citizenry. The shared nature of common heritage resources necessitates that there is some entity to protect the interests of the beneficiaries. Article 137 identifies the ISA as that entity. What article 137(2) does not specify is whether this provision would entitle the ISA to claim compensation for damage to common heritage of humankind (CHH) resources (i.e. polymetallic nodules, polymetallic sulphides and cobalt-rich crusts or CHH resources) or damage to the marine environment or both.

A narrow interpretation is that article 137 (2) would only be the legal basis for the ISA claiming for damage to CHH resources. This reading reflects the specific reference to the 'resources' of the Area in article 137, which are defined as the *in situ* mineral resources of the seabed. In other words, the right of standing should be restricted to the shared resources. The SDC appears to differentiate between

[159] *Activities in the Area* Advisory Opinion (n 39) paras 179–180.
[160] UNCLOS (n 10) art 176.
[161] ibid art 157.
[162] ibid art 162(2)(u).

damage to 'the common heritage of mankind' and 'damage to the marine environment'. Moreover, the marine environment in ABNJ is not subject to the common heritage of humankind principle.[163]

On the other hand, it is not clear whether compensable damage to CHH resources and compensable damage to the marine environment can be meaningfully separated.[164] The obligation to protect the marine environment in article 145 also includes 'natural resources of the Area'. Damage to the marine environment may result in damage to the resources subject to the CHH principle and vice versa. It therefore may be difficult to separate compensable damage to the marine environment from damage to CHH resources. It would be conceivable for the ISA to rely on article 137 (2) of UNCLOS to bring a claim for damage to CHH resources which may arguably be easier to quantify, and which would still result in compensation for damage to the marine environment.[165] In addition, UNCLOS states that 'the *Area* and its resources are the common heritage of mankind (emphasis added)',[166] which would at least encompass the marine environment of the seabed. The broad definition of marine environment in the Exploration Regulations and current Draft Exploitation Regulations (DER) would encompass CHH resources.[167]

The basis of the ISA's standing to bring claims for environmental damage should not be restricted to article 137(2), but rather ought to be understood in light of the other provisions addressing the role and functions of the ISA. A further foundation for the ISA's standing to bring claims for damage to the marine environment is its obligations relating to the protection of the marine environment, particularly article 145 which provides:

> Necessary measures shall be taken in accordance with this Convention with respect to activities in the Area to ensure effective protection for the marine environment from harmful effects which may arise from such activities. To this end the Authority shall adopt appropriate rules, regulations and procedures for *inter alia*:
>
> (a) the prevention, reduction and control of pollution and other hazards to the marine environment, including the coastline, and of interference with the ecological balance of the marine environment, particular attention being paid to the need for protection from harmful effects of such activities as

[163] See discussion in Tara Davenport, 'Responsibility and Liability for Damage Arising Out of Activities in the Area: Potential Claimants and Possible Fora' (Legal Working Group on Liability for Environmental Harm from Activities in the Area, Liability Issues for Deep Seabed Mining Series, Paper No 5, February 2019) 4–9.

[164] See discussion in Chapter 3.

[165] For example, it may be possible to determine the value of common heritage of mankind resources on the basis of the market value of the resource in questions, that is, polymetallic nodules, polymetallic sulphides and cobalt-rich crusts, as noted in Chapter 3.

[166] UNCLOS (n 10) art 136.

[167] See, for example, International Seabed Authority (ISA), 'Regulations on Prospecting and Exploration for Polymetallic Nodules in the Area' (13 July 2000) Doc No ISBA/6/A/18 (PMN) reg 1(3)(c); ISA, 'Draft Regulations on Exploitation of Mineral Resources in the Area' (2019) ISBA/25/C/WP.1 (DER) schedule 1.

drilling, dredging, excavation, disposal of waste, construction and operation or maintenance of installations, pipelines and other devices related to such activities.

(b) the protection and conservation of the natural resources of the Area and the prevention of damage to the flora and fauna of the marine environment.

This provision 'assigns the primary responsibility for preventing environmental harm resulting from mining activities in the Area to the ISA' and affords the ISA 'a general and far-reaching environmental mandate'.[168] A purposive interpretation of article 145 is that an essential component of the ISA's obligation to protect and preserve the marine environment is its ability to initiate claims against actors that have caused environmental harm arising from activities in the Area. This entitlement is essential to deter wrongful activities and incentivize greater care by the relevant actors. Further, UNCLOS recognizes that the ISA 'shall have the right to take at any time any measures provided for under [Part XI] to ensure compliance with its provisions and the exercise of the functions of control and regulation assigned to it thereunder or under any contract'.[169] This, read together with the ISA's incidental powers that are necessary for the exercise of those powers and functions with respect to activities in the Area, suggests that the ISA has the legal authority to initiate proceedings for harm to the marine environment as part of its measures to ensure compliance with the provisions on the protection of the marine environment.[170]

It is also relevant that under the Exploration Regulations, the Council has the authority to issue measures in response to an emergency (on the recommendation of the Council) and if the Contractor fails to comply with these measures, the Council shall take by itself or through arrangements with others on its behalf, such practical measures necessary to prevent harm to the marine environment.[171]

The ISA does not face barriers relating to access to courts and tribunals – it has access to the dispute settlement mechanisms under section 5 of Part XI of UNCLOS, although its access to domestic courts will depend on the relevant national procedures.[172] The issue of what to do with any compensation that is received from legal proceedings is also surmountable in that the SDC in its 2011 Advisory Opinion recommended the establishment of a trust fund and this is envisaged in the current DER which contain provisions on the establishment of the Environmental Compensation Fund (see discussion in Chapter 8).[173] Any compensation received by the ISA can be directed to this fund. The DER state that one of

[168] Aline L Jaeckel, *The International Seabed Authority and the Precautionary Principle: Balancing Deep Seabed Mineral Mining and Marine Environmental Protection* (Brill 2017) 123–124.

[169] UNCLOS (n 10) art 153(5).

[170] ibid art 157(2).

[171] PMN Regulations (n 167) reg 33(7).

[172] See discussion in Chapter 7.

[173] *Activities in the Area* Advisory Opinion (n 39) para 205; DER (n 167) regs 54–56.

the sources of the Fund will consist of amounts recovered by the ISA as a result of legal proceedings in respect of a violation of the exploitation contract.[174]

While the ISA would seem the most logical actor to initiate proceedings given its mandate to organize, carry out and control 'activities on the Area' on behalf of humankind, there is no guarantee that it will do so. It is conceivable that the Legal and Technical Commission (LTC) could recommend not initiating proceedings and/or the Council could veto a decision to institute proceedings for a claim for damage to the marine environment before the SDC,[175] leading to a situation where damage remains uncompensated. Under UNCLOS, the decision to initiate proceedings requires a consensus in the Council at first, failing which a decision shall be taken by a two-thirds majority of members present and voting, provided that such decisions are not opposed by a majority in any of the voting chambers.[176] This potentially means that states with a direct interest in mining or states with an interest in revenue-sharing can potentially block a decision, even if it is contrary to the benefit of humankind.[177] Another issue is that the ISA *itself* may also be responsible for damage to the marine environment, or there may be multiple parties responsible for the environmental harm. If the ISA engaged in wrongful acts that contributed to damage to the marine environment, it may have fewer incentives to pursue claims against other responsible parties.

6.3.2.2 States

The standing of states in relation to deep seabed mining will depend upon the nature of the harm suffered. Most straightforwardly, there will be states whose economics interests are affected by environmental harm from deep seabed mining. This could take a number of forms, such as interference with a state's direct interest in deep seabed mining or other established resource rights, such as fisheries, as well as a sponsoring state who has sponsored a contractor which has had to stop activities and/or suffered damage to CHH resources in their contract area as a result of another contractor's activities and has resultantly lost a potential stream of revenue. As observed by the SDC, coastal states would also be entitled to bring claims for damage to the marine environment, presumably on the basis that coastal states have

[174] DER (n 167) reg 56(c).

[175] The LTC recommends to the Council that proceedings be instituted on behalf of the ISA before the SDC: UNCLOS (n 10) art 165(i). The Council has the power to institute proceedings on behalf of the ISA before the SDC for cases of non-compliance: UNCLOS (n 10) art 162(2)(u).

[176] Agreement relating to the Implementation of Part XI of the United Nations Convention on the Law of the Sea (adopted 28 July 1994, entered into force 28 July 1996) 1836 UNTS 3 (1994 Implementation Agreement) Annex, section 3(5).

[177] For a discussion of the inherent tensions in the mandate of the ISA, see Richard Collins and Duncan French 'A Guardian of Universal Interest or Increasingly Out of Its Depth? The International Seabed Authority Turns 25' (2019) Int Organ Law Review 1.

suffered damage to the marine environment in areas under national jurisdiction (for example, in the EEZ or continental shelf).[178] While the coastal state has sufficient legal interest to bring a claim as it has sustained direct injury, it only has access to the SDC for claims against the sponsoring State,[179] the ISA[180] and state contractors,[181] but not against non-state contractors and their ability to bring proceedings against any of these actors in national courts will depend on the applicable procedures of the relevant national court.[182]

The ability of states to recover for restoration of environmental resources in ABNJ is less certain. Unlike the Antarctic Liability Annex, there is no clear authority for states to unilaterally undertake restoration actions and recover from the responsible party. In these instances, states would need to argue that they are acting under a general obligation to protect the environment as found in Part XII of UNCLOS,[183] and by incurring restoration costs are specially affected. However, these states would still need to overcome the obstacles associated with differentiating between officious and necessitous interventions.[184] In the case of deep seabed mining, this question is further complicated by the presence of the ISA, which has the ability (and possibly obligation) to make emergency orders, in the face of environmental incidents, which undermines the argument that a unilateral clean-up by a state is necessary.

As indicated by the SDC, the alternative basis for standing lies in the doctrine of *erga omnes* obligations.[185] The SDC does not elaborate on its reasoning, but as noted, the *erga omnes* nature of obligations to protect the marine environment is supported (albeit implicitly) in the *Whaling in the Antarctic* case and *South China Sea Arbitration*.[186] There remains a windfall gain problem, which suggests that a litigant should not be able to keep the compensation for its own uses and it is even questionable whether that state party should have full discretion on what to do with the funds. A potential solution would be a fund mechanism (as is the case under the Antarctic Liability Annex) that is collectively managed for the benefit of the affected environment. Claims based on *erga omnes* obligations would be limited to claims against other states, as the obligations flow from common membership in the UNCLOS.

Finally, non-states parties to UNCLOS, which could include other users of the sea or coastal states as identified by the SDC above, may also suffer direct losses arising from damage to the marine environment as a result of activities in the Area (for example, the costs of reasonable preventive or response measures), but

[178] *Activities in the Area* Advisory Opinion (n 39) para 179.
[179] UNCLOS (n 10) art 187(a).
[180] ibid art 187(b).
[181] ibid art 187(a).
[182] See discussion in Chapter 7.
[183] UNCLOS (n 10) arts 192 and 209.
[184] See discussion in Section 6.2.1.1.
[185] *Activities in the Area* Advisory Opinion (n 39) para 180.
[186] See discussion in Section 6.2.1.1.

non-parties will not have any access to UNCLOS dispute settlement. Their ability to bring proceedings against any of these actors in national courts will depend on the applicable procedures of the relevant national court.[187]

6.3.2.3 Non-state Actors (Including Contractors)

It is possible that contractors may incur direct costs because of an incident (which can be attributable to another contractor, sponsoring state or the ISA) and which can be classified as harm to the marine environment, for example, the costs of reasonable response or preventive measures or the cost of assessing the damage. Contractors may also suffer damage to CHH resources which fall within their contract area. To the extent that the contractor has suffered direct injury, it will have sufficient legal interest against the ISA and the sponsoring state based on its contractual rights to exploit seabed resources (and access to the dispute settlement procedures in section 5 of Part XI of UNCLOS). Other non-state actors operating in the Area (including other users of the sea) may also incur direct losses because of activities in the Area, but have no access to dispute settlement procedures in section 5 of Part XI of UNCLOS. While recognition of the specific interests in question will then be a matter for the domestic courts, there is no principled barrier to domestic courts to recognizing legal interests (such as rights to exploit marine living resources) that relate to ABNJ.[188]

A thornier question, in the context of activities in the Area, is whether non-state actors including international organizations and non-governmental organizations have standing to bring claims for environmental harm when they have not suffered direct damage. It is a complex question because the 'Area and its resources are the common heritage of mankind' and governance of the exploration and exploitation of CHH resources are carried out for the benefit of mankind as a whole.[189] While it has been argued that humankind has emerged as a subject of international law given its frequent invocation in various fields,[190] there is still considerable debate on its parameters.[191] During the negotiations of Part XI of UNCLOS, there were some attempts to confine the concept of 'mankind' to just states parties but this did not get strong support and was considered to be contrary to the 1970 Declaration of Principles.[192] It has also been held by the ICJ that 'mankind necessarily entails both

[187] See discussion in Chapter 7.

[188] This is further elaborated upon in Chapter 7.

[189] UNCLOS (n 10) arts 136 and 140(1).

[190] Antônio Augusto Cançado Trindade, *International Law for Humankind: Toward a New Jus Gentium* (Martinus Nijhoff 2005) 287.

[191] Kemal Baslar, *The Concept of the Common Heritage of Mankind in International Law* (Martinus Nijhoff 1998) 70–76.

[192] ED Brown, *The Area beyond the Limits of National Jurisdiction: Sea-Bed Energy and Mineral Resources and Law of the Sea* (Martinus Nijhoff 1986) vol II 3.29. Although note that article 82, which obliges the coastal state to make payments or contributions for exploitation of the

present and future generations'.[193] It is clear that humankind extends beyond states. In recognition of this, the DER have defined 'stakeholder' as 'a natural or juristic person or an association of persons with an interest of any kind in, or who may be affected by, the proposed or existing Exploitation Activities under a Plan of Work in the Area, or who has relevant information or expertise'.[194] The ISA recognizes that these 'stakeholders' have an interest in the administration of the CHH and are, at the very least, entitled to participate in the policy making of the ISA.[195]

Do such non-state actors have sufficient legal interest to bring claims for environmental harm in ABNJ from activities in the Area considering the harm done to collective interests? An argument could be made that such NGOs or equivalent bodies have standing given the intrinsic relationship between CHH resources and the marine environment (the preservation for future generations is said to be an essential component of the CHH principle) and the protection of the marine environment from activities in the Area is also for the benefit of the collective interests of humankind.[196] Recognition of the rights of NGOs in domestic courts to represent public interests are statutory creations, but the competence of a state to extend standing to areas outside of its territory is doubtful. In addition, there may be questions of the basis and legitimacy of a claim by an NGO to represent the interests of humankind as a whole.[197]

6.3.3 *High Seas*

The question of which actor has standing for environmental harm in the high seas will largely be determined by the default rules, which already have been discussed in Section 6.2. Nonetheless, it is useful to consider in more depth the specific aspects of the legal regimes governing the high seas that may influence questions of standing.

outer continental shelf which are to be distributed by the Authority on the basis of equitable sharing criteria, only specifies that the Authority shall distribute them to States Parties (rather than mankind as a whole).

193 See, for example, *Gabčíkovo-Nagymaros Project (Hungary v Slovakia)* (Judgment) [1997] ICJ Rep 7, para 140.

194 DER (n 167) schedule 1.

195 For example, in the context of developing the Exploitation Regulations, the ISA has recognized the need to develop an effective 'communications and engagement strategy' for the ISA to ensure active stakeholder participation in the development of a minerals code (see Kristian Telicki, 'Developing a Communications and Engagement Strategy for the International Seabed Authority to Ensure Active Stakeholder Participation in the Development of a Minerals Exploitation Code' (2016) ISA Discussion Paper No 3. The ISA conducted a series of 'stakeholder surveys' in 2014, 2015, 2016 and 2017, in which it received submissions for various actors, including IOs, NGOs and individuals.

196 See Section 6.2.1.3.

197 ibid.

There are a variety of international organizations that have mandates in the high seas, for example, various RFMOs, regional seas organizations and sectoral organizations.[198] It is conceivable that environmental harm in the high seas could impact the interests of such international organizations and fall under their relevant mandate. In such cases, standing is dependent on two key factors. First, whether the constitutive instrument endows the international organization with international legal personality and capacity to bring international claims. Second, whether the mandate and powers conferred on the institution provide either a direct legal interest in the high seas environment or responsibilities that would include incidental powers to pursue compensation – the most salient of these, perhaps, being the ability to take response measures to protect the marine environment. Applying these factors to the existing institutions governing the high seas, there are no institutions, except for the ISA, discussed above, that would appear to have standing to pursue claims for environmental harm in the high seas. Many of the institutional structures, such as regional seas commissions, do not have separate legal personality and are intended to function as coordinating bodies for state-led activities. Even where institutions have legal personality, as is the case with some RFMOs,[199] the mandate of the body concerned (for example, as described in relation to the CCAMLR Commission) does not disclose an intention to provide these institutions with legal interests in resources or the authority to initiate response measures. The institutional structures established under the newly agreed upon agreement on the conservation and sustainable use of marine biological diversity of areas beyond national jurisdiction (2023 BBNJ Agreement),[200] consisting of a conference of parties, a scientific and technical body, clearing-house mechanisms and a secretariat, are similarly constrained.[201] In earlier discussions leading up to the 2023 BBNJ Agreement, there were suggestions that states parties should seek compensation from private entities for environmentally harmful activities involving biodiversity beyond national jurisdiction.[202] There was also mention of obtaining guidance from 'conventional regimes

[198] See, for example, 'Mapping Governance Gaps on the High Seas' (The Pew Charitable Trusts, March 2017) available at <www.pewtrusts.org/-/media/assets/2017/04/highseas_mapping_governance_gaps_on_the_high_seas.pdf> accessed 1 September 2022.

[199] On the legal status and degree of institutionalization of regional fisheries management organizations and arrangements, see James Harrison, 'Key Challenges Relating to the Governance of Regional Fisheries' in Richard Caddell and Erik J Molenaar (eds), *Strengthening International Fisheries Law in an Era of Changing Oceans* (Hart Publishing 2019) 79–102. Harrison notes that 'it is more important to consider the detailed functioning of an organization or arrangement, rather than its formal designation or status'.

[200] Draft agreement under the United Nations Convention on the Law of the Sea on the conservation and sustainable use of marine biological diversity of areas beyond national jurisdiction, Advance, Unedited text, 4 March 2023 ('BBNJ Agreement'), Part VI.

[201] David S Berry, 'Unity or Fragmentation in the Deep Blue: Choices in Institutional Design for Marine Biological Diversity in Areas beyond National Jurisdiction' (2021) 8 Front Mar Sci 1, 7–11.

[202] Chair of Preparatory Committee, 'Chair's Non-Paper on Elements of a Draft Text of an International Legally Binding Instrument under the United Nations Convention on the Law

addressing liability', which could refer to the civil liability conventions adopted under the International Maritime Organization. The International Union for Conservation of Nature (IUCN) put forward the most detailed proposal on responsibility and liability which entailed a recognition that states, and competent international organizations, are entitled to invoke the responsibility of another state that has breached its obligations and that redress of environmental damage shall prioritize recovery of ecological integrity as determined by the use of best available science.[203] Ultimately, as explained in Chapter 1, responsibility and liability for environmental damage under the 2023 BBNJ Agreement is only addressed in the preamble which affirmed that states are responsible for the fulfilment of their international obligations concerning the protection and preservation of the marine environment and may be liable in accordance with international law.

In light of the absence of institutions with standing to pursue environmental claims for harm to the high seas, it would fall to states or non-state actors to bring such claims. International instruments addressing rights in the high seas, principally UNCLOS,[204] determine the nature of the interests that may be protected, but do not advance the rules on standing which are determined by the general approaches discussed above.

6.4 CONCLUSIONS

The essence of determinations of standing is which interests are recognized as worthy of legal protection and who may prosecute those interests. As these questions relate to environmental harm in ABNJ, there is little doubt in both international and domestic law that environmental resources are worthy of legal protection. The UNCLOS and the Antarctic Protocol not only identify the centrality of environmental interests, they identify responsibility and liability as key approaches to protecting those interests. The challenge lies with the second question, and in particular, with the question of who may pursue communal legal interests. There are, of course, private interests (whether of states or non-state actors) that are subject to harm in ANBJ, but for the most part the challenge here relates to access to courts, not standing.

International institutions or organizations can play a direct and indirect role in ensuring that recognized environmental interests in ABNJ can be protected. The

of the Sea and the Conservation and Sustainable Use of Marine Biological Diversity of Areas beyond National Jurisdiction' (28 February 2017) 111 Part X.

[203] International Union for Conservation of Nature (IUCN), 'Submission by IUCN following the Second Session of the Preparatory Committee on the Development of an International Legally Binding Instrument under the United Nations Convention on the Law of the Sea on the Conservation and Sustainable Use of Marine Biological Diversity of Areas beyond National Jurisdiction' (5 December 2016) <www.un.org/depts/los/biodiversity/prepcom_files/rolling_comp/IUCN.pdf > accessed 1 September 2022.

[204] UNCLOS (n 10) art 87.

direct role is exemplified by the ISA, which maintains a trust-like role in relation to the common heritage of humankind that provides it with a sufficient legal interest to pursue claims. The role of the ATCM is more indirect. It does not have the capacity to bring claims in its own right, but facilitates claims by states through the maintenance of a fund and by acting as a decision-making body in relation to determining the costs of a response action to be paid into the fund. In both cases, the international institution plays an important role in representing the community interest. The absence of any institutional structure in relation to the high seas (and the absence of ratification of the Antarctic Liability Annex) illustrates the limited willingness of states to concede these roles to institutions.

The standing of states to pursue claims for harm to communal interests is complicated by two areas of ambiguity. First, it is unclear under what conditions a state can undertake response measures unilaterally and seek compensation from the responsible entity. We have argued that international law ought to recognize that the obligation of states to preserve and protect the environment in ABNJ includes the ability to undertake responsible response measures. This remains, of course, an untested proposition. Second, the implications of many obligations concerning the commons environment having an *erga omnes partes* or *erga omnes* character appears to provide a clear basis for standing, but the form of reparations under these conditions may be constrained. The ILC's indication that reparations may be sought 'in the interest . . . of the beneficiaries of the obligation breached' provides a basis for claiming damages that is broadly consistent with the idea of *erga omnes* obligations. The problem of windfall gains remains a concern.

Finally, we note that both international organizations and states are likely to be imperfect guardians of the commons environment. This has certainly been the case in relation to many domestic and international environmental issues and has led to a profusion of innovative approaches to standing with domestic legal systems. While approaches based in trusteeship or the extension of rights to natural objects remain confined to domestic legal systems, the trajectory of the approach is towards broad and remedial rules of standing, which has growing relevance for the global commons.

7

Access to Remedies

7.1 INTRODUCTION

A major obstacle to ensuring that environmental harm in areas beyond national jurisdiction (ABNJ) is compensated is challenges associated with access to remedies. In relation to damage caused by pollution in the marine environment in ABNJ, article 235 (2) of the 1982 United Nations Convention on the Law of the Sea (UNCLOS) obliges states to provide recourse within their domestic legal systems as well as requires states to cooperate to implement and develop relevant rules of international law.[1] Access to remedies includes facilitating access to international and national courts to initiate claims for environmental harm, but also requires consideration of the associated rules that may constrain the ability of the court or tribunal in question to provide relief, such as jurisdiction over the subject matter of disputes and over certain defendants, rules on the choice of law and the recognition and enforcement of judgments rendered in such cases. As with other parts of this book, identifying the law addressing access to remedies depends on whether the claims for compensation are being pursued under international law or domestic law.

Under international law, liability and compensation for environmental harm will be determined by international dispute settlement mechanisms, and while such mechanisms include non-adversarial approaches (i.e. negotiation, mediation and conciliation), our focus here is on access to international courts or tribunals. In connection with domestic liability rules, the focus shifts to the competencies of domestic courts, which are, of course, principally a matter of national law. However, international law also places duties on states to ensure access to remedies within their domestic legal systems in order to ensure remedies are available to injured parties.[2] Pursuant to this general

[1] United Nations Convention on the Law of the Sea (adopted 10 December 1982, entered into force 16 November 1994) 1833 UNTS 397 (UNCLOS).

[2] See, for example, International Law Commission (ILC), 'Draft Principles on the Allocation of Loss in the Case of Transboundary Harm Arising Out of Hazardous Activities, with

obligation, an important element of international civil liability rules is directed towards removing barriers to access to remedies within domestic legal systems through harmonized rules governing access to courts and the availability of effective remedies. Such rules have, to date, been enacted through civil liability treaties, which may provide useful lessons for implementing the general obligation to ensure access to remedies in the commons context.

This chapter begins with a discussion of the general rules and principles concerning access to remedies under the rules of state responsibility and domestic civil liability, respectively, before turning to the specific rules in ABNJ. This chapter addresses the substantial additional challenges that each of these sets of rules pose to realizing the goals of liability regimes, including the need to prevent environmental harm and restore the environment, to provide for effective deterrence of risky behaviour, to ensure a level playing field and to ensure adequate and prompt compensation.[3]

7.2 GENERAL APPROACHES TO ACCESS TO REMEDIES

7.2.1 *International Forums*

There are an increasing number of international courts and tribunals that can hear environmental disputes between states, including claims relating to environmental harm.[4] These include forums with general subject matter jurisdiction, such as the International Court of Justice (ICJ) and inter-state arbitral tribunals, as well as forums established under specialized treaty regimes or branches of international law, including international courts and tribunals with jurisdiction to hear disputes under Part XV of UNCLOS (UNCLOS forums).[5] Specialized claims commissions

Commentaries' (2006) UN Doc A/61/10 (Draft Principles), principle 4 and commentary to principle 4, 76–83, paras 1–39. Whether the principle of equal access to remedies and non-discrimination is an accepted principle in international law is debatable. The ILC observed that it is an 'aspect which is gaining increasing acceptance in State practice' (see Draft Principles, commentary to principle 6, 8, para 5). Birnie, Boyle and Redgwell have said that it is not possible to get a clear picture on state practice on the basis that equal access to remedies is difficult to reconcile with the 'principle of *forum non conveniens*, the denial of jurisdiction in actions affecting foreign land, or the refusal to allow transboundary access to administrative proceedings on the ground that national legislation does not have extraterritorial application'. Patricia Birnie, Alan Boyle and Catherine Redgwell, *International Law and the Environment* (4th edn, OUP 2021) 326. However, Birnie and others also state that 'it can probably be assumed that it already reflects existing international law'. ibid 325.

3 See discussion in Chapter 2.

4 See generally Tim Stephens, *International Courts and Environmental Protection* (CUP 2009) 21–61. He notes at 27 that the '[t]he expansion in the number of and variety of adjudicative options in international environmental law is in large part a function of the growth of international adjudicative bodies more generally'.

5 UNCLOS (n 1) art 287. Under article 287, states parties can choose between four different forums: the International Tribunal for Law of the Sea (ITLOS); the ICJ; an arbitral tribunal

with competence, *inter alia*, in relation to environmental claims have also been established, such as the United Nations Compensation Commission (UNCC).[6]

The fundamental principle in international dispute settlement is that states must consent to the jurisdiction of that court or tribunal. The ICJ will only have jurisdiction over an inter-state dispute relating to environmental harm in ABNJ if the disputing states have consented to refer such a dispute either by special agreement, in a treaty compromissory clause, or through acceptance of the Court's jurisdiction by way of declaration under article 36 (2) of the ICJ Statute.[7] The ICJ has had fourteen cases submitted to it that involved environmental elements and, to date, the majority of them have been via the optional clause declaration instead of special agreements.[8] As the ICJ is a court of general subject matter jurisdiction, it has broad competence to hear disputes concerning state responsibility for environmental harm to the global commons, albeit that such claims may raise questions relating to standing in the context of potential challenges to jurisdiction and admissibility.[9]

As an alternative to the ICJ, states could agree, either ad hoc or through a treaty compromissory clause, to submit a dispute concerning liability for environmental harm in ABNJ to inter-state arbitration. There are several examples of arbitration of environmental disputes,[10] and Stephens has suggested that within environmental arbitration practice, 'states favour the *ad hoc* determination of specific disputes rather than institutional arbitration where the procedures are agreed in advance'.[11] Numerous multilateral environmental agreements make reference to arbitration of disputes concerning the interpretation or application of the agreement, although submission of a dispute to arbitration under these provisions often requires additional specific consent of the states parties to the dispute.[12] It has been widely

constituted under Annex VII of UNCLOS; and an arbitral tribunal constituted under Annex VIII for special categories of disputes.

6 See UN Compensation Commission (UNCC) Website <www.uncc.ch/> accessed 27 August 2022.

7 Statute of the International Court of Justice (ICJ) art 36(1) (ICJ Statute). To date, seventy-four states have made optional clause declarations, some of which have included reservations excluding either environmental disputes or certain types of environmental disputes. See ICJ Website <www.icj-cij.org/en/declarations> accessed 27 August 2022.

8 See also Tim Stephens, 'The Development of International Environmental Law by the International Court of Justice' in Douglas Fisher (ed), *Research Handbook on Fundamental Concepts of Environmental Law* (2nd edn, Edward Elgar 2022) 184.

9 On the standing of states to bring claims related to damage to areas beyond national jurisdiction (ABNJ), see Chapter 6.

10 Stephens, *International Courts* (n 4) 28. These include the *Bering Fur Seals Arbitration* Award RIAA vol XXVII, 263 (1893); *Trail Smelter Arbitration* (1949) RIAA vol III 1905 (1941); *Lake Lanoux Case* RIAA vol XII 281 (1957).

11 Stephens, *International Courts* (n 4) 29.

12 The most common dispute settlement mechanism found in environmental treaties is compulsory referral to conciliation of disputes not able to be settled by negotiation, with an ability for parties to optin by declaration to compulsory referral to the ICJ or arbitration: See Anais

observed that states may prefer to submit disputes to arbitration, rather than judicial settlement, due to the perceptions of enhanced party control over arbitral proceedings – for example in terms of arbitrator selection and the specification of procedural rules.[13] In particular, arbitration might enable parties to a dispute to exclude rules allowing third party intervention or other forms of participation such as *amicus curiae* submissions. For this reason, while arbitration may be well-suited to bilateral disputes, one matter of principle that might arise in relation to claims for environmental harm in ABNJ is whether arbitration is appropriate for disputes that engage wider questions of interest to the international community.[14]

The most promising avenue for inter-state claims on environmental harm to the marine environment in ABNJ is recourse to UNCLOS forums to hear disputes on the interpretation or application of UNCLOS.[15] Under article 287, states parties can choose between four different forums: the International Tribunal for Law of the Sea (ITLOS); the ICJ; an arbitral tribunal constituted under Annex VII of UNCLOS; and an arbitral tribunal constituted under Annex VIII for special categories of disputes relating to fisheries, protection and preservation of the marine environment, marine scientific research and navigation. Annex VII arbitration is the default procedure if the parties to a dispute have not accepted the same procedure or if the parties have not made a declaration.[16] Given that any dispute on responsibility for environmental harm to the marine environment will involve the application of provisions concerning state duties to protect the environment under UNCLOS, the UNCLOS forums have broad plenary jurisdiction to hear claims relating to environmental harm in ABNJ. The application of the UNCLOS compulsory dispute settlement to liability claims for environmental harm in specific regimes applicable in ANBJ is addressed in Section 7.3.

There are several points of general application to be considered in relation to the use of international courts and tribunals to litigate claims relating to environmental harm in ANBJ.

Kedgley Laidlaw and Shaun Kang, 'The Dispute Settlement Mechanisms in Major Multilateral Treaties', NUS Centre for International Law Working Paper 18/02 (2018) 40 <https://cil.nus.edu.sg/wp-content/uploads/2018/10/NUS-CIL-Working-Paper-1802-The-Dispute-Settlement-Mechanisms-in-Major-Multilateral-Treaties.pdf> accessed 25 August 2022.

[13] Loretta Malintoppi, 'Methods of Dispute Resolution in Inter-State Litigation – When States Go to Arbitration Rather than Adjudication' (2006) 5 LPICT 133.

[14] Neil Craik, 'Recalcitrant Reality and Chosen Ideals: The Public Function of Dispute Settlement in International Environmental Law' (1997) 10 Geo Int'l Envtl L Rev 551.

[15] UNCLOS (n 1) art 286. There are both compulsory and optional exceptions to the submission of disputes to compulsory binding dispute settlement procedure under arts 297 and 298, respectively.

[16] ibid arts 287(3) and (4).

7.2.1.1 Parties

The inter-state dispute settlement forums discussed above are only open to states. Only states have access to the contentious jurisdiction of the ICJ.[17] Similarly, the compulsory procedures in Part XV of UNCLOS (with the exception of disputes relating to activities in the Area) are only open to UNCLOS states parties,[18] and to international organizations that are parties to UNCLOS (presently, only the EU).[19] In general, arbitral proceedings are more flexible and there is scope for international organizations, non-governmental organizations (NGOs) and corporate actors to be parties to arbitral proceedings with states, subject to the agreement of the parties to the dispute.[20] Given that the primary perpetrators of environmental damage (in ABNJ or otherwise) are non-state actors, the ICJ and UNCLOS forums would primarily be used for claims to hold states accountable for oversight failures.[21] This substantive limitation means that recourse to inter-state claims will only capture a portion of potential environmental harm, and would on its own fail to hold other responsible parties accountable.[22]

While one-off instances of environmental harm in ABNJ may be attributable to one state, there may also be cases of cumulative harm attributable to the conduct of several or even multiple states (or the private actors over which they have to exercise due diligence), and hence it may be necessary to initiate proceedings against more than one state.[23] The ICJ Statute does envisage multi-party proceedings in cases where several parties have the same legal interest, and the ICJ may also direct that

[17] ICJ Statute (n 7) art 34. Under article 35(1) the Court is open to states parties to the ICJ Statute. Other states may also have access in accordance with article 35(2).

[18] UNCLOS (n 1) art 291. In consensual proceedings brought before the International Tribunal for the Law of the Sea (ITLOS), the statute of ITLOS recognizes that potential parties can also include international organizations, non-governmental organizations and private actors. Article 20(2) of the ITLOS Statute provides that '[t]he Tribunal shall be open to entities other than States Parties in any case expressly provided for in Part XI *or in any case submitted pursuant to any other agreement conferring jurisdiction on the Tribunal which is accepted by all the parties to that case* (emphasis added)': Statute of the International Tribunal for the Law of the Sea, UNCLOS (n 1), Annex VI (ITLOS Statute).

[19] UNCLOS (n 1) art 305(1)(f) and Annex IX.

[20] See, for example, Dane P Ratliff, 'The PCA Optional Rules for Arbitration of Disputes Relating to Natural Resources and/or the Environment' (2001) 14 LJIL 887 which *inter alia*, can be utilized by non-State actors (international organizations, NGOs and corporations).

[21] See discussion in Chapters 4 and 5.

[22] See discussion in Chapter 4.

[23] Note the *Monetary Gold* principle, whereby an international court or tribunal cannot resolve a dispute in which the legal interests of a state that is not a party to the proceedings 'would not only be affected by a decision, but would form the very subject-matter of the decision', may also be a barrier to international courts and tribunals exercising jurisdiction (see *Monetary Gold Removed From Rome in 1943 (Italy v France, United Kingdom and United States)* Judgment [1954] ICJ Rep 19). However, this principle has been applied unevenly by courts and tribunals and has come under increasing criticism: see, for example, Zachary Mollengarden and Noam Zamir, 'The Monetary Gold Principle: Back to Basics' (2021) 115(1) AJIL 41.

proceedings in two or more cases be formally joined or litigated together without formal joinder.[24] UNCLOS forums also envisage the possibility of multiple parties to proceedings.[25] The possibility of multiple parties either being claimants or respondents in state-to-state arbitration is also feasible if consent of all relevant parties is given,[26] but as the number of parties increase the likelihood of all parties consenting decreases. There is no doubt, however, that inter-state arbitration, the ICJ and to a large extent ITLOS are primarily designed for the resolution of bilateral disputes. As currently conducted, international adjudication appears ill-suited to determine liability for diffuse environmental harms to the commons, such as ocean acidification or marine plastics pollution, that is attributable to a multitude of different actors, and which clearly goes beyond the actions of state actors alone.

Claims grounded in *erga omnes* standing raise further issues as to which parties are entitled to participate in proceedings that involve shared legal interests.[27] Cases that seek to hold one or more states responsible for environmental harm in ABNJ may have legal consequences for the broader community of states that use or benefit from the resources found therein. One potential avenue to increase participation would be through the rules of intervention in proceedings in the ICJ or ITLOS.[28] Both bodies require states seeking intervention to have 'an interest of a legal nature which may be affected by the decision in the case', and confer broad discretion on the ICJ or ITLOS to decide upon the request.[29] Interventions do not generally confer party status on intervenors and would not broaden the availability of remedies to other affected states, but would allow states that have an interest in the judicial determination of collective interests to present their views to the court. States have in other contexts sought to intervene in cases where community interests are at stake. New Zealand, for example, successfully intervened in the *Whaling Case*,[30] although it relied on article 63 of the ICJ Statute, which allows intervention as of right to states in proceedings involving the construction of a convention to which they are a party.[31] In the dispute on the *Application of the Convention on the Prevention and*

[24] ICJ Statute (n 7) art 31(5); Rules of the ICJ Court (ICJ Rules) arts 36 and 47.

[25] For ITLOS, see ITLOS Statute (n 18) arts 17(5) and 47; For Annex VII Arbitration, see UNCLOS (n 1) Annex VII art 3(g); For Annex VIII Arbitration, see UNCLOS (n 1) Annex VIII art 2(g).

[26] For example, the various optional rules adopted by the Permanent Court of Arbitration (PCA) contain guidelines for their adaptation to multi-party proceedings: See Guidelines for Adapting the Permanent Court of Arbitration Rules to Disputes arising under Multilateral Agreements and Multiparty Contracts. The Optional Rules on Natural Resources also are designed to accommodate multi-party proceedings.

[27] This is further discussed in Chapter 6.

[28] ICJ Statute (n 7) arts 62 and 63; ITLOS Statute (n 18) arts 31 and 32.

[29] ibid.

[30] *Whaling in the Antarctic (Australia v Japan)*, Declaration of Intervention of New Zealand, Order of 6 February 2013, ICJ Reports 2013, p. 3.

[31] ICJ Statute (n 7) art 63(2); the ITLOS Statute (n 18) contains a similar provision in art 32(3).

Punishment of the Crime of Genocide (The Gambia v Myanmar), the Maldives,[32] Canada and the Netherlands indicated an intention (not yet pursued at the time of writing) to intervene in those proceedings 'which are of concern to all humanity', raising the potentiality of interventions rooted in obligations *erga omnes*.[33] The legal basis of the proposed interventions – article 62 or 63 ICJ Statute – was not stated. In *Allegations of Genocide under the Convention on the Prevention and Punishment of the Crime of Genocide (Ukraine v Russia)* dispute, by August 2022, four states had filed declarations of intervention under article 63 ICJ Statute.[34] More than forty states issued a joint statement indicating an intention to intervene.[35] Interventions in liability cases, even where the harm is alleged to have impacted a shared resource, may raise concerns about the equality of the parties, particularly where intervenors seek quite specifically to support one party or another.[36]

Non-state actors, such as intergovernmental organizations (other than parties to UNCLOS), NGOs and other non-state entities are unable to initiate proceedings in international courts against states alleged to be responsible for environmental harm in ABNJ in UNCLOS forums.[37] As discussed in Chapter 6, there are conflicting views on whether such non-state actors *should* have the right to initiate proceedings in international courts and tribunals. On the one hand, it is argued that relevant international organizations and NGOs should have standing or legal interest to bring claims on behalf of the environment as they represent the 'public interest' or that they are 'global guardians of environmental values'.[38] This is a logical extension of the principle of participation in environmental decision-making first articulated in Principle 10 of the Rio Declaration and entrenched in subsequent

[32] Ministry of Foreign Affairs, 'Maldives Welcomes the Joint Statement by Canada and the Kingdom of the Netherlands Announcing Their Intention to Intervene in *The Gambia v Myanmar* case at the International Court of Justice' (4 September 2020) <www.gov.mv/en/news-and-communications/maldives-welcomes-the-joint-statement-by-canada-and-the-kingdom-of-the-netherlands-announcing-their-intention-to-intervene-in-the-gambia-v-myanmar-case-at-the-international-court-of-justice> accessed 4 September 2020.

[33] 'Joint Statement of Canada and the Kingdom of the Netherlands Regarding Intention to Intervene in *The Gambia v Myanmar* case at the International Court of Justice' (2 September 2020) <www.government.nl/documents/diplomatic-statements/2020/09/02/joint-statement-of-canada-and-the-kingdom-of-the-netherlands-regarding-intention-to-intervene-in-the-gambia-v.-myanmar-case-at-the-international-court-of-justice> accessed 29 August 2022.

[34] *Allegations of Genocide under the Convention on the Prevention and Punishment of the Crime of Genocide (Ukraine v Russia)*. See Declarations of Intervention by Latvia, Lithuania, New Zealand and the United Kingdom <www.icj-cij.org/en/case/182/intervention> accessed 5 August 2022.

[35] UK Foreign, Commonwealth and Development Office, 'Support for Ukraine's Application before the International Court of Justice against Russia: Joint Statement', Press Release (13 July 2022), <www.gov.uk/government/news/joint-statement-of-support-for-ukraines-application-before-the-international-court-of-justice-against-russia> accessed 5 August 2022.

[36] See, for example, *Whaling* (n 30), Declaration of Judge Owada.

[37] See discussion in Chapter 6.

[38] Birnie and others (n 2) 266; Stephens, *International Courts* (n 4) 265.

environmental treaties.[39] Indeed, this argument has some resonance for environmental harm in ABNJ where no state has suffered a direct injury – arguably giving international organizations and non-state actors' access to international courts or tribunals increases the chances that environmental harm will not go unaddressed. Indeed, in national jurisdictions, government agencies play a crucial role in protecting shared environmental resources, for example, through their *parens patriae* jurisdiction.[40] The closest analogy to this role is the trustee-like role conferred on the International Seabed Authority (ISA) under article 137 of the UNCLOS.[41] In some states, NGOs are increasingly the actors that are holding states (and private actors) accountable for failing to meet their environmental obligations, although in most cases it is because national legislation permits certain non-state actors to have access to national courts.[42] Quite aside from the standing of these entities to pursue claims for environmental harm, there remains a lack of capacity for non-state actors to initiate or participate in international adjudicatory processes. If states wanted to confer authority on international organizations, such as regional fisheries management organizations (RFMOs) or regional seas commissions, to play a greater role in protecting the ABNJ environment, access to international judicial forums would need to be addressed.

Another route to expanding participation in environmental liability disputes in international courts and tribunals would be through more liberal intervention rules that allow courts and tribunals to receive *amici curiae* submissions from non-state actors, which are said to 'improve the quality of judicial analysis and reduce judicial error, enhance the legitimacy and authority of international judicial decision-making and thereby strengthen the influence of these decisions on the behavior of governments and other actors'.[43] The ABNJ context, which is likely to involve novel legal and policy questions, would benefit from the diversity of perspectives that *amici curiae* could provide. Indeed, the concept of common heritage of humankind in Part XI of UNCLOS suggests a set of interests that transcend state interests and would provide an opportunity for those views to be presented to the court or tribunal in question. Presently, in contentious cases, the ICJ and ITLOS permit submissions from intergovernmental organizations only.[44] Arbitration, either ad hoc or under

[39] See, for example, the United Nations Economic Commission for Europe Convention on Access to Information, Public Participation in Decision-Making and Access to Justice in Environmental Matters (adopted 25 June 1998, entered into force 30 October 2001) 2161 UNTS 447, 38 ILM 517 (Aarhus Convention).

[40] See discussion in Chapter 6.

[41] ibid.

[42] ibid.

[43] Stephens, *International Courts* (n 4) 268. On *amicus curiae* submissions in international dispute settlement, see generally Astrid Wijk, *Amicus Curiae before International Courts and Tribunals* (Nomos/Hart 2018).

[44] See ICJ Statute (n 7) art 34(2); ICJ Rules (n 24) arts 69(2) and (4); ITLOS Rules, rule 84. Christine M Chinkin and Ruth Mackenzie, 'Intergovernmental Organizations as "Friends of Courts"' in Laurence Boisson de Chazournes, Cesare PR Romano and Ruth Mackenzie (eds),

UNCLOS, does not expressly address *amici curiae* submissions.[45] Despite the lack of procedures authorizing *amicus curiae* interventions, NGOs have sought to participate in the proceedings before the ITLOS in the *Activities in the Area* Advisory Opinion and the *Arctic Sunrise* case. In both instances, the request for formal participation was refused but the briefs were circulated to the parties.[46] In some instances, international courts have invited or permitted specific *amicus curiae* submissions when called upon to address novel questions of international law, or when certain issues may not be argued by parties to the dispute.[47] This *amicus* function might be relevant in the context of ABNJ disputes where wider community or intergenerational interests may be invoked.

7.2.1.2 Available Remedies

The ICJ, arbitral tribunals and UNCLOS forums all clearly have the authority to order remedies for environmental harm that takes place in ABNJ.[48] Under the International Law Commission's (ILC) 2001 Draft Articles on Responsibility of States for Internationally Wrongful Acts (ASR), full reparation for the injury caused by the internationally wrongful act shall take the form of restitution, compensation and satisfaction.[49] Environmental disputes in international courts to date have generally focused on securing the prevention or cessation of activities giving rise to environmental harm and/or on satisfaction in the form of declarations of illegality, rather than on monetary compensation as such, but more recent practice may

International Organisations and International Dispute Settlement: Trends and Prospects (Brill 2002) 135, 140–141. The Court did not accept an NGO submission in the Gabčikovo-Nagymaros Case.

45 Ruth Mackenzie, Cesare Romano, Yuval Shany and Philippe Sands, *The Manual on International Courts and Tribunals* (2nd edn, OUP 2010) 117, para 4.24. The question of possible *amicus curiae* submissions in UNCLOS Annex VII arbitration was raised in the *South China Sea Arbitration (The Republic of Philippines v The People's Republic of China)* (Award) (2016) Oxford Reports on ICGJ 495 (PCA) before an Arbitral Tribunal Constituted under Annex VII to the 1982 UNCLOS (*South China Sea Arbitration)*, paras 40–42.

46 *Responsibilities and obligations of States with respect to activities in the Area* (Advisory Opinion, 1 February 2011) ITLOS Reports 2011 10 (*Activities in the Area* Advisory Opinion) paras 17 and 182; *Arctic Sunrise Case (Netherlands v Russia)* (Order of 22 November 2013) ITLOS Reports 2013, para 18.

47 See, for example, the International Criminal Tribunal for the Former Yugoslavia and the Special Court for Sierra Leone. See Wijk (n 43) 312–313, and Sarah Williams, Hannah Woolaver and Emma Palmer, *The Amicus Curiae in International Criminal Justice* (Hart Publishing 2020), at 118–120.

48 The rules on state responsibility provide that 'it is equally well-established that an international court or tribunal which has jurisdiction with respect to a claim of State responsibility has, an aspect of that jurisdiction, the power to award compensation for damage suffered': ILC, 'Draft Articles on the Responsibility of States for Internationally Wrongful Acts, with Commentaries,' (2001) UN Doc A/56/10 (ASR) commentary to art 36, 99, para 2.

49 ASR (n 48) art 34, 95.

indicate a move towards awards of such compensation.[50] The obligation to compensate for the damage caused (insofar as the damage is not made good by restitution) would 'cover any financially assessable damage including loss of profits insofar as it is established'.[51] As explored in Chapter 6, damages may not be available, however, in circumstances where the plaintiff is relying on *erga omnes* standing to bring claims for environmental harm.[52] The approach of the ILC is to allow for the possibility of reparations, but only where the state seeking reparations can demonstrate that the claim is being made in the interests of the beneficiaries of the obligation. The law on this point is unclear, with the ILC expressly noting that article 48(2)(b) of the ASR represents 'a measure of progressive development'.[53] The unanswered question is what steps a claimant state or states would need to take to show that the reparations are being used to protect the community interest.

7.2.1.3 Enforcement and Recognition

The ICJ, inter-state arbitral tribunals and ITLOS all provide for judgments or awards that are final and binding and that must be complied with.[54] That said, unlike the judgments of national courts, commercial arbitral tribunals and even investor–state dispute settlement, there is no overarching multilateral system of enforcement and recognition of judgments or awards issued by the ICJ, inter-state arbitral tribunals or UNCLOS forums, with the exception of the Seabed Disputes Chamber (SDC) of ITLOS.[55] The decisions of the SDC or any court or tribunal having jurisdiction over the rights and obligations of the ISA and the contractor (discussed in Section 7.3) are to be enforceable in the territory of the state party in the same manner as judgments or orders of the highest court of that state party.[56] While there is possible recourse to the Security Council in the event of non-compliance with an ICJ judgment, the Security Council's powers under article 94(2) UN Charter have

[50] *Certain Activities Carried Out by Nicaragua in the Border Area (Costa Rica v Nicaragua), Compensation owed by the Republic of Nicaragua to the Republic of Costa Rica* [2018] ICJ Rep 15; *Armed Activities on the Territory of the Congo (Democratic Republic of the Congo v Uganda)*, (Order of 8 September 2020) [2020] ICJ Rep 264, (Order of 12 October 2020) [2020] ICJ Rep 295; see also Chapter 3.

[51] ASR (n 48) art 36, 98.

[52] Discussed in Chapter 6.

[53] ASR (n 48) commentary to art 48, 127, para 12.

[54] United Nations Charter UKTS 67 (1946) art 94(1); UNCLOS (n 1) art 296(1), ITLOS Statute (n 18) art 33(1); UNCLOS (n 1) Annex VII art 11.

[55] See generally Ralf Michaels, 'Recognition and Enforcement of Foreign Judgments' in Rüdiger Wolfrum (ed), *Max Planck Encyclopedia of Public International Law* (OUP 2009). Jan Kleinheisterkamp, 'Recognition and Enforcement of Foreign Arbitral Awards' in Rüdiger Wolfrum (ed), *Max Planck Encyclopedia of Public International Law* (OUP 2008).

[56] ITLOS Statute (n 18) art 39; UNCLOS (n 1) Annex III art 21(2); *Activities in the Area* Advisory Opinion (n 46) para 235.

never been used.[57] The lack of enforcement and recognition of judgments and awards of the ICJ, ad hoc arbitral tribunals and UNCLOS forums undermines the utility of using these courts and tribunals to bring a claim for environmental harm in ABNJ.

7.2.1.4 Evidentiary Issues

Disputes concerning liability for environmental damage in ABNJ are likely to require consideration of complex scientific evidence. This has been discussed in Chapter 3 and will not be revisited here except to reiterate that based on practice to date, there have been questions about the extent to which international courts and tribunals are equipped to deal with such evidence.[58] These concern, amongst other things, the way in which expert evidence has been treated in international courts and tribunals, and the limited use that the ICJ in particular has made of its power to appoint its own experts to assist with evaluation of scientific data.[59] Further consideration is likely to be needed to improve this aspect of the practice and procedure of international courts.

7.2.1.5 An International Court for the Environment?

In light of the perceived shortcomings of existing international courts and tribunals in dealing with the nature and scope of environmental claims, as discussed above, there have been calls for the establishment of a specific international environmental court by academics, grassroots and environmental organizations, as well as some legal practitioners.[60] The arguments for an international environmental court relate to the ineffectiveness of existing dispute settlement forums in addressing the complexities of environmental disputes, the lack of scientific and technical knowledge on the part of judges and arbitrators and the lack of standing for non-state actors before such international courts and tribunals.[61] However, an international environmental court has not been established and seems unlikely to be established in the

57 ICJ Statute (n 7) art 94 (2). Also see Mackenzie and others (n 45) 34.

58 See Chapter 3, Section 3.4.

59 For example, ICJ Statute (n 7) art 50.

60 The call for an international environmental court began in the late 1980s led by Amedeo Postiglione, founder of the International Court of the Environment Foundation, which has now been succeeded by the International Court for the Environment Coalition. See <www.icecoalition.org/> accessed 27 August 2022. For a history of the movement for an international environmental court, see Ole W Pedersen, 'An International Environmental Court and International Legalism' (2012) 24(3) JEL 547, 547–553.

61 Pedersen (n 60) 550–552. Also see Alexander M Solntsev, 'The International Environmental Court – A Necessary Institution for Sustainable Planetary Governance in the Anthropocene' in Michelle Lim (ed), *Charting Environmental Law Futures in the Anthropocene* (Springer 2019) 129–137.

near future.[62] Indeed, to date, even specialized chambers for environment-related disputes within existing courts, such as the ICJ or ITLOS, have either been abandoned or have not yet been utilized.[63]

7.2.1.6 Advisory Opinions?

An advisory opinion from either the ICJ or ITLOS is a non-binding court process open to states but their utility in determining liability and compensation for environmental harm in ABNJ may be limited.[64] Advisory opinions from ITLOS and its SDC have already contributed in elucidating the content of states' due diligence obligations, and aspects of the liability rules under Part XI UNCLOS. Undoubtedly, advisory opinions have certain advantages over contentious litigation in that they avoid procedural obstacles related to contentious jurisdiction and standing, allow states and relevant international organizations to participate and have an authoritative (yet non-binding) character.[65] This has led to them being one of the avenues explored to clarify the obligations of states in relation to climate change, including the impact of climate change on the oceans, as exemplified by the recent requests for advisory opinions to ITLOS and the ICJ from the Commission of Small Island States on Climate Change and International Law and General Assembly, respectively.[66] Notably, both advisory opinions explicitly or implicitly ask questions which may require ITLOS and the ICJ to decide on the existence of liability of states for breaches of obligations to protect the marine environment from anthropogenic greenhouse gas emissions. However, it is uncertain how these international courts will respond to such requests. Undoubtedly, advisory opinions can contribute

62 For a discussion of why, see Stephens, *International Courts* (n 4) 58–61; Birnie and others (n 2) 267–268; Pedersen (n 60) 548–543.

63 See, for example, the ICJ's special chamber for environmental cases established under article 26(1) of the ICJ Statute which was not utilized and eventually abolished; the special chamber for marine environmental disputes set up within ITLOS whose use was subject to the agreement of states in disputes on the interpretation or application of UNCLOS marine environmental protection provisions and disputes under treaties referred to in article 237 or that confer jurisdiction on ITLOS; the special arbitral tribunal established pursuant to Annex VIII of UNCLOS to hear disputes relating to the protection and preservation of the marine environment.

64 ICJ Statute (n 7) arts 65–68; ITLOS Rules art 138.

65 See, for example, *Dispute Concerning Delimitation of the Maritime Boundaries between Mauritius and Maldives* (Mauritius/Maldives), Preliminary Objections, ITLOS Judgment of 28 January 2021, Case No. 28, paras 140–215.

66 Request for Advisory Opinion to ITLOS from the Commission of Small Island States on Climate Change and International Law, 12 December 2022; General Assembly, Request for An Advisory Opinion of the International Court of Justice on the Obligations of States in Respect of Climate Change, A/77/L.58, 1 March 2023. See also, for example, Margaretha Wewerinke-Singh, Julian Aguon and Julie Hunter, 'Bringing Climate Change before the International Court of Justice: Prospects for Contentious Cases and Advisory Opinion' in Ivano Alogna, Christine Bakker and Jean-Pierre Gauci (eds), *Climate Change Litigation: Global Perspectives* (Brill 2021) 393–414.

significantly to clarifying primary obligations of states, any gaps in the law, and may also affirm the existence and/or principles of liability for breaches of these primary obligations, but courts rendering advisory opinions may be reluctant to go as far as determining which states are specifically liable, the extent of liability and corresponding compensation, particularly in relation to environmental harm in ABNJ.[67]

7.2.2 *Domestic Forums*

Another approach to access to remedies in respect of liability for environmental harm has been for recourse to be directed through domestic legal systems. In cases of transboundary harm, this approach has the principal virtue of allowing direct recovery to those who have sustained losses because of environmental harm from those most directly responsible for causing the harm. The challenge is, of course, that each system entails different rules and requirements that will impact the ability of victims of environmental harm from being able to pursue and recover damages (which will be explored in the following sections). A primary role of international law has been to seek greater consistency with domestic legal systems in how they approach the various elements of access to remedies.

7.2.2.1 International Obligation on Access to Remedies

The principle on access to remedies in domestic legal systems forms an integral part of the general requirement for states to put in place measures to ensure that prompt and adequate compensation is available. The ILC's 2006 Draft Principles on the Allocation of Loss (Draft Principles) require that

> [s]tates shall provide their domestic judicial and administrative bodies with the necessary jurisdiction and competence to ensure that these bodies have prompt, adequate and effective remedies available in the event of transboundary damage caused by hazardous activities located within their territory or otherwise under their jurisdiction or control.[68]

Where the general obligation addresses the substantive requirements for redress, the access to remedies principle seeks to establish minimum procedural standards, at the heart of which is to ensure that the courts of the state that have jurisdiction or control over the activity resulting in harm have the competence to entertain claims for redress. This builds upon Principle 10 of the 1992 Rio Declaration which is

[67] For example, in the *Wall* Advisory Opinion, the ICJ considered it appropriate for Israel to pay compensation but refrained from specifying the quantum: *Legal Consequences of the Construction of a Wall in the Occupied Palestinian Territory*, (Advisory Opinion) [2004] ICJ Rep 136. See also Jason Rudall, *Compensation for Environmental Damage under International Law* (Routledge 2020) 13–14.

[68] 2006 Draft Principles (n 2) principle 6(1), 85.

understood as laying the foundations of 'environmental democracy' consisting of access to information, access to public participation and access to justice in environmental matters.[69] Principle 10 specifically provides that 'effective access to judicial and administrative proceedings including redress and remedy, shall be provided'. While the Draft Principles are confined to transboundary harm, there is no principled reason to distinguish between transboundary harm and harm to the global commons in the context of access to remedies. The location of the activity or the harm, whether in another state or in ABNJ, should not impact the ability of the victim to seek redress.

The application of the obligation to provide access to remedies in the commons is reflected in article 235 (2) of UNCLOS, which as mentioned above, obliges states to ensure that recourse is available in accordance with their legal systems for prompt and adequate compensation or other relief in respect of damage caused by pollution of the marine environment by natural or juridical persons under their jurisdiction, without differentiating between damage within or beyond national jurisdiction.[70] The SDC identified the obligation to provide recourse under article 235 (2) as an element of a sponsoring state's due diligence obligation that serves the purpose of ensuring that the sponsoring state meets it broader liability obligations where its wrongful acts cause damage.[71] However, given that UNCLOS acknowledges the need for 'further development of international law relating to responsibility and liability for assessment of and compensation of damage', it is not clear how stringently this obligation would be interpreted.[72] The structure of article 235(2) suggests that the content of the obligation to ensure recourse must be assessed in light of the specific requirements of each state's domestic legal system, complicating the identification of minimum standards. Neither article 235 nor the Draft Principles enumerate minimum standards, leaving states with significant discretion in how this obligation is implemented.

The Draft Principles also include a non-discrimination requirement whereby foreign victims of transboundary damage should have non-discriminatory or equal access to remedies in the state of origin that are no less prompt, adequate and effective than those afforded to those that suffer damage within the state's territory.[73] The application of non-discrimination to the global commons could be designed to afford victims of harm in the commons that same treatment as that provided to

[69] United Nations Environment Programme, *Environmental Courts & Tribunals – A Guide for Policy Makers* (2016) 3–4 <https://wedocs.unep.org/handle/20.500.11822/10001> accessed 29 August 2022.

[70] The origins of all paragraphs of article 235 can be traced back to Principle 22 of the Stockholm Declaration: Myron H Nordquist, Shabtai Rosenne and Louis Sohn, *United Nations Convention on the Law of the Sea 1982, Volume V: A Commentary* (Martinus Nijhoff 1989) commentary to arts 235, 401.

[71] *Activities in the Area* Advisory Opinion (n 46) para 140.

[72] ibid paras 139–140, 236; UNCLOS (n 1) art 235(3).

[73] Draft Principles (n 2) principle 6 (2), 85; see also discussion in note 2 above.

victims of non-transboundary harm. The difficulty, of course, is that non-discrimination only provides as much access to remedies as those available to domestic litigants, which may be insufficient to ensure an objective level of prompt and adequate relief, and to protect and restore the environment. As a central objective of UNCLOS is to provide a common standard of behaviour in relation to protection of the marine environment, an approach that seeks to harmonize domestic practice may be preferable. In this regard, it is noteworthy that article 235 does not contain a non-discrimination provision, and the prevailing approach within civil liability regimes has been the identification of harmonized standards governing domestic legal procedures. In considering what reasonable steps a state may have to take to ensure recourse in its domestic legal system, it is instructive to consider the types of obstacles that are likely to arise for litigants seeking damages for harm in ABNJ through domestic courts.

7.2.2.2 Choice of Forum

Private international law generally provides victims with some discretion in terms of where they can initiate proceedings. In the case of harm that occurs in ABNJ, claimants cannot initiate claims where the damage occurred, and would generally be restricted to their home courts or the jurisdiction of the defendant.[74] Article 235 (2) indicates that the *state of the operator* that caused damage to the environment is required to ensure within its legal system that there is recourse for prompt and adequate compensation or other relief. This is slightly different from the Draft Principles where the emphasis is on 'hazardous *activities* located within its territory or otherwise under its jurisdiction or control' rather than 'natural or juridical persons under its jurisdiction'. The benefit of requiring the state of the operator to provide access to its courts rests on the assumption that operators' assets are more likely to be located in their home state, thus avoiding the need for further recognition of any judgment in other jurisdictions. It may also reflect an ethical obligation on states that benefit from environmentally risky activities to ensure that operators can be held accountable where those risks manifest themselves. The approach in article 235, which focuses on 'natural or juridical persons under [the responsible state's] jurisdiction' requires that there must be some link (usually incorporation) between the perpetrator and the state. This is unlikely to be straightforward in many cases.

For example, states that would *prima facie* have the obligation to ensure that recourse is available in their domestic systems for pollution caused to the marine environment in ABNJ by natural or juridical persons under their jurisdiction are the

[74] Birnie and others (n 2) 332; Draft Principles (n 2) commentary to art 6, 87, para 8. The Draft Principles acknowledge that claims can be brought in the state of origin, that is, the state which in the territory or otherwise under the jurisdiction or control of which the hazardous activity is carried out.

courts of the flag state if a vessel was involved in the incident leading to marine environmental harm.[75] However, the existence of flags of convenience means that the actual perpetrators may not have any link with the flag state, and may not have assets in the jurisdiction to satisfy a judgment. Moreover, the perpetrator may be a multinational corporation with subsidiaries in several jurisdictions.[76] The difficulty in unravelling causation may lead to multiple defendants, only some of whom the court in question may compel to participate in the proceedings, which in the absence of channelling, may lead to multiple proceedings. This could also open the possibility of courts using the doctrine of *forum non conveniens* to decline jurisdiction, since article 235 does not confer exclusive jurisdiction on the state with jurisdiction over the defendant which could result in the same defendant being exposed to several proceedings arising out of the same incident.[77] In determining whether it would accept jurisdiction, the court will look at contextual factors to see which legal system is better placed to decide the case.[78] The doctrine of *forum non conveniens* has been critiqued as directly impacting the access to justice of victims of environmental damage and allowing corporations (often the perpetrators of environmental damage) to escape liability, and is said to be 'obsolete in a world in which markets are global and in which ecologists have documented the delicate balance of all life on this planet'.[79]

Harmonization through civil liability treaties can clarify choice of forum questions. For example, the 1992 Protocol to the 1969 Convention on Civil Liability for Oil Pollution Damage (1992 Oil Pollution Liability Convention) provides that 'where an incident has caused pollution damage in the territory including the territorial sea or exclusive economic zone of one or more contracting states, actions

75 Sarah Gahlen, *Civil Liability for Accidents at Sea* (Springer-Verlag 2015) 283.

76 While the place where the defendant is domiciled is often considered the most appropriate as the defendant is best able to defend itself in the courts of the state in which it is domiciled, coupled with the ease of enforcement of judgments, the question of whether that state is the domicile of the operator is usually left to the law of that state. Further, when multinational corporations with different subsidiaries established in several jurisdictions are responsible for environmental damage, determining the true domicile of the defendant becomes more difficult. Moreover, national courts are traditionally reluctant to 'pierce the corporate veil' to find the parent company liable, allowing parent companies in group structures to evade liability: See Amanda Perry-Kessaris, 'Corporate Liability for Environmental Harm' in Malgosia Fitzmaurice, David M Ong and Panos Merkouris (eds), *Research Handbook on International Environmental Law* (Edward Elgar 2010) 360.

77 For example, the classic statement of the UK approach to *forum non conveniens* is found in the leading case of *Spiliada*, namely, that a case may be dismissed from a domestic court where there is another available forum with competent jurisdiction 'in which the case may be tried more suitably for the interests of the parties and ends of justice'. See *Spiliada Maritime Corp v Cansulex Ltd* [1986] UKHL 10, [1987] AC 460.

78 Accordingly, in the famous Bhopal litigation (the disaster happened in India), the US court referred the case against Union Carbide to Indian courts on the basis that the design, safety standards and management of the plant were based in India.

79 *Dow Chemical Co v Aifares* 286 SW2d 674, 688–689 (Tex 1990) (Droggett J).

for compensation may only be brought in the courts of any such contracting state'.[80] Other forums such as the domicile of the defendant or the place where the vessel was arrested have been excluded. Under article V (III), the shipowner has the right to establish the fund in any of the contracting states in which an action is brought against the shipowner, or if no claim is brought, in any of the contracting states in which a claim could be brought. Article IX (3) of the 1992 Oil Pollution Liability Convention states that only the court of the place where the fund has been constituted is competent to decide on the apportionment and distribution of the fund and all claims for payments must in the end be addressed to this court. Most claims addressed to the Fund are settled amicably without the necessity for the intervention of courts and courts will usually intervene for purposes of reviewing the initial decisions taken by the Fund.[81] The choice of forum and determination of parties is further simplified through the channelling of liability to operators.[82]

The 2010 Protocol to the 1996 Convention on Liability and Compensation for Damage in Connection with the Carriage of Hazardous and Noxious Substances (2010 HNS Convention) adopts different jurisdictional provisions due to its geographical scope.[83] The 2010 HNS Convention applies to (1) all damage on the territory and in the territorial sea of a state party; (2) to damage by contamination of the environment of a state party's exclusive economic zone (EEZ) or corresponding zone; (3) any damage *other than environmental impairment* outside the territory and territorial sea of any state if it has been caused by a substance carried on board a ship registered in a state party, or, in the case of an unregistered ship on board a ship entitled to fly the flag of a state party (emphasis added).[84] Thus, the 2010 HNS Convention also applies to property, personal injury and death claims that occur on the high seas but not to damage by contamination of the environment that occurs in the high seas. Where an incident has caused damage in the territory, territorial sea or EEZ of a state party, actions for compensation may be brought against the registered owner of the ship or other person providing financial security for the owner's liability only in *the courts of the state party that has suffered damage*.[85] Where an incident

[80] International Convention on Civil Liability for Oil Pollution Damage (adopted 29 November 1969, entered into force 19 June 1975) 973 UNTS 3, 9 ILM 45 (1970) (1969 Oil Pollution Liability Convention) art IX (1) as amended by the 1992 Protocol to Amend the International Convention on Civil Liability for Oil Pollution Damage (adopted 27 November 1992, entered into force 30 May 1996) 1956 UNTS 255 (1992 Oil Pollution Liability Convention) art VIII.

[81] Gahlen (n 75) 75.

[82] See Chapter 4.

[83] Convention on Liability and Compensation for Damage in Connection with the Carriage of Hazardous and Noxious Substances by Sea (adopted 3 May 1996, not yet entered into force) 35 ILM 1415 (1996 HNS Convention), as amended by the International Convention on Liability and Compensation for Damage in Connection with the Carriage of Hazardous and Noxious Substances by Sea (adopted 30 April 2010, not yet entered into force) (2010 HNS Convention).

[84] 2010 HNS Convention (n 83) art 3.

[85] ibid art 38(1).

has caused damage outside the territory and territorial sea of any state, actions for compensation may be brought against the registered owner of the ship or person providing financial security for the owner's liability only in the courts of (a) the state where the ship is registered (or in the case of an unregistered ship, the state party whose flag the ship is entitled to fly); or (b) the state party where the owner has habitual residence or where the principal place of business of the owner is established; or (c) the state party where a fund has been constituted by the owner either where an action has been brought or if no action is brought, with any court in a state party in which an action can be brought under article 38.[86] The 1999 Protocol on Liability and Compensation for Damage Resulting from the Transboundary Movement of Hazardous Wastes and Their Disposal (1999 Basel Liability Protocol) also recognizes that claims may be brought in the courts of a contracting party where (1) the damage was suffered; (2) the incident occurred; or (3) where the defendant has his habitual residence or his principal place of business.[87] These conventions provide a potential model for appropriate national courts for a civil liability regime for environmental harm in ABNJ, namely one which focuses on the nationality of the flag or where the defendant has his habitual residence.

7.2.2.3 Parties to the Proceedings

When one considers the likely plaintiffs in cases involving harm to the commons environment *per se*, further complications arise. As discussed in the previous chapter, non-state actors are less likely to have standing to pursue claims in relation to environmental harm *per se* to ABNJ. However, the ability of foreign states and international organizations to access domestic courts of another state may be affected by rules on judicial recognition of whether such international actors can pursue remedies in the national courts of another state, which will be unique in their application within each state. In the United States, for example, foreign states are granted access to US courts as a matter of comity, and as such access may be limited to 'governments recognized by the United States and at peace with [the United States]'.[88] While this is a fairly narrow constraint, there is also a line of cases in the United States that constrain the ability of sovereigns from bringing cases in foreign (US) courts where the standing of the government is rooted in their *parens patria* jurisdiction to pursue claims on behalf of their nationals.[89] Claims grounded

[86] ibid art 38(2).

[87] Basel Protocol on Liability and Compensation for Damage Resulting from Transboundary Movement of Hazardous Wastes and their Disposal (adopted 10 December 1999) UNEP/CHW.1/WG/1/9/2 art 4 (1999 Basel Liability Protocol).

[88] *Pfizer, Inc v Government of India* 434 U.S. 308 at 319–320. See also Hannah Buxbaum, 'Foreign Governments as Plaintiffs in U.S. Courts and the Case against "Judicial Imperialism"' (2016) 73 Wash Lee L Rev 653.

[89] Buxbaum (n 88) 662–665.

in a state or international organization's rights to claim on behalf of the international community appear to fall outside the basis of judicial recognition of foreign governments or international organizations' rights to pursue remedies. At a minimum, such claims would be dependent upon the rules of standing in relation to make claims on behalf of collective interests in the jurisdiction in question.

The international rules concerning sovereign immunities will also act to shield foreign governments and international organizations as defendants. Here the law quite clearly prevents foreign governments from being subject against their will to the proceedings of another state.[90] For example, UNCLOS contains a blanket immunity against claims for failing to protect the marine environment for 'any warship, naval auxiliary, other vessels or aircraft owned or operated by a State and used, for the time being, only on governmental non-commercial service'.[91] The restrictive approach to immunity would allow for a commercial exception, so a state agency or enterprise engaged in a commercial activity that causes harm in ABNJ may not be able to claim immunity.[92] However, characterizing activities as either commercial or governmental in ABNJ, such as scientific research, harvesting marine genetic resources or engaging in marine geoengineering activities, is not straightforward. Even seemingly commercial activities like deep seabed mining may be undertaken for non-commercial reasons, such as securing a supply of critical minerals for defence purposes.

Civil liability conventions can direct parties to ensure that domestic courts have jurisdiction over parties that may not otherwise be recognized by domestic courts. For example, the 1992 Protocol on the International Convention on the Establishment of an International Fund for Compensation for Oil Pollution Damage (1992 Fund Convention) has specific provisions requiring that states grant the International Oil Pollution Compensation Funds (IOPC Funds) the right to intervene in domestic legal proceedings and, as a corollary, provides that decisions undertaken with proper notice shall be binding on the Fund.[93] In relation to defendants, article XI of the 1992 Oil Pollution Liability Convention requires that state-owned ships used for commercial purposes be subject to suit in courts hearing

[90] The base rule is found in *The Schooner Exchange v McFadden* (1812) 7 Cranch 116.

[91] UNCLOS (n 1) art 236, although note art 31 which states that the flag state shall bear international responsibility for any loss or damage resulting from the non-compliance by a warship or other government ship operated for non-commercial purposes with the provisions of UNCLOS or other rules of international law.

Warships and other state-owned non-commercial ships retain their immunity under the 1992 Oil Pollution Liability Convention.

[92] On the contours of the current approach to sovereign immunity, see Hazel Fox and Philippa Webb, *The Law of State Immunity* (3rd edn, OUP 2015); James Crawford, *Brownlie's Principles of Public International Law* (9th edn, OUP 2019) 470ff.

[93] 1992 International Convention on the Establishment of an International Fund for Compensation for Oil Pollution (adopted 27 November 1992, entered into force 30 May 1996) 1953 UNTS 330 (1992 Fund Convention) arts 7(4) and (6).

compensation claims that the state 'shall waive all defences based on its status as sovereign state'.[94]

Some civil liability conventions also address multiplicity of proceedings. In the 1992 Oil Pollution Liability Convention, in cases where damage affects more than one state, claimants can choose where to bring their claims.[95] Although there is no *lis pendens* rule in the 1992 Oil Pollution Liability Convention (whereby proceedings in one contracting state could be stayed in favour of earlier proceedings in another contracting state), there will ultimately be a final bundling of claims when it comes to the distribution of the limitation fund established by the shipowner. In situations where damage affects more than one state, the claimant and the shipowner could potentially 'forum shop' and choose a forum that is favourable to them, given that there may be differing interpretations of the Convention's provisions in different contracting states, although the likelihood of this is said to be small.[96] The 1999 Basel Liability Protocol addresses the situation where there may be a multiplicity of proceedings in different forums. Related actions are those which are so 'closely connected that it is expedient to hear and determine them together to avoid the risk of irreconcilable judgments resulting from separate proceedings'.[97] It gives courts (other than the court first seized) the power to stay proceedings while actions are pending at first instance as well as the authority to decline jurisdiction if another court has jurisdiction and the law of that court permits the consolidation of related actions.[98]

7.2.2.4 Choice of Law

Generally, the principle used to determine the law applicable to a tort is the place where the damage occurred (*lex loci delicti*). If the event leading to environmental harm took place solely in ABNJ, the *lex loci delicti* rule does not apply, as there is no state in which the tort was committed. There is no clear conflict-of-laws rule that has developed in relation to environmental harm in ABNJ, arguably because not many claims have been made in national courts.[99] Some parallels may be drawn from conflict-of-laws rules for other torts that occur on the high seas where national forums have adopted different types of rules for maritime torts on the high seas, depending on the type of tort and whether it is damage occurring outside the ship or on the ship.[100] For example, English courts apply the 'general maritime law as

94 1992 Oil Pollution Liability Convention (n 80) art XI.

95 Gahlen (n 75) 72–73. 1992 Oil Pollution Liability Convention (n 80) art XI.

96 ibid.

97 1999 Basel Liability Protocol (n 87) art 18(3).

98 ibid arts 18(1) and (2).

99 One case is the 'Red Sludge Case' which concerned Italian flagged vessels dumping waste into the high seas of the Mediterranean, 40 km from the French island of Corsica, which gave rise to proceedings in the courts of Italy and France: See Gahlen (n 75) 284.

100 Gahlen (n 75) 317–320.

administered in England', which under English law happens to be the *lex fori* and this is also applied to collisions on the high seas involving two flags.[101] In France, maritime torts involving one ship are governed by the law of the flag.[102] Other jurisdictions determine the applicable law based on the law which has the most connection with the case, which would lead to different results depending on the circumstances of the case.[103] A different outcome might occur if the event giving rise to environmental harm in ABNJ occurred in areas under the national jurisdiction of the coastal state.

The willingness of a court to entertain a case or apply the law of the forum will also depend on the nature of the rights being protected. Rights of an economic nature, such as a right to engage in fisheries or to conduct certain scientific research, may have a close connection to the issuing jurisdiction despite the activity being undertaken in ABNJ. On the other hand, protecting the collective interests in the environment outside the territory of the state raises complex questions on the extraterritorial application of domestic law to what may amount to a shared property interest.[104]

Civil liability conventions can clarify the determination of applicable law in two ways. First, the treaty or subsidiary rules often provide substantive rules, governing the claim. Second, the treaty may identify the applicable domestic law that is to be applied to matters not specifically regulated by the treaty itself.[105]

7.2.2.5 Recognition and Enforcement

Finally, there may also be issues related to recognition and enforcement of judgments, the rules of which will differ from jurisdiction to jurisdiction and will also depend on whether there is a bilateral or multilateral instrument between the relevant countries. Recognition of foreign judgments is a matter of judicial comity, which injects a degree of discretion into proceedings for recognition.[106] Awards for damage to ABNJ areas may be perceived as raising public policy issues that may influence the receiving court's determination of recognition. For example, awards for damages may turn on a foreign court's understanding of the legal status of a

[101] ibid 320.

[102] ibid 321.

[103] ibid 324–325.

[104] In the event the interests in the commons are characterized as interests in immovable property, the spectre of the *Mozambique Rule* is raised, where the House of Lords held that it had no jurisdiction to entertain certain claims in respect of foreign land, including for the recovery of damages for trespass to immovable property, *British South Africa Co v Companhia de Moçambique* [1893] AC 602 (HL).

[105] 1999 Basel Liability Protocol (n 87) art 19 (providing that the applicable law for matters of procedure or substance which are not specifically addressed under the Protocol and to be governed by the law of the competent court).

[106] See, for example, *Hilton v Guyot* (1895) 159 US 113.

particular commons resource that may not be universally held. Moreover, would a court recognize a judgment awarded to an officious state or private actor that initiated an environmental clean-up that it was under no legal duty to undertake? Civil liability conventions, on the other hand, contain provisions on mutual recognition and enforcement of judicial decisions rendered by a court within the jurisdiction of a contracting party.[107]

There are several key lessons for ABNJ liability regimes that may be drawn from the experience of other civil liability regimes. First, there is a clear recognition of the need to address access to remedies issues through the establishment of harmonized rules. In the context of elaborating on the content of what steps may amount to due diligence in ensuring access to remedies, the approaches adopted within civil liability regimes provide a useful indication of reasonable steps states are willing to take to facilitate claims. Second, there are likely limits on the degree of generalizability of such rules, as the approaches adopted will reflect the structural features of the civil liability regime in question, such as the degree of channelling and the presence of a fund.

7.3 SPECIFIC APPROACHES TO ACCESS TO REMEDIES IN ABNJ

7.3.1 *Antarctic*

Annex VI to the Environmental Protocol on Liability Arising from Environmental Emergencies (Liability Annex)[108] adopts a dual system of forums, providing for international forums to address inter-state claims and domestic forums for claims against non-state operators. Until such time as the Liability Annex comes into force, any incident arising in the Antarctic will be governed by the general principles discussed in Section 7.2. The discussion in the following sections therefore focuses on how the Liability Annex addresses access to remedies.

7.3.1.1 International Forums

Claims against state operators by another state party to the Liability Annex for reimbursement costs responding to an environmental emergency are to be decided by state-to-state dispute settlement mechanisms including any enquiry procedure decided by the parties, as well as any dispute settlement procedures provided for in articles 18, 19 and 20 of the Protocol on Environmental Protection to the Antarctic

[107] 1992 Oil Pollution Liability Convention (n 80) art X; 1999 Basel Liability Protocol (n 87) art 21.

[108] Annex VI to Protocol on Environmental Protection to the Antarctic Treaty on Liability Arising from Environmental Emergencies (adopted 17 June 2005, not entered into force) 45 ILM 5 (Liability Annex).

Treaty (1991 Antarctic Protocol).[109] Article 18 stipulates that if a dispute arises out of the Antarctic Protocol, the parties to the dispute shall, at the request of any one of them, consult amongst themselves with a view to having the dispute resolved by negotiation, inquiry, mediation, conciliation, arbitration, judicial settlement or other peaceful means to which the parties agree. In the event that the parties cannot agree to a form of dispute settlement, the Antarctic Protocol provides for mandatory dispute settlement in articles 19 and 20. These provisions address, *inter alia*, the interpretation or application of article 15, which relate to emergency response action taken by the parties, and any Annex, including the Liability Annex, in the event that it enters into force, and provides that if states parties have not agreed on a means of resolving the dispute within twelve months of the request for consultation pursuant to article 18, they can choose either the ICJ or an Arbitral Tribunal to be established pursuant to the Schedule to the Antarctic Protocol.[110] The Arbitral Tribunal is the default option if a state party has not made a declaration on choice of procedure or if the parties to the dispute have not chosen the same procedure.

The application of the Antarctic Protocol's mandatory dispute settlement provisions is confirmed in the Liability Annex,[111] but is restricted to circumstances, anticipated under article 6(1) of the Liability Annex, where a party has undertaken a response action to address an environmental emergency arising from the activities of another state operator that failed to take a response action. Regarding liability of state operators for payment of the costs of response action into the fund, the identification of the state which has standing to initiate proceedings is more complex. Since there is no injured state *per se*, the negotiating states 'thought it undesirable to allow all other [States] Parties the simultaneous ability to bring dispute settlement actions against the responsible State operator'.[112] Therefore, rather than identifying the state that could invoke dispute settlement procedures, the Liability Annex leaves the settlement of disputes to the Antarctic Treaty Consultative Meeting (ATCM). The amount of the costs of the response action is to be approved by a decision of the ATCM with advice of the Committee on Environmental Protection where appropriate.[113] Further, the

[109] Protocol on Environmental Protection to the Antarctic Treaty (adopted 4 October 1991, entered into force 14 January 1998) 30 ILM 1461 (1991 Antarctic Protocol). It remains an open question whether the dispute settlement provisions in the Antarctic Protocol would provide an avenue for liability claims outside the procedures of the Liability Annex. The reference to article 15, on response actions, in the dispute settlement provisions indicates that the parties contemplated that the duty to provide for prompt and effective response action to environmental emergencies could give rise to a claim. Although the obligation in article 15 does not clearly identify responsible parties or indicate to whom the duty is owed, making the formulation of a claim that involves the 'interpretation or application' of article 15 difficult at best.

[110] ibid art 20.

[111] Liability Annex (n 108) art 7(4).

[112] Michael Johnson, 'Liability for Environmental Damage in Antarctica: The Adoption of Annex VI to the Antarctic Protocol' (2006) 19(1) Geo Int'l Envtl L Rev 33 at 48. Also see Chapter 6.

[113] Liability Annex (n 108) art 7(5)(b).

determination of liability of the state operator is to be resolved by the ATCM.[114] Decisions of the ATCM are taken by consensus so there is the possibility that a Consultative Party can block a decision related to its own liability. However, if a dispute remains unresolved, the dispute can go to the dispute settlement mechanism in articles 18, 19 and 20 of the Antarctic Protocol, although the Liability Annex still does not identify which state would have standing to invoke the dispute settlement mechanism.[115]

The jurisdiction to pursue claims against state operators appears to be exclusive to the international forums discussed above and precludes the initiation of proceedings against state operators in domestic forums. There is also no provision for the ATCM to be held liable in any way, which reflects the ATCM's lack of legal personality, (unlike the ISA), as well as the absence of any clear legal duties on the ATCM to protect the Antarctic environment (again, unlike the ISA).

7.3.1.2 Domestic Forums

With regard to non-state operators, the issue of which actor has standing to bring an action depends on whether it is an action for liability for reimbursement costs or if it is an action for liability for payment of costs of response actions into the fund.[116] In connection with liability for reimbursement costs, the only actor that can bring a claim against the non-state operator is the state party which has taken a response action.[117] The forum where such action could be taken was subject to debate and ultimately, two options were established in the Liability Annex. First, a state party can bring an action in the state where the non-state operator is incorporated or has its principal place of business or his habitual place of residence.[118] Second, if this fails because the non-state operator is not incorporated in a state party or does not have its habitual residence in a state party, then states parties can bring an action in the courts of the state party that authorized the activity.[119] States parties shall ensure that its courts possess the necessary jurisdiction to entertain these actions, although the precise requirements are not identified.[120]

With regard to actions for payment of the costs of response actions into the fund, it was also not immediately clear which actor would have standing to bring a claim

114 ibid art 7(5)(a).

115 ibid. Johnson notes that recourse to the dispute settlement mechanisms in the Antarctic Protocol was included late in negotiations and this may be why the issue of the state which could invoke dispute settlement mechanisms was not elaborated on, but that it should be possible for the ATCM to determine how the mechanism will be invoked. See Johnson (n 112) 49.

116 See Chapter 6.

117 Liability Annex (n 108) art 7(1).

118 ibid.

119 ibid art 7(2).

120 ibid.

and therefore the issue of standing is not explicitly addressed.[121] Instead, states parties only have an obligation to ensure that there is a domestic law mechanism that exists for the enforcement of a claim against a non-state operator that did not undertake a response action and is therefore liable to pay an amount equal to the costs of the possible response action into the Fund.[122] The Liability Annex contemplates that such actions may be brought by the party of the operator or another party, leaving it to the relevant parties to determine who should take the enforcement action.[123]

The limited scope of the Liability Annex leaves the question of recovery of damages for harm that falls outside a response action unaddressed. There is clear potential for general losses to be suffered. For example, oil spills from ships could interfere with tourism operators or with the conduct of scientific research. In such instances, access to remedies would be governed by general principles.

7.3.2 *Deep Seabed*

Claims for liability for environmental harm arising out of activities in the Area can be brought under special dispute settlement mechanisms established under section 5 of Part XI of UNCLOS. There is also the possibility of domestic courts hearing such claims but as discussed below, domestic courts face the same challenges here as domestic forums discussed in Section 7.2.2.

7.3.2.1 International Forums

The SDC is the primary forum to decide disputes relating to activities in the Area.[124] While article 187 of UNCLOS describes the SDC's jurisdiction in considerable detail, the only reference to claims for liability is found in article 187 (e), which refers to disputes between the ISA, a state party and a contractor where it is alleged that the ISA has incurred liability 'for any damage arising out of wrongful acts in the exercise of its powers and function'. However, article 187 could be interpreted broadly to cover most claims for compensable damage for environmental harm. For example, damage resulting from the 'wrongful acts' of the contractor and the ISA will necessarily require an interpretation of Part XI, the Annexes, the regulations, rules and procedures of the ISA, as well as any contractual arrangements, all of which are *prima facie* covered by articles 187(a) to (e). The SDC determines its own

121 Johnson (n 112) 48.
122 Liability Annex (n 108) art 7(3).
123 Johnson (n 112) 48. See art 7(3) which provides 'where there are multiple *Parties* that are capable of enforcing art 7(2)(b)' against non-State operators: Liability Annex (n 108) art 7(3).
124 UNCLOS (n 1) art 87, but see also art 188, which provides for the possibility of a more limited role for other disputes settlement bodies, such as a special chamber of the ITLOS, an ad hoc Chamber of the SDC or commercial arbitration.

jurisdiction and may be inclined to take a broad approach to the jurisdictional provisions of section 5 given that the objective of section 5 of Part XI is to confer primary jurisdiction on the SDC to promote uniformity in jurisprudence.[125] This remains, however, an untested question of interpretation.

Accepting that the SDC has jurisdiction over certain disputes concerning environmental liability arising from activities in the Area, the question then becomes which actor can utilize the SDC to bring claims against the actor responsible for environmental harm. States parties, the ISA, the Enterprise and the contractors have access to the SDC, making the SDC unique amongst international courts.[126] In the event that a contractor has suffered direct losses as a result of environmental harm because of the actions of the ISA, it could potentially fall within articles 187 (c) and (e) of UNCLOS and the SDC would have jurisdiction. Sponsoring states and other states parties could bring claims against the ISA in the event ISA's actions have resulted in environmental harm, and could do so for direct losses they have suffered or potentially for pure environmental damage in light of the SDC's finding that 'each state party may also be entitled to claim compensation in light of the *erga omnes* character of the obligations relating to preservation of the environment of the high seas and in the Area'.[127] Claims against sponsoring states for their failure to exercise due diligence were expressly noted by the SDC to fall under the SDC's jurisdiction under article 187(b)(1).[128] The ISA can also initiate claims in the SDC against contractors and sponsoring states for environmental harm, including pure environmental damage, given its broad mandate to protect and preserve the marine environment.[129]

However, the SDC does not have jurisdiction over all claims between the above-mentioned actors. A contractor that has suffered losses as a result of environmental harm due to the actions of another contractor would not be able to utilize the SDC, unless both contractors are states parties, in which case, article 187 (a) could conceivably be relied upon. It is also not clear whether the SDC would have jurisdiction over disputes between contractors and other sponsoring states with

[125] As observed by Alan Boyle, '[E]verything turns in practice not on what each involves but on how the issues are formulated. Formulate them wrongly and the case falls outside compulsory jurisdiction. Formulate the same case differently and it falls inside'. Alan Boyle, 'Dispute Settlement and the Law of the Sea Convention: Problems of Fragmentation and Jurisdiction' (1997) 46(1) ICLQ 37, 38. One of the primary concerns of the group of legal experts, as well as negotiators of UNCLOS, was to ensure uniformity of jurisdiction and jurisprudence. See in general, Report of the Chairman of the Group of Legal Experts on the Settlement of Disputes Relating to Part XI of the Informal Composite Negotiating Text, Doc No. A/CONF.62/C.1/L.25 and Add. 1, Official Records of the Third United Nations Conference on the Law of the Sea, Volume XI, 117.

[126] UNCLOS (n 1) Annex VI art 37.

[127] *Activities in the Area* Advisory Opinion (n 46) para 180. UNCLOS (n 1) arts 187(b) and (e).

[128] ibid para 230.

[129] UNCLOS (n 1) arts 187(b) and (c). Also see discussion in Chapter 6.

whom they are not in a contractual relationship.[130] The SDC does not have jurisdiction over claims for environmental harm brought by states that are non-parties to UNCLOS, or by non-state actors (such as shipowners, fishermen, cable owners, owners/operators of installations operating in the high seas or in areas under national jurisdiction) or jurisdiction over claims brought against other non-state actors that may actually be responsible for the damage (such as subcontractors, agents, employees of contractors; owners or operators of vessels or installations involved in activities in the Area; manufacturer of equipment or parent corporations of contractors that are privately owned). Moreover, the jurisdiction of the SDC might give rise to incomplete or fragmented jurisdiction where a single incident gives rise to environmental damage to the Area and to the high seas water column.

Nonetheless, the SDC does have its advantages as a forum to hear disputes relating to environmental harm. Not only does it have jurisdiction over the primary actors involved in activities in the Area, including (importantly) the ISA, but it can appoint experts to give expert and technical advice on the complex issues relating to determining environmental harm.[131] Referring claims to the SDC would also have the benefit of developing uniformity in jurisprudence, particularly given the centrality of the SDC in disputes relating to activities in the Area.[132] Moreover, with regard to recognition and enforcement, UNCLOS affirms that any final decision rendered by the SDC relating to the rights and obligations of the ISA and the contractor (notably excluding the sponsoring state) shall be enforceable in the territory of each state party.[133] The SDC in its Advisory Opinion observed that legislation of sponsoring states should include provisions to ensure that any final decision rendered by a court or tribunal under UNCLOS relating to the rights and obligations of the ISA and contractor shall be enforceable in the territory of each state party.[134]

One potential restriction of the SDC's jurisdiction to hear claims is the limitation found in article 189, which provides that the SDC 'shall have no jurisdiction with regard to the exercise by the Authority of its discretionary powers in accordance with this part'.[135] The nature of a liability claim against the ISA for its failure to exercise due diligence in its duty to protect the marine environment may require the SDC to determine whether actions taken by the ISA, which could be understood to be discretionary, meet the requisite standard. The analogy would be to restrictions in common law courts in reviewing the policy decisions of public authorities as a

[130] ibid art 187(c) which covers disputes between states parties and contractors and only applies to contractual disputes.

[131] UNCLOS (n 1) art 289. See Section 7.2.1.4, and Chapter 3, Section 3.4.

[132] Indeed, even if disputes are referred to commercial arbitral tribunals, the SDC retains essential jurisdiction over disputes that involve a question of interpretation of Part XI and the annexes thereto: UNCLOS (n 1) art 188(2).

[133] ibid Annex III art 21(2); ITLOS Statute (n 18) art 39.

[134] UNCLOS (n 1) Annex III art 21(2); *Activities in the Area* Advisory Opinion (n 46) para 235.

[135] UNCLOS (n 1) art 189.

source of tort liability.[136] The rationale for this limited immunity is to avoid judicial interference with the legislative branches of government; a rationale that appears to underlie article 189. The wording of article 189, which affirms the jurisdiction of the SDC to decide cases involving 'claims for damages to be paid or other remedy to be given to the party concerned for the failure of the other party to comply with its contractual obligations or its obligations under this Convention', which would allow for claims against the ISA where it exceeds its jurisdiction. However, the SDC may still be constrained in reviewing the actions of the ISA on a reasonableness standard, which is in effect what a claim for a failure of the ISA to exercise due diligence would require.[137]

7.3.2.2 Domestic Forums

UNCLOS does not explicitly mention domestic courts as a forum for deciding claims related to activities in the Area. However, article 235 (2) would, at the very least, require sponsoring states to ensure recourse within their courts for victims of environmental damage caused by sponsored contractors; a point confirmed by the SDC in its Advisory Opinion.[138] According to the SDC, the sponsoring state has a certain measure of discretion with regard to the adoption of laws and regulations and the taking of administrative measures in support of its general obligation of due diligence, but its discretion is not absolute – it must act in good faith, taking 'the relevant options into account in a manner that is reasonable, relevant and conducive to the benefit of mankind as a whole'.[139]

In principle, national courts of sponsoring states should have jurisdiction to decide claims relating to activities in the Area, including those related to environmental harm. They may prove particularly useful for actors that do not have access to the SDC, ITLOS special chamber or SDC ad hoc chamber or commercial arbitral tribunals constituted under section 5 of Part XI. These include the vessel owners, cable owners, fishing companies and non-party states to UNCLOS, as well as subcontractors, agents, employees of contractors; owners or operators of vessels or installations involved in activities in the Area; manufacturer of equipment or parent corporations of contractors that are privately owned. However, the same issues relating to the implications for access to remedies of non-harmonization of liability

[136] *Anns v Merton London Borough Council* [1977] UKHL 4; *Just v British Columbia* [1989] 2 SCR 1228.

[137] For a general discussion, see James Harrison, 'Checks and Balances on the Regulatory Powers of the International Seabed Authority' in A Ascencio Herrera and MH Nordquist (eds), *The United Nations Convention on the Law of the Sea Part XI Regime and the International Seabed Authority: A Twenty-Five Year Journey* (Brill 2022) 151–173.

[138] *Activities in the Area* Advisory Opinion (n 46) para 139.

[139] ibid paras 227 and 230.

for environmental harm in the commons generally (as outlined in Section 7.2.2) would also apply to activities in the Area.

There are also specific challenges related to having two levels of forums to decide environmental harm claims. It may lead to inconsistent decisions relating to deep seabed mining and a fragmentation of interpretation of 'the constitution' of the oceans. The drafters of UNCLOS felt it important enough to reserve the jurisdiction of the SDC to decide issues of interpretation or application of UNCLOS even in the context of commercial arbitration. There is no such review by the SDC when it comes to decisions of national courts even if they may decide matters that address UNCLOS and/or activities in the Area that are carried out for the benefit of humankind. Indeed, it has been argued that 'it should be recognized that if jurisdiction over "activities in the Area" is fragmented, the importance of the Chamber and the authority of its decisions risks being diluted'.[140] Moreover, having two forums may result in actors such as the contractor being potentially exposed to liability in two different forums for the same wrongful acts.

7.3.3 *High Seas*

Absent a specific international regime, or sectoral regimes for specific hazardous activities applicable in relation to the high seas, liability for environmental harm in the high seas is currently subject to the general rules and considerations concerning access to remedies discussed in Section 7.2 of this chapter, particularly the discussion relating to Part XV dispute settlement procedures under UNCLOS.

The recently agreed upon text of the agreement on the conservation and sustainable use of marine biological diversity of areas beyond national jurisdiction (2023 BBNJ Agreement) provides that disputes concerning the interpretation or application of the 2023 BBNJ Agreement shall be settled in accordance with Part XV of UNCLOS, and again the discussion in Section 7.2 of this chapter is relevant.[141] One potential issue is that the delimitation of jurisdiction between the SDC conferred pursuant to Part XI of UNCLOS and dispute settlement mechanisms in the 2023 BBNJ Agreement may be complex in relation to cases involving both harm to marine biodiversity and to the Area and its resources. For example, one suggestion has been that the negotiators, or ITLOS on its own initiative, might establish a standing chamber in ITLOS for disputes on marine biodiversity in ABNJ

[140] Herbert Smith Freehills, 'Dispute Resolution Considerations Arising under the Proposed New Exploitation Regulations' (Discussion Paper No 1, ISA, 12 February 2016) 9 at para 4.7 <www.isa.org.jm/wp-content/uploads/2022/12/DP1.pdf> accessed 29 August 2022.

[141] Draft agreement under the United Nations Convention on the Law of the Sea on the conservation and sustainable use of marine biological diversity of areas beyond national jurisdiction, Advance, Unedited text, 4 March 2023 ('BBNJ Agreement'), Part XI.

jurisdiction, but this may lead to additional questions concerning which body has jurisdiction to determine disputes.[142]

A new dimension has been added to the 2023 BBNJ Agreement in terms of non-adversarial dispute settlement mechanisms. An Implementation and Compliance Committee will be established 'to facilitate and consider the implementation of and promote compliance with' the provisions of the BBNJ Agreement, along with a provision that parties may refer disputes concerning a matter of a technical nature to an ad hoc expert panel which shall 'confer with the Parties concerned and shall endeavour to resolve the dispute expeditiously without recourse to binding procedures' established under Part XV of UNCLOS.[143] These non-adversarial processes could present possible opportunities for consideration of issues relating to liability for environmental harm in the high seas if it relates to the interpretation or application of the 2023 BBNJ Agreement, or its implementation and compliance.

It is also worth noting the 2023 BBNJ Agreement endows the conference of parties with competence to request advisory opinions from ITLOS 'on a legal question on the conformity with this Agreement of a proposal before the Conference of the Parties on any matter within its competence'.[144] As in the case of the SDC's advisory jurisdiction, such requests may provide an opportunity to seek elucidation of relevant rules concerning liability for environmental harm in the high seas.

7.4 CONCLUSIONS

While claimants for environmental harm in ABNJ potentially have both international and national forums in which they can pursue remedies, both sets of forums present numerous challenges. International and national forums are not mutually exclusive and the suitability of either will depend on a range of factors. However, what is clear is that neither are perfect solutions to address claims in respect of environmental harm in the ABNJ. Undoubtedly, international forums specifically catered to address activity-based harm (such as activities in the Area and activities in Antarctica) and which have an institutional mechanism or structure that

[142] Liesbeth Lijnzaad, 'Dispute Settlement for Marine Biodiversity beyond National Jurisdiction: Not an Afterthought' in Helene Ruiz Fabri, Erik Franckx, Marco Benatar and Tamar Meshel (eds), *A Bridge over Troubled Waters: Dispute Resolution in the Law of International Watercourses and the Law of the Sea* (Brill 2020) 169–171. In respect of the division of competence, Lijnzaad notes that '[w]hether the environmental *consequences* and harmful effects *directly resulting* from "activities in the Area" – such as mining activities having a direct impact on marine biodiversity – therefore also fall within the jurisdiction of the [SDC], or should be addressed by the Tribunal (as pertaining to Part XII), or could indeed be under the jurisdiction of a future "BBNJ Chamber" is – to my mind – not fully clear' (at 176).

[143] BBNJ Agreement (n 141) arts 53 ter and 54 ter.

[144] ibid art 48 (6); and see ITLOS Statute (n 18) art 21; ITLOS, Rules of the Tribunal, ITLOS/8 25 March 2021, art 138.

can initiate claims for environmental harm have specific advantages over regimes which lack such an institutional mechanism. However, it is inescapable that the utilization of any of these forums for litigating claims depends on the willingness of states (or the relevant institutional mechanism) to bring such claims. Indeed, 'states have historically shown a great reluctance to initiate proceedings even where environmental damage is very severe'.[145] The practice of civil liability regimes demonstrates that many of the issues associated with domestic claims can be addressed through harmonization of claims procedures. However, there is little appetite to develop civil liability regimes that would cover environmental harm in ABNJ. This raises larger questions of whether courts and tribunals (whether national or international) are appropriate to address environmental harm in ABNJ given problems associated with standing, an absence of interest in utilizing them, issues relating to expertise in evaluating environmental harm and recognition and enforcement of judgments. Indeed, courts and tribunals may be particularly unsuitable for addressing cumulative, long-term environmental harm and other mechanisms such as funds (explored in the next chapter) may provide an appropriate alternative.

[145] Stephens, *International Courts* (n 4) 69.

8

Insurance and Compensation Funds

8.1 INTRODUCTION

Financial assurances, typically in the form of mandatory insurance or the creation of a compensation fund, have played a central role in international liability schemes since their inception. The presence of financial assurances responds to the overarching legal obligation to provide 'prompt and adequate compensation' for environmental harm by securing potential future liabilities,[1] since compensation is only adequate if it is available. Such arrangements address the concern that operators or other persons responsible for environmental harm may not have sufficient funds to cover the losses associated with an environmental incident. This concern has, of course, been borne out by the occurrence of major oil spills where there were insufficient funds to address the increasingly stringent demands for clean-up and compensation for economic losses associated with the incidents.[2]

[1] United Nations Convention on the Law of the Sea (adopted 10 December 1982, entered into force 16 November 1994) 1833 UNTS 397 (UNCLOS) art 235. See also International Legal Commission (ILC), 'Draft Principles on the Allocation of Loss in the Case of Transboundary Harm Arising Out of Hazardous Activities, with Commentaries' (2006) UN Doc A/61/10 (Draft Principles) principle 4, 76; for a general discussion, see René Lefeber, *Transboundary Environmental Interference and the Origin of State Liability* (Kluwer Law International 1996) ch 7.

[2] The *Torrey Canyon* incident in 1967 spurred the development of the International Convention on Civil Liability for Oil Pollution Damage (adopted 29 November 1969, entered into force 19 June 1975) 973 UNTS 3 (1969 Oil Pollution Liability Convention), amended by Protocol to Amend (adopted 27 November 1992, entered into force 30 May 1996) 1956 UNTS 255 (1992 Oil Pollution Liability Convention), followed by the International Convention on the Establishment of an International Fund for Compensation for Oil Pollution Damage (adopted 18 December 1971, entered into force 16 October 1978) 1110 UNTS 57, amended by Protocol of 1992 to Amend (adopted 27 November 1992, entered into force 30 May 1996) 1953 UNTS 330 (1992 Fund Convention). Subsequent incidents, such as the *Erika* and *Prestige*, in 1999 and 2002, respectively, gave rise to new concerns over the adequacy of the 1992 Oil Pollution Liability Convention and the 1992 Fund Convention, resulting in the

In order to provide a complete picture of the existing and emerging liability schemes for areas beyond national jurisdiction (ABNJ), this chapter details the legal and institutional frameworks associated with the provision of financial assurances as part of international civil liability schemes. The focus is on the requirements as they are set out in relation to ABNJ, with some focus on the yet to be implemented or proposed requirements of the Antarctic and deep seabed mining regimes, respectively. However, given the absence of experience in operational assurance schemes, this chapter also draws upon the existing practices of other international civil liability regimes to draw out some of the potential challenges with the implementation of financial assurances that respond to the unique legal and physical characteristics of areas beyond national jurisdiction.

8.2 THE PURPOSE OF FINANCIAL ASSURANCE

The primary purpose of financial assurances is to implement the more general obligation of ensuring 'prompt and adequate compensation', through the provision of security that is independent of the person responsible for providing compensation. Adequacy implies having accessible pools of funds available to satisfy successful claims.[3] The requirement that the compensation also be 'prompt' speaks to the need for claims to be assessed and, where eligible, paid out in a manner that avoids protracted and burdensome legal proceedings.[4] Financial assurances may be responsive to this objective by providing for more efficient processes for claims administration. For example, the International Oil Pollution Compensation Funds (IOPC Funds) set time frames for addressing claims and has processes to fast track certain claims to avoid undue delays.[5]

Securing compensation has direct and indirect effects on the ability of liability regimes to preserve and restore the environment, and much of the design of financial assurances is oriented towards meeting this objective. As a direct matter, financial assurances secure funds for post-incident preventive measures and for restoration of degraded environmental resources. The extent of coverage required through mandatory insurance is tied to the scope of damages and limitations on recovery amounts identified in the scheme, such that there is limited scope for

negotiation of the Protocol of 2003 to the International Convention on the Establishment of an International Fund for Compensation for Oil Pollution Damage (adopted 16 May 2003, entered into force 3 March 2005) 92FUND/A.8/4 Annex I (2003 Supplementary Fund Convention). See also Philippe Sands and Jacqueline Peel, *Principles of International Environmental Law* (4th edn, CUP 2018) ch 16.

3 Draft Principles (n 1) principle 4, 76.

4 ibid commentary to principle 4, 77, para 7 (noting the extensive length of time to resolve large-scale, often transnational, environmental litigation, such as the *Exxon Valdez*, *Amoco Cadiz*, the Bhopal Incident and *Trail Smelter Arbitration*).

5 International Oil Pollution Compensation Funds (IOPC Funds), *Claims Manual* (IOPC Funds 2019) 21.

unsecured liabilities under the recovery cap.[6] However, the willingness of assurance providers to accept certain risks may influence the outcome of coverage decisions. It has been observed that regulators are reluctant to define the extent of liability without 'first obtaining a commitment from the insurance industry to the effect that coverage commensurate to the intended new level of liability will be available'.[7] The extent of insurability has been an important concern in the negotiation of international liability conventions.[8] For example, in the Antarctic, the liability limits set out in the Liability Annex to the 1991 Protocol on Environmental Protection to the Antarctic Treaty (1991 Antarctic Protocol) were set to coincide with the levels identified in the Convention on Limitation of Liability for Maritime Claims (LLMC), which established baseline coverage amounts accepted by the insurance industry.[9] A central factor in assessing insurability is the ability of the insurer to accurately predict and quantify risks. This leads to a rejection of certain forms of damages that are contingent or abstract. For example, as discussed in Chapter 3, the IPOC Funds' refusal to entertain pure ecological damage relates to the open-ended nature of calculating damages not firmly rooted in actual costs.[10]

Indirectly, financial assurances, particularly insurance, contribute to the internalization of risk by providing a vehicle for pricing risk and having the operator bear

6 For example, 1992 Oil Pollution Liability Convention (n 2) art VII(1); International Convention on Liability and Compensation for Damage in Connection with the Carriage of Hazardous and Noxious Substances by Sea (adopted 3 May 1996) 35 ILM 1415 (1996 HNS Convention) art 12(1).

7 W Pfennigstorf, 'Policy Considerations for Insurers Engaging in Environmental Liability Insurance' in H Bocken and D Ryckbost (eds), *Insurance of Environmental Damage* (Story-Scientia 1991) 269, 273.

8 This relationship between limitations and insurability lies at the centre of the Convention on Limitation of Liability for Maritime Claims (adopted 19 November 1976, entered into force 1 December 1986) 1456 UNTS 221 (1976 LLMC), and Protocol of 1996 to Amend the 1976 Convention on Limitation of Liability for Maritime Claims (adopted 2 May 1996, entered into force 13 May 2004) Can TS 2008 No 18 (1996 LLMC); see the Travaux Préparatoires of the LLMC Convention 1976 and of the Protocol of 1996 (CMI 2000) 124. See also ATCM, 'Liability – Report of the Group of Legal Experts' (1998) XXII ATCM/WP1, para 36 (noting the need to consult with insurance industry on fixing limits of insurance); CropLife International, 'Implementation Guide to the Nagoya-Kuala Lumpur Supplementary Protocol' (2013) 16 <https://croplife.org/wp-content/uploads/2014/04/Implementation-Guide-to-the-Nagoya-Kuala-Lumpur-Supplementary-Protocol-on-Liability-and-Redress-to-the-Cartagena-Protocol-on-Biosafety.pdf> accessed 29 August 2022.

9 Protocol on Environmental Protection to the Antarctic Treaty (adopted 4 October 1991, entered into force 14 January 1998) (1991) 30 ILM 1461 (1991 Antarctic Protocol); Annex VI to the Protocol on Environmental Protection to the Antarctic Treaty on Liability Arising from Environmental Emergencies (adopted 17 June 2005) 45 ILM 5 (Liability Annex) art 9; discussed in ATCM, Final Report of the Fortieth Antarctic Treaty Consultative Meeting (vol I, ATCM 2017) paras 30 and 139 (referring to Informational Paper (IP) 87 'Liability Annex: Financial Security' submitted by the International Group of P&I Clubs).

10 IOPC Funds 2019 (n 5) 14 (noting that 'compensation is not paid in respect of claims for environmental damages based on abstract quantification calculated in accordance with theoretical models').

those costs through mandatory coverage requirements. Insurance, because it allocates risk amongst a class of insured entities, supports the polluter-pays principle by providing an efficient mechanism for risk internalization. Insurers, in order to control their own risk exposure, can encourage environmental risk reduction measures by requiring appropriate measures to be taken as a condition of insurance, through increasing premiums to reflect riskier behaviours or by withdrawing coverage altogether.[11] The deterrent effect of insurance may, however, cut in both directions, insofar as coverage shields operators from the catastrophic losses, and may thereby encourage risks that would not otherwise be undertaken – presenting what economists refer to as a 'moral hazard'.[12] The incentive for insurance to promote risk is moderated by the use of deductibles, premium adjustments and exclusions within the insurance contract.

It ought, however, to be recognized that encouraging certain kinds of risk is an intended and central objective of financial assurances. Where there are socially (economically) beneficial activities that present liability risks that could not otherwise be borne by the operator, financial assurances distribute that risk amongst other entities, creating conditions for the viability of the activity.[13] Risk distribution requires that there be a sufficient number of insured entities engaged in activities that present similar risks.[14] This requirement suggests that novel activities, such as deep seabed mining or marine bioprospecting, that have few initial participants, may raise insurability challenges.

Mandatory insurance addresses the competitive implications of internalizing risk-related costs by requiring all the participants in the activity to bear similar cost burdens. Uniformity discourages a 'race to the bottom' whereby some jurisdictions seek to attract participants through lower regulatory burdens, including the costs associated with liability coverage. The goal of uniformity is especially important in transnational activities, such as shipping dangerous goods, where the operators may have some freedom of choice in terms of the jurisdiction regulating their activity, and where the consequences of an accident are not contained to the overseeing jurisdiction.[15]

A final objective of financial assurances is that, where there are public concerns over the acceptability of risks associated with an activity, the presence of assurances

[11] Benjamin Richardson, *Environmental Regulation through Financial Organizations* (Kluwer Law International 2002) 330.

[12] See Joseph Stiglitz, 'Risk Incentives and Insurance: The Pure Theory of Moral Hazard' (1983) 8 GRIR 4.

[13] Draft Principles (n 1) commentary to principle 4, 81 para 30.

[14] Richardson (n 11) 329.

[15] Uniform rules respecting liability are expressly identified as a goal within the preambles of the various IMO civil liability conventions. See, for example, 1992 Oil Pollution Liability Convention (n 2); 1996 HNS Convention (n 6); and the International Convention on Civil Liability for Bunker Oil Pollution Damage (adopted 23 March 2001, entered into force 21 November 2008) UKTS No 47 (2001 Bunker Oil Convention).

provides credibility to operator claims that it will be in a position to address any harms that arise, contributing to greater public and political acceptance (often referred to as a 'social license to operate') of the activity.[16] In this regard, it is not uncommon for risky industries to self-organize in order to create requirements and processes for liability coverage, even in the absence of regulatory requirements to do so. For example, the oil transport industry had several industry-led schemes prior to the implementation of the current international rules.[17] Similar initiatives have also arisen in relation to the offshore oil and gas industry and in relation to the transboundary movement of living modified organisms.[18]

8.3 FORMS OF ASSURANCE

There are four distinct forms of financial assurances that are identified in various civil liability regimes: insurance, bonds or financial guarantees, compensation funds and state guarantees. These are often combined to provide alternative or tiered forms of security within a single civil liability regime. Third party insurance is the default form of assurance, and typically provides the baseline coverage for the liabilities identified in the regime. Insurance in civil liability regimes is mandatory and the amount of insurance required is specified, and typically matches the caps on liability identified in the treaty.[19] International civil liability rules do not specify the provider of insurance but will usually require some form of certification demonstrating that the coverage is adequate. The certification structure is central to the ability of states to ensure compliance with the financial security requirements, particularly in the shipping context, as states typically require proof of coverage as a condition of entry into their ports.[20]

Typically, the insurer is a commercial entity or a form of mutualized insurance whereby the operators may create a form of pooled self-insurance, such as protection and indemnity (P&I) clubs, which play a prominent role in insuring shipping

[16] For a discussion of the social lisence to operate in the oceans context, see Michelle Voyer and Judith van Leeuwen, '"Social Licence to Operate" in the Blue Economy' (2019) 62 Resour Pol'y 102.

[17] Most notably in the context of oil transport are the Tanker Owners Voluntary Agreement Concerning Liability for Oil Pollution (TOVALOP) and Contract Regarding a Supplement to Tanker Liability for Oil Pollution (CRISTAL) arrangements.

[18] See Offshore Pollution Liability Agreement (OPOL), and second amended version of 'The Compact: A Contractual Mechanism for Response in the Event of Damage to Biological Diversity Caused by the Release of a Living Modified Organism' (2012) <www.isaaa.org/workshop/2012-01-10-bangkok/download/liability_and_redress/Compact.pdf> accessed 29 August 2022.

[19] With the exception of the Nagoya-Kuala Lumpur Supplementary Protocol on Liability and Redress to the Cartagena Protocol on Biosafety (adopted 15 October 2010, entered into force 5 March 2018) 50 ILM 105 (2010 Nagoya-Kuala Lumpur Supplementary Protocol) art 10.

[20] See, for example, Marine Liability Act, SC 2001, c 6, s 55 (Canada).

activities.[21] Declarations of self-insurance are generally not permitted, except where the operator is a state or state enterprise.[22] Since there can be no guarantee of the availability of commercial, third party insurance, most civil liability treaties provide that operators may use bonds or other guarantees as an alternative to insurance. The financial burden of posting this type of security in amounts necessary to cover the liability caps is significant and may be unfeasible in many cases. As such, insurance has been the predominant form of assurance used in civil liability conventions.[23]

Compensation funds provide a further risk-pooling mechanism that can provide enhanced coverage and, depending on its contribution structure, spread the burden of securing liability obligations to other actors in the risk chain. As developed under the oil pollution regime, the oil pollution fund is primarily structured to provide further tiers of coverage in recognition that insurance coverage will not be sufficient in some instances to cover high-cost claims. Where claims are anticipated to exceed first tier coverage, the fund assesses contributions (usually on an *ex-post* basis) that are then used to settle claims. The use of funds to provide enhanced coverage recognizes the limited capacity of the insurance industry to bear catastrophic losses. The fund also provides coverage for claims not otherwise covered by insurance (for example, due to a policy exception, successfully raised defence or bankruptcy of the insurer).

In the case of oil pollution, shipowners are responsible for acquiring insurance, but the source of fund contributions comes from the oil receivers (generally large refining interests) in member states.[24] Such a structure requires the presence of another sufficiently uniform (in terms of risk) class of participants in the risk chain. Thus, funds can contribute to further risk spreading by providing for a wider base of contributors, but the presence of a fund complicates ratification, as it requires states to negotiate with domestic contributors (such as oil receivers) that will be subject to additional financial burdens. There is a third tier of coverage in the oil liability regime, which covers losses beyond those in the first two tiers.[25] Fund coverage is residual in nature, covering only those costs not addressed by the tier below.

Funds have been proposed in a number of other regimes beyond oil transport, including the 1996 International Convention on Liability and Compensation for Damage in Connection with the Carriage of Hazardous and Noxious Substances by Sea (1996 HNS Convention) (carriage of hazardous and noxious substances), the

[21] Charles Anderson and Colin de la Rue, 'The Role of the P&I Clubs in Maritime Pollution Incidents' (2011) 85 Tul L Rev 1257.

[22] See, for example, Liability Annex (n 9) art 11(3).

[23] But see discussion on potential uses of bonds in the deep seabed context in Sarah Hoyt, Cindy Van Dover, Samantha Smith and Linwood Pendleton, 'Closing the Liability Gap: A Review of Liability Alternatives for the Emerging Seafloor Mineral Extraction Industry' (2016) <https://dukespace.lib.duke.edu/dspace/bitstream/handle/10161/11881/MP_FINAL.pdf?sequence=1> accessed 29 August 2022.

[24] 1992 Fund Convention (n 2) art 10.

[25] 2003 Supplementary Fund Convention (n 2).

1999 Basel Protocol on Liability and Compensation for Damage Resulting from Transboundary Movement of Hazardous Wastes and their Disposal (1999 Basel Liability Protocol) (transboundary movement of hazardous waste) and the Liability Annex to the 1991 Antarctic Protocol.[26] The 1996 HNS Convention adopts a similar structure to the 1992 Fund Convention, and is contemplated (upon coming into force) on being managed by the IOPC Funds, the international organization set up to manage the oil fund conventions.[27] Because the 1996 HNS Convention covers a variety of substances with different risk profiles, the fund is segregated by substance to avoid cross-subsidization across sectors.[28] The 1999 Basel Liability Protocol does not create a new fund, but rather extends the role of the existing Technical Co-operation Trust Fund to include taking 'additional and supplementary measures'.[29] There is no new funding mechanism to support this role; instead the Basel Convention Technical Co-operation Trust Fund relies on voluntary contributions.[30] The designation of the fund as a 'trust' fund speaks to the broader, but more ambiguous, role of the fund beyond providing compensation. The fund under the Antarctic Liability Annex, discussed below, is structured to collect funds from operators who fail to take required response actions, and use those funds to reimburse parties who undertake response actions in relation to other incidents.

A final form of assurance, found in the conventions addressing liability for damage arising from nuclear installations, takes the form of a state commitment to make public funds available to cover claims in excess of insurance coverage.[31] This approach is effectively a form of state guarantee, whereby installation states agree to cover the liabilities associated with operators within their jurisdiction. Unlike the oil pollution regime, the approach in the first instance is not tiered. Instead, the nuclear liability regime identifies overall liability limits, but leaves the amount to be covered by insurance in the hands of the installation state. The installation state must then agree to cover the uninsured portion through public funds. There is a further tier of compensation available under a separate treaty, the Convention on Supplementary Compensation for Nuclear Damage, which is financed collectively by the parties to

[26] 1996 HNS Convention (n 6); Basel Protocol on Liability and Compensation for Damage Resulting from Transboundary Movement of Hazardous Wastes and their Disposal (adopted 10 December 1999) UNEP/CHW.1/WG/1/9/2 (1999 Basel Liability Protocol); Liability Annex (n 9).

[27] 1996 HNS Convention (n 6) art 13.

[28] ibid art 19.

[29] 1999 Basel Liability Protocol (n 26) art 15 (indicating the use of 'existing mechanisms' to provide supplemental compensation measures).

[30] See Jutta Brunnée, 'Of Sense and Sensibility: Reflections on Environmental Liability Regimes as Tools for Environmental Protection' (2004) 53 ICLQ 351, 361.

[31] Vienna Convention on Civil Liability for Nuclear Damage (adopted 21 May 1963, entered into force 12 November 1977) 1063 UNTS 265, amended by Protocol to Amend the Vienna Convention on Civil Liability for Nuclear Damage (adopted 12 September 1997, entered into force 4 October 2003) 2241 UNTS 270 (1997 Vienna Convention) art VII.

that treaty.[32] The contributions are based on a formula that accounts for the installed nuclear capacity of the state and its capacity to pay (using the UN rate of assessment). By providing a guarantee of compensation, participating states are providing a form of indirect subsidy to the nuclear sector. The acceptability of this subsidy reflects the unique conditions surrounding nuclear installations, in terms of their risk profile and the central role of the state in the industry.

8.4 FINANCIAL ASSURANCE OBLIGATIONS IN ABNJ

The inclusion of financial assurances as a fundamental element of most civil liability structures raises the question of whether the provision of financial assurances is a legal requirement or simply a matter of sound policy and political preference. As noted, the requirement to provide financial assurances is framed within civil liability regimes as an element of the requirement to provide 'prompt and adequate compensation'. In situating this requirement in the context of activities occurring in areas beyond national jurisdiction, the starting point is article 235 (2) of the 1982 UN Convention on the Law of the Sea (UNCLOS),[33] which provides a standard for the minimum measures that a state must enact, at least insofar as those measures are necessary to address damage caused by pollution to the marine environment. The obligation to ensure the availability of 'prompt and adequate compensation' is an emerging international legal standard, but its precise contents remain ambiguous. Amongst the outstanding questions is whether this standard includes a positive obligation to provide financial assurances within domestic legal systems or through international cooperation.

Lefeber notes that the requirement for prompt and adequate compensation has both procedural and substantive dimensions. The procedural dimensions require equal access to legal mechanisms and procedures for the recognition and enforcement of judgments, while the substantive dimensions speak to the rules and procedures governing recovery, including financial security.[34] Similarly, amongst the measures identified as necessary to ensure prompt and adequate compensation, the International Legal Commission (ILC) includes the requirement for financial security on the basis that security is necessary to ensure that sufficient funds are available to meet claims.[35] Both Lefeber and the ILC note that there is extensive treaty practice in support of the inclusion of financial security requirements in civil liability treaties. In and of itself, it may be hard to draw any firm conclusions on the presence of a generalized obligation to provide security from such a practice, given

[32] Convention on Supplementary Compensation for Nuclear Damage (adopted 12 September 1997, entered into force 15 April 2015) 36 ILM 1473 (1997 Nuclear Supplementary Fund Convention).

[33] UNCLOS (n 1) art 235.

[34] Lefeber (n 1) 270 et seq.

[35] Draft Principles (n 1) principle 4(3), 76.

that the requirement has only been accepted in a relatively limited number of activities (nuclear installations, and oil and HNS transport).

The Seabed Disputes Chamber (SDC) in its 2011 Advisory Opinion on *Activities in the Area* identifies the requirement for 'prompt and adequate compensation' as a constituent element of a sponsoring state's due diligence obligations, specifically related to its obligation to ensure that a contractor meets its liability obligations under Annex III, article 22, but does not specify the content of that obligation.[36] In particular, the SDC does not speak to the requirement for assurances, except to note the utility of compensation funds, as contemplated in article 235(3).[37] However, understood as a matter of due diligence, the requirement for financial security comes down to the foreseeability of contractors having insufficient funds to cover potential liabilities and what might be understood to be the accepted practices of good governance in this context.[38] The consistent practice of states indicates the foreseeability of operators having insufficient funds (also identified as being foreseeable by the SDC in its Advisory Opinion), and points to the requirement of financial securities as an accepted practice to address those circumstances. Thus, where the provision of prompt and adequate compensation is required, including in marine areas beyond national jurisdiction, and adequacy is assessed on the basis of due diligence, there is support in favour of a standard that requires assurances. The recognition of compulsory insurance and compensation funds in article 235(3) strengthens the claim that securing compensation is an integral element of adequate compensation, whether implemented domestically or through international cooperation. However, the qualified wording of article 235(3) suggests a high degree of flexibility and discretion in implementing that requirement.

The situation in relation to the Antarctic is less clear. The 1991 Antarctic Protocol contains similar wording in article 15, where the parties agree to provide for 'prompt and effective response action' to environmental emergencies. However, the liability provision does not identify any particular standard for compensation.[39] In the Liability Annex, which includes a requirement for financial security, the issue of liability is linked directly to response measures, but there is little evidence that the content of the Liability Annex was driven by an understanding that the requirements for compensation, including assurances, had to satisfy minimum legal requirements,

[36] *Responsibilities and Obligations of States Sponsoring Persons and Entities with Respect to Activities in the Area* (Advisory Opinion of 1 February 2011) ITLOS Reports 2011 (*Activities in the Area* Advisory Opinion) para 140.

[37] ibid para 205.

[38] ILC, 'Draft Articles on Prevention of Transboundary Harm from Hazardous Activities, with Commentaries' (2001) UN Doc A/56/10 (Draft Articles on Prevention of Transboundary Harm), commentary to art 3, 155, para 17 (noting 'the main elements of the obligation of due diligence involved in the duty of prevention could thus be stated: the degree of care in question is that expected of a good Government').

[39] 1991 Antarctic Protocol (n 9) art 16.

as evidenced by the restrictive approach to coverage in the Liability Annex.[40] There was discussion amongst the parties concerning insurance in the lead-up to the adoption of the Liability Annex in 2005.[41] However, this discussion centred on the need to adjust the Annex in order for the requirements to align with insurability constraints, which suggests that the financial assurance provision was driven by practical concerns rather than a belief that there were minimum international requirements respecting assurances. The Convention on the Regulation of Antarctic Mineral Resource Activities (CRAMRA) also addresses liability issues and provides a reference to the development of a fund to assure response actions and compensation obligations.[42]

8.5 FINANCIAL ASSURANCES IN LIABILITY STRUCTURES IN ABNJ

8.5.1 *Antarctic*

The Liability Annex adopts an insurance-based approach to assurance but includes provisions for the creation of a compensation fund that is funded through the recovery of amounts equal to the funds that ought to have been paid to address environmental emergencies. The more flexible application of compensation fund contributions provides a novel and administratively oriented approach to securing compensation. The other unique aspect of the Liability Annex is its differential treatment of state and private operators, discussed below, which illustrates some of the difficulties in imposing liability requirements on state actors, even under the limited and well-defined operating conditions in the Antarctic.

Because the liabilities to be secured under the Liability Annex are limited to the costs of 'response actions' to 'environmental emergencies',[43] the principal obligation is for the operator to undertake prevention and restoration actions in response to environmental emergencies, with liability flowing from their failure to do so.[44] In the event that the operator fails to undertake response actions in accordance with the requirements of the Annex (i.e. it is not 'prompt and effective'), a response action may be undertaken by the party of the operator or another party. In those instances,

40 Liability Annex (n 9) art 6 (restricting liability to costs associated with response measures). There is overlap between article 235 and the Antarctic Liability regime, insofar as both address requirements for compensation in relation to Antarctic waters, but this does not appear to have been a factor in the development of the liability rules: see Patrizia Vigni, 'The Interaction between the Antarctic Treaty System and the Other Relevant Conventions Applicable to the Antarctic Area: A Practical Approach versus Theoretical Doctrines' in JA Frowein and Rüdiger Wolfrum (eds), *Max Planck Yearbook of United Nations Law* (Kluwer 2000) 481.

41 ATCM, 'Liability – Report of the Group of Legal Experts' (n 8) para 36.

42 Convention on the Regulation of Antarctic Mineral Resource Activities (adopted 2 June 1988) 27 ILM 868 (CRAMRA) art 8(7).

43 Liability Annex (n 9) art 2.

44 ibid art 5(1).

the operator is liable for the costs of the response action undertaken by the party in question.[45] In the event that no response action was taken (by either the operator or a party), the operator shall be liable for the amount equal to the costs of the response action that should have been undertaken.[46] This second form of liability is unique in that it does not address a specific attributable loss, but rather recognizes a general loss to the Antarctic environment. This is a noteworthy innovation, as it decouples liability for environmental losses from restoration activities undertaken and, as discussed below, makes funds available for future uncovered losses.

Operators are required to maintain insurance cover in amounts equal to the liability limits identified in the Annex to address response actions undertaken.[47] However, insurance is not mandatory to cover liability flowing from the second circumstance where no response action was taken, but rather the question of insurance coverage is left to the state party with jurisdiction over the operator in question.[48] The insurance requirements lack the same level of detail seen in other civil liability regimes, which typically specify the requirements of certificates of insurance and provide for claims to be brought directly against the insurer. The absence of a requirement for certificates of insurance reflects the difficulties of enforcement where there is no port state jurisdiction.[49] Instead, the enforcement of the insurance requirements is again the responsibility of the party of the operator.[50] The inability under the Liability Annex to claim directly against insurers creates a potentially significant liability gap since direct claims against insurers prevent the frustration of compensation where the operator becomes bankrupt or is otherwise unable to be subject to an action. The defences available to the insurer are not specified, and could, therefore, include broader exemptions than those specified for operators under the Annex.[51] No attempt is made to impose insurance requirements on non-parties through requiring proof of insurance for entry into Antarctic waters in a manner analogous to port state entry requirements. This is not surprising given the interference that such a requirement would have on the right of free navigation.

The required coverage is identified with different caps being specified for accidents involving ships and those that do not.[52] Unlike the oil pollution liability

45 ibid art 6(1).
46 ibid art 6(2).
47 ibid art 11(1).
48 ibid art 11(2).
49 See, for example, International Maritime Organization, Resolution A.1155(32), 'Procedures for Port State Control, 2021' (adopted 15 December 2021) para 2.2.3 and Annex 12 (listing various certificates of insurance required to be produced and examined by port state control officers).
50 Liability Annex (n 9) art 11(1).
51 ibid art 8 (setting out liability exemptions). Of particular note in relation to P&I insurers is the 'pay to be paid' clause, which relieves insurers of an obligation to pay claims unless, and until, the insured has first satisfied the claim. For general discussion of 'pay to be paid' clauses, see Jody Schisel-Meslin, 'Out of the Club? Out of Luck: Complexities Facing Injured Third Parties Seeking Recovery from P&I Clubs' (2019) 43 Tul Mar L J 319.
52 Liability Annex (n 9) art 9.

regime, the Annex does not displace other international conventions affecting shipowner liability, particularly the LLMC.[53] When the Annex was negotiated, the limits on liability identified in the Annex were set to match the 1996 LLMC but since that time, new limits have come into effect under further amendments to the LLMC,[54] leading to the possibility of different operators being subject to different limitations depending on the version of the LLMC, if any, to which the party with jurisdiction over the operator is bound.[55] For non-shipping operators, liability is capped at three million special drawing rights. It is less clear whether there is commercially available insurance for non-shipowners.[56] However, state operators are permitted to self-insure.[57]

Where no response action is taken, the amounts collected under article 6(2) are to be paid into a fund created under article 12 of the Annex. The purpose of the fund is to provide for the 'reimbursement of the reasonable and justified costs incurred by a party or parties in taking response actions pursuant to article 5(2)'.[58] Instead of contributions being directed towards addressing the incident that gives rise to the liability, they provide a source of funding to address future liabilities that arise and may otherwise go unaddressed. The contemplated circumstances under which the fund might provide reimbursement include where the identity of the operator is unknown or not subject to the Annex, the unforeseen failure of an insurer or exemptions relieving the operator of liability obligations.[59] Reimbursement proposals may be submitted by any party and will be subject to the approval of the Antarctic Treaty Consultative Meeting (ATCM).

The ability to collect funds that can then be applied to other incidents is unique but reflects the collective status of the Antarctic environment. Unlike losses to specific victims or states, where restitution requires that the compensation be directed to the victim of the loss suffered, in the Antarctic, the loss (where no response action is taken) is suffered collectively. Allowing for funds to be used in relation to a different incident maintains the underlying environmental purposes of the scheme. The Secretariat of the Antarctic Treaty is anticipated to administer the

[53] 1996 LLMC (n 8). Article 3 of the 1996 LLMC exempts claims under the 1992 Oil Pollution Liability Convention (n 2) from the limitations contained within the LLMC 1996.

[54] Amendments to the Protocol of 1996 to Amend the Convention on Limitation of Liability for Maritime Claims, 1976 (adopted 19 April 2012, entered into force 8 June 2015) IMO Resolution LEG.5(99).

[55] This has been the subject of several reports to the ATCM from the International Group of P&I Clubs; see ATCM (n 8) and ATCM, Final Report of the Forty-Second Antarctic Treaty Consultative Meeting (vol I, ATCM 2019) paras 167–168 (referencing IP 101 'Annex VI to the Protocol on Environmental Protection to the Antarctic Treaty: Financial Security' submitted by the International P&I Clubs).

[56] ibid.

[57] Liability Annex (n 9) art 11(3).

[58] ibid art 12(1).

[59] ibid art 12(3).

fund created under the Liability Annex, with the ATCM providing the decision-making authority required.[60]

Unlike the fund created under the oil pollution regime, the Antarctic fund is not tiered and only indirectly provides supplemental coverage, insofar as the ATCM could approve reimbursements for response actions that exceed the coverage limitations provided under article 9. The structure of the Annex is such that insurers may be required to cover amounts sought to be recovered from operators and paid into the fund. Because recovery in these instances is based on the costs of a response action not actually undertaken, the calculation of damages differs slightly from the reinstatement coverage under other civil liability regimes, which is based on the costs of only those reinstatement actions that are actually undertaken, although the coverage is similarly restricted to 'reasonable measures'.[61]

8.5.2 *Deep Seabed*

At the time of writing, the International Seabed Authority (ISA) has enacted regulations governing the exploration phase of deep seabed mining, which include insurance requirements. The current practice, under the Exploration Regulations, provides a requirement that the contractor 'maintain appropriate insurance policies with internationally recognized carriers, in accordance with generally accepted international maritime practice'.[62] The requirement does not specify what coverage is 'appropriate', and the reference to 'generally accepted international maritime practice' is not further elaborated upon.[63] It is unclear what these standards might refer to, particularly in relation to the extent of liability coverage in areas beyond national jurisdiction. In addition, in the absence of operational extensions, maritime coverage would not address damage arising from non-shipping-related, operational accidents (i.e. during equipment testing). While exploration activities appear low-risk, the exploration regulations clearly foresee the potential for damage to the marine environment.

In relation to the exploitation phase, the 2019 Draft Exploitation Regulations (DER) include reference to both insurance requirements and the creation of a fund. The DER include an obligation on contractors to maintain appropriate insurance policies but have not specified any details.[64] The DER make reference to applicable 'international maritime practice, consistent with Good Industry Practice', as the basis for insurance requirements.[65] At the present time, there is no endemic

60 ibid arts 12(1) and (2).

61 ibid art 2(f).

62 See, for example, International Seabed Authority (ISA), 'Regulations on Prospecting and Exploration for Polymetallic Nodules in the Area' (2013) ISBA/19/C/17 (PMN), Annex IV, s 16.5.

63 This wording does suggest that the limits contained in the 1996 LLMC (n 8) would apply.

64 ISA, 'Draft Regulations on Exploitation of Mineral Resources in the Area' (2019) ISBA/25/C/WP.1 (DER) reg 36 (but the draft regulations anticipate that particulars will be addressed in a Guideline).

65 ibid.

insurance market for operational aspects of deep seabed mining, and the commercial availability of such insurance is an open question. Self-insurance is a possibility, particularly for contractors that are state agencies or state-owned entities, but this may raise competitiveness concerns, particularly in light of the attention given to non-discrimination in Part XI of UNCLOS.[66]

The application of financial assurance requirements to seabed mining ought to consider the specific liability provisions applicable to activities in the Area. The wording of Annex III, article 22, which indicates that 'liability in every case shall be for the actual amount of damage', could be interpreted as a constraint on the parties' ability to impose liability caps, which could potentially conflict with current maritime insurance practices that accept limitations as a necessary element of insurability. Much, of course, would depend upon how damages are defined in this context, but the wording raises the possibility of an uninsured portion of losses.

The DER also call for the creation of an 'Environmental Compensation Fund' (ECF), the main purposes of which include assuring 'necessary measures designed to prevent, limit or remediate any damage to the Area arising from activities in the Area', where the costs cannot otherwise be recovered from contractors or sponsoring states, but also providing funds for matters such as research, education and training and general restoration and rehabilitation of the Area.[67] The funding sources identified for the ECF reflect its mixed mandate, and include a percentage of fees and penalties, in addition to 'monies paid into the Fund at the Direction of the Council'. The latter source provides a potential basis for imposing contributions to the ECF on contractors, or other actors involved in deep seabed mining. There are jurisdictional limitations on the ability of the ISA to impose requirements on entities, such as mineral processors, operating outside the Area.[68] As a result, the likely contributors would be contractors and potentially sponsoring states, which may raise concerns about the ability of the ECF to accumulate sufficient funds in the early stages of mining, when only one or two contractors are operating.

The structure has some similarities to the fund created under the Antarctic Liability Annex insofar as the fund is not tied directly to compensating individual losses but provides potential coverage for general harm to the Area. The potential contours of the ECF have been explored in a technical study prepared under the direction of the ISA, which addresses a range of implementation issues associated with compensation funds.[69] Notably, the Study advises that pure environmental damage be excluded from the fund, citing considerations respecting financial

66 UNCLOS (n 1) art 152. See also Agreement Relating to the Implementation of Part XI of the United Nations Convention on the Law of the Sea (adopted 28 July 1994, entered into force 28 July 1996) 1836 UNTS 3 (1994 Implementation Agreement) Annex, s 6 (1)(c).

67 DER (n 64) reg 55.

68 *Activities in the Area* Advisory Opinion (n 36) para 95.

69 ISA 'Study on an Environmental Compensation Fund for Activities in the Area' (2021) ISA Technical Study No. 27.

viability. More broadly, liability caps can address viability concerns, although there is a significant challenge associated with establishing caps under the uncertain operational and environmental conditions that prevail in the Area. The operational modalities of the ECF, including identifying eligible claimants, claims procedures and fund administration, will need to be addressed.

8.6 FUTURE PROSPECTS FOR THE USE OF FINANCIAL ASSURANCE IN ABNJ

Given the central role that insurance and compensation funds have played in protecting and restoring the coastal marine environment from environmental harm, and the contemplated extension of financial assurances in the Antarctic and deep seabed mining contexts, it is reasonable to anticipate increased interest in broadening the coverage of financial assurances to address the evolving range of activities in areas beyond national jurisdiction, such as those contemplated under the negotiation process for a new instrument governing for marine biodiversity of areas beyond national jurisdiction.[70]

Understanding the insurability of risks arising in areas beyond national jurisdiction is complicated by the restricted application of civil liability regimes to only pollution damage that occurs in the territorial sea and exclusive economic zone of parties.[71] Since insurance requirements under liability regimes are tied to the scope of liability under the treaty in question, coverage for damage to the high seas is not required under most existing civil liability treaties. The one exception to this limitation is in relation to compensation for preventive measures, which may be undertaken on the high seas, but only in relation to the prevention or minimization of harm to the territorial sea or exclusive economic zone.[72] Where the attention on compensation focused primarily on the economic losses associated with incidents, treating areas beyond national jurisdiction differently was understandable. As the compensation and financial assurances in support of compensation increasingly address environmental damage, this different treatment is increasingly difficult to justify. P&I coverage and other forms of maritime insurance are not similarly restricted to territorial areas or exclusive economic zones, since liability risks (for

[70] The issue of developing some form of liability funding mechanism has been raised in the negotiations for an internationally binding legal instrument for marine biodiversity of areas beyond national jurisdiction, but the issue has not formed part of the negotiating drafts. See Earth Negotiations Bulletin, 'Summary of the Second Session of the Intergovernmental Conference on an International Legally Binding Instrument under the UN Convention on the Law of the Sea on the Conservation and Sustainable Use of Marine Biodiversity of Areas Beyond National Jurisdiction: 25 March–5 April 2019' (2019) vol 25 no 195 (noting the discussion on responsibility and liability).

[71] See, for example, 1992 Oil Pollution Liability Convention (n 2) art II; 1996 HNS Convention (n 6) art 3; 1999 Basel Liability Protocol (n 26) art 3.

[72] See, 1992 Oil Pollution Liability Convention (n 2) art II(b).

example, collisions at sea) exist in areas beyond national jurisdiction.[73] As a result, there is a demand for coverage in areas beyond national jurisdiction, which is addressed in existing insurance arrangements for shipping, but not in accordance with any uniform requirements.

There is no jurisdictional bar to the imposition of mandatory insurance in areas beyond national jurisdiction through an international agreement. However, it has been noted that the extension of existing mandatory insurance requirements of the various civil liability conventions to areas beyond national jurisdiction may likely be viewed by some states as an undesirable intrusion on high seas freedoms, and if enforced unilaterally (through port entry requirements), may result in opposition from non-signatories.[74] Nonetheless, there are clearly areas where the nature of the activity and its associated risks have given rise to demands for harmonized financial assurance requirements; for example, the extension to mandatory insurance to shipping (and other) activities in the Antarctic was accepted by the parties.

There are several practical challenges connected to the provision of insurance in areas beyond national jurisdiction. First, insurability requires that the insurer be able to calculate the risks subject to coverage.[75] Making this determination requires the development of an understanding of the operational risks, the environmental harm that may arise from those risks and the costs associated with addressing those harms. A number of the proposed activities that might be subject to liability rules in areas beyond national jurisdiction, such as deep seabed mining and marine bio-prospecting, are novel with unclear operational risks. There are also high levels of scientific uncertainty in relation to the potential environmental impacts of incidents in the high seas, deep seabed and Antarctic environments, which further weaken the ability of insurers to quantify risks. In the face of risk uncertainty, insurability can be enhanced using liability caps, which are a consistent feature of civil liability regimes, as well as limitations on recovery for certain types of damages.[76] However, the appropriateness of these limitations to ABNJ needs to be carefully considered. For example, the exclusion of using offsets or abstract calculations to assess pure ecological losses may be considered overly restrictive in environments where remediation requirements may be technically and economically challenging.[77]

73 See, for example, the conditions for coverage relating to oil pollution in the Gard AS, *Gard Rule Book* (2020) <www.gard.no/Content/33063275/cache=20221803124344/Gard%20Rules%202022_web.pdf> accessed 4 September 2022. See also The Shipowner's Club, *Club Rules 2020* (2020) <www.shipownersclub.com/media/2020/01/Club_Rules_2020_Web.pdf> accessed 4 September 2022.

74 Nicholas Gaskell, 'Liability and Compensation Regimes: Pollution of the High Seas' in Robert Beckman and others (eds), *High Seas Governance: Gaps and Challenges* (Brill Nijhoff 2019) 229, 246.

75 Richardson (n 11) 329.

76 The restrictions on recoverability of restoration costs to reimbursing only the 'reasonable' costs of actions actually undertaken. See, for example, 1992 Oil Pollution Liability Convention (n 2) art 1 (6); see also Liability Annex (n 9) art 2 (restricting response actions to reasonable measures).

77 See discussion in Chapter 3.

A second condition that facilitates insurance is the ability for risk spreading; that is, it is desirable for there to be a sufficiently large number of insureds to allow the insurer to allocate its risks across operators. This, in turn, promotes the economic feasibility of the insurance arrangement as the costs of accidents (reflected in premiums) are shared. In the case of mutual insurance (i.e. through P&I clubs), risk spreading is fundamental to the viability of the arrangement. In the case of shipping, the risks involved may be spread amongst large numbers of actors. As such, the provision of insurance for Antarctic shipping activities does not appear to present viability concerns. The same cannot be said (at this time) for deep seabed mining or other novel ocean-based industries, where there are only a small number of operators (some of which may be able to self-insure as state enterprises). The situation in deep seabed mining is further complicated by the presence of private corporations, state enterprises and state agencies as contractors.

Given the specificity of operational risks, liability rules and associated insurance requirements are typically sector-based, with key stakeholders (operators, insurers) being consulted in the shaping of the rules, as opposed to being geographically oriented. The Antarctic Liability Annex is the exception, where the liability rules address both terrestrial and maritime activities, but even here, the parties developed separate shipping requirements aligned with existing industry standards. In other areas where non-sectoral liability regimes have been developed, such as general environmental liability rules under the Lugano Convention or under regional seas conventions, the insurance (or other financial security) provisions have provided parties with near complete discretion to determine the requirements.[78] Thus, including insurance or other security requirements in a treaty of general application would not likely yield a uniform and harmonized result.

A condition for the implementation of compensation funds in the oil and HNS context has been the presence of other actors beyond the operator (shipowner) who are prepared to make contributions to the fund. In these cases, the justification for imposing contribution obligations on the receivers of oil or HNS flows from their role in driving the demand for the risky activity. The small number of receivers and the relatively low cost of the contribution in relation to the overall cost of the substance receiver, as well as the desire on the part of the receivers for a social licence to operate, facilitate the acceptability of the arrangement.[79] The extension of

[78] Lugano Convention on Civil Liability for Damage resulting from Activities Dangerous to the Environment (adopted 21 June 1993) 32 ILM 1228 art 12; UNEP, 'Guidelines for the Determination of Liability and Compensation for Damage Resulting from Pollution of the Marine Environment in the Mediterranean Sea' (2008) UNEP(DEPI)MED IG.17/10 Annex V, para 28.

[79] See Nicholas Gaskell, 'Compensation for Offshore Pollution: Ships and Platforms' in Malcolm Clarke (ed), *Maritime Law Evolving* (Hart Publishing 2013) 63, 67 (noting the low cost of the impost per tonne of oil). See also John Morrison, 'Global Approval Not Enough, Businesses Need Social License' (2014) YaleGlobal Online <https://archive-yaleglobal.yale.edu/content/government-approval-not-enough-businesses-need-social-license> accessed 4 September 2022.

the fund coverage from the oil and HNS funds to areas beyond national jurisdiction is possible, but may face opposition from some states and receivers on both jurisdictional grounds (on the issue of interference with the freedom of navigation) and on the basis of concerns over increased exposure. There are parallels between receivers of seabed minerals and receivers of oil and HNS that suggest mineral processors as a potential source of contributions to deep seabed mining. The need for further risk spreading would depend upon whether the assurance demands exceeded the capacity of contractors to provide. Even if this step were desirable, such an arrangement would require the agreement of processor states who would need to impose the contribution requirements.[80]

The other potential sources of contributions to the fund would be the operators themselves or states. The creation of an operator-funded structure would effectively be a form of mutual insurance but could address types of compensation that commercial insurers are unwilling to cover. State contributions or guarantees could be sourced from states whose nationals are benefitting from a risky activity, such as sponsoring states in the deep seabed mining context, or even a broader constellation of states, on the basis that the fund would accrue to the benefit of all states insofar as the fund would be used to protect and preserve the marine environment. The willingness of states to become the effective insurers of activities in areas beyond national jurisdiction is doubtful, as the risks presented differ considerably from those relating to nuclear installations (the only example where states have agreed to make public funds available to address liability claims). In the nuclear context, the risks are both potentially catastrophic in scale and directly impact the core economic and human security interests of the states. In the global commons context, the risks are more remote and therefore less politically salient, making it more difficult to justify what amounts to a subsidy.

Determining the form of assurance, and in particular, the desirability of a compensation fund, depends very much on the adequacy of first tier financial assurances. Adequacy, in turn, is a function of whether the amount of compensation required will exceed the limits of insurance coverage, or if there is a (political) desire to address certain forms of harm for which insurance cover is unavailable. The precise driver of the need for second tier coverage will again be sector-specific. The high potential for damage from oil pollution or nuclear incidents clearly influenced the demand for financial assurances that supplement the limited capacity of insurance.

Based on the approach of the Antarctic and the emerging approach for deep seabed mining, there may be a need for greater flexibility in the design of fund mechanisms in areas beyond national jurisdiction, owing to the shared nature of the environmental resources and the diffuse nature of the activities posing risk of harm.

80 As noted above, the ISA is constrained in its ability to impose obligations on activities outside the Area.

The ability to use funds collected in relation to one incident in connection with another may facilitate a more environmentally responsive approach to compensation. For example, greater flexibility may allow for the use of offsets or other environment enhancing tools, where the focus is on the net environmental benefits, as opposed to compensating victims. These more diffuse approaches to fund coverage may also play a role in addressing cumulative and other forms of harm that are not easily attributable.

The challenge of hard to attribute losses may benefit from developments of innovative insurance and risk pooling products, such as parametric insurance, being developed under the Paris Agreement's loss and damage structures. The challenges that face climate-vulnerable states differ from the principal risks facing the environment in ABNJ, but both contexts involve moving away from the tight coupling of operator fault and compensable losses towards a more collectivist approach to addressing losses.[81]

Finally, the creation of a fund requires an institutional structure to manage the fund and claims against it, including determining the contributions required and assessing whether the claims made meet the requirements for payout under the liability rules in question. The IOPC Funds, which plays this role in relation to the oil pollution and HNS regimes, is an intergovernmental organization with a governing assembly and sophisticated secretariat, with an active role in negotiating and litigating settlements. The ATCM and the ISA can perform this role in relation to the Antarctic and deep seabed mining, respectively, although the extent of that role is not yet clear. The extension of assurances to address a broader set of claims in areas beyond national jurisdiction would require the creation of an institution with similar powers to manage claims on behalf of state and private interests: an act that would require significant political capital.[82]

8.7 CONCLUSIONS

It is premature to arrive at firm conclusions on the future direction of financial assurances in activities in areas beyond national jurisdiction beyond those covered

[81] In the climate context, parametric insurance is currently being developed as a risk pooling measure to protect against certain catastrophic impacts, which may be triggered by exceedances of predetermined thresholds (such as wind speed or precipitation associated with extreme weather events). While parametric insurance does not provide full indemnification of losses, the scheme provides greater certainty and prompt payouts, which may be critical in addressing catastrophic events. See Patricia Galvao Ferreira, 'Arrested Development: The Late and Inequitable Integration of Loss and Damage Finance into the UNFCCC' in Meinhard Doelle and Sara Seck (eds), *Research Handbook on Climate Law and Loss and Damage* (Edward Elgar 2021) 127.

[82] For example, the nature of any treaty institutions developed in connection with the BBNJ ILBI has been a source of contention amongst states. Discussed in Margaret Young and Andrew Friedman, 'Biodiversity beyond National Jurisdiction: Regimes and Their Interaction' (2018) 112 AJIL Unbound 123.

by the Liability Annex, but some general observations may be made. First, states are under a due diligence obligation to take steps to ensure that adequate and prompt compensation is available in the event of pollution events. While the provision of financial assurances cannot be said to be a binding legal requirement, it is increasingly understood as a standard response to the very foreseeable circumstance of responsible parties being unable or unwilling to meet their liability obligations. As such, at a minimum, in the development of rules governing liability for new activities involving risk to the environment, there will be a strong normative expectation that some form of financial security arrangement be included.

Second, insurance will most likely form the centrepiece of financial assurance arrangements. Insurance is the default form of assurance across civil liability regimes and has proven to be an effective and sufficiently versatile product. Commercial availability may be an issue for novel activities, but insurers have adapted to provide cover for new risky activities, such as offshore oil and gas, in the past.[83] Past practice shows that there is a degree of collaboration amongst states, operators and the insurance industry, in developing rules that will facilitate insurance cover. The necessity for supplementary coverage depends on the adequacy of first tier assurance, and as was the case with the oil pollution regime may first require some demonstration of the inadequacy of insurance before being agreed to.

Third, there may be some reluctance to embrace an ambitious approach to liability cover in areas beyond national jurisdiction. The Antarctic Liability Annex adopts a cautious approach by carefully conscribing liability and by matching the limits of liability with existing industry standards, which has given a high priority to insurability. The Antarctic compensation fund is designed with similar constraint, offering some greater flexibility to the parties, but not increasing the amount of coverage available. The limited ambition has raised questions regarding whether the Liability Annex was a missed opportunity.[84] However, the slow pace of ratification suggests that a more ambitious approach was not likely to succeed. There was an indication that negotiations on extending the liability rules (beyond environmental emergencies) would be resumed at a further date, but there is no indication of when or whether such negotiations will occur.[85]

Finally, the Liability Annex points to a willingness by states to view compensation mechanisms as more than simply a means to achieve restitution to victims, but as part of the broader regulatory toolkit at their disposal. This reflects the shared nature

[83] Gaskell, 'Compensation for Offshore Pollution' (n 79).

[84] Rüdiger Wolfrum, 'Liability for Environmental Damage in Antarctica: Supplement to the Rules on State Responsibility or a Lost Opportunity?' in Isabelle Buffard (ed), *International Law between Universalism and Fragmentation: Festschrift in Honour of Gerhard Hafner* (Martinus Nijhoff 2008) 817.

[85] ATCM, Final Report of the Twenty-Eighth Antarctic Treaty Consultative Meeting (vol I, ATCM 2015) para 126. Discussed in Alan Hemmings, 'Liability Postponed: The Failure to Bring Annex VI of the Madrid Protocol into Force' (2018) 8 Polar J 315.

of resources in areas beyond national jurisdiction, which allows for the more flexible application of compensation funds to achieve net environmental benefits. Such an approach opens up the use of financial assurances to providing compensation tied to liability but applying those funds in ways that can further the environmental purposes of the regime. This is an innovation with broader significance to liability in areas beyond national jurisdiction, as it decouples the availability of funding for harm to the environment from individualized losses. These approaches may be supplemented by innovative risk pooling measures, such as trust funds, which can distribute risk amongst a wider range of private and public actors with interests in ABNJ activities.

9

Conclusion

9.1 INTRODUCTION

The puzzle that sits at the heart of liability for environmental harm in the global commons is that there is broad acceptance of the underlying principle that states and non-state actors that contribute directly or indirectly to environmental harm are legally responsible for the consequences of that harm. This principle is captured in broad strokes in the no-harm principle, and more specifically in Principle 13 of the Rio Declaration and article 235 of the 1982 UN Convention on the Law of the Sea (UNCLOS) – both of which call for the development of liability rules to address environmental harm in areas beyond national jurisdiction (ABNJ).[1] Yet the implementation of this principle has proven to be elusive. So much so that when the International Law Commission (ILC) started work on liability for environmental harm, it simply bracketed the issue of liability for environmental harm in the global commons. Forty years later, the issue of environmental harm to the ocean commons is widely acknowledged as a crisis;[2] prompting, amongst other things, the negotiation of a new treaty specifically addressing environmental protection of areas beyond national jurisdiction. Yet even within the context of this negotiation, there is little appetite amongst states to develop liability rules and procedures.

[1] United Nations General Assembly, 'Report of the United Nations Conference on Environment and Development' (3–14 June 1992) UN Doc A/Conf.151/26/Rev.1 (1992) Annex I (1992 Rio Declaration); United Nations Convention on the Law of the Sea (adopted 10 December 1982, entered into force 16 November 1994) 1833 UNTS 397 (UNCLOS).

[2] Declaration of the 2022 United Nations Oceans Conference: Our Ocean our future, our responsibility, 17 June 2022, UN Doc. a/conf.230/2022/12, noting '[w]e are therefore deeply alarmed by the global emergency facing the ocean. Sea levels are rising, coastal erosion is worsening, and the ocean is warmer and more acidic. Marine pollution is increasing at an alarming rate, a third of fish stocks are overexploited, marine biodiversity continues to decrease and approximately half of all living coral has been lost, while alien invasive species pose a significant threat to marine ecosystems and resources'.

The continuing reluctance of states to address liability suggests that the international community has made little progress over the past forty years towards realizing the goals of developing liability rules for ABNJ. Indeed, if one looks solely at the limited number of ABNJ specific liability regimes, and the explicit exclusion of ABNJ from other sector-specific civil liability regimes, there may be good reason to question whether liability is a useful tool to address environmental harm in ABNJ. This was the conclusion of Alan Boyle in 1997, who suggested that criminal responsibility may be a more realistic pathway than state responsibility or civil liability approaches.[3] Jutta Brunnée expressed similar reservations in 2004, noting that 'it seems unlikely that liability regimes will play a significant role as a tool for environmental protection'.[4]

Our conclusion on this threshold question is more optimistic but remains equivocal. There have been legal advances in approaches to damages and standing that provide important building blocks for the extension of liability to areas beyond national jurisdiction. In addition, the international community has developed some legal innovations within specific regimes that should have more general application to the ABNJ context. At the same time, there remain significant challenges that are scientific, legal and political in nature that must be overcome if liability is to meaningfully contribute to the environmental management of the global commons. In the discussion that follows we take stock of the key developments identified in the preceding chapters and the substantial challenges that remain. We then address what we believe are some potential pathways forward towards more effective liability rules in ABNJ.

9.2 KEY DEVELOPMENTS

9.2.1 *The Purpose of Liability Rules*

As a starting observation, we note that the demand for liability in ABNJ is likely, in the short- to medium-term, to relate more to the environmental protection and prevention goal of liability regimes, than the compensation and loss allocation goal.

[3] Alan Boyle, 'Remedying Harm to International Common Spaces and Resources: Compensation and Other Approaches' in Peter Wetterstein (ed), *Harm to the Environment: The Right to Compensation and Assessment of Damages* (OUP 1997) 83–100. There is growing support for making serious breaches of environmental obligations an international crime. For example, a non-governmental Independent Expert Panel was established to develop the definition of ecocide and in 2021, the Panel defined it as 'unlawful or wanton acts committed with knowledge that there is substantial likelihood of severe and either widespread or long-term damage to the environment being caused by those acts': See <www.stopecocide.earth/expert-drafting-panel> accessed 30 September 2022.

[4] Jutta Brunnée, 'Of Sense and Sensibility: Reflections on Environmental Liability Regimes as Tools for Environmental Protection' (2004) 53 ICLQ 351, 367 (addressing environmental harm generally, not simply to areas beyond national jurisdiction).

The emphasis on environmental protection is in keeping with the environmentally focused approach in the 1991 Antarctic Protocol and in article 235 of UNCLOS but is also supported by several conditions present in the ABNJ context. First, there is limited exposure for private losses in ABNJ.[5] This is a function of both the nature and intensity of activities currently being carried out in ABNJ, and the limited presence of private legal rights in ABNJ. These rights are not wholly absent. There are, for example, private rights in relation to deep seabed mining, submarine cables and in fisheries that may affect or be affected by environmental damage. Second, while there is scope for public losses that require compensation, for example, for reinstatement and restoration costs, these relate primarily to the environmental protection objective of liability.

The demand for liability rules and processes as an element of environmental prevention reflects the need to promote due care from both states and operators in connection with risky activities. Liability, if properly structured, can play an important role in providing incentives for environmentally sound behaviour. The identification, by the Seabed Disputes Chamber (SDC), of the state obligation to provide recourse under article 235 as an element of due diligence in relation to the duty to protect and preserve the marine environment indicates a recognition of liability as an integral element of environmental management.[6] This is an important finding that ought to be understood as forming part of the customary rules concerning environmental due diligence.

Liability rules are intended to play a crucial role in providing funds for the restoration of the environment. While the duty to prevent harm is prospective, this aspect of liability relates directly to the duty of responsible parties to restore the environment, which flows from the duty to make reparations.[7] As discussed in Chapters 2 and 3, the obligation to make reparations is qualified by a principle of proportionality. In the absence of reparations, environmental harm to ABNJ is externalized and borne by the international community as a whole and not by the responsible party, contrary to the polluter-pays principle.

There are several important implications that flow from the prioritization of the environmental protection goal of liability in ABNJ over the compensation goal. First, focusing on environmental purposes provides a stronger basis for strict liability, and operation of the polluter-pays principle, since the underlying goal is directed more to the question of remedying harm than to correcting (morally) wrongful acts.

5 Protocol on Environmental Protection to the Antarctic Treaty (adopted 4 October 1991, entered into force 14 January 1998) (1991) 30 ILM 1461 (1991 Antarctic Protocol).

6 *Responsibilities and Obligations of States Sponsoring Persons and Entities with Respect to Activities in the Area* (Advisory Opinion of 1 February 2011) ITLOS Reports 2011 (*Activities in the Area* Advisory Opinion), paras 139–140.

7 ILC, 'Draft Principles on the Allocation of Loss in the Case of Transboundary Harm Arising Out of Hazardous Activities, with Commentaries' (2006) UN Doc A/61/10 (Draft Principles) principle 3, commentary 2.

This is reflected in the approach to operator liability under the Antarctic Liability Annex, but not under the current approach to contractor liability under the Exploration Regulations for deep seabed mining, which still requires a wrongful act.[8] Second, because the emphasis on liability in ABNJ is on the environment itself, irrespective of the identity of the victim, the approach to standing ought to reflect the community interests in the shared environmental resources and functions. Finally, focusing on the environment provides justification for a more inclusive approach to damages that includes damages to the environment *per se*, and not simply the instrumental value of environmental resources to identified victims.

Turning from the purposes of liability rules to their substance, we identified (in Chapter 2) several potential approaches to environmental liability that may be relevant to addressing environmental harm in ABNJ. The first of these is what we termed 'unharmonized domestic liability'. We identified numerous barriers, including standing and immunity, jurisdiction (subject matter and personal) and choice of law issues that indicate that domestic courts are poorly suited to adjudicate on liability for environmental harms arising in ABNJ. Given the near absence of private interests affected by environmental incidents in ABNJ, there has been little recourse to domestic courts. The predominance (at this time) of public interests in the ABNJ environment indicate that liability approaches in this context will require state cooperation through state responsibility or civil liability approaches.

9.2.2 *State Responsibility*

There have been several developments in the law of state responsibility that improve the prospects for state liability for environmental harm, although the limits of due diligence and the politics of state responsibility will likely render state responsibility a secondary approach. The first significant development is the elaboration of the due diligence obligation on states to protect and preserve the environment. The obligation for states to exercise reasonable care to prevent activities under its jurisdiction from harming the environment, including the environment in ABNJ, has a long pedigree in international environmental law. However, the Advisory Opinions in the *Activities in the Area* and *Sub-Regional Fisheries Commission* cases, and the decision in the *South China Sea Arbitration* clarify a number of critical points. First, these cases make it clear that states are under an obligation to 'exercise effective jurisdiction and control in administrative matters', which includes obligations to investigate and take necessary actions, if appropriate.[9] There is a clear emphasis on the

8 See discussion Chapter 5, Section 5.4.2.

9 *Request for an Advisory Opinion Submitted by the Sub-Regional Fisheries Commission (SRFC)* (Advisory Opinion of 2 April 2015) ITLOS Reports 2015 (SRFC Advisory Opinion), para119; *The South China Sea Arbitration (The Republic of Philippines v The People's Republic of China)* (Award) (2016) Oxford Reports on ICGJ 495 (PCA) (*South China Sea Arbitration*), paras 964–966.

responsibility of states to actively oversee activities that are formally under their control, whether through sponsoring state or flag state jurisdiction. This was particularly evident in the *Activities in the Area* Advisory Opinion, where the SDC was not willing to lessen the responsibilities of sponsoring states considering the presence of the ISA or in light of the sponsoring state's development status. In the *South China Sea Arbitration* knowledge of illegal activities was an important factor,[10] although the due diligence standard generally suggests that wilful blindness cannot act as a defence. As the ICJ in the *Pulp Mills* case noted, a degree of active vigilance is required.[11]

This latter point is especially significant in the ABNJ context because of the remoteness of activities and their impacts. When considered in concert with the dicta in the *Activities in the Area* Advisory Opinion concerning the application of the precautionary principle to due diligence,[12] a rigorous standard of oversight of risky activities is clearly emerging in international law. This standard requires an appreciation of the risks involved in activities undertaken, and must account for scientifically uncertain, yet plausible, risks. The content of due diligence must account for scientific and technological advances, which, given the rapidly changing knowledge environment in ABNJ, suggests an obligation to incorporate new knowledge and new technologies that will improve oversight and monitoring of remote activities.

The second substantive legal development of relevance is the more inclusive and comprehensive approach to damages. There are two advances of note. First, the clear acceptance of 'pure environmental losses' as a compensable head of damage will more effectively capture the harm in ABNJ, which in many cases will not have a substantial economic component or be subject to restoration. As a matter of principle, these losses are real, and as detailed in Chapter 3, are increasingly understood as compensable. The practice of the International Oil Pollution Compensation Funds (IOPC Funds) of not compensating these losses is a policy decision that is out of step with the prevailing approaches in international law.[13] While valuation of pure environmental losses will remain a significant challenge, recognizing this form of environmental damage will facilitate methodologies and approaches that reflect the actual losses – the challenge is an evidentiary one, not a substantive legal barrier.

The impracticality or disproportionality of restoration and reinstatement measures presents a further bar to recovery. A second development that has potential to

10 *South China Sea Arbitration*, para 962.

11 See *Pulp Mills on the River Uruguay (Argentina v Uruguay)* (Judgment) [2010] ICJ Rep 14, para 197 ('It is an obligation which entails not only the adoption of appropriate rules and measures, but also a certain level of vigilance in their enforcement . . .').

12 *Activities in the Area* Advisory Opinion (n 6), para 131.

13 *Guidelines for Presenting Claims for Environmental Damage* (2018 edn, International Oil Pollution Compensation Funds, 2018), para 4.1; see also discussion, Chapter 3, Section 3.2.2.5.

contribute to effectively addressing environmental losses is the acceptance of other proxies for valuing and addressing unremediated harms. For example, the approach under the Antarctic Liability Annex is to require operators to undertake response measures, but in the face of a failure to do, there is a further obligation to pay the equivalent costs of the response measure (not undertaken) into a fund. In effect, the estimated cost of restoration becomes a proxy for the loss to the environment. The funds are then available to address future environmental emergencies.

The use of proxies is also reflected in the emerging practice of using environmental offsets or equivalent ecosystem components as an alternative to restoration measures. The concept of offsets as a response to ecosystem losses has extensive recognition within biological diversity approaches and is acknowledged as a potential response by the ILC in its Draft Principles on Loss Allocation.[14] The practice of using offsets as an alternative to harm avoidance or mitigation in the planning stages of resource development is controversial, but in the context of liability offsets ought to be understood as a proportional response to a loss that has already occurred, even if they may not fully compensate losses. The use of proxies is facilitated by the presence of trust funds in the Antarctic Liability Annex and is also reflected in the structure of the proposed Environmental Compensation Fund (ECF) in the deep seabed mining regime.[15] Trust funds allow for a decoupling of compensation from the specific incident, which can be seen as an acceptance of the global commons environment as an indivisible whole, while allowing for a more flexible and pragmatic approach to restoration.

There have also been important developments in the law of standing that may broaden the use of state responsibility as an effective accountability tool in ABNJ. While there are no contentious cases explicitly endorsing the idea that obligations to protect the environment in ABNJ are obligations *erga omnes partes*, the concept has been the subject of increasing judicial recognition and would appear to underlie the rights of the applicant states in the *Whaling in the Antarctic* case and *South China Sea Arbitration*.[16] The difficulty with standing based on obligations *erga omnes* has less to do with establishing that the obligation protects a collective interest and more with who will have sufficient political interest to initiate such claims, the modalities of reparations as a remedy and the avoidance of what may appear to be windfall gains. Conferring the authority on the competent international organization (as is the case with the ISA), coupled with the establishment of trust funds or other collective mechanisms provide a potential avenue for satisfying the requirement

[14] Draft Principles (n 7) commentary to principle 3, 74, 7 ('Where restoration or reinstatement is not possible, it is reasonable to introduce the equivalent of those components into the environment').

[15] See Chapter 8.

[16] See Chapter 6.

that the compensation sought is in the interest of the beneficiaries of the obligation that has been breached (see discussion in Section 9.2.4).[17]

Another significant development that bears on the issue of standing concerns the question of when a state or other actor may undertake response measures. In areas within national jurisdiction, the right of a state to respond to environmental harm and to seek compensation from those responsible is broadly accepted as a corollary of state sovereignty over its territory. In ABNJ, the right of a state to intervene to respond to environmental harm and to seek compensation is ambiguous. In the deep seabed mining context, the ISA Council has the ability to respond to emergencies that are 'necessary to prevent, contain and minimize' serious environmental harm where a contractor does not comply with an emergency order.[18] Under the Antarctic Liability Annex, parties have the ability to take response measures where an operator fails to take action, subject to notifying the party of the operator, and only in the face of imminent harm.[19] While the right for third party states or international institutions to take response measures is constrained, the acknowledgment of this ability is an important legal innovation as it is premised on the idea that states have an interest and corresponding right to protect the commons environment, and can be compensated for their reasonable actions. These treaty rules cannot be generalized, but they are consistent with existing international rules that provide that states are under a general obligation to protect and preserve the marine environment,[20] and are analogous to a line of domestic law cases providing recovery for 'necessitous interventions'.[21]

Our broader point here is not that the law of state responsibility provides a clear and effective approach to compensation. As we outline below, there remain numerous obstacles, and, notwithstanding those obstacles, state responsibility is at best a partial response. Nonetheless, states play a critically important role in the environmental management of ABNJ. State responsibility is a crucial element in promoting the accountability of states that engage in or have jurisdiction over risky activities in ABNJ.

9.2.3 *Civil Liability Approaches*

Turning to civil liability approaches, direct developments here are still emerging, but appear modest in their scope. There has been little progress in extending civil

[17] ILC, 'Draft Articles on Responsibility of States for Internationally Wrongful Acts, with Commentaries' (2001) UN Doc A/56/10 (ASR), art 48, 126.

[18] International Seabed Authority, Regulations on Prospecting and Exploration for Polymetallic Nodules in the Area (2013) ISBA/19/C/17 (PMN), reg 33(7).

[19] Annex VI to the Protocol on Environmental Protection to the Antarctic Treaty on Liability Arising from Environmental Emergencies (adopted 17 June 2005) (2006) 45 ILM 5 (Liability Annex) (not in force), art 5.

[20] UNCLOS (n 1) art 192.

[21] John McCamus, 'Necessitous Intervention: The Altruistic Intermeddler and the Law of Restitution' (1979) 11 Ottawa L Rev 297; discussed in Chapter 3, Section 3.2.2.3.

liability structures to ABNJ generally. A key difference between the deep seabed and Antarctic, on the one hand, and the high seas, on the other, is the discrete and contained nature of activities in the former, as compared to the highly heterogeneous nature of high seas activities. The sector-specific nature of most civil liability regimes, which allows for a degree of risk sharing (in the case of funds) and requirements, such as exclusions, caps and insurance that can be tailored to specific risk profiles, suggests that there is unlikely to be a general civil liability structure for the high seas. The absence of civil liability rules in the high seas may also be a function of demand. Much of the international movement on civil liability, for example, in oil pollution and nuclear facilities, was preceded by very visible incidents that influenced public and state perceptions of risk. The environmental risks in ABNJ, especially marine areas, are less visible and less direct.

Another possibility would be to extend the existing civil liability regimes, particularly for shipping related activities, to the high seas areas.[22] There appears little interest in such a reformation, which would require addressing a range of issues, including reconsideration of the approach to damages, clarity on the right of states or other actors to undertake response measures on the high seas and addressing choice of law and forum issues. It is worth recalling that one response to tanker accidents in areas within national jurisdiction is to tow the ship further away from shore, often into the high seas, to mitigate harm. This practice may be sensible as a harm minimization measure, but it also speaks to the economic and state-centric bias of existing civil liability structures that make them poorly suited to addressing the more ecological interests at stake in ABNJ.

The Antarctic Liability Annex, should it come into effect, contains many of the key elements of civil liability regimes, such as channelling, strict liability and insurance requirements, although the scope of the regime is limited to environmental emergencies. At present, the deep seabed mining regime does not contemplate a stand-alone liability regime but would address contractor liability through insurance and the development of an environmental compensation fund through the Exploitation Regulations.[23] Unlike the Antarctic Liability Annex, the deep seabed mining liability structure is directed to both private economic harms and public losses, although there is an indication that the coverage may exclude pure environmental losses, which would serve to limit the scope of available compensation.[24] Neither the Antarctic nor the deep seabed mining regimes exclude the possibility of state liability. Instead, the approach to channelling is, in principle,

[22] See Nicholas Gaskell, 'Liability and Compensation Regimes: Pollution of the High Seas' in Robert Beckman and others (eds), *High Seas Governance: Gaps and Challenges* (Brill Nijhoff 2019) 229.

[23] ISA, 'Draft Regulations on Exploitation of Mineral Resources in the Area' (2019) ISBA/25/C/WP.1 (DER).

[24] ISA, 'Study on an Environmental Compensation Fund for Activities in the Area' (2021) ISA Technical Study No 27, p. 37.

non-exclusive. This speaks to the important role that states continue to play in overseeing activities in the commons.

9.2.4 *Institutional Mechanisms*

On the key issues of defining harm and structuring rules of standing, these liability regimes provide different avenues for recovery. The Antarctic, with its focus on remediation, places primary responsibility on operators to address emergencies, with oversight falling to the state of the operator, but ultimately empowering all parties to take action. The Antarctic treaty bodies play an important but secondary role in collectively determining the liability of state operators, through the Antarctic Treaty Consultative Meeting (ATCM) or through the Antarctic dispute settlement processes. Non-state operator liability is addressed through domestic processes. The deep seabed mining regime has two distinct institutional advantages. First, the presence of the ISA, which is empowered to take enforcement actions, can potentially simplify liability proceedings, at least in relation to some remediation efforts, through administrative (emergency) orders.[25] Administrative orders allow the ISA to address remediation directly and with a degree of precision that is not readily available through compensation mechanisms. In addition, the ISA may be empowered to undertake some restoration actions on its own, providing a clearer mechanism for standing to pursue claims against contractors.[26] The ability of individual states to initiate response actions or to pursue claims for environmental harm to ABNJ arising from deep seabed mining is much more ambiguous, as there is no direct authority for states to undertake response actions arising from the actions of third parties. Second, the deep seabed mining regime benefits from the presence of the mandatory dispute settlement mechanisms, which encompass the ISA, states parties and contractors, albeit in a complicated matrix of jurisdictional competences.[27]

The presence of institutions in the Antarctic and deep seabed mining liability regimes is crucial, as is their nature and functions. Where those institutions have legal personality and a broad remedial mandate, as is the case with the ISA, they can intervene directly on behalf of collective interests. The ISA and the ATCM are anticipated to play important roles in managing compensation funds, which are key elements in both regimes that allow for more flexible responses and add credibility by addressing liability gaps or insufficiencies in first tier sources of compensation (for example, insurance). The IOPC Funds play a similar indispensable role in under the oil pollution and HNS Conventions. The existing high seas institutions, such as regional fisheries management organizations or regional seas commissions are poorly suited to contribute to enhanced liability. The prospects of new institutions playing

[25] UNCLOS (n 1), art 162(2)(w).
[26] PMN (n 18), reg 33(7).
[27] See Chapter 7.

this role in the context of the recent agreement on the conservation and sustainable use of marine biological diversity of areas beyond national jurisdiction (2023 BBNJ Agreement) are diminished by the exclusion of express liability provisions in the agreement, apart from a reference to responsibility and liability in the preamble.

9.3 CHALLENGES

The most far-reaching and difficult to overcome challenge to addressing liability in ABNJ is the substantial tension between the environmental risks that many activities in or affecting ABNJ pose, which are long-term, cumulative and uncertain, and the practicalities of applying liability rules, which require a degree of immediacy, clear attribution and predictability. Principally, this is an issue of the nature of the major threats to the global commons environment, such as ocean acidification, plastics pollution and illegal, unreported and unregulated fishing which have multiple, and difficult to attribute, sources. Liability rules, at their centre, concern individualized responsibility, but much of the harm to the commons environment is collective in nature. These are not entirely novel issues. For example, some forms of widespread environmental harm have been addressed in domestic legal settings through innovative approaches to causation, such as probabilistic harm.[28] But the scale of global environmental harms from cumulative sources makes the adaptation of these approaches to ABNJ unlikely, if not impossible.

Another major source of potential harm from activities in ABNJ comes from operational harm, as opposed to accidents. This is best exemplified by deep seabed mining, where much of the concern is related less to accidents, such as unintended releases (from ships or mining equipment), and more from when intended operational activities result in higher than predicted environmental harm.[29] For example, it is anticipated that there will be an acceptable level of harm to the marine environment (presumably below the threshold of significance) from authorized deep seabed mining activities. Operators that comply with regulatory standards are typically not held liable for anticipated levels of harm, but the approach is complicated by cumulative effects and unpredicted harms. The harm that arises under these conditions may be unforeseeable and may be as much a result of the regulator's deficiencies or lack of precaution as that of the operator. The presence of uncertainty militates in favour of a strict approach to liability – indeed foreseeability concerns were at the heart of Goldie's original analysis of standards of liability in international law.[30] Yet, operational harms raise difficult questions about the extent to which operators may reasonably rely on international and national approval

[28] See Chapter 4, Section 4.2.

[29] Lisa Levin, Diva J Amon and Hannah Lily, 'Challenges to the Sustainability of Deep-Seabed Mining' (2020) 3 (10) Nature Sustainability 784.

[30] LFE Goldie, 'Liability for Damage and the Progressive Development of International Law' (1965) 14(4) ICLQ 1189; discussed in Chapter 5, Section 5.2.

authorities and collectively agreed upon standards, which is as much a question of allocation, as it is one of the appropriate standard of liability.

A second challenge concerns the central role of institutions in liability structures for ABNJ. The juridical aspect of this challenge relates to the ability of interested parties, whether state or non-state, to access forums for relief. Domestic forums face a host of limitations in adjudicating over claims in the global commons.[31] Agreements on reciprocal access, such as those found in the Antarctic Liability Annex, may address some of these constraints, but may need to be supplemented by further rules addressing standing, choice of law and enforcement of judgments. International courts and tribunals, particularly if they are clothed with mandatory jurisdiction over key actors, provide opportunities to extend standing and access to remedies to states and international organizations. However, as the complicated jurisdictional rules of Part XI of the UNCLOS show, providing forums that can adjudicate complex, multi-party claims remains exceptional in international law.

Fundamentally, the nature of rights in the commons requires the creation of a collective body to act on behalf of the shared environmental interests. As such, institutions with administrative powers are the lynchpin of international liability structures. There is, however, a political aspect to this challenge insofar as there appears to be limited willingness on the part of states to create institutions that are able to constrain state activities in ABNJ.[32] The ISA, which is unique in international law, may be a product of a particular political moment that resulted in the common heritage status of the seabed.[33] Even accounting for this, states maintain a high level of control through the ISA Council (and its voting chambers) and the ISA Assembly. Decisions to pursue actions against contractors, many of whom have close ties to their sponsoring state, are subject to political control. This may result in the ability of a state that is itself, or through a sponsored contractor, subject to potential liability exposure, being able to vote on, and possibly block decisions.[34] A similar degree of control arises under the Antarctic Liability Annex, where decisions about state operator liability are made by the ATCM on the basis of consensus.[35]

This points to a final challenge to effective liability structures in international law, which is the complex politics of state responsibility in the global commons. States are imperfect protectors of the global commons, as they benefit from risk-based activities under their jurisdiction, and even in circumstances where pursuing damages against another state may be appealing, states must weigh the costs of such actions in the context of broader state interdependencies. Despite broad recognition of the growing

[31] See Chapter 7.

[32] On a wider scale, the tensions surrounding institutional empowerment have been evident in the negotiations on the treaty structures under the new international legally binding instrument for marine biodiversity beyond national jurisdiction.

[33] Surabhi Ranganathan, 'Global Commons' (2016) 27 EJIL 693.

[34] See Chapter 6, Section 6.3.2.1.

[35] See Chapter 7.

environmental crisis facing areas beyond national jurisdiction, cooperative forms of environmental management, such as the approaches favoured by states in the 2023 BBNJ Agreement (for example, environmental impact assessment, area-based management tools and capacity building), remain preferred over the more confrontational approach inherent to liability processes. Privatizing liability through channelling responsibility to operators has been the preferred avenue to avoid interstate disputes, but these opportunities are more limited in the global commons.

9.4 MOVING FORWARD

Reflecting on these challenges, it is important to be realistic about the limitations of liability structures to address collective harms in ABNJ. Liability as an approach to environmental protection remains centred on individuated legal responsibility that links victims to those responsible for the harm in question. Problems such as ocean acidification or ocean-based plastics pollution may be so diffuse in their origins as to make traditional liability approaches ill-suited to achieving the aims of compensation and environmental protection. Alternative approaches, such as the loss and damage provision found in Article 8 of the Paris Agreement under the UN Framework Convention on Climate Change, may provide for more efficient and effective mechanisms to remedy certain environmental harms. Looking ahead, an important task will be to identify areas of collective responsibility that may best be addressed through alternative remedial mechanisms and differentiating these areas from circumstances that demand the direct form of legal accountability that liability structures provide. In this regard, it is critical to identify areas better suited to alternatives to liability provisionally and without prejudice to future legal and scientific developments that could overcome the existing barriers to effective liability regimes. In drawing this distinction, we do not want to suggest a binary approach. Indeed, there are some elements of modern liability structures, such as insurance products and trust funds that provide a basis for collective responsibility. The particular advantage of loss and damage approaches is that they allow for environmental harm to be treated as legally significant notwithstanding the inability to attribute that harm to a specific defendant.

Despite these limitations, there are opportunities to strengthen the rules and practices respecting compensation for environmental harm within liability structures. A sensible starting point would be the extension of the ILC Draft Principles on Loss Allocation to include areas beyond national jurisdiction. The original justification for excluding ABNJ from the ILC's work on liability, which was based on the uncertain nature of states' rights and the cumulative nature of environmental impacts in the global commons,[36] ought to be revisited in light of the developments on standing and damage discussed above. Extending the ILC's work to include

[36] ILC, 'First Report on Prevention of Transboundary Damage from Hazardous Activities, by Mr. Pemmaraju Sreenivasa Rao, Special Rapporteur' (1998) UN Doc A/CN.4/487, paras 106–110;

ABNJ would recognize and solidify existing legal developments and provide guidance to states in relation to future legal developments.[37] This is a modest and incremental suggestion as extending the Draft Principles to ABNJ largely reflects existing customary law on the duty to provide adequate and prompt compensation (Principle 4) and access to remedies (Principle 6).[38]

One particular benefit of extending the Draft Principles is in broadening the scope of Principle 5 on response measures. In its current (transboundary) context, the right of the affected state to mitigate damages in its own territory is clear. In the commons context, this would best be extended as a right of any state or competent international organization to take appropriate response measures, subject to consultation, in the face of imminent harm. Such an approach would place states and competent international organizations in the same position of Parties under the Antarctic Liability Annex. Extending Principle 5 in this manner would reflect the legal interest that all states have in the ABNJ environment; an interest that has been implicitly accepted in the emerging approach to standing to seek remedies for breaches of obligations *erga omnes*. Principle 5 does not expressly include a right for states that undertake response measures to seek compensation, but such a right is assumed in the commentaries.[39]

A final area of considerable promise that falls outside the Draft Principles is the use of trust funds or related concepts as a collective basis for recovery. As discussed in Chapter 6, the concept of trusteeship has received increasing attention in relation to the global commons, including the climate. As a specific domestic legal concept, the notion of public trusteeship is tied to sovereign authority, which limits its direct application in ABNJ. However, the concept has a wider history as a general principle of international law and has specific application in underlying the relationship of commons institutions like the ISA towards the beneficiaries of shared environmental resources. Trust-like structures can be created by states to direct compensation towards environmental restoration of commons resources, overcoming windfall concerns and allowing for collective decision-making. The indication by the ISA of the creation of an environmental compensation fund is a promising development that has potential to facilitate the harm prevention and restoration goals of international liability structures.[40]

see also ILC, 'Report of the International Law Commission on the Work of Its Forty-Second Session' (1 May–20 July 1990) UN Doc A/45/10. Discussed in c 2, Section 9.3.1.

37 Draft Principles (n 7), general commentary, 59, para 5 (describing the intent of the Principles as being 'intended to contribute to the process of development of international law ... by providing appropriate guidance to States in respect of hazardous activities not covered by specific agreements and by indicating the matters that should be dealt with in such agreements').

38 In fact, the ILC cites UNCLOS, art 235 in support of principle 4.

39 Draft Principles (n 7), commentary to principle 5, 85, 10.

40 ISA, Technical Study No 27 (n 24); Another relevant model is the funding mechanism to address loss and damage under the Paris Agreement, Decision - CP.27, -/CMA.4, 'Funding arrangements for responding to loss and damage associated with the adverse effects of climate change, including a focus on addressing loss and damage', 20 November 2022.

Of course, the concept of trusts carries with it the question of the identity of the beneficiaries. There are multiple and competing understandings of who ought to be the beneficiaries of the commons environment. The unique status of the seabed as the common heritage of mankind presents a non-statist understanding of the commons, but this approach has not been adopted outside of the deep seabed context, and even there, states remain at the political centre. Liability, as a legal tool to preserve and protect the environment, is interesting because it forces courts and decision-makers to focus on who has suffered a loss. There has been a historic tendency of international law to treat environmental losses in the global commons as a nullity, but this legal understanding is increasingly at odds with our scientific understanding of the commons environment. However, the legal recognition of environmental losses within state territory signals a closing of the gap between the legal and scientific understanding of environmental damage. It is not tenable, scientifically or legally, that this gap will continue to exist in the global commons. Thus, we are hopeful that as our understanding of the global commons environment and the impact of human activities on its functions develops, the international law of liability will follow.

Bibliography

Adshead J, 'The Application and Development of the Polluter-Pays Principle across Jurisdictions in Liability for Marine Oil Pollution: The Tales of the "Erika" and the "Prestige"' (2018) 30 JEL 425

Aguon J and Hunter J, 'Second Wave Due Diligence: The Case for Incorporating Free, Prior and Informed Consent into the Deep Seabed Mining Regulatory Regime' (2019) 38 Stan Envtl L J 3

Albers J, *Responsibility and Liability in the Context of Transboundary Movements of Hazardous Wastes by Sea* (Springer-Verlag 2015)

Allen J, 'Points of Law' in Cymie Payne and Peter Sand (eds), *Gulf War Reparations and the UN Compensation Commission: Environmental Claims* (OUP 2011) 141

Ameye EM, 'United States and India: Two Nuclear States with Legislation that Truly Holds Responsible Parties Liable in Case of a Nuclear Accident' (2015) 18(8) Journal of Risk Research 1070

Anderson C and de la Rue C, 'The Role of the P&I Clubs in Maritime Pollution Incidents' (2011) 85 Tul L Rev 1257

Anton D, 'The Principle of Residual Liability in the Seabed Disputes Chamber of the International Tribunal for the Law of the Sea: The Advisory Opinion on Responsibility and Liability for International Seabed Mining (ITLOS Case No. 17)' (2012) 7(2) JSDLP-RDPDD 241

Badia A, *Piercing the Veil of State Enterprises in International Arbitration* (Wolters Kluwer 2014)

Bailey SH and Bowman MJ, 'The Policy/Operational Dichotomy – A Cuckoo in the Nest' (1986) 45(3) CLJ 430

Barboza J, *The Environment, Risk and Liability in International Law* (Brill 2011)

Barrett J, 'The Antarctic Treaty System' in Karen N Scott and David L VanderZwaag (eds), *Research Handbook on Polar Law* (Edward Elgar 2020) 40

Baslar K, *The Concept of the Common Heritage of Mankind in International Law* (Martinus Nijhoff 1998)

Bentata P and Faure M, 'The Role of ENGOs in Environmental Litigation: A French Case Study' (2015) 25 EPG 459

Bergkamp L, *Liability and Environment: Private and Public Law Aspects of Civil Liability for Environmental Harm in an International Context* (Kluwer Law International 2001)

Berry DS, 'Unity or Fragmentation in the Deep Blue: Choices in Institutional Design for Marine Biological Diversity in Areas beyond National Jurisdiction' (2021) 8 Front Mar Sci 1

Birnie P, Boyle A and Redgwell C, *International Law and the Environment* (4th edn, OUP 2021)

Blokker N, 'International Organizations: The Untouchables?' (2013) 10 Int Organ Law Rev 259

'International Organizations or Institutions, Implied Powers' (last updated December 2021) in Anne Peters and Rüdiger Wolfrum (eds), *Max Planck Encyclopedia of Public International Law* (OUP 2008)

Blum J, *The End of the Old Order in Rural Europe* (Princeton University Press 1978)

Blumm M and Guthrie R, 'Internationalizing the Public Trust Doctrine: Natural Law and Constitutional and Statutory Approaches to Fulfilling the Saxion Vision' (2012) 45 UC Davis L Rev 741

Boon KE, 'Are Control Tests Fit for the Future? The Spillage Problem in Attribution Doctrines' (2014) 15 MJIL 1

Bosselmann K, *Earth Governance: Trusteeship of the Global Commons* (Edward Elgar 2015)

Bourrel M, Thiele T and Currie D, 'The Common Heritage of Mankind as a Means to Assess and Advance Equity in Deep Sea Mining' (2018) 95 Mar Pol'y 311

Bowman M and Boyle A (eds), *Environmental Damage in International and Comparative Law: Problems of Definition and Valuation* (OUP 2002)

Boyle A, 'State Responsibility and Liability for Injurious Consequences of Acts Not Prohibited by International Law: A Necessary Distinction?' (1990) 39 ICLQ 1

'Dispute Settlement and the Law of the Sea Convention: Problems of Fragmentation and Jurisdiction' (1997) 46(1) ICLQ 37

'Remedying Harm to International Common Spaces and Resources: Compensation and Other Approaches' in Peter Wetterstein (ed), *Harm to the Environment: The Right to Compensation and Assessment of Damages* (OUP 1997) 83

'Reparation for Environmental Damage in International Law: Some Preliminary Problems' in Michael Bowman and Alan Boyle (eds), *Environmental Damage in International and Comparative Law: Problems of Definition and Valuation* (OUP 2002) 17

'Globalising Environmental Liability: The Interplay of National and International Law' (2005) 17 JEL 3

Brans E, *Liability for Damage to Public Natural Resources: Standing, Damage and Damage Assessment* (Kluwer Law International 2001)

Brent K, 'Solar Radiation Management Geoengineering and Strict Liability for Ultrahazardous Activities' in Neil Craik, Cameron SG Jefferies, Sara L Seck and Tim Stephens (eds), *Global Environmental Change and Innovation in International Law* (CUP 2018) 161

Brondizio ES, Settele J, Díaz S and Ngo HT (eds), *Global Assessment Report on Biodiversity and Ecosystem Services of the Intergovernmental Science-Policy Platform on Biodiversity and Ecosystem Services* (IPBES Secretariat 2019)

Brown ED, *The Area beyond the Limits of National Jurisdiction: Sea-Bed Energy and Mineral Resources and Law of the Sea* (Martinus Nijhoff 1986) vol II

Brunnée J, 'Of Sense and Sensibility: Reflections on Environmental Liability Regimes as Tools for Environmental Protection' (2004) 53 ICLQ 351

Buck S, *The Global Commons: An Introduction* (Island Press 2012)

Burdon P and Williams C, 'Rights of Nature: A Constructive Analysis' in Douglas Fisher (ed), *Research Handbook on Fundamental Concepts of Environmental Law* (Edward Elgar 2016) 196

Burmester HC, 'Liability for Damage from Antarctic Mineral Resource Activities' (1989) 29 Va J Int'l L 621

Buxbaum H, 'Foreign Governments as Plaintiffs in U.S. Courts and the Case against "Judicial Imperialism"' (2016) 73 Wash Lee L Rev 653
Calabresi G and Melamed AD, 'Property Rules, Liability Rules, and Inalienability: One View of the Cathedral' (1972) 85 Harv L Rev 1089
Chao W, *Pollution from the Carriage of Oil by Sea: Liability and Compensation* (Kluwer Law International 1996)
Charme J, 'Transnational Injury and Ultra-hazardous Activity: An Emerging Norm of International Strict Liability' (1989) 4 J L & Tech 75
Chinkin C and Mackenzie R, 'Intergovernmental Organizations as "Friends of Courts"' in Laurence Boisson de Chazournes, Cesare PR Romano and Ruth Mackenzie (eds), *International Organisations and International Dispute Settlement: Trends and Prospects* (Brill 2002) 135
Chow PY, 'On Obligations Erga Omnes Partes' (2021) 52 Geo J Int'l L 469
Churchill R, 'Facilitating (Transnational) Civil Liability Litigation for Environmental Damage by Means of Treaties: Progress, Problems, and Prospects' (2001) 12 Yrbk Int'l Env Law 3
Churchill R and Ulfstein G, 'Autonomous Institutional Arrangements in Multilateral Environmental Agreements: A Little-Noticed Phenomenon in International Law' (2000) 94(4) AJIL 623
Collins R and French D, 'A Guardian of Universal Interest or Increasingly Out of Its Depth? The International Seabed Authority Turns 25' (2019) 17(3) Int Org Law Rev 1
Convey P and Peck LS, 'Antarctic Environmental Change and Biological Responses' (2019) 5 Science Advances 11
Craik N, 'Recalcitrant Reality and Chosen Ideals: The Public Function of Dispute Settlement in International Environmental Law' (1997) 10 Geo Int'l Envtl L Rev 551
Crawford J, *The International Law Commission's Articles on State Responsibility: Introduction, Text and Commentaries* (CUP 2002)
'State Responsibility' in Rüdiger Wolfrum (ed), *Max Planck Encyclopedia of Public International Law Online* (OUP September 2006)
State Responsibility (CUP 2013)
Brownlie's Principles of Public International Law (9th edn, OUP 2019)
Creutz K, *State Responsibility in the International Legal Order: A Critical Appraisal* (CUP 2020)
Daugirdas K, 'How and Why International Law Binds International Organizations' (2016) 57 Harv Intl L J 325
Davenport T, 'Responsibility and Liability for Damage Arising Out of Activities in the Area: Potential Claimants and Possible Fora' (Legal Working Group on Liability for Environmental Harm from Activities in the Area, Liability Issues for Deep Seabed Mining Series, Paper No 5, February 2019)
de La Fayette L, 'The Concept of Environmental Damage in International Liability Regimes' in Michael Bowman and Alan Boyle (eds), *Environmental Damage in International and Comparative Law: Problems of Definition and Valuation* (OUP 2002) 149
'International Liability for Damage to the Environment' in Malgosia Fitzmaurice, David M Ong and Panos Merkouris (eds), *Research Handbook on International Environmental Law* (Edward Elgar 2010) 320
de Smedt K, Wang H and Faure M, 'Towards Optimal Liability and Compensation for Offshore Oil and Gas Activities' in Michael Faure (ed), *Civil Liability and Financial Security for Offshore Oil and Gas Activities* (CUP 2016)
Doeker G and Gehring T, 'Private or International Liability for Transnational Environmental Damage – The Precedent of Conventional Liability Regimes' (1990) 2(1) JEL 1

Doelle M and Seck S, 'Introducing Loss and Damage' in Meinhard Doelle and Sara Seck (eds), *Research Handbook on Climate Change Loss and Damage* (Edward Elgar 2021) 1

Dubois SM and Mayer B, 'Liability and Compensation for Marine Plastic Pollution: Conceptual Issues and Possible Ways Forward' (2020) 114 AJIL Unbound 206

Duvic-Paoli L, *The Prevention Principle in International Environmental Law* (CUP 2018)

Elliot L, *International Environmental Politics: Protecting the Antarctic* (Palgrave MacMillan 1994)

Ellis J, 'Extraterritorial Excuse of Jurisdiction for Environmental Protection: Addressing Fairness Concerns' (2012) 25 LJIL 397

Evans M, '*Parens Patriae* and Public Trust: Litigating Environmental Harm *Per Se*' (2016) 12 (1) MJSDL 1

Fasia E, 'No Provision Left Behind – Law of the Sea Convention's Dispute Settlement System and Obligations *Erga Omnes*' (2021) 20 LPICT 519

Fasoli E, 'The Possibilities for Nongovernmental Organizations Promoting Environmental Protection to Claim Damages in Relation to the Environment in France, Italy, the Netherlands and Portugal' (2017) 26(1) RECIEL 30

Faure M, 'Attribution of Liability: An Economic Analysis of Various Cases' (2016) 91(2) Chi-Kent L Rev 603

(ed), *Civil Liability and Financial Security for Offshore Oil and Gas Activities* (CUP 2016)

Faure M and Vanden Borre T, 'Compensating Nuclear Damage: A Comparative Economic Analysis of the US and International Liability Schemes' (2008) 33 Wm & Mary Envtl L & Pol'y Rev 219

Faure M, Jing L and Wang H, 'Analysis of Existing Regimes' in Michael Faure (ed), *Civil Liability and Financial Security for Offshore Oil and Gas Activities* (CUP 2016) 68

Feichtner I, 'Community Interests' in Rüdiger Wolfrum (ed), *Max Planck Encyclopedia of Public International Law* (OUP 2007)

Feldthusen B, 'Public Authority Immunity from Negligence Liability: Uncertain, Unnecessary, and Unjustified' (2014) 92(2) Can Bar Rev 211

Ferreira PG, 'Arrested Development: The Late and Inequitable Integration of Loss and Damage Finance into the UNFCCC' in Meinhard Doelle and Sara Seck (eds), *Research Handbook on Climate Law and Loss and Damage* (Edward Elgar 2021) 127

Fitzmaurice M, 'Liability for Environmental Damage Caused to the Global Commons' (1996) 5 RECIEL 305

Fleming JG, 'Probabilistic Causation in Tort Law' (1989) 68(4) Can Bar Rev 661

Foster C, 'The ILC Draft Principles on the Allocation of Loss in the Case of Transboundary Harm Arising Out of Hazardous Activities: Privatizing Risk?' (2005) 14 RECIEL 265

Science and the Precautionary Principle in International Courts and Tribunals: Expert Evidence, Burden of Proof and Finality (CUP 2011)

'New Clothes for the Emperor? Consultation of Experts by the International Court of Justice' (2014) 5 JIDS 139

Fox H and Webb P, *The Law of State Immunity* (3rd edn, OUP 2015)

Freestone D, 'International Governance, Responsibility and Management of Areas Beyond National Jurisdiction' (2012) 27 IJMCL 191

Fry J, 'Attribution of Responsibility' in André Nollkaemper and Ilias Plakokefalos (eds), *Principles of Shared Responsibility in International Law* (CUP 2014)

Gahlen S, *Civil Liability for Accidents at Sea* (Springer-Verlag 2015)

Gaskell N, 'Compensation for Offshore Pollution: Ships and Platforms' in Malcolm Clarke (ed), *Maritime Law Evolving* (Hart Publishing 2013) 63

'Liability and Compensation Regimes: Pollution of the High Seas' in Robert Beckman, Millicent McCreath, J Ashley Roach and Zhen Sun (eds), *High Seas Governance: Gaps and Challenges* (Brill 2019) 229

Glasby GP, 'Deep Seabed Mining: Past Failures and Future Prospects' (2002) 20(2) Marine Georesources & Geotechnology 161

Goldie LFE, 'Liability for Damage and the Progressive Development of International Law' (1965) 14(4) ICLQ 1189

'Concepts of Strict and Absolute Liability and the Ranking of Liability in Terms of Relative Exposure to Risk' (1985) 16 NYIL 175

Handl G, 'Liability as an Obligation Established by a Primary Rule of International Law: Some Basic Reflections on the International Law Commission's Work' (1985) 16 NYIL 49

'Marine Environmental Damage: The Compensability of Ecosystem Service Loss in International Law' (2019) 34 IJMCL 602

Hanley N, 'The Economic Valuation of Environmental Damage' in Michael Bowman and Alan Boyle (eds), *Environmental Damage in International and Comparative Law: Problems of Definition and Valuation* (OUP 2002) 27

Harden-Davies H and others, 'Rights of Nature: Perspectives for Global Ocean Stewardship' (2020) 122 Mar Pol'y 104059

Harpwood VH, *Modern Tort Law* (7th edn, Routledge-Cavendish 2008)

Harrison J, 'The Law of the Sea Convention Institutions' in Donald R Rothwell, Alex G Oude Elferink, Karen N Scott and Tim Stephens (eds), *Oxford Handbook on the Law of the Sea* (OUP 2014) 373

'Key Challenges Relating to the Governance of Regional Fisheries' in Richard Caddell and Erik J Molenaar (eds), *Strengthening International Fisheries Law in an Era of Changing Oceans* (Hart Publishing 2019) 79

'Checks and Balances on the Regulatory Powers of the International Seabed Authority' in A Ascencio Herrera and MH Nordquist (eds), *The United Nations Convention on the Law of the Sea Part XI Regime and the International Seabed Authority: A Twenty-Five Year Journey* (Brill 2022) 151

Heller K, 'Specially-Affected States and the Formation of Custom' (2018) 112(2) AJIL 191

Hemmings A, 'Liability Postponed: The Failure to Bring Annex VI of the Madrid Protocol into Force' (2018) 8(2) Polar J 315

Hinteregger M, 'Environmental Liability' in Emma Lees and Jorge E Viñuales (eds), *Oxford Handbook of Comparative Environmental Law* (OUP 2019) 1025

Hoyt S, Van Dover C, Smith S and Pendleton L, 'Closing the Liability Gap: A Review of Liability Alternatives for the Emerging Seafloor Mineral Extraction Industry' (2016) <https://dukespace.lib.duke.edu/dspace/bitstream/handle/10161/11881/MP_FINAL.pdf?sequence=1>

Huguenin M, Donlan M, van Geel A and Paterson R, 'Assessment and Valuation of Damage to the Environment' in Cymie Payne and Peter Sand (eds), *Gulf War Reparations and the UN Compensation Commission: Environmental Claims* (OUP 2011) 67

Hylton K, *Tort Law: A Modern Perspective* (CUP 2016)

Intergovernmental Panel on Climate Change, *Special Report on the Ocean and Cryosphere in a Changing Climate* (CUP 2019)

Special Report on the Ocean and Cryosphere in a Changing Climate (CUP 2022)

Jaeckel A, Ardron J and Gjerde K, 'Sharing Benefits of the Common Heritage of Mankind – Is the Deep Seabed Mining Regime Ready?' (2016) 70 Mar Pol'y 198

Jaeckel A, *The International Seabed Authority and the Precautionary Principle: Balancing Deep Seabed Mineral Mining and Marine Environmental Protection* (Brill 2017)

Jaeckel A, Gjerde K and Ardron J, 'Conserving the Common Heritage of Humankind – Options for the Deep Seabed Mining Regime' (2017) 78 Mar Pol'y 150

Jarrett M, *Contributory Fault and Investor Misconduct in Investment Arbitration* (CUP 2019)

Jenks CW, 'The Scope and Nature of Ultra-Hazardous Liability in International Law' (1968) 117 Recueil de Cours 99

Johnson M, 'Liability for Environmental Damage in Antarctica: The Adoption of Annex VI to the Antarctic Environmental Protocol' (2006) 19(1) Geo Int'l Envtl L Rev 33

Joyner C C, 'Legal Implications of the Concept of the Common Heritage of Mankind' (1986) 35(1) ICLQ 190

'The Antarctic Legal Regime: An Introduction' in Christopher C Joyner and Sudhir K Chopra (eds), *The Antarctic Legal Regime* (Martinus Nijhoff 1988) 2

Governing the Frozen Commons: The Antarctic Regime and Environmental Protection (University of South Carolina Press 1998)

Kees A, 'Responsibility of States for Private Actors' in Rüdiger Wolfrum (ed), *Max Planck Encyclopedia of Public International Law Online* (OUP 2011)

Kindje K and Faure M, 'Assessing Reparation of Environmental Damage by the ICJ: A Lost Opportunity?' (2019) 57 QILJ 5

Klabbers J, 'Formal Intergovernmental Organizations' in Jacob Katz Cogan, Ian Hurd and Ian Johnstone (eds), *The Oxford Handbook on International Organizations* (OUP 2016) 133

Klein P, 'Responsibility' in Jacob Katz Cogan, Ian Hurd and Ian Johnstone (eds), *The Oxford Handbook on International Organizations* (OUP 2016) 1026

Laidlaw AK and Kang S, 'The Dispute Settlement Mechanisms in Major Multilateral Treaties' NUS Centre for International Law Working Paper 18/02 (2018) <https://cil.nus.edu.sg/wp-content/uploads/2018/10/NUS-CIL-Working-Paper-1802-The-Dispute-Settlement-Mechanisms-in-Major-Multilateral-Treaties.pdf>

Lanovoy V, 'Causation in the Law of State Responsibility' (2022) British Yearbook Intl L 1

Lefeber R, *Transboundary Environmental Interference and the Origin of State Liability* (Kluwer Law International 1996)

'The Liability Provisions of Regional Seas Conventions: Dead Letters in the Sea?' in Davor Vidas and Willy Østreng (eds), *Order for the Ocean at the Turn of the Century* (Kluwer Law International 1999) 507

Leigh K, 'Liability for Damage to the Global Commons' (1992) 14 Aust YBIL 129

Levin L and others, 'Defining "Serious Harm" to the Marine Environment in the Context of Deep-Seabed Mining' (2016) 74 Mar Pol'y 245

Levin L, Amon D and Lily H, 'Challenges to the Sustainability of Deep Seabed Mining' (2020) 3 Nature Sustainability 784

Lijnzaad L, 'Dispute Settlement for Marine Biodiversity beyond National Jurisdiction: Not an Afterthought' in Helene Ruiz Fabri, Erik Franckx, Marco Benatar and Tamar Meshel (eds), *A Bridge over Troubled Waters: Dispute Resolution in the Law of International Watercourses and the Law of the Sea* (Brill 2020)

Loan J, 'The Common Heritage of Mankind in Antarctica: An Analysis in Light of the Threats Posed by Climate Change' (2004) 1 NZ Yearbook Intl L 149

Lodge M, 'The Common Heritage of Mankind' (2012) 27 IJMCL 733

Lohan D and Johnston S, *Bioprospecting in Antarctica* (UNU-IAS 2005) <www.cbd.int/financial/bensharing/g-absantarctic.pdf>

Long R, 'Restoring Marine Environmental Damage: Can the *Costa Rica v Nicaragua* Compensation Case Influence the BBNJ Negotiations?' (2019) 28 RECIEL 244

Long R and Sun Z (eds), *Workshop Report: Biodiversity beyond National Jurisdiction: Towards the Development of a Balanced, Effective and Universal International Agreement* (World Maritime University 2020)

Mace MJ and Verheyen R, 'Loss, Damage and Responsibility after COP21: All Options Open for the Paris Agreement' (2016) 25 RECIEL 197

Mackenzie R, Romano C, Shany Y and Sands P, *The Manual on International Courts and Tribunals* (2nd edn, OUP 2010)

Malintoppi L, 'Methods of Dispute Resolution in Inter-state Litigation – When States Go to Arbitration Rather than Adjudication' (2006) 5 LPICT 133

'Fact-Finding and Evidence before the International Court of Justice (Notably in Scientific-Related Disputes)' (2016) 7 JIDS 421

Marjanac S and Patton L, 'Extreme Weather Event Attribution Science and Climate Change Litigation: An Essential Step in the Causal Change' (2018) 36 (3) J Energy Nat Resources Law 265

McCamus J, 'Necessitous Intervention: The Altruistic Intermeddler and the Law of Restitution' (1979) 11 Ottawa L Rev 297

Messineo F, 'The Invocation of Member State Responsibility before National and International Courts' (2015) 12 Int Org Law Rev 484

Mickelson K, 'Rereading Trail Smelter' (1994) 31 Canadian YBIL 219

Minnerop P and Friederike O, 'Climate Change and Causation: Joining Law and Climate Science on the Basis of Formal Logic' (2019) 27 Buff Env L J 49

Mitchell C and Swadling W (eds), *Restatement (Third) of Restitution and Unjust Enrichment* (Bloomsbury Publishing 2013)

Mollengarden Z and Zamir N, 'The Monetary Gold Principle: Back to Basics' (2021) 115(1) AJIL 41

Morrison J, 'Global Approval Not Enough, Businesses Need Social License' (2014) YaleGlobal Online <https://archive-yaleglobal.yale.edu/content/government-approval-not-enough-businesses-need-social-license>

Musiker D, France T and Hallenbeck L, 'The Public Trust and *Parens Patriae* Doctrines: Protecting Wildlife in Uncertain Political Times' (1995) 16 Pub Land L Rev 87

Nandan S, Lodge MW and Rosenne S (eds), *United Nations Convention on the Law of the Sea 1982: A Commentary*, vol VI (Brill 2002)

Nigar M, 'Environmental Liability and Global Commons: A Critical Study' (2018) 60(2) IJLMA 435

Niner H. and others, 'Deep-sea mining with no net loss of biodiversity—an impossible aim' (2018) 5 Front Mar Sci 53

Nollkaemper A, 'Internationally Wrongful Acts in Domestic Courts' (2007) 101(4) AJIL 760

Nollkaemper A and Jacobs D, 'Shared Responsibility in International Law: A Conceptual Framework' (2013) 34 Mich J Intl L 359

Nollkaemper A and others, 'Guiding Principles on Shared Responsibility in International Law' (2020) 31 EJIL 15

Nordquist MH, Rosenne S and Sohn L, *United Nations Convention on the Law of the Sea 1982: A Commentary*, vol V (Martinus Nijhoff 1989)

Okowa P, *State Responsibility for Transboundary Air Pollution in International Law* (OUP 2000)

'Responsibility for Environmental Damage' in Malgosia Fitzmaurice, David M Ong and Panos Merkouris (eds), *Research Handbook on International Environmental Law* (Edward Elgar 2010) 303

Oral N, 'The South China Sea Arbitral Award, Part XII of UNCLOS and the Protection and Preservation of the Marine Environment' in S Jayakumar, Tommy Koh, Robert

Beckman, Tara Davenport and Hao Duy Phan (eds), *The South China Sea Arbitration: The Legal Dimension* (Edward Elgar 2018) 223
Ostrom E, *Governing the Commons: The Evolution of Institutions for Collective Action* (CUP 1990)
'From Domestic to Global? Recent Trends in Environmental Liability from a Multilevel and Comparative Law Perspective' (2015) 24(3) RECIEL 289
Owens J, 'Comparative Law and Standing to Sue: A Petition for Redress for the Environment' (2001) 7 Envtl Law 321
Pala C, 'Can Mining the Seabed Help save the Planet?' Foreign Policy, 7 November 2021 <https://foreignpolicy.com/2021/11/07/seabed-mining-marine-life-climate-change-electric-cars-pacific-nauru/>
Pardo A, 'Law of the Sea Conference – What Went Wrong' in Robert L Friedheim (ed), *Managing Ocean Resources: A Primer* (Westview Press 1979) 137
Parsons C, 'Moral Hazard in Liability Insurance' (2003) 29 Geneva Papers on Risk and Insurance: Issues and Practice 448
Pasquet L, 'Litigating the Immunities of International Organizations in Europe: The "Alternative Remedy" Approach and Its Humanizing Function' (2021) 36(2) Utrecht J Int Eur Law 192
Payne C, 'Mastering the Evidence: Improving Fact Finding by International Courts' (2011) 41 Envtl L 1191
'Negotiation and Dispute Prevention in Global Cooperative Institutions: International Community Interests, IUU Fishing and the Biodiversity Beyond National Jurisdiction Negotiation' (2020) 22 Int C L Rev 428
Pedersen O, 'An International Environmental Court and International Legalism' (2012) 24 (3) JEL 547
Pekkarinen V, Toussaint P and van Asselt H, 'Loss and Damage after Paris: Moving beyond Rhetoric' (2019) 13 CCLR 31
Perry-Kessaris A, 'Corporate Liability for Environmental Harm' in Malgosia Fitzmaurice, David M Ong and Panos Merkouris (eds), *Research Handbook on International Environmental Law* (Edward Elgar 2010)
Pfennigstorf W, 'Policy Considerations for Insurers Engaging in Environmental Liability Insurance' in H Bocken and D Ryckbost (eds), *Insurance of Environmental Damage* (Story-Scientia 1991) 269
Plakokefalos I, 'Causation in the Law of State Responsibility and the Problem of Overdetermination: In Search of Clarity' (2015) 26(2) EJIL 471
'Environmental Protection of the Deep Seabed' in André Nollkaemper and Ilias Plakokefalos (eds), *The Practice of Shared Responsibility in International Law* (CUP 2017) 380
Plakokefalos I and Schechinger J, 'Liability for Transboundary Harm' in André Nollkaemper and Ilias Plakokefalos (eds), *The Practice of Shared Responsibility in International Law* (CUP 2017) 1051
Peel J, 'New State Responsibility Rules and Compliance with Multilateral Environmental Obligations: Some Case Studies of How the New Rules Might Apply in the International Environmental Context' (2001) 10(1) RECIEL 82
Peel J and Lin J, 'Transnational Climate Litigation: The Contribution of the Global South' (2019) 113(4) AJIL 679
Ragazzi M, *The Concept of International Obligations Erga Omnes* (Clarendon Press 1997)
Rao C and Gautier P, *The International Tribunal for the Law of the Sea: Law, Practice and Procedure* (Edward Elgar 2018)

Ratliff D, 'The PCA Optional Rules for Arbitration of Disputes Relating to Natural Resources and/or the Environment' (2001) 14 LJIL 887

Redgwell C, *Intergenerational Trusts and Environmental Protection* (Manchester UP 1999)

'The Wrong Trousers: State Responsibility and International Environmental Law' in Malcolm Evans and Panos Koutrakos (eds), *The International Responsibility of the European Union: European and International Perspectives* (Hart Publishing 2013) 257

Regalia J, 'The Public Trust Doctrine and the Climate Crisis: Panacea or Platitude?' (2021) 11(1) MJEAL 1

Reid E, 'Liability for Dangerous Activities: A Comparative Analysis' (1999) 48 ICLQ 731

Reinisch A, 'Privileges and Immunities' in Jacob Katz Cogan, Ian Hurd and Ian Johnstone (eds), *The Oxford Handbook on International Organizations* (OUP 2016) 1048

Reis TH, *Compensation for Environmental Damages under International Law: The Role of the International Judge* (Wolters Kluwer 2011)

Richardson B, *Environmental Regulation through Financial Organizations* (Kluwer Law International 2002)

Robles Jr A, 'The 1994 Agreement on Deep Seabed Mining: Universality vs. the Common Heritage of Humanity' (1996) 12 World Bulletin 20

Rojas AS and Philips FK, 'Effective Control and Deep Seabed Mining: Toward a Definition' Centre for International Governance Innovation, Liability Issues for Deep Seabed Mining Series, Paper No 7, February 2019

Rosas A, 'Issues of State Liability for Transboundary Environmental Damage' (1991) 60 Nord J Intl L 29

Rudall R, *Compensation for Environmental Damage under International Law* (Routledge 2020)

Sachariew K, 'The Definition of Thresholds of Tolerance for Transboundary Environmental Injury under International Law: Development and Present Status' (1990) XXXVII NILR 193

Sand PH, 'The Rise of Public Trusteeship in International Environmental Law' (2014) 44(1) EPL 210

Sands P and Peel J, *Principles of International Environmental Law* (4th edn, CUP 2018)

Sax J, 'The Public Trust Doctrine in Natural Resource Law: Effective Judicial Intervention' (1969) 68 Mich L Rev 571

Schisel-Meslin J, 'Out of the Club? Out of Luck: Complexities Facing Injured Third Parties Seeking Recovery from P&I Clubs' (2019) 43 Tul Mar L J 319

Schuda R, 'The International Maritime Organization and the Draft Convention on Liability and Compensation in Connection with the Carriage of Hazardous and Noxious Substances by Sea: An Update on Recent Activity' (1992) 46 U Miami L Rev 1009

Schwartz P, 'The Polluter-Pays Principle' in Ludwig Krämer and Emanuela Orlando (eds), *Principles of Environmental Law* (Edward Elgar 2018) 264

Scott K, 'Geoengineering and the Marine Environment' in Rosemary Rayfuse (ed), *Research Handbook on International Marine Environmental Law* (Edward Elgar 2015) 451

Scott K and VanderZwaag D, 'Polar Oceans and Law of the Sea' in Donald Rothwell, Alex Oude Elferink, Karen Scott and Tim Stephens (eds), *The Oxford Handbook of the Law of the Sea* (OUP 2015) 724

'Ocean Acidification: A Due Diligence Obligation under the LOSC' (2020) 35 IJMCL 382

Scott S, 'Australia's Decision to Initiate Whaling in the Antarctic: Winning the Case versus Resolving the Dispute' (2014) 68(1) Aust J Int'l Aff 1

Scovazzi T, 'The Mediterranean Guidelines for Determination of Environmental Liability and Compensation: The Negotiations of the Instrument and the Question of Damage that Can Be Compensated' (2009) 13 Max Planck UNYB 183

Shavell S, 'Strict Liability versus Negligence' (1980) 9 *JLS* 1
Shibata A (ed), *International Liability Regime for Biodiversity Damage: The Nagoya-Kuala Lumpur Supplementary Protocol* (Routledge 2014)
Siegele L, 'Loss and Damage (Article 8)' in Daniel Klein, María Pía Carazo, Meinhard Doelle, Jane Bulmer and Andrew Higham (eds), *The Paris Agreement on Climate Change: Analysis and Commentary* (OUP 2017) 224
Soares G and Vargas E, 'The Basel Liability Protocol on Liability and Compensation for Damage Resulting from Transboundary Movements of Hazardous Wastes and Their Disposal' (2001) 12(1) Yearbook Int Environ Law 69
Sohn L, 'The Stockholm Declaration on the Human Environment' (1973) 14 Harv Int'l L J 423
Solntsev AM, 'The International Environmental Court – A Necessary Institution for Sustainable Planetary Governance in the Anthropocene' in Michelle Lim (ed), *Charting Environmental Law Futures in the Anthropocene* (Springer 2019)
Steffen W, Richardson K, Rockström J and Cornell SE, 'Planetary Boundaries: Guiding Human Development on a Changing Planet' (2015) 347 (6223) Science 736
Stephens T, *International Courts and Environmental Protection* (CUP 2009)
'Environmental Litigation by Asia Pacific States at the International Court of Justice' (2021) 21 MJIL 653
'The Development of International Environmental Law by the International Court of Justice' in Douglas Fisher (ed), *Research Handbook on Fundamental Concepts of Environmental Law* (2nd edn, Edward Elgar 2022) 184
Stiglitz J, 'Risk Incentives and Insurance: The Pure Theory of Moral Hazard' (1983) 8 GRIR 4
Stone C, 'Should Trees Have Standing – Toward Legal Rights for Natural Objects' (1972) 45 S Cal L Rev 450
Tams C, *Enforcing Obligations Erga Omnes in International Law* (CUP 2005)
Tanaka Y, 'Reflections on *Locus Standi* in Response to a Breach of Obligations *Erga Omnes Partes*: A Comparative Analysis of the *Whaling in the Antarctic* and *South China Sea* Cases' (2018) 17 LPICT 527
'The Legal Consequences of Obligations Erga Omnes in International Law' (2021) 68(1) NILR 1
'Temporal Elements in the Valuation of Environmental Damage: Reflections on the *Costa Rica v Nicaragua* Case before the International Court of Justice' (2021) 90 Nord J Intl L 257
Tarver D, '"Hunnuh Mus Tek Cyare da Root fa Heal da Tree": Saving the South Carolina Lowcountry from Overdevelopment through Judicial Application of a Modern Public Trust' (2017) 68 S C L Rev 1047
Taylor P, 'The Concept of the Common Heritage of Mankind' in Douglas Fisher, (ed), *Research Handbook on Fundamental Concepts of Environmental Law* (Edward Elgar 2016) 306
Taylor P and Stroud L, *Common Heritage of Mankind: A Bibliography of Legal Writing* (Fondation de Malte 2013)
Telesetsky A, 'The 2010 Nagoya-Kuala Lumpur Supplementary Protocol: A New Treaty Assigning Transboundary Liability and Redress for Biodiversity Damage Caused by Genetically Modified Organisms' (2011) 14 ASIL Insight 2
Telicki K, 'Developing a Communications and Engagement Strategy for the International Seabed Authority to Ensure Active Stakeholder Participation in the Development of a Minerals Exploitation Code' (2016) ISA Discussion Paper No 3
Toussaint P, 'Loss and Damage and Climate Litigation: The Case for Greater Interlinkage' (2022) 30(1) RECIEL 16

Trindade AAC, *International Law for Humankind: Toward a New Jus Gentium* (Martinus Nijhoff 2005)

Turnipseed M and others, 'Reinvigorating the Public Trust Doctrine: Expert Opinion on the Potential of Public Trust Mandate in US and International Environmental Law' (2010) 52(5) Environment: Science and Policy for Sustainable Development 7

UNEP-WCMC, 'Governance of Areas beyond National Jurisdiction for Biodiversity Conservation and Sustainable use: Institutional Arrangements and Cross-sectoral Cooperation in the Western Indian Ocean and the Southeast Pacific' (UN Environment World Conservation Monitoring Centre 2017)

Urs P, 'Obligations *Erga Omnes* and the Question of Standing before the International Court of Justice' (2021) 34(2) LJIL 505

Vanden Borre T, 'Shifts in Governance in Compensation for Nuclear Damage 20 Years after Chernobyl' in Michael Faure and Albert Verheij (eds), *Compensation for Environmental Damage* (Springer 2007) 262

Van Dover CL and others, 'Biodiversity Loss from Deep Sea Mining' (2017) 10 Nat Geosci 464

Vierucci L, 'NGOs before International Courts and Tribunals' in Pierre-Marie Dupuy and Luisa Vierucci (eds), *NGOs in International Law: Efficiency in Flexibility?* (Edward Elgar 2008)

Vigni P, 'The Interaction between the Antarctic Treaty System and the Other Relevant Conventions Applicable to the Antarctic Area: A Practical Approach versus Theoretical Doctrines' in JA Frowein and Rüdiger Wolfrum (eds), *Max Planck Yearbook of United Nations Law* (Kluwer 2000) 481

Vogler J, *The Global Commons: A Regime Analysis* (Wiley & Sons 1995)

The Global Commons: Environmental and Technological Governance (2nd edn, Wiley 2000)

Vönecky S, 'The Liability Annex to the Protocol on Environmental Protection to the Antarctic Treaty' in Doris König, Peter-Tobias Stoll, Volker Röben and Nele Matz-Lück (eds), *International Law Today: New Challenges and the Need for Reform?* (Springer 2007) 186

Voyer M and van Leeuwen J, '"Social License to Operate" in the Blue Economy' (2019) 62 Resour Pol'y 102

Weinrib EJ, 'Corrective Justice in a Nutshell' (2002) 52 UTLJ 349

The Idea of Private Law (rev edn, OUP 2012)

Wetterstein P (ed), *Harm to the Environment: the Right to Compensation and Assessment of Damages* (OUP 1997)

'Pure Environmental Damage' in Günther Handl and Kristoffer Svendsen (eds), *Managing the Risk of Offshore Oil and Gas Accidents* (Edward Elgar 2019) 305

Wewerinke-Singh M and others, 'Bringing Climate Change before the International Court of Justice: Prospects for Contentious Cases and Advisory Opinion' in Ivano Alogna, Christine Bakker and Jean-Pierre Gauci (eds), *Climate Change Litigation: Global Perspectives* (Brill 2021) 393

Wijk A, *Amicus Curiae before International Courts and Tribunals* (Nomos/Hart 2018)

Wilde M, *Civil Liability for Environmental Damage: A Comparative Analysis of Law and Policy in Europe and the United States* (Kluwer Law International 2004)

Wilder M, 'The Settlement of Disputes under the Protocol on Environmental Protection to the Antarctic Treaty' (1995) 31(179) Polar Rec 399

Williams S, Woolaver H and Palmer E, *The Amicus Curiae in International Criminal Justice* (Hart Publishing 2020)

Wolfrum R, 'Purposes and Principles of International Environmental Law' (1990) 33 GYIL 308

'Liability for Environmental Damage in Antarctica: Supplement to the Rules on State Responsibility or a Lost Opportunity?' in Isabelle Buffard (ed), *International Law between Universalism and Fragmentation: Festschrift in Honour of Gerhard Hafner* (Martinus Nijhoff 2008) 817

Wood MC and Woodward IV CW, 'Atmospheric Trust Litigation and the Constitutional Right to a Healthy Climate System: Judicial Recognition at Last' (2016) 6 Wash J Envtl L & Pol'y 634

Wouters J and Odermatt J, 'Assessing the Legality of Decisions' in Jacob Katz Cogan, Ian Hurd and Ian Johnstone (eds), *The Oxford Handbook on International Organizations* (OUP 2016) 1006

Wright RW, 'Causation, Responsibility, Risk, Probability, Naked Statistics and Proof: Pruning the Bramble Bush by Clarifying the Concepts' 73 Iowa L Rev (1987–1988) 1001

Wright G, Rochette J, Gjerde K and Seeder I, 'The Long and Winding Road: Negotiating a Treaty for the Conservation and Sustainable Use of Marine Biodiversity in Areas beyond National Jurisdiction' IDDRI Study No 18, August 2018 <www.iddri.org/sites/default/files/PDF/Publications/Catalogue%20Iddri/Etude/201808-Study_HauteMer-long%20and%20winding%20road.pdf>

Xue H, *Transboundary Damage in International Law* (CUP 2003)

Yang X, *State Immunity in International Law* (CUP 2012)

Young M and Friedman A, 'Biodiversity beyond National Jurisdiction: Regimes and Their Interaction' (2018) 112 AJIL Unbound 123

Zhang H, 'The Obligation of Due Diligence in Regulating the Marine Genetic Resources in Areas beyond National Jurisdiction' in Keyuan Zou (ed), *Global Commons and the Law of the Sea* (Brill Nijhoff 2018) 286

Index

www.ingramcontent.com/pod-product-compliance
Lightning Source LLC
LaVergne TN
LVHW011807200926
848484LV00005B/1089
* 9 7 8 1 1 0 8 4 9 6 2 2 3 *